STUDIES IN THE SOCIAL HISTORY OF MODERN EGYPT

Publications of the Center for Middle Eastern Studies, Number 4
The University of Chicago

WILLIAM R. POLK, GENERAL EDITOR

STUDIES IN THE SOCIAL HISTORY OF MODERN EGYPT

GABRIEL BAER

THE UNIVERSITY OF CHICAGO PRESS
CHICAGO AND LONDON

Publications of the Center for Middle Eastern Studies

Number 1: *Beginnings of Modernization in the Middle East: The Nineteenth Century*, edited by William R. Polk and Richard L. Chambers

Number 2: *The Mosque in Early Ottoman Architecture*, by Aptullah Kuran

Number 3: *Economic Development and Regional Cooperation: Kuwait*, by Ragaei El Mallakh

Number 4: *Studies in the Social History of Modern Egypt*, by Gabriel Baer

Library of Congress Catalog Card Number 69–17537

THE UNIVERSITY OF CHICAGO PRESS, CHICAGO 60637
THE UNIVERSITY OF CHICAGO PRESS, LTD., LONDON W.C.1

Published 1969

Printed in the United States of America

Contents

General Editor's Preface

The Center for Middle Eastern Studies at the University of Chicago was founded in October, 1965. The more than two dozen members of its faculty offer courses on subjects ranging from the geography of Morocco to the literature of Iran, and from the beginnings of the Muslim state in the time of Muhammad to contemporary political problems. The Center, when combined with the Oriental Institute, which deals with the more ancient periods of the Near East, enables the University to offer one of the most complete programs on the Middle East available anywhere in the world.

It is the purpose of the Center to encourage and disseminate scholarly work on the Middle East. To this end, the Center provides fellowships and research funds and brings to the University visiting scholars. The author of the following book, Professor Gabriel Baer of the Hebrew University of Jerusalem, visited the University of Chicago in the fall of 1966. This and other forthcoming volumes of the series will show the extent and diversity of the interests of the members of the Center for Middle Eastern Studies at the University of Chicago.

William R. Polk
Director
Center for Middle Eastern Studies

General Editor's Introduction

As painfully—and realistically—aware as we are of the inadequacies of our understanding of the history of Asia and Africa in the "dark age" between the cultural pronouncements of classical times and the strident headlines of today, scholars can take comfort—and enrichment—from the progress of the past decade. It is precisely that decade of essays of a leading social and economic historian of the modern Middle East which this volume assembles.

At the beginning of the decade, the great Orientalist Professor Sir Hamilton Gibb could reasonably question whether among the scholars of the Middle East there were true historians. This, above all other questions, is surely answered by Professor Baer's thirteen essays.

I emphasize this point strongly for, as a student of Middle Eastern history myself during this period, I have been personally touched by the considerable intellectual transformation as well as the more obvious contribution to knowledge these essays represent. The two are, obviously, closely related, but it is only when their relationship is appreciated that the essays can be put in a proper focus.

Let me, then, try to set out some notions of this relationship.

Twenty years ago—twice the age of the first essay in this collection—when both Professor Baer and I were beginning our studies of Arab history, only a handful of non-Arabs had sufficient mastery of Arabic to be regarded as literate in that language. Achievement of literacy was, indeed, regarded as so high and unusual an achievement as to confer upon—and demand from—its possessor a sort of universal expertise. The Arabist *knew*, or was expected to know, the Arabs, their language, their mores, their acts, their thoughts, their very Arabness in all of its dimensions. In the broad, humanistic view of this lens could be seen all facets of life, and each viewer felt compelled to attempt to focus on a whole civilization—from the declension of the verb to the declaration of Islam, from the campfires of the beduin poet to the cinema of the Egyptian playwright, and from pre-Islamic times through conquest, caliphates, crusades to modern coups. If few can aspire to be Renaissance men in their own cultures, it is obviously much less likely in an exotic civilization. While the greatest performed remarkable feats of scholarship, even they necessarily were forced to pay in depth for their gains in breadth of vision. Obviously, in such views of a vast, evolving, multi-dimensional culturescape, no one element could be given a satisfactorily craftsmanlike treatment. And when a period had to be neglected, it was usually the modern or comparatively modern period when great literature was not being written in Arabic, when religion was apparently fully established and "evolved," and when Arab governments were no longer engaged in world conquest. This period was not only less majestic and creative but also far more confusing and obscure. Many scholars contributed portions of their effort to it, but most regarded the past three centuries as only a small and not exciting part of the vast scholarly challenge facing the Orientalist.

It was the quest of a new depth of understanding, a new craftsmanship, and a greater fund of information which has encouraged the substitution of the more selective lenses of the separate disciplines of the social sciences and humanities for the wide-angled lens of the Orientalist. This new specialization has been made possible both by the relative abundance of resources and by the relative growth of interest in the several facets of modern Middle Eastern life.

One of the things that set the new specialists on Arabic civilization apart from the Orientalists was the kind of questions they posed. In general the new specialists have tended to be less concerned with the process of the transmission of knowledge than with the message conveyed, more with the concept and content than with morphology and grammar of the language, less interested in description of action than in the analysis of social organization, the distribution of the rewards of society, and the mobilization of groups within society to perform political tasks. As a consequence, they turned from those aspects in Islamic society which were regarded as legitimate, as moral, and as more permanent to those aspects which, even in Muslim eyes, appeared often tyrannical, capricious, temporary, or even unworthy of serious scholarly study. Their attention turned from the philosopher-king to the merchant–tax collector, from the romantic warrior-poet to the earthbound peasant, and from the theological treatise to the tax register.

Some Orientalists have feared that the new specialization would result in gross distortions because a perspective of the majestic whole would be lost in concentration on the ephemeral part. In some cases this prophecy has proved correct.

A holistic view is the more crucial for a civilization as rooted in, and conscious of, a complex and coherent tradition as is Islam, and much generalization has been tried on narrow bases. Yet new perspectives, even if limited, and new accumulations of information on specific issues have forced us all, humanist or social scientist, generalist or specialist, native or foreigner, to rethink and reformulate our intellectual portraits of the past. In work on early history, for example, it is clear that radically different sorts of questions—questions often posed by detailed study of modern politics, economics, sociology, military affairs, and propaganda—need to be asked if our history is to be more than a refined translation of Arabic chronicles, chronicles indeed often written and interpreted by men whose scholarly and personal preferences similarly removed them from the stimulus of the politics of their times.

The new disciplinary challenge to established notions has provoked a kind of academic cloudburst from which torrents of discussion have eroded the familiar landscape of the unified field of Orientalism. Much that was silly and some that was of real value have been washed away, but in the intellectual battle, as in the battles of the pagan Arab tribes, a new "culture" has begun to be created: we are all profiting from one another as never before. The political scientist or sociologist must be literate and well-read; the historian is stimulated by categories of thought which were not of imperative interest a generation ago; while the student of the literary culture will today find inspiration in literary criticism and philosophy remote from the lexicography and grammar which seemed, in the past, sufficient founts of wisdom. From the challenge of the new professionalism, which inevitably produced a division of functions and interests, a new scholarly synthesis is beginning to develop.

Among the examples of this new kind of scholar, Professor Baer is notable. As will be seen in the following essays, he is able to bring to bear on a few pivotal topics a concentration of talents and resources not only to elucidate specific issues but also to illuminate a far broader vista of Middle Eastern history.

The problems addressed by this collection of essays are those arising from the transformation of medieval Islamic society to something else—just *what* else is still by no means clear. In part, the impulses of modernization or mutation have come from the West; in part, they are continuations or accentuations of existing tendencies. And, scattered among the many, obvious, mutations are elements which continue almost unchanged.

To put the essays, which deal with the several facets of this transformation, in perspective, a brief review may be useful to the reader.

The year 1798 is one of those which appear to mark major turning points in history. In that year, Napoleon led a French expedition into Egypt. After shattering the Mamluk medieval cavalry at the Battle of the Pyramids just outside Cairo, the French occupied the whole of Egypt. During their four-year occupation, the French undertook a series of ventures, each magnificently documented by members of the expeditionary force, which, on the surface, appeared dramatically to alter the life of the country.

If there was a turning point which could be pinpointed in history, this surely was it. In comparison with most other major dates in history, that of the occupation of Egypt was a remarkably precise and dramatic turning point.

But was it actually?

What was Egypt really like in the eighteenth century? Were its population, its legal system, its administration, its culture, its mores, and its political life really static? Was there a discernible direction of change? Was Egypt in 1804 really so different from Egypt in 1796. If so, how? What kinds of tendencies had been set in motion, what others had been accentuated, what others acted as brakes on the process of change?

Similarly, at the end of the nineteenth century—roughly at the outbreak of the First World War—had everything changed, as some writers have said, or almost nothing, as the mystique of the "changeless East" would suggest. Clearly, much had. But what, affecting whom, in what ways and degrees and with what effects?

These, in ever increasing degrees of sophistication, are the kinds of questions before historians. Thus, while the general outlines of the history of the period are easily discernible—indeed, easily described in political, economic, or military terms—the nuances of accentuation and style engage the craftsmanship of the historian. It is precisely the points at which evaluation or measurement can take place to which Professor Baer has addressed himself.

To show what these points are, one need only relate the chapter headings of this book to the major problems of the history of the period.

Let me take them in the order in which they appear in this book.

The beduin, whose apparently romantic way of life has ever caught the fancy of travelers, soldiers, and scholars, lived, after the early years of Islam, largely outside the culture and the society of the Middle East. They were ever in conflict with the urban societies which, as producers and keepers of written records, are known to us historically and continuously. Economically, the beduin were of marginal importance—they furnished transport and animal products. In short, as I have suggested elsewhere, they were to the deserts what fishermen were to the seas. However, the fishermen exacted a high price for their product in that they combined piracy with fishing. The city governments feared the beduin and sought various ways to defeat, tame, or incorporate them. In Toynbee's term, it was the challenge of the beduin in earlier centuries which had motivated the Meccan "response" and thus created early Arabian urban society. But, if the beduin were the fishermen and the pirates—"bad neighbors," as the Caliph Harun a-Rashid called them—their abrasive presence was so strongly felt by one another (as well as by the settled folk) that groups were constantly driven away from the finite and fragile resources of the desert. Still others were lured by the softer life of the town and village. Thus, settlement was a continuous process from the earliest recorded times.

What was the effect of the settlements? Arab scholars—notably the great North African Ibn Khaldun—have held that the beduin have been historically a reservoir of new blood: History is written as a rhythm of desert impulses and urban disintegrations. This interpretation, while intellectually provocative and productive of many insights into Islamic history, is clearly insufficient in any given case and irrelevant in some. In any event, as governments, based upon the urban culture, began to mobilize wealth and power in the nineteenth century, the scope of the beduin became increasingly constricted. The squeezing out of the beduin occurred, obviously, first among the weaker and more exposed tribes. The "sedentarization" of these tribes was both a familiar process, known throughout history, and the beginning of a tendency on such a large scale as to be comparable only to the early Islamic wars of conquest. In the modern example, however, the beduin came more as refugees than as conquerors: to inhabit the hovels, not to sack the palaces.

Thus, in his first essay, Professor Baer hits upon a problem which is both "classical" and modern, both a continuation of a process and the beginning of a new development. From this starting point, he moves in the next five essays into the vexing problem of the peasant, his community, his leaders, his land, his religious organization, and his attitudes.

The peasant is the neglected—indeed, despised—actor on the Middle Eastern stage. Bound to the land, chained to the plow, circumscribed by a village, he partook neither of the pride and civilization of the desert nor of the stimulus and learning of the town. Yet, the peasant is the hub of the Middle Eastern wheel: from him, his plow, and his land radiated the economic spokes which supported both the urban and desert civilizations. Rightly, therefore, if we wish to understand the social and economic life of the Middle East—as distinct from its cultural outpourings—we must come to know the peasant in his village.

But how?

The peasant has left us little in the way of written records. Even his villages are flimsy and amoeba-like, constantly growing and dying house-by-house on the same site. Oddly, it is usually in his fields that the peasant has left his signature most permanently. Thus, the land records are often the best we have. But here the art of the historian is put to its test: from the scanty materials must be derived a series of deductions. It is to this task that Baer devotes the central portions of his book.

In his discussion of the "dissolution of the village community," the author notes changes in what he regards as the three fundamental aspects of the village community, periodic redistribution of lands held in common, collective responsibility for public works and joint liability for taxes. The gradual growth of private land holdings, individualized tax responsibilities, and, under the influence of European liberalism, the transformation of forced labor for public works to an individual rather than a collective obligation—all these constituted a revolution. In the loss of these elements of community sharing of obligations, Professor Baer asserts, is the cause of the transformation of the Egyptian village from community to unformed social mass.

What then, Professor Baer next asks, was the principal unifying factor of village life? He finds his answer in the role of the village shaykh or *ʿumda*. The shaykh was a contact point between the external forces of government —defense, police, and taxation—and the villager. To the government, he was responsible for all village actions and culpable inactions; to the villagers, his was the voice of authority in the allocation of obligations and privileges.

While the growth of the number and range of governmental functions has necessitated the appointment of other officials at the village level, the village shaykh has retained a surprisingly large role. Like all rural Egyptians, the village shaykh made every effort to perpetuate his power and status by the control of ownership of land. It is, thus, to the development of private landed property that Professor Baer turns in his fourth essay.

Socially, as he points out, a major aspect of the long rule of Muḥammad ʿAlī in Egypt was the destruction of large agglomerations of land control. These agglomerations resembled in some ways the fiefs of European feudalism but lacked, in Egypt, both the social dimension expressed as the fealty of the population and the security of geographical delineation upon which fealty depended. It was relatively easy, consequently, for a strong centralized government to destroy its rivals and to absorb overall landownership. But there were countervailing tendencies, as we have seen, and these, a decade after Muḥammad ʿAlī's death, caused the Egyptian government to create a new landownership pattern to encourage the development of agriculture. To increase production, the government sought to give increased property security and expanded rights over the land to those who used it effectively.

While the Egyptian Land Law of 1858 appeared only a few months after the Ottoman Land Law, and the two have often been equated in historical writings, Professor Baer points out the obviously diametrically opposite goals sought by the Ottoman and Egyptian governments. As we have seen, the purpose of the Egyptian government, which had already overcome its internal rivals, was to facilitate development by granting owners more security and flexibility; the Ottoman government, still struggling against regional and ethnic particularism, sought, in the Ottoman Land Law of 1858, a means of restricting the rights of cultivators over the land.

A major social consequence has followed from the ways in which the land laws of 1858 were implemented: in Egypt, where private property became accepted, Islamic laws of inheritance promoted extreme fragmentation of ownership. In other areas of the Ottoman Empire, notably modern Iraq, Syria, and Lebanon, land was not regarded as private property but rather as the preserve of the state (*miri*), over which individuals had limited rights and control. There, Islamic law (and the nature of agriculture) did not promote excessive fragmentation. For this latter-day social reprieve, a price was clearly paid. Syria and Iraq developed slowly, whereas Egypt became agriculturally "modern" a century ago.

Throughout Islamic history, landowners have sought to evade the demands of the state tax collector and the leveling and scattering aspects of Islamic inheritance law by creating pious foundations (*awqaf*). Periodically, when excessive amounts of land were alienated from public commerce, when governments were in dire need, or when the prize was too tempting, rulers have moved to confiscate pious-foundation property. In the year 1812, when Muḥammad ʿAlī confiscated them, the *awqaf* controlled well over a quarter of the lands of Egypt. A century later, the factors which had impelled earlier creation of pious foundations had again asserted themselves so that approximately the same amount of land, over half a million acres, was again controlled by pious foundations. (They were to undergo confiscation again somewhat later.)

Turning from the aspects of governmental control over the peasant through taxation, landownership, village institutions, and his shaykh, Professor Baer next discusses one of the most complex and controversial aspects of social analysis—national characteristic traits. Most of us are at once enthralled and repelled by the notion of a national personality. Egypt is said to have such a personality, with submissiveness before authority as the most notable feature. The Egyptians, it has often been said by foreigners, have so long been ruled by others that they have lost not only the ability but also the will to rule themselves. But is this merely an "external" view? If not, how do we judge? Ignorance of the motivations and temperament of the Egyptian peasantry was not restricted to superficial foreigners, as Professor Baer points out, but was general among their fellow countrymen. Indeed, the most literate of the Egyptian observers were those with least contact with the village community. If the more facile of the national personality trait theory were correct, Professor Baer asks, how can we explain the rebellions of the Egyptian peasantry over the past two centuries?

Having shown the propensity of the "submissive" peasant to take violent action against his government, his landlord, his oppressors, and his fellows, Professor Baer next turns to the development of a penal code designed to restrain social violence.

On the "wheel" of Middle Eastern civilization, if the hub is the peasant, then on opposite sides of the rim are the beduin and the urban society. It is to various aspects of this urban society—its growth, its socio-craft-religious organizations, its government, its laws, and its servitude—that Professor Baer next turns.

In his first essay, he deals with the growth of the city, pointing to the intimate, indeed crucial, relationship of urbanization and modernization. By relating growth of population to development of transportation systems, improvements in agriculture, and the beginnings of industrialization, Professor Baer is able to establish a relationship between intensification of modernization and a movement of the population away from the agricultural areas into the cities.

But, the new urbanism was markedly different from the old. At the same time that countrymen were flocking into the cities, one of the most characteristic of medieval Muslim institutions was in its death throes. As a result, Professor Baer believes, "of the influx of European goods and of Europeans settling in Egypt, the change of its commercial system, the growth of its towns, and the reorganization of its administration," the guild system was rapidly undermined. Contrary, however, to the opinion of many previous writers, Professor Baer shows that the guild system remained more or less intact until the 1880's. Indeed, not only were they not destroyed at an earlier date as is usually averred but, in the second half of the nineteenth century, the guilds were actively employed by the Egyptian government to mobilize and control the labor force. In part, Baer believes, the guilds' survival was due to their relative flexibility and lack of economic differentiation: unlike the situation in the more familiar European guilds, in Egypt "there was no rigid system of apprenticeship, no clear-cut distinction between apprentice and journeyman . . . no sharp economic or social differentiation . . . between the guilds' masters and the shaykhs, whose economic and social position did not rise much above that of other members of the guilds, but rather depended upon the position of the guild as a whole." Rival institutions, trade unions, and chambers of commerce and industry were, essentially, a twentieth-century development. Indeed, "by 1911 there were no more than eleven unions, some of them with exclusively foreign membership." The guilds collapsed but not, as in Europe, to be replaced by structurally similar institutions. Two major causes of their decline and fall, singled out by Baer, are the replacement of local products by European imports, a change socially "unproductive" in Egypt whatever the effects in Europe, and the growth and diversification of the state, notably its assumption of such new activities as rendered superfluous the labor mobilization role of the guild system.

Changes in the character of the labor force are perhaps most sharply pinpointed in the issue of slavery. Slavery, indeed, was one of the most remarkable institutions in premodern Egypt: at the one social and political extreme, Egypt "had been ruled for about six hundred years by an elite of soldiers who had been white slaves, the mamluks." While the power of the mamluks was broken and many were massacred in 1811 by Muḥammad ʿAlī, new mamluks continued to be imported, and they, and their descendants, continued to occupy important positions in the Egyptian army and bureaucracy. At the other —lower—end of the social spectrum, significant numbers of slaves performed domestic household chores or were the concubines of the wealthier classes. For the most part, Egyptians did not, as did Americans and Europeans, employ slaves as field, industrial, or mining laborers.

Given the closed nature of the Islamic family system, it was extremely difficult for representatives of the government or others to collect information on the "mass" of the slaves—household slaves. It was only when they were transported or sold that these slaves emerged from seclusion and were publicly accountable. From their prices and the numbers imported, it is possible to infer a certain amount about the social status of different classes, colors, and sexes of slaves. The most valuable were the Circassian women who found their ways in to the harems of the wealtheir Egyptians; black women, men, eunuchs, boys, the elderly—each category had a place in the human market. While the number of slaves imported yearly into Egypt and their prices varied considerably over the course of the century, the institution of slavery remained an even more accepted and integral part of the social system than in the United States. Slaves were much more closely incorporated into the family structure, enjoying many of the privileges of kinship, and if this tie was inaffective, until the very end of the century, there was almost no opportunity for outside employment. This was true because of the exclusive nature of the guild structure. Thus, while repeatedly throughout the century regulations were passed, diplomatic activity was undertaken, and even forcible military interventions were made to prevent the transfer or sale of slaves as to encourage manumission, slavery persisted.

Perhaps the major blow to the importation of slaves in Egypt was the uprising of the Mahdi in the Sudan. This cut off the route of importation of the largest number of slaves—central African Negroes—into Egypt. Despite extensive government efforts to effect manumission, particularly after the British invasion of Egypt in 1882, and government decrees of severe punishments of those who traded in slaves, slavery remained an integral institution for many years. Indeed, slaves who had been manumitted often returned to the status of slavery because until the development of a free labor market in Egypt toward the end of the nineteenth century, there was literally no employment available for most of the former slaves.

Gradually, however, as a free labor market developed, particularly after the decline of the guild system, former slaves could find their way into the mainstream of society. At about this time also the reformist Islamic movement began to press for the abolition of slavery. In Cairo in 1891, the noted Egyptian writer Ahmad Shafiq published a book in which he argued that slavery, as practiced in Egypt, was a violation of Islamic law and that all slaves should be set free. The end was in sight. It came quietly and almost unnoticed. By the end of the century, Professor Baer concludes, slavery was dead in Egypt.

Islam was above all an urban civilization; yet, as Professor Baer points out, "the Islamic city never developed into an autonomous league of citizens or attained corporate status or rights." Unlike the European city, which, to stimulate its commerce, had been granted special privilages, the Islamic city was not set apart, even in privilege, from the totality of Islamic society but was the quintessence of Islamic society. In Egypt, always highly centralized, "no traces of urban popular autonomy or municipal development could be detected." Government in Egypt was always imposed from above—sometimes *for* the people but never of or by the people. When, in the sixth decade of the nineteenth century, modest efforts began to be made toward creating an institution of municipal administration, it was paradoxically inhibited by the Europeans themselves, the source of the modernizing stimulus, who viewed the growth of any municipal activity as an encroachment on their special essentially extraterritorial privileges. It was only when their business interests were directly affected by inattention to local facilities, particularly the roadways of Alexandria, that the merchants reconciled themselves to the payment of voluntary contributions to support certain limited urban activities.

From these modest beginnings was formed, in 1890, the Alexandria municipality. Not only were the beginnings modest, however; they were unnational: since the majority of the revenues came initially and throughout the important stages of the development of municipal legislation from foreigners, the foreigners insisted on dominating the institution. As late as 1912 only one of the fourteen elected members of the Alexandria council was Egyptian. And only 357 Egyptians were to be counted among the 2,173 registered voters.

These facts were to have most important consequences in the development of Egyptian involvement in government. Whereas in Europe men had learned gradually over long periods of time to take responsibility for their neighborhoods and their towns before assuming the overwhelming tasks of ruling their nations, in Egypt the pattern was almost exactly the reverse. Consequently, the average Egyptian, even of the well-to-do and well-educated classes, had little feeling of responsibility for, or experience in, managing any affairs outside his own front door. When finally he chose, modestly, to make a few tentative steps, he found his way blocked by foreigners, whose only interest lay in the affairs directly influencing their commercial activities and who sought to prevent the development of other urban activities or institutions. These two facts—inexperience in public responsibility on a local level, and exclusion by Europeans from control over the most obvious and immediate "national" tasks—have had profound consequences in more recent history.

About such issues as these, of burning importance to the past three generations, sources are copious. Indeed, relative to information on the peasant or the beduin, the historian is here in what the Arab poets would call the "upland meadows" of source materials. It was the urban civilization which created and preserved documents. Within the sheltering walls, the city encouraged men to think of the past and the future—the one to study, and the other to impress. Thus, it is appropriate that after a concluding essay, in effect summarising the sweep of change in the Egyptian society in the first "modern" century, Professor Baer should end his volume by considering how and what we can *know* from one of the potential sources, the "jottings" of ʿAlī Mubārak.

In reading these essays, I believe one will not only be impressed by their scope and penetration but will find within and between them both explicit and implicit suggestions for the sort of further research upon which alone a more comprehensive view of modern Middle Eastern history can be built.

In a companion volume, also published by the University of Chicago Press for the Center for Middle Eastern Studies, are other probings into the *Beginnings of Modernization*. This is an area, as the reader will realize, on which much remains to be undertaken, but the fact that a quantum jump forward has been made in the short span of a decade will be equally evident.

William R. Polk

STUDIES IN THE SOCIAL HISTORY OF MODERN EGYPT

1

The Settlement of the Beduins

There can be no doubt that the liquidation of the problem of nomadic tribes was one of the most radical changes in Egypt's social structure during the nineteenth century. Unfortunately, it is impossible to illustrate this process by figures. Estimates for the beginning of the nineteenth century are contradictory and ambiguous—in most cases only the number of horsemen is given and it is not clear whether semi-nomads are included in the estimates or not. Moreover, we have come to the conclusion that all published population estimates for the early nineteenth century are much too low,[1] and we suspect that one of the main reasons for these low figures is a too small estimate of the number of beduins. On the other hand, figures published for the end of the century probably are too high. The population census of 1897 has 70,472 nomads living in tents, 290,075 "fixed beduins" living in villages, and 240,880 living dispersed among the fellahs; but these figures have been described as "inflated," because many fellahs claimed to be "*ʿarab*" (nomads) in order to be exempted from military service.[2] It seems, therefore, that the decline in the number of Egypt's beduins during the nineteenth century was considerably greater than published figures would suggest.

However that may be, sedentarization obviously took place, involving, at the same time, settlement of real nomads and detribalization and assimilation of semi-nomads. The Hanādī section of the Western Desert nomads was transferred to Sharqiyya province and settled there by

Originally published as "Some Aspects of Bedouin Sedentarization in 19th Century Egypt," *Die Welt des Islams*, n.s., 5, nos. 1–2 (1957): 84–98. (Here expanded and reedited.)

[1] See chapter 8, below.
[2] G. W. Murray, *Sons of Ishmael*, London, 1935, p. 31.

Muḥammad ʿAlī;[3] the Fawāʾid branch of the Libyan Barāghīth, who came to Egypt together with the Hanādī during the turbulent period of the eighteenth century and raided Gīza province as late as February, 1813,[4] settled in the nineteenth century in the provinces of Fayyūm, Banī Suwayf, and Minyā;[5] the powerful Hawwāra, the real rulers of Upper Egypt in the eighteenth century, were crushed by Muḥammad ʿAlī's son Ibrāhīm in 1813,[6] and by the beginning of the twentieth century were "lost in the fellahin,"[7] and the Ḥabāʾiba, who dominated the Delta in the eighteenth century, are no longer mentioned by writers of the late nineteenth and the twentieth centuries. An illuminating example of sedentarization is given by the assimilation of Ahl al-ʿĀʾidh in the Sharqiyya province at the beginning of the nineteenth century. When Muḥammad ʿAlī came to power, they were, in Mubārak's words, *fī khushūnat al-ʿarab*, that is, "coarse nomads", and they had many feuds with other beduin tribes and none of the obligations of the fellahs, "and they frequently raided neighbouring people and villages."[8] By building roads, Muḥammad ʿAlī forced them into submission,

> and they were given the choice between exemption from treatment as fellahs along with expropriation of their lands and date-palms, like other nomads who inhabit hills and live in crude tents, and treatment as fellahs along with permission to keep their property. They chose the fellahs' way of life and were considered as Egyptian fellahs and treated like them in all matters, such as taxes, digging of canals, etc.[9]

From then on, and during the nineteenth century, many of the more important ʿĀʾidh shaykhs would found new villages and settle there with their families and attendants: Shaykh Ibrāhīm al-ʿĀʾidhī, who died in 1836–37, founded Kafr Ibrāhīm; two of the Abāẓas are mentioned by Mubārak as founders of villages: Baghdādī (died 1858–59) and Ḥusayn b. ʿAbd al-Raḥmān (died 1865–66); and ʿIyād Kuraym al-Mihannāwī (died 1846) founded the village which still bears his name (about twelve kilometers northeast of Bilbays).[10]

In 1854 Hekekyan, a perceptive Armenian engineer who was employed by Muḥammad ʿAlī and his successors, described this process as follows in his journal:

[3] Cf. Murray, pp. 294–96; ʿAbbās M. ʿAmmār, *The People of Sharqiya*, Cairo, 1944, 1:39–40.

[4] ʿAbd al-Raḥmān al-Jabartī, *ʿAjāʾib al-āthār fīʾl-tarājim waʾl-akhbār*, Cairo-Būlāq, 1297 A.H./1880, 4:174 (15–18). Figures in parentheses show number of lines.

[5] ʿAlī Pasha Mubārak, *al-Khiṭaṭ al-tawfīqiyya al-jadīda*, Cairo-Būlāq, 1304–5 A.H./1886–89, 17:33 (1–2).

[6] Jabartī, 4:185 (4–20).

[7] Murray, p. 297.

[8] Mubārak, 14:3 (5–6).

[9] Mubārak, 14:3 (8–11).

[10] Mubārak, 14:3 (13); 5 (6–7; 16; 19). Cf. Robert Montagne, *La Civilisation du désert*, Paris, 1947, p. 201.

M. A. was the first who, in modern times, permitted the roaming Arab to cultivate the skirts of the valley provided they kept the predatory Arabs from making incursions into the valley. As the new settlers became rich, the Pasha required of them the payment of a small annual land tax—and gradually increased their liabilities until he reduced them to the same conditions as fellahs. In the time of Abbas some of the bedoween villages were disarmed—in the same manner as all the fellah villages had been, and conscripts for the army and forced labour were required of them in the same proportion as from the other inhabitants of the valley. They built houses, but were ever ready to quit them when compelled by the state of affairs in the valley. . . .[11]

Sedentarization was the general trend affecting all groups of the population with some kind of tribal organization; its symptoms differed, of course, according to the different stages of transition which had been reached by different tribes at the beginning of the century: from the complete nomadism of the Western Desert beduin to the advanced assimilation of tribes settled in the Delta. Moreover, local conditions played their part in determining the actual form of transition to agriculture. Thus many of the camel-breeding tribes of the Western Desert, who, by the end of the century, still moved regularly between the Nile Valley and the oases, began at the same time to acquire agricultural skills and to rent land from the fellahs in order to cultivate it.[12] On the other hand, a tribe like Ahl al-Hilla, which had apparently settled near Ṭahṭā as early as in the twelfth century, continued up to Mubārak's time to consider agricultural work as disgraceful and did not till their fields themselves—like many of the settled beduins of "noble origin" in Syria of the twentieth century.[13] This attitude toward agriculture, however, was of course not confined to the settled tribes, but hampered considerably the attempts of Muḥammad ʿAlī and his successors to settle some of the fully nomadic tribes of the Egyptian deserts. They were given land for cultivation, but instead of settling down to cultivate it, they persisted in their roaming life while leasing the land to fellahs for half the proceeds. This practice was forbidden again and again by decrees of 1837, 1846, and 1851, but some of the beduins concerned did not give it up until the second half of the nineteenth century.[14]

Muḥammad ʿAli furthered his purpose of assimilating the tribes and breaking up their cohesion by appointing their chiefs, for the first time, to government offices. Until 1833 all offices higher than the village *ʿumda* (mayor) were held by non-Egyptians; from that year on, native Egyptians, mainly *ʿumdas* and beduin shaykhs, were appointed to be *nāẓir qism* or

[11] Hekekyan Papers, vol. 7, British Museum Add. 37454, f. 363.
[12] Mubārak, 17:33 (15–16).
[13] Mubārak, 17:23 (36). Cf. Montagne, p. 215.
[14] Cf. Yacoub Artin-Bey, *La Propriété foncière en Egypte*, Cairo, 1883, pp. 261–64.

ma'mūr.[15] By the time Clot-Bey wrote his *Aperçu général*, in the late thirties, all posts of *ma'mūr* were in native hands, but the *mudīrs* (governors of provinces) were still "Turks."[16] Later, higher positions were also filled with native Egyptians, among whom we find notables of beduin origin and *mashāyikh al-ʿarab* (beduin sheykhs) of formerly semi-sedentary important families, as, for instance, the Abāẓas and Shawāribīs.[17] This policy could lead only to the estrangement of shaykhs from their tribes; but it seems to have been carried out effectively, in contrast with Iraq, where Midḥat and his successors failed, half a century later, to implement a similar policy by appointing one faction of the Saʿdūns as Ottoman officials in order to tame the Muntafiq tribes.[18]

In consequence of their service in the administration some of the shaykhs had to move into towns: the Abāẓas, for instance, most of whom were born in Kafr Abāẓa, moved to different towns of Sharqiyya and other provinces.[19] Others were brought to Cairo by Muḥammad ʿAlī as hostages:

> Depuis lors les Bédouins ont été soumis au vice-roi. En faisant la paix avec eux, celui-ci a voulu que leurs grand-cheiks habitassent le Caire, où ils lui servent d'otages et sont responsables de toutes les infractions que leurs tribus peuvent faire au bon ordre. Ils reçoivent d'ailleurs un traitement.[20]

Again others settled in provincial towns as a sign of their enhanced social position. Thus Shaykh al-Saʿdāwī al-Jibālī of the Ḥarābī, who was made chief of all the tribes in the Fayyūm by Muḥammad ʿAlī, established himself in Madīnat al-Fayyūm.[21] By the beginning of the twentieth century many of the shaykhs were town dwellers: the Lamlūms of the Fawā'id lived in Maghāgha (Minyā) and in Cairo, the Sayf al-Naṣrs of the Tarhūna in Mallawī (Asyūṭ), and so on.[22] The separation of the shaykhs from the way of life of the other members of the tribe led to further disintegration of tribal unity.

But perhaps the most important factor in the disruption of the social

[15]Mubārak, 14:38 (6): "*ʿfī awwal jaʿl nuẓẓār al-aqsām min awlād al-ʿarab sanat 1249.*" Cf. 17:21 (31), and E. W. Lane, *The Manners and Customs of the Modern Egyptians,* Everyman's Library, London, 1944, p. 129: "the change was made very shortly before my second visit to this country"—i.e., before 1834. *Nāẓir qism* and *ma' mūr* were officials in charge of a district.

[16]A. B. Clot-Bey, *Aperçu général sur l'Egypte*, Paris, 1840, 2:186–87.

[17]Mubārak, 14:3–5; 116–17; cf. also 17:20–25; 10:70 (1–5); 11:99 (14–18).

[18]Cf. S. H. Longrigg, *Four Centuries of Modern Iraq*, Oxford, 1925, pp. 308–9.

[19]Cf. Mubārak, 14:3–5.

[20]Clot, 2:121. Cf. Jabartī, 4:150 (7); C. B. Klunzinger, *Upper Egypt: Its People and Its Products,* London, 1878, p. 255.

[21]Mubārak, 17:33 (7–9).

[22]A similar trend has been observed half a century later in the Syrian-Iraqi Jazīra by Montagne, p. 203.

fabric of nomads and semi-nomads was the socio-economic differentiation among the members of the tribe which took place in the course of the nineteenth century in Egypt. Such a differentiation was made possible by the enormous development of agriculture during that period. The cultivated area of Egypt grew from about three million feddans[23] at the beginning of the century to about five million feddans at the end of it, while the crop area was enlarged more than threefold, from less than two millions to about seven million feddans. Through the introduction of perennial irrigation an increasing part of the crop area was planted with cash crops, especially sugar and cotton, whose export grew more than tenfold between the twenties and the eighties and doubled again by the end of the century. The development of cash crops and the rising prices of agricultural products, whose upward trend was stronger than that of most other commodities,[24] gave the higher strata of Egyptian society, and among them the "Arab Shaykhs,"[25] a powerful incentive to acquire large tracts of land. This tendency was facilitated in the nineteenth century by Egypt's rulers, who were interested in the extension of agricultural production—mainly in order to increase the state revenue from taxes. In view of this aim large areas of uncultivated lands were granted as full private property to members of the viceregal family, officials, notables, and shaykhs, while usufruct rights in other lands (*athariyya, kharājiyya*) were gradually extended until they virtually became full property of their holders by the end of the century.[26]

Thus, at the end of the nineteenth century, shaykhs of formerly nomadic and semi-nomadic tribes emerged as big landowners, while other members of the tribe "were lost among the fallāḥīn." In his report on the situation of Egypt after the British occupation, Lord Dufferin wrote on the beduins: "Many of their Sheikhs have become the owners of estates."[27] Among the most prominent of such land-owning shaykhs we find the Abāẓas of Ahl al-ʿĀ'idh.[28] According to Mubārak, the first important shaykh of the Abāẓa family was Ḥasan Āghā, who was appointed in 1812 as *shaykh mashāyikh niṣf al-Sharqiyya* by Muḥammad ʿAlī's son Ibrāhīm. At the time of his death in 1265 A.H./1848–49, his landed property amounted to about

[23]One feddān = 1.038 acres.

[24]Cf. Yacoub Artin Pacha, "Essai sur les causes du renchérissement de la vie matérielle au Caire dans le courant du XIXe siècle (1800–1907)", *Mémoires présentés à l'Institut Egyptien*, tome 5, fasc. 2, Cairo, 1907, pp. 107, 131.

[25]But not only "Arab shaykhs"; see, for instance, Mubārak, 3:54 (31)–55 (9) and 15:96 (8–10) for the increasing acquisition of agricultural lands by rich merchants.

[26]See chapter 4 below.

[27]Dufferin to Granville, Cairo, February 6, 1883, *Further Correspondence respecting Reorganization in Egypt*, Egypt No. 6 (1883), C. 3529, p. 69.

[28]The following data are based on Mubārak's biography, 14:3 (16)–5 (17), the figures being probably his estimates.

four thousand feddans. One of his sons, al-Sayyid Pasha, who served Saʿīd as *mudīr* of Buḥayra province, owned at the time of his death in 1292 A.H./1875–76 six thousand feddans. The second son of Ḥasan Agha, Sulaymān Pasha, acquired about two thousand feddans in Sharqiyya province, where he established irrigation pumps and cotton ginneries. Other big landowners of the Abāẓa family mentioned by Mubārak are Baghdādī, Ḥasan's brother, whose estate covered five hundred feddans, while Ḥasan's cousin Ḥusayn b. ʿAbd al-Raḥmān managed to accumulate about two thousand feddans. Of seven thousand feddans of Qalyūb, four thousand were owned, at the time when Mubārak wrote his book, by the Shawāribīs, the hereditary *mashāyikh al-ʿarab* of that region.[29] The estate of ʿAlīwa abū Kuraysha, the chief of a number of villages called ʿArrābat abī Kuraysha in Girgā province, was estimated by Mubārak at sixteen thousand feddans.[30] Even one of the Hawwāra shaykhs, who formerly were important *multazims* (tax farmers) in Upper Egypt but whose lands had been completely confiscated by Muḥammad ʿAlī in 1812,[31] acquired again, in the nineteenth century, a sugar plantation covering three hundred feddans.[32] Among the shaykhs of beduin origin still prominent as big landowners in the twentieth century there are the Lamlūms of the Fawā'id tribe, notorious for their violent opposition to the implementation of the Agrarian Reform Law of 1952 in its initial stages.[33]

Large agricultural estates were concentrated in the hands of shaykhs in several ways. First, there were lands called *aṭyān al-ʿarab* on which only half the tax was imposed. It is not clear at which time such lands were given to beduins, but apparently some areas were classified in this category when Muḥammad ʿAlī carried out his new cadastral survey;[34] it was not mentioned any more by name in later works on land tenure in Egypt, such as Artin's book[35] but Muḥammad al-Shawāribī, for instance, who died in 1855–56, owned about one thousand seven hundred feddans of *aṭyān al-ʿarab*.[36]

Other lands became the property of shaykhs as a result of the *ʿuhda* system introduced by Muḥammad ʿAlī's decree of 19 Muḥarram 1256 A.H./March

[29] Mubārak, 14:116–17, especially 117 (11–13).
[30] Mubārak, 14:38 (4–7).
[31] Jabartī, 4:183 (27–29).
[32] Mubārak, 14:69 (5).
[33] See *al-Ahrām*, September 15, 1952 and October 28, 1952; *Middle East Journal*, 7 (1953): 74.
[34] Mubārak, 14:116 (31–32).
[35] Cf., however, Saʿīd's décret dated 8 Jumādā al-ūlā 1271 A.H./January 27, 1855, where lands exploited by beduins on which half the tax is imposed are mentioned (Artin, *Propriété foncière*, pp. 262–63).
[36] Mubārak, 14:116 (31–32).

23, 1840. According to this system notables, army officers, beduin shaykhs, and others were charged with collecting the taxes of a village or villages whose tax arrears they had to pay and whose future taxes they guaranteed. As a reward they received a tax-free tract of private land to be tilled by the fellahs of the *ʿuhda*. The reason for the introduction of this system was a tremendous decrease in the revenue because of wars and years of low Nile. But when the system was abolished many of the *mutaʿahhidīn* (the receivers of *ʿuhdas*) became the virtual owners of the village or villages given to them as *ʿuhda*.[37] Thus the above mentioned al-Sayyid Pasha Abāẓa was given twenty villages as *ʿuhda* by Muḥammad ʿAlī and Ibrāhīm,[38] and the lands of Qalyūb owned by the Shawāribīs at the end of the century were given to them as *ʿuhda* by Muḥammad ʿAlī and again by Ismāʿīl.[39]

A third kind of land given to beduin shaykhs, especially those of the Western Desert, were the so-called *abāʿid* (sing. *ibʿādiyya*). These were surveyed but uncultivated lands which had not been included in Muḥammad ʿAlī's land register.[40] But in contrast with the other notables who were granted *abāʿid* in order to cultivate them, the beduins did not receive at once full property rights to these lands, and only gradually they passed into their complete private ownership.[41] Such an *ibʿādiyya* was granted, for instance, to Shaykh ʿAbdallāh Bayāḍ of the Barāʿiṣa tribe near Ṣinarū[42] (about ten kilometers northwest of Madīnat al-Fayyūm), where the tribe settled after having been driven from Cyrenaica in 1830;[43] some other *abāʿid* were granted to Shaykh al-Saʿdāwī al-Jibālī of the Ḥarābī tribe, also in the Fayyūm.[44]

In addition to receiving these grants of different kinds, some of the rich beduin shaykhs bought lands from other landowners and from the fellahs,[45] while others, like Ḥusayn ʿAbd al-Raḥmān Abāẓa, "took hold" (*istaḥwadha ʿalā*) of large stretches of land.[46]

It should be noted that the transformation of beduin and semi-nomadic shaykhs into big landowners is not a peculiar feature of Egyptian society in the nineteenth century. Similar processes have been observed in all other

[37] For details see Artin, *Propriété foncière*, pp. 128–32; Artin, "Essai," pp. 72–73. Cf. G. Baer, *A History of Landownership in Modern Egypt, 1800–1950*, London, 1962, pp. 13–16.

[38] Mubārak, 14:3 (28).

[39] Mubārak, 14:116 (30; 36).

[40] Clot, 2:264; Artin, *Propriété foncière*, pp. 95, 334.

[41] For details of the legal development of the beduin *abāʿid*, see Artin, *Propriété foncière*, pp. 261–64; Gouvernement Égyptien, *La Législation en matière immobilière en Égypte*, Cairo, 1901, p. 205.

[42] Mubārak, 17:33 (6–7).

[43] Murray, p. 290.

[44] Mubārak, 17:33 (7–8).

[45] Mubārak, 17:33 (16–17).

[46] Mubārak, 14:5 (15).

parts of the Middle East where sedentarization of beduin tribes has taken place, such as Syria, Iraq, and Persia.[47] It seems, however, that the main means by which the Egyptian shaykhs acquired large estates differed from those prevalent in the northern Arab countries. As we have seen, the new landed property of the Egyptian shaykhs had been received by them mainly as grants from Egypt's rulers because they, the shaykhs, were able to care for its cultivation or to guarantee its revenue to the state. Additional lands were bought by the shaykhs themselves. But none of the sources mentions the existence, in Egypt, of one of the main causes for the accumulation of landed property in the hands of the Syrian and Iraqi beduin shaykhs, namely, the confused conditions of land registration, which enabled them to register large tracts of land in their own names. When Midḥat Pasha introduced the Tapu system into Iraq, great or small tracts of state land were sold "to holders of the doubtfully valid farmans and buyurildis of an earlier age . . . and, most important, to the shaykhs of tribes for their tribal areas." The Saʿdūns of the Muntafiq, for instance, "made haste to buy the rights over vague estates in the tribal dirah."[48] Thus, "many villages appear to have been wholly or partially registered as the personal possessions of local notables, without any consideration of the immemorial rights of those who had regularly occupied or tilled the land or pastured their flocks thereon,"[49] and in the tribal areas it was the beduin shaykhs in whose name the land was registered.[50] Very much the same conditions existed on the borderlands of the Syrian Desert. As early as the second half of the nineteenth century it was "the intention of the authorities . . . that the tribesmen should be settled on these lands. What in fact happened was that the shaykhs had the land registered in their own names, and thus became big landowners."[51] In the twentieth century, beduin chiefs continued to encroach on the unregistered and uncultivated lands on the fringe of the desert classified as *mawāt*. The situation was aggravated by Order No. 275 of May 5, 1926, which excluded most of these lands from the public domain, and Order LR/132 of June 4, 1940, which gave the beduins rights over the lands outside the *bādiya* (desert) line, and it was remedied only by Legislative Decree No. 135 of October 29, 1952, which included the *mawāt* lands

[47] Cf. Montagne, pp. 201–2; Jacque Weulersse, *Paysans de Syrie et du Proche Orient*, Paris, 1946, pp. 117–18; A. K. S. Lambton, *Landlord and Peasant in Persia*, London, 1953, p. 289.

[48] Longrigg, pp. 306, 308.

[49] Sir Ernest Dowson, *An Inquiry into Land Tenure and Related Questions*, Government of el-ʿIraq, Letchworth, England, 1932, p. 20.

[50] Fadhel Jamali, *The New Iraq: Its Problem of Beduin Education*, New York, 1934, p. 82.

[51] Norman N. Lewis, "The Frontier of Settlement in Syria 1800–1950," *International Affairs*, 31, no. 1 (January, 1955): 55.

in the public domain and defined the rights of their occupation:[52] "Taking advantage of the complexity and confused state of the law on land tenure, influential shaykhs have found it possible . . . to appropriate for their personal aggrandizement large areas of the public domain."[53]

The main reason for this difference between the Egyptian way of transformation of nomad and semi-nomad shaykhs into big landowners, on the one hand, and the Syrian and Iraqi way, on the other hand, was the complete and uncomplicated, if primitive, land registration carried out by Muḥammad ʿAlī and Saʿīd.[54] Thus property rights in Egypt were well defined by the middle of the nineteenth century, while they were not in Iraq until the thirties and not in Syria until the middle of the twentieth century. Notwithstanding this difference—since the result was much the same it led to similar social consequences in the different regions of sedentarization.

First of all, the growing wealth of shaykhs, a result of developing agriculture and their new landed property, found its expression in the establishment of a luxurious household. The Egyptian beduin chiefs of the nineteenth century, of course, were not yet able to enjoy the luxury of the motor car, one of the main pleasures of their counterparts in the Syrian Jazīra in the twentieth century. But like them, many built themselves a castle (*qaṣr*), generally at a strategic point near the track of their tribes' movements.[55] Fawā'id shaykhs of the Lamlūm family, for instance, occupied in the second half of the nineteenth century a castle called Qaṣr Lamlūm situated in the Western Desert. Al-Saʿdāwī al-Jibālī, shaykh of the Ḥarābī and the owner of several *abāʿid*, even managed to build several *quṣūr*, one in Madīnat al-Fayyūm and two others in the countryside of the same province.[56] (Both of the mentioned tribes settled in Egypt during the nineteenth century). Another sign of increasing wealth was the growing number of slaves and servants: when ʿAlīwa abū Kuraysha went for a ride many of his slaves used to ride behind him.[57] Some of the shaykhs began to indulge in a voluptuous life, like Ismāʿīl abū Nuṣayr of the Hilla, who was favored by Ibrāhīm Pasha after he had taken part in the expedition against the Wahhābīs and fought

[52] See text and explanation of Legislative Decree No. 135, October 29, 1952, *Official Gazette of the Syrian Republic*, no. 64 (Nov. 3, 1952); *Middle East Journal* 7 (1953): 69.

[53] Adnan Mahhouk, "Recent Agricultural Development and Beduin Settlement in Syria," in *Middle East Journal* 10 (1956): 174.

[54] Cf. Jabartī, 4:183 (27–28); 203 (16–18); 208 (21–26); Artin, *Propriété foncière*, pp. 90, 100, 123–24, 289, 311–14, 326.

[55] Cf. Montagne, pp. 215–16.

[56] Mubārak, 17:33 (8–9).

[57] Mubārak, 14:38 (7). Cf. Montagne, pp. 199–200.

well, and another Hilla shaykh of the same family.[58]

Furthermore, the economic and social interests common to the shaykhs and their tribes weakened more and more. The shaykhs joined the new ruling class of rich landowners, to whom they became linked by many ties. One of the most characteristic features of their new attachments was their intermarriage with rich peasants, townpeople, and especially with the ruling element. When the Iraqi Shammar began to settle, their shaykh, Farḥān, "gave offence in his tribe by his Turkish airs and town-bred wives."[59] Similarly the Abāẓas of Ahl al-ʿĀ'idh married Circassian women in the time of Muḥammad ʿAlī.[60] Descendants of another branch of ʿĀ'idh shaykhs became related to the family of Muḥammad ʿĀlī: Mubārak mentions as one of the most famous ʿĀ'idh chiefs ʿIyād Kuraym, at one time *ma'mūr* of Bilbays, who died in 1262 A.H./1846. His eldest son was ʿAbdallāh b. ʿIyād (died 1875–76).[61] One of ʿAbdallāh's grandsons, ʿĀdil b. ʿIyād, married Princess ʿAyn al-Ḥayāt Ibrāhīm, the granddaughter of Ibrāhīm Aḥmad—a grandson of Muḥammad ʿAlī's son Ibrāhīm.[62] It should be mentioned that near Bilbays, the center of this branch of ʿĀ'idh shaykhs, the Ibrāhīm Aḥmad branch of Muḥammad ʿAlī's family owned, in the nineteenth century, a number of large estates, such as Mīt Jābir and vicinity, al-Zankalūn, and al-Jūsaq (5 km west of Bilbays, the estate of Princess ʿAyn al-Ḥayāt in the twentieth century).[63]

This crystallization of a separate social class within the tribe, contrary to all traditional values of beduin society, was bound to create friction between the shayks and their tribesmen—as it did in the Muntafiq province of Iraq:

> The degradation in status of the tribesmen to tenants, . . . together with the necessity of paying both rent to the newly created Saʿdūn landlords—who formerly had exercised only a form of lordship over the Muntafiq and had held none of the land as private property—and revenue to the Government in the form of shares of their crops, stirred tribal feeling to revolt in which they were joined by the party of landless Saʿdūn hostile to the Government. An era of bitter strife ensued between tribesmen and landlords, many of whom lived in the towns . . . and between tribesmen and the Government.[64]

[58] Mubārak, 17:21 (22–23, 26).

[59] Longrigg, p. 309.

[60] ʿAmmār, p. 43, n. 2.

[61] Mubārak, 14:5 (17–22).

[62] Cf. *al-Ahrām*, January 21, 1954.

[63] *al-Ahrām*, January 21, 1954 and Mubārak, 11:98 (35–36); 14:4 (29); 16:60 (26); 64 (17); 19:58; 60; 61.

[64] P. W. Ireland, *ʿIrāq: A Study in Political Development*, London, 1937, pp. 92–93. Cf. also Longrigg, pp. 308, 309.

Although not many such incidents have become known, the following one related by Mubārak seems to indicate that similar conflicts were brought about by sedentarization in Egypt of the nineteenth century. After his description of the transformation of Ahl al-ʿĀʾidh at the time of Muḥammad ʿAlī, as a result of which they were treated as fellahs, taxes were imposed on them and they had to do *corvée* labor—Mubārak goes on to tell the story of the different ʿĀʾidh shaykhs, beginning with Ibrāhīm al-ʿĀʾidhī, chief shaykh of the ʿĀʾidh at that time. Ibrāhīm was made a government official by Muḥammad ʿAlī, first *nāẓir qism* and then *maʾmūr* of Bilbays. But after some time the people revolted against him, claiming that he had deprived them of their possessions. His attempts to appease his tribe and to rehabilitate his honor failed, and he was dismissed from office.[65]

An interesting cultural aspect of sedentarization is reflected in Mubārak's description of Ahl al-Hilla.[66] According to their tradition they had come to Egypt in the twelfth century and settled near Ṭahṭā (Girgā province), on lands formerly occupied by the Juhayna. After fierce clashes with the Juhayna the Hilla succeeded in conquering half of their former lands, and further acquisitions augmented the agricultural area of the Hilla to over twenty thousand feddans, in addition to their *abāʿid.* Although they were already settled by the beginning of the nineteenth century, they had retained many typical traits of beduin life and tribal organization. They divided into five *badanāt*, each *badana* being led by a chief (*kabīr*). Accordingly all their lands were divided into five parts.[67] All of their shaykhs are described by Mubārak as very courageous, generous, and hospitable, and some of them still used to live in a tent during summer.[68] Until the time of Muḥammad ʿAlī crimes and disputes were tried by shaykhs according to tribal laws and customs.[69] One of their shaykhs, Ismāʿīl abū Nuṣayr, bred horses for the army of Muḥammad ʿAlī's son Ibrāhīm.[70] As we have mentioned above, agriculture was not held by them in esteem.

During the nineteenth century the Hilla passed through an important process of cultural change.[71] Traditionally they were known as insolent,

[65] Mubārak, 14:3 (11–13).

[66] Mubārak, 17:20–25.

[67] Mubārak, 17:24 (1–12). In Qurna near Luxor the *badana* consists of ten to twenty related families. See H. Fathy, "Planning and Building in the Arab Tradition: The Village Experiment at Gourna," in M. Berger (ed.), *The New Metropolis in the Arab World,* Delhi, 1963, p. 220. Similarly, before 1911 some of the larger groups of the Sudanese Baggara were known by the term *bedana*, implying agnatic kinship. Cf. I. Cunnison, *Baggara Arabs*, Oxford, 1966, p. 8, n. 25.

[68] Mubārak, 17:21 (1–2).

[69] Mubārak, 17:22 (2–7).

[70] He was supplied with the horses, their fodder, and land for grazing; of the foals, the female remained his property. Mubārak, 17:21 (17–18).

[71] The following account is a summary of Mubārak, 17:25 (9–22) and 22 (14–16).

haughty, and ignorant: the story went that they claimed to have been mentioned in the Qur'ān, because, at recitals of the holy book, they heard the passage *yas'alūnaka ʿan-il-ahilla*;[72] they did not teach their children to read because they thought that education would weaken their courage and disqualify them for raids and fights; *imāms* were brought from the towns for display only, but they themselves had no use for prayers and religion.[73] This attitude seems to have changed in the nineteenth century: they became gentle and kindly, many of them established schools near their houses, and some went to al-Azhar. Most of those who kept guest houses (*maḍāyif*) provided them with a mosque and hired an *imām* who was considered as being attached to the guest house and who had the same obligations as other servants, in addition to instructing the children in the Qur'ān. Religion, apparently, gained an important place in the lives of the formerly tribal Ahl al-Hilla and especially of their notables and shaykhs.

If Mubārak's account of the Hilla is correct—and, allowing for some exaggerations, there is no reason to doubt the faithful reflection of the general trend—it constitutes an interesting parallel to developments observed elsewhere. Describing the sedentarization of the Shammar of the Syrian-Iraqi Jazīra, Montagne observes:

> Près de la tente du cheikh s'élève celle du cafetier, indispensable à l'hospitalité, et aussi le tente d'une personne religieuse, le mollah. . . . Ce personnage mettra son pouvoir sur les hommes au service du chef de tribu. . . . Le nombre des pèlerins croît en tribu, et à leur retour de la Mecque ce sont eux qui dans les campement président la prière, naguère presque inconnue au temps des ghazous. . . .[74]

Again the perusal of Mubārak's encyclopedia reveals aspects of the social transformation of Egyptian tribes in the nineteenth century corresponding to similar ones in the Syrian Desert many decades later.

Why, then, did Egypt's sedentarization and its corollaries precede those of Syria and Iraq by more than half a century or even by a whole century? Various reasons seem to have contributed to this difference. First of all, geographically and economically Egypt is better suited for a strong central government than the Fertile Crescent: the Nile serves at one and the same time as a natural way of communication between the different parts of the country and as a single factor on which the whole economy is dependent. As a matter of fact, such a strong central government was established in

[72] Qur'ān, 2:189 ("They will ask thee concerning the phases of the moon").

[73] For other examples of the beduins' ignorance in matters of religion, see Clot, 2:115; Klunzinger, p. 264; and F. Mengin, *Histoire de l'Egypte sous le gouvernement de Mohammed-Aly*, vol. 2, Paris, 1823, p. 304.

[74] Montagne, pp. 200, 204.

Egypt at the beginning of the nineteenth century by Muḥammad ʿAlī—at least indirectly as a result of the undermining of the old order by the French expedition. As against this, effective control of the vast Ottoman Empire was difficult, if not virtually impossible, at that time, especially control of the Arabian Peninsula—the reservoir of beduin tribes and migrations. The main attempt made in the nineteenth century to bring about the settlement and assimilation of tribes—that of Midḥat Pasha in Iraq—initially led to similar results as Muḥammad ʿAlī's policy in Egypt, but in the long run it failed. The old order had not been undermined by Western occupation, and its reform was slow and often ineffective. Political conditions favorable to sedentarization were created only by the dismemberment of the Ottoman Empire and the establishment of European mandates over its northern Arab countries. One of the most important means by which these new regimes succeeded in gaining decisive military superiority over the beduin was the airplane.

There was a similar time gap between the various stages of economic development in Egypt, on the one hand, and the northern Arab countries, on the other. We have seen that exact land registration was completed in Egypt much earlier than in either Syria or Iraq. Full private property rights, an important incentive for beduin shaykhs to settle down, were granted to Egyptian landowners in the nineteenth century, while in the northern Arab countries the state retained certain rights to all agricultural lands—though the extent of these rights was diminishing. Moreover, Egyptian agriculture developed tremendously in the nineteenth century: the cultivated area expanded, the irrigation system was transformed, and cash crops were grown instead of cereals for subsistence. This had a twofold effect on the nomadic population: on the one hand, it transformed the desert into "the sown" and thus deprived the beduins of their livelihood and closed the breaches through which they had infiltrated into the settled region;[75] on the other hand, it served as an incentive for beduins to acquire land and become farmers. And finally, transport developed in nineteenth-century Egypt as it did not develop in most other countries of the world, and certainly not in the Fertile Crescent: by 1913 Egypt had 108 kilometers of railways per thousand square kilometers and 356 kilometers per million inhabitants, while the respective figures for Asiatic Turkey were only two and 199.[76] This development hit severely one of the most important branches of beduin economy. This is particularly true with regard to the

[75]For the transformation of nomads' pasture grounds into private and government owned agricultural land, see, for instance, Mubārak, 12:133 (7–10).

[76]See Charles Issawi, "Asymmetrical Development and Transport in Egypt," in W. R. Polk and R. L. Chambers (ed.), *Beginnings of Modernization in the Middle East*, The University of Chicago Press, 1968, p. 394.

Eastern Desert beduins, whose livelihood was ruined by the establishment of the Suez railway and the Suez Canal. No similar revolution has ever been witnessed in the Arab countries of the Fertile Crescent, and insofar as comparable progress was initiated its achievements were not effective before the second quarter of the twentieth century. In this period all those signs of sedentarization appeared in Syria and Iraq which were perceptible in Egypt already in the nineteenth century.

2

The Dissolution of the Village Community

The existence of the village community in medieval and modern Egypt found its tangible expression in the following three phenomena: (a) village lands were held in common and periodically redistributed among the peasants; (b) the village was a fiscal unit, that is, its inhabitants were collectively responsible for the payment of taxes; and (c) the village as a whole, not the individual peasant, was held responsible for the maintenance of irrigation works or the furnishing of labor for any public works required. The importance of public works was by far greater than in Syria, but otherwise the Egyptian village community was similar to that of Syria. However, while at the beginning of the twentieth century the Syrian village community was still almost completely intact and *mushāʿ* (the common tenure and periodical redistribution of village lands) was predominant during the early decades of the present century, in Egypt the three tangible attributes of the village community referred to above had gone by then, leaving no trace whatever. The purpose of this chapter is to find out, as accurately as possible, at what historical stage each of them had disappeared.

In his book *Feudalism in Egypt, Syria, Palestine, and the Lebanon*, A. N. Poliak maintains that the Egyptian village community dissolved under Ottoman rule. He tries to prove this thesis with regard to each of the three aspects of the village community mentioned above. Of common tenure and periodical redistribution of the village lands, he says:

> . . . in Egypt at the end of the eighteenth century the private holdings of peasants were already separated by fixed boundary marks, except in some regions of Upper Egypt, where the annual redivisions still existed, but every member of the community had already a fixed share.

Originally published as "The Dissolution of the Egyptian Village Community," *Die Welt des Islams*, n.s., 6, nos. 1–2 (1959): 56–70. (Here corrected, with additional material.)

And in the next sentence he speaks about the "disappearance of the land comunity."[1] The only authority on which Poliak founds this opinion is General Reynier. Unfortunately, he does not say to what passage in which of Reynier's works he is referring. In his study only Reynier's *De l'Egypte après la bataille d'Héliopolis* is mentioned (as quoted by Dr. Worms in *Journal Asiatique*).[2] But the source of Poliak's opinion is another work of Reynier, namely his contribution to the collection of articles called *Mémoires sur l'Egypte*,[3] which is also quoted by Dr. Worms but without reference.

However that may be, there can be no doubt that, at the end of the eighteenth century, village lands in Upper Egypt were still periodically redistributed among the peasants. M. Lancret writes:

> Dans toute la partie de la haute Egypte comprise depuis Girgeh jusqu'aux cataractes de Syène, les terres dépendantes de chaque village n'appartiennent pas par portions distinctes aux divers fellâh, comme dans l'Égypte inférieure: elles sont, en quelque sort, le bien commun de tous, et sont distribuées à chacun selon ses moyens de culture; et comme le nombre des cultivateurs est presque toujours trop petit pour la quantité de terres cultivables, un fellâh, de quelque lieu qu'il soit, peut participer à la distribution. On appelle ces terres *b'el-mesâha*, terres par la mesure.
>
> Ce mode de propriété ne cesse pas brusquement à Girgeh; il s'étend dans toutes les provinces inférieures où les propriétés distinctes sont aussi connues; et plus on approche du Caire, plus celles-ci sont en grand nombre.
>
> Dans tous les villages du haut Sa'yd, et dans ceux de la moyenne Égypte, où les terres appartiennent par indivis à tous les habitans, elles leur sont distribuèes, chaque année, par les cheykhs.[4]

Thus, periodical redistribution of the village lands seems to have prevailed not only in Upper Egypt proper but also in some areas of Middle Egypt. According to Comte Estève, another contributor to the *Description de l'Égypte*, village lands were annually redistributed in the provinces of Qenā, Isnā, Girgā, Asyūṭ, Manfalūṭ, and Minyā.[5]

In Lower Egypt, on the other hand, village lands apparently were not redistributed periodically among the peasants. This does not mean, however, that they were, at the end of the eighteenth century, the private

[1] A. N. Poliak, *Feudalism in Egypt, Syria, Palestine, and the Lebanon, 1250–1900*, London, 1939, pp. 69–70.

[2] In the following we quote the English translation: General Reynier, *State of Egypt after the Battle of Heliopolis*, London, 1802. Poliak's reference is on p. 67 of his study.

[3] L. Reynier, "Considérations générales sur l'agriculture de l'Egypte, et sur les améliorations dont elle est susceptibles," *Mémoires sur l'Egypte*, Paris, vol. 4, an XI, pp. 25–26. As we shall see below, Reynier's statements in his two works are mutually contradictory.

[4] M. A. Lancret, "Mémoire sur le système d'imposition territorial et sur l'administration des provinces de l'Egypte," in *Description de l'Egypte, état moderne*, 1, Paris, 1809, pp. 246, 247.

[5] Le Comte Estève, "Mémoire sur les finances de l'Egypte," in *Description de l'Egypte, état moderne*, 1:321–22.

property of individual fellahs. True, M. Lancret, in his contribution to the *Description de l'Égypte*, reiterates again and again that the fellahs were proprietors (*possesseurs*, *propriétaires*) of their land and that they had the right to sell it or transfer it through inheritance.[6] The same is said by Reynier in his article in *Mémoires sur l'Égypte* quoted above: "... le fellah ... transmet son héritage à ses héritiers, il peut même l'aliéner par vente, ou par bail emphytéotique; mais ces mutations doivent obtenir l'agrément du mukhtesim [*sic*]." However, in his *State of Egypt* Reynier contradicts his own statement as follows: "They indeed possess and transmit to their children the land allotted to their families; but they cannot alienate them, and scarcely can let any part without the permission of their lord".[7] Presumably, Lancret's and Reynier's first statements were founded on a misunderstanding, which can be cleared up by the following passages from Girard and Chabrol, two other contributors to the *Description de l'Égypte*:

> ... Tel est encore l'état de ce qu'on appelle ici *propriétés particulières*: elles restent dans la même famille, moins par un droit de succession, que comme un témoignage de la faveur du Gouvernement, qui conserve toujours la faculté d'en disposer à son gré. Ces propriétés ne sont, comme on voit, que des espèces de fiefs amovibles, et par cela même, inaliénables.
>
> Aussi ne faut-il pas attacher ici à l'expression *vente d'un fonds de terre* l'idée d'une cession perpétuelle et absolue, mais seulement temporaire pour une somme d'argent reçue à titre de prêt.
>
> La terre est possédée au même titre par le prêteur, jusqu'au remboursement, époque à laquelle l'usufruitier rentre en jouissance de la terre qu'il avait engagée.[8]

> Quelques individus, sous le nom de *moultezim*, ont la propriété effective du territoire de ces villages: les *fellâh* sont censés la partager entre eux. ...
>
> Un cultivateur transmet à ses enfans le droit d'ensemencer la terre qu'il a fait valoir. Ceux-ci doivent préablement payer au moultezim une espèce de droit d'investiture ... si le fellâh qui doit hériter, refusait de payer, malgré les sommations du propriétaire, celui-ci pourroit l'y contraindre, en lui refusant la jouissance de la ferme paternelle. ...
>
> ... un fellâh n'a pas le pouvoir de vendre la terre qu'il cultive ... cependant il est libre de l'engager pour un temps, et conserve toujours le droit d'y renter.[9]

And Chabrol adds that it was the task of the *shaykh al-balad* to furnish the *multazim* with new fellahs in lieu of those who failed to pay. Thus, in Lower Egypt the custom seems to have been to let holdings be passed down in the

[6] Lancret, pp. 235, 246.

[7] Reynier, *State of Egypt*, p. 60.

[8] P. S. Girard, "Mémoire sur l'agriculture, l'industrie et le commerce de l'Egypte," in *Description de l'Egypte, état moderne*, 2 (1), Paris, 1812, p. 585.

[9] De Chabrol, "Essai sur le moeurs des habitans modernes de l'Egypte," in *Description de l'Egypte, état moderne*, 2 (1), pp. 479 80.

family from generation to generation, without the family acquiring any legal right of property to the land its members tilled; the land could be pawned but not sold; the *multazim* could deprive a fellah of his land if he failed to make the payments due to him and give the land to another fellah for cultivation; and it was the village headman, the *shaykh al-balad*, whose task it was to carry out these transactions. Therefore, not only did the fellahs, at the end of the eighteenth century, have no property rights to the lands they tilled, but the village, represented by the *shaykh al-balad*, had a certain status in connection with these lands. True, in Lower Egyptian villages land was not redistributed periodically,[10] but there is no proof whatever that under Mamluk rule such redistribution existed in Lower Egypt. Consequently, with regard to the first aspect of the village community, the common tenure of village lands, no basic change occurred after the Ottoman conquest of Egypt or before the end of the eighteenth century.

The same holds for the second aspect of the village community, namely, collective responsibility for the payment of taxes. All sources known to the present writer agree that at the end of the eighteenth century the village was the common unit of taxation in Egypt.[11] In his report on taxation and administration, M. Lancret writes: "On répartit le myry non par feddân de terres mais par villages. . . . C'est cette première répartition du myry sur les villages qui subsiste encore aujourd'hui".[12]

The same is stated again especially for the Fayyūm,[13] and on another page Lancret explains that a village has to pay taxes even for those of its lands which have been occupied by beduins.[14] When fellahs deserted their villages because of the oppressive tax burden, the remaining population had to make up their part:

> The Fellahs who remain in a village partially deserted by the cultivators are more unfortunate than the fugitives. They are compelled to support all the labour and pay all the dues of the fugitives; and, often reduced to despair, they entirely abandon the village, and engage themselves as domestics of the Arabs of the desert, if they can find no other secure refuge.[15]

This evidence would seem to contradict Poliak's claim that as a fiscal unit the village was replaced as early as the sixteenth century by the *qīrāṭ*,

[10]The reason for this difference between Upper and Lower Egypt, according to Reynier, was the fact that, because of the differences in the yearly inundation in Upper Egypt, different plots remained uncultivated, while in Lower Egypt the cultivated area was more or less stable from year to year. See *Mémoires sur l'Egypte*, 4:25.

[11]Cf. H. A. R. Gibb and H. Bowen, *Islamic Society and the West*, I, 1, London, 1950, p. 262, where several sources are mentioned.

[12]Lancret, p. 237.

[13]Lancret, p. 247.

[14]Lancret, p. 250.

[15]Reynier, *State of Egypt*, p. 60.

which was no longer a share in the common land of a village but a certain delimited piece of land.[16] The argument that there were *iltizāms* which contained only a *qīrāṭ* or half a *qīrāṭ*[17] is not convincing, since it is not stated at all that these were delimited pieces of land and not portions of a greater fiscal unit. On the contrary, according to Jabartī the *mīrī* (land tax) and the *fā'iz* (profit of *multazim*) were imposed on each *ḥiṣṣa* (portion), [18] and the *ḥiṣṣa* (another name for *iltizām*[19]) was very often identical with a whole village: among the *ḥiṣaṣ al-iltizām* of Shaykh al-Sādāt's wife were the (apparently entire) villages of Qalqashanda (Qalyūbiyya province) and Sawāda and Difrīna in Upper Egypt;[20] and about Shaykh Muḥammad al-Mahdī Jabartī relates: "*iltazama bi'iddat ḥiṣaṣ bi'l-Buḥayra mithla Shābūr wakhilāfihā* . . ."[21]—that is to say, the village of Shābūr was a *ḥiṣṣat iltizām*. Accordingly Jabartī tells us that in 1184 A.H./1770–71 ʿAlī Bey imposed on every village a tax of a hundred riyāl; similarly, two events in the year 1202 A.H./1787–88 related by Jabartī include information about the imposition of a tax of 110 dīnār and 100 riyāl and a camel respectively on every village.[22]

Similarly, there is nothing to show that in the Ottoman period supplying labor for irrigation dams and canals and other public works became the individual responsibility of the fellah. In the passage indicated in Poliak's footnotes, Jabartī only says that, when the Nile began to rise, the fellahs used to repair their irrigation works: ". . . *fī mabādi' ziyādat al-nīl . . . yuṣliḥūna jusūrahum waḥubūsahum*. . . ."[23] Nothing is said about whose responsibility this was, let alone that it was the responsibility of each fellah. On the other hand, we have his evidence that when it was necessary to repair a dike (*jisr*) the fellahs for the work were recruited through the village shaykh,[24] as well as Reynier's statement, quoted above, that fellahs who remained in a partially deserted village had to supply all the labor of the fugitives. This seems to prove that, at the end of the eighteenth century, the village as a whole and not the individual fellah was responsible for the provision of labor for public works.

We have tried to show that it is wrong to place the dissolution of the Egyptian village community under Ottoman rule. Surprisingly, no

[16] Poliak, pp. 49–50, 70. The *qīrāṭ* is one-twenty-fourth part of a unit.

[17] Jabartī, 4:204 (2). *Iltizām* is the system of tax farming, as well as the land made over to a *multazim*.

[18] Jabartī, 4:123 (23).

[19] Cf. Poliak, p. 50.

[20] Jabartī, 4:197 (3–4).

[21] Jabartī, 4:234 (2).

[22] Jabartī, 1:351 (31–2); 2:154 (3), 159 (24).

[23] Jabartī, 4:293 (3–6).

[24] Jabartī, 2:93 (32–3).

fundamental change occurred in this respect during the whole of the first half of the nineteenth century, until the rule of Saʿīd. Under Muḥammad ʿAlī a cadastral survey was carried out, but the land was not registered in the name of each individual fellah. *Kharāj* lands (which were the majority in existing villages) were ". . . enregistrées au nom des communes et distribuées aux habitants".[25] An old fellah, who related to D. Mackenzie Wallace his reminiscences, told him that in Muḥammad ʿAlī's days, ". . . when the head of the family died, the land which he possessed was distributed . . . with a regard to the welfare of the community rather than to any supposed rights of inheritance. . . ."[26] According to Artin, during that period the *shaykh al-balad*, and later the *mudīr*, decided who was to receive the land of a deceased fellah.[27]

In Upper Egypt the periodical redistribution of village lands was observed during the whole of the first half of the nineteenth century. As late as 1855 a French physician who worked as health inspector at Asyūṭ told N. W. Senior that ". . . in many cases . . . the land surrounding a village is held in common by its inhabitants, and a new allotment of it is made, family by family, every year";[28] and Hekekyan Bey told the same author: "Few of them [the fellahs] have land of their own or temporary rights to a portion of the common land belonging to a village".[29]

Similarly, no change occurred in the system of tax collection from the villages before the accession of Saʿīd to the office of *wālī* of Egypt. During Muḥammad ʿAlī's rule the tax was imposed on the village as a whole, and the local authorities divided it among the various inhabitants, according to their means, the *shaykh al-balad* being responsible for the collection of the taxes.[30] Apparently it was not always easy to implement this principle: as a result of recruitment to the army, public works, or industry, as well as after an epidemic, the population of some villages shrank to such a degree that it became impossible to collect the former tax assessments from them. The reaction of the authorities, however, was not to make each individual

[25] M. K. Moursy, *De l'Etendue du droit de propriété en Egypte*, Paris, 1914, p. 104.

[26] D. Mackenzie Wallace, *Egypt and the Egyptian Question*, London, 1883, p. 263.

[27] Y. Artin-Bey, *La Propriété foncière en Égypte*, Cairo, 1883, p. 276. On pp. 90, 100, and 124 of his book, Artin claims that land registration at the time of Muḥammad ʿAlī was in the name of individual fellahs. This seems to us extremely improbable and inconsistent with what we know about property rights at that time. Moreover, we have quoted above a number of sources for the opposite view. That the land was registered in the name of the village, not the individual fellah, is also stated in the following official publication: Gouvernement Egyptien, Ministère des Finances, *La Législation en matière immobilière en Egypte*, Cairo, 1901, p. 10 n.

[28] N. W. Senior, *Conversations and Journals in Egypt and Malta* [1855–56], London, 1882, 1:111.

[29] Senior, p. 280.

[30] Cf. J. Nahas, *Situation économique et sociale du fellah Egyptien*, Paris, 1901, p. 44; A. E. Crouchley, *The Economic Development of Modern Egypt*, London, 1938, p. 110.

responsible for his taxes but to extend the range of collective tax responsibility to whole districts. In his famous *Report on Egypt and Candia*, John Bowring writes: "A well-grounded cause of complaint . . . is the making a district responsible in mass for the amount of its taxes. . . ."[31] And on September 15, 1835 Patrick Campbell, the British Agent and Consul General in Egypt, wrote to Lord Palmerston: "The Egyptian system of liability is well known—the son is responsible for the debts of the father, the village for every one of its inhabitants, and ultimately the Province is responsible for all its villages. . . . The debts of the dead [of the plague] were then an additional burthen upon those that survived."[32] Similarly, Clot-Bey wrote in his *Aperçu général sur l'Égypte*: "Un rigoureux système de solidarité entre les habitants du même village, entre les villages compris dans le même canton, entre les cantons du même département, etc., assure au trésor la rentrée des contributions qu'il a fixées."[33]

At the end of the 1830's, British representatives in Egypt were under the impression that this state of affairs was undergoing a change: on May 12, 1836 Mr. Sloane, British Vice Consul at Alexandria, mentioned in a report to Lord Palmerston

> . . . the more liberal plan which he [Muḥammad ʿAlī] has lately adopted by the abolishment of the system of mutual liability . . . the Government has paid to the peasantry the amount of their respective credits for the cotton, grain and other produces . . . remitting for ever the debts of those who died by the plague during the last year. . . .[34]

Mentioning collective responsibility for the payment of taxes in his Report of July 1840, Patrick Campbell believed that ". . . in fact this responsibility is but little enforced".[35]

In 1840, however, the accumulation of considerable tax arrears induced the government not to abolish the system of mutual liability but instead to introduce the *ʿuhda* system: high officials were compelled by the Pasha to accept responsibility (which developed later into property rights) for whole villages and to guarantee payment of arrears and future taxes.[36] Not unlike the former *iltizāms*, the *ʿuhda* was again based on the village as a unit. The villages al-Balyanā (Girgā province), Fazāra (Asyūṭ province), and Zayniyya (Qenā province) were all *ʿuhda* of Salīm Pasha al-Siliḥdār;[37]

[31] J. Bowring, *Report on Egypt and Candia*, London, 1840, p. 15.
[32] Public Record Office, FO 78/257.
[33] A.-B. Clot-Bey, *Aperçu général sur l'Egypte*, Paris, 1840, 2:206.
[34] PRO, FO 78/285.
[35] Campbell Report, PRO, FO 78/408B.
[36] Cf. Artin, p. 128–29. According to A. A. al-Hitta (*Taʾrīkh al-zirāʿa al-miṣriyya fī ʿahd Muḥammad ʿAlī*, Cairo, 1950, p. 51), some *ʿuhdas* had been given before 1840, during the 1830's.
[37] Mubārak, 9:82 (26–27); 11:99 (21–25); 14:75 (19–20).

Qalyūb was *ʿuhda* of Muḥammad al-Shawāribī;[38] Samannūd (Gharbiyya) of al-Badrāwī;[39] and so on.

Moreover, reading Hekekyan Bey's diary one cannot but come to the conclusion that in the years 1843 to 1854 the village continued to function as a fiscal unit whose population was collectively responsible for the payment of taxes. The flight of fellahs from their villages increased the tax burden of the remaining residents; Hekekyan mentions a number of villages that were some years behind in their payments; he also noted that the village shaykhs were responsible for payment of the village assessment.[40] Finally, the penal code published as late as the first year of Saʿīd's rule (January 24, 1855) provided for the punishment of shaykhs who distributed unjustly the tax to be paid by their village.[41]

The recruitment of fellahs for public works, the factories, and the army of Muḥammad ʿAlī was carried out rather arbitrarily, and not on the basis of consistent village quotas. In some cases all the able-bodied men in the village were taken away.[42] A certain change occurred in this respect during the rule of ʿAbbās, when a set quota was imposed on each village and the village shaykhs were entrusted with the duty of carrying out the conscription (instead of the army).[43] The functioning of this system has been vividly described by Hekekyan Bey in his diaries. Writing about the village of Manṣūriyya in July, 1854, that is, the last month of ʿAbbās' rule, he says:

> . . . It is a certain fact that the number of hands this village alone sends for forced labour in the Pasha's palaces . . ., to the bridges of the Delta (the barrages), the Railway—and the viceregal farms, amounts to 450 . . . The labourers are maintained by the village; and they are relieved once a month; so that nearly a thousand of the male population are almost constantly on the move out of their village. It is the policy of the Government to keep the villages down by always keeping a certain number of their population away as hostages. On my arrival in the village I found the sheikhs organizing a body of 600 men, women and children . . . for the strengthening of a transverse dike. . . . These Sheikhs are the medium between the Government and the village. It is the Sheikhs who pay the taxes—choose the men to be sent to the public works etc.[44]

In the 1850's, therefore, the supply of labor for public works was the

[38] Mubārak, 14:116 (28–37).

[39] Hekekyan Papers, vol. 3, British Museum Add. 37450, ff. 70, 193.

[40] Hekekyan Papers, vol. 2, B.M. Add. 37449, f. 120 (for the year 1843); f. 259–60 (1844); vol. 3, B.M. Add. 37450, ff. 153, 164 (1846); vol. 7, B.M. Add. 37454, f. 366a (1854); etc.

[41] See *Qānūn-nāmeh al-Sulṭānī*, F. Jallad, *Qāmūs al-idāra wa'l-qaḍā'*, Alexandria, 1890, 2:99. Also A. von Kremer, *Aegypten*, Leipzig 1863, 2:63. For details about this code, see below, chapter 7.

[42] Cf. J. A. St. John, *Egypt and Mohammed Ali*, London, 1834, 2:176.

[43] Bayle St. John, *Village Life in Egypt*, London, 1852, 2:82–85.

[44] Hekekyan Papers, vol. 7, B.M. Add. 37454, ff. 365a–66a. For the development of the office, the tasks, and the social position of the *shaykh al-balad* in Egypt, see chapter 3, below.

responsibility of the village and its shaykh or shaykhs. Although this was not exactly the case in the days of Muḥammad ʿAlī, at that time too it was not the individual fellah who had been held responsible for a certain share in the maintenance of irrigation works or for a certain amount of labor for public works. We may therefore conclude our review of this period with the observation that no fundamental change occurred before the middle of the nineteenth century in any of the three aspects of the Egyptian village community referred to at the beginning of this study.

It was in the reign of Saʿīd (1854–63) that the decisive measures were taken which led to the elimination of two of the three attributes of the Egyptian village community dealt with here. As early as the first year of his reign, on January 27, 1855, Saʿīd enacted a law according to which male descendants of a fellah (and, under certain circumstances, also female descendants) acquired the legal right to inherit his lands. No such rights had ever existed in Egypt under Muslim rule. Furthermore, the same law provided that transfers of land from one peasant to another be certified by an official document (*ḥujja*) issued by the *mudīriyya* (governor's office), thereby depriving the *shaykh al-balad* of his arbitrary power in all matters regarding the peasant's lands.[45] This law put an end to the old custom of the village community according to which the village headman decided who was to receive the land of a deceased fellah.

Even more decisive was the second step in the same direction, namely, Saʿīd's Land Law of 24 Dhū al-Ḥijja 1274 A.H./August 5, 1858. This law extended considerably the fellah's property rights to the land he held. Article 1 applied the Muslim laws of inheritance to all such land. Articles 4 and 5 laid down the principle that a person who had held a certain plot of *kharājiyya* land[46] for five consecutive years, tilled it and paid its taxes, acquired irrevocable ownership of it. Article 8 permitted the owner of *kharājiyya* land to mortgage it, sell it, exchange it, or transfer it to somebody else, provided he informed the local authorities so that the change in ownership could be registered. Article 9 allowed the owner of such land to lease it—on condition the contract was made with the knowledge of the local authorities. According to Article 11 full property rights were acquired by the owners of *kharājiyya* land if they had erected a building, installed a *sāqiya* (water-raising apparatus for irrigation), or planted trees on it.[47] All these provisions aimed at consolidating the fellah's property rights to his

[45] Artin, pp. 101–2.

[46] At that time, most of the village lands in Egypt were *kharājiyya*, that is, land over which the government reserves certain rights of ownership.

[47] Artin, pp. 103–4; Gouvernement Egyptien, *La Législation en matière immobilière en Egypte*, pp. 3–4, 39. See also chapter 4, below.

land and thus weakened or abolished altogether the rights and the tasks of the village community to these lands. Moreover, to the best of the present writer's knowledge, after the 1850's the periodical redistribution of village lands in Upper Egypt was not mentioned again by any author or observer writing anything about contemporary Egypt.

Another significant change was brought about by Article 12 of Saʿīd's Land Law, which dealt with the expropriation of land by the state for public purposes (roads, canals, etc.). Until that time not only were the former owners of *kharājiyya* land expropriated for public purposes not entitled to compensation for such land, but even the tax on the land was not relinquished: it was imposed collectively on the remaining lands of the village community. The change introduced by Saʿīd's Land Law was that *kharājiyya* lands expropriated for public purposes were no longer taxable.[48]

This last provision of Saʿīd's Land Law was only a natural corollary of a much more profound development that had taken place in connection with the second aspect of the village community: Saʿīd had abolished the principle of collective village responsibility for tax payment.[49] This fundamental change has been observed by many authors who visited and described Egypt in Saʿīd's days. We will content ourselves with two examples. In 1858 P. Merruau wrote: ". . . Les cotes étant établies par avance et personnelles à chaque cultivateur, l'intermédiaire du chef de village est devenu inutile."[50] And A. von Kremer observed in his book *Aegypten*, published in 1863: "Die Steuern werden nun für jedes Individuum von der Mudirijje festgesetzt. . . . Die Steuern sind persönlich auf den Namen eines jeden eingetragen, nicht, wie früher, wo nur die Steuer des gesammten Dorfes eingeschrieben war, für welche alle Dorfbewohner solidarisch haften mussten".[51]

Thus the abolition of village responsibility for the payment of taxes, which seems to have already begun in the last years of the reign of Muḥammad ʿAlī, was completed in the 1850's. In Ismāʿīl's days the levying of taxes may have been a cruel affair, as shown, for instance, in Klunzinger's *Upper Egypt*,[52] but the tax assessments were individual, not by villages.

Only the third function of the Egyptian village community remained intact during the reign of Saʿīd and even of Ismāʿīl: the supply of labor for public works, the *corvée*, did not become the individual duty of each fellah but remained the responsibility of the village until foreign control was

[48] The right to compensation for such land was recognized only years later. Cf. Artin, pp. 203–9; *La Législation en matière immobilière*, p. 317.

[49] Cf. Nahas, p. 44; Crouchley, p. 110.

[50] P. Merruau, *L'Egypte contemporaine 1840–1857*, Paris, 1858, p. 63.

[51] Von Kremer, 1:256; 2:13.

[52] C. B. Klunzinger, *Upper Egypt: Its People and Its Products*, London, 1878, p. 69.

imposed on Egypt's finances and administration. Every village, or every proprietor of a village, had to furnish a certain quota. For instance, in a letter from the Egyptian Foreign Minister to the British Consul General, dated July 10, 1860, we read about a decree of the Viceroy which contained instructions to estate owners ". . . afin qu'ils fournissent le contingent d'hommes nécessaire tant pour le service militaire que pour tous autres services publics, conformément aux lois locales. . . ."[53] And von Kremer, who also describes Saʿīd's days, writes:

> Es sind daher in dem District, wo ein Kanal gegraben oder ausgebessert wird, die Dörfer fast ganz verlassen. Die Einwohner eines jeden Dorfs haben eine bestimmte Strecke zu bearbeiten und werden erst dann entlassen, wenn sie dieselbe beendigt haben. . . . Das System der Zwangsarbeiten, wobei meistens die Bezahlung nicht erfolgt, hat leider auch jetzt noch nicht aufgehört. . . . Von dem nächsten besten Dorfe werden so und so viel Mann requirirt.[54]

This principle was not abandoned in Ismāʿīl's days either. As late as the last year of his rule, the Commission Supérieure d'Enquête stated in its preliminary report to the Khedive that if a fellah deserted from the *corvée* and his family was unable to pay indemnity, the village was liable to pay.[55] McCoan (1877) says that the burden of the *corvée* is allotted by the *shaykh al-balad*.[56] Further proof that the *corvée* was not an individual duty was the fact that there were villages whose inhabitants were liable to forced labor, while other villages were exempt from it. Laborers on *ibʿādiyya*[57] estates, for instance, were exempt:

> This privilege naturally attracted the fellahs of the neighbouring lands, who, in order to escape the "corvée", squatted in large numbers on the various "Abadiehs."[58]
>
> . . . il suffit à un indigène, pour se soustraire aux charges de la prestation, imposées aux habitants des villages (balad), d'entrer au service d'un propriétaire d'Abadieh (Esbeh et Koufour).[59]

And even as late as 1882 a fellah from Minūfiyya province told Mr. Villiers Stuart the following, when asked about the *corvée*:

53 Cherif to Colquhoun, July 10, 1860, PRO, FO 141/37.

54 Von Kremer, 1:166, 257. It should be noted that, at the time of Saʿīd, recruitment for the army was also the collective responsibility of the village and not the individual duty of each fellah. See, for instance, Amīn Sāmī, *Taqwīm al-Nīl*, part 3, vol. 1, Cairo, 1936, pp. 239–40.

55 Egypt no. 2 (1879), C. 2233, p. 245.

56 J. C. McCoan, *Egypt as It Is*, London, n.d. [1877], pp. 182, 186.

57 See chapter 1, above.

58 Mr. Vivian to the Marquis of Salisbury, February 15, 1879, Egypt No. 5 (1879), C. 2397, p. 23.

59 *Moniteur Egyptien*, February 11, 1879. Inclosure in Vivian to Salisbury.

> ... the Sheikh el Beled used to fix who was to work and who was to be exempt and those who could bribe him to let them off did so. But since three years this has been changed. Now the villagers settle amongst themselves who is to go and they relieve each other at the work.[60]

Meantime, however, Anglo-French Dual Control had been imposed on Egypt's finances, and under its influence a decree was issued on January 25, 1881 according to which forced labor for public works became the individual obligation of every male person in Egypt, except certain groups explicitly mentioned in the decree—like all kinds of people occupied in religious offices, craftsmen, watchmen, inhabitants of towns, sick people, and so on. Everyone was permitted to send somebody else as a substitute, and inhabitants of certain kinds of settlements could pay an indemnity instead.[61] Additional decrees of the years 1887 and 1895 required every *shaykh al-balad* or *ʿumda* to supply the *mudīriyya* with a *nominal* list of men in their villages liable to recruitment for forced labor.[62] During that period forced labor was gradually abolished; what remained was the obligation to turn out for fighting locusts, strengthening dams in case of floods, and so on, which became, of course, the individual duty of each person and ceased to be the collective responsibility of the village.[63]

One might ask whether during the Mamluk and Ottoman period the Egyptian village as such ever was a strong and cohesive social unit. The sources contain too little material on the village for a definite answer to this question; they contain almost no material at all which would enable us to compare it with modern sociological research. Whatever the answer may be, the preceding analysis shows that during the nineteenth century the Egyptian village lost a number of functions which must have had the effect of creating a certain village solidarity: common tenure and the periodical redistribution of village lands, and common responsibility for the payment of taxes and the supply of labor. This development may be one of the reasons for the lack of any social coherence in the Egyptian village in our days:

> Le village égyptien n'est pas une commune au sens civique du mot, pas un organisme, mais une masse.[64]

> Wir finden auch keinerlei organische Zusammengehörigkeit der Bauernschaft eines Dorfes ... keinerlei Vertretung der Dorfgemeinschaft, keinerlei Ältestenrat,

[60] *Reports by Mr. Villiers Stuart respecting Reorganization in Egypt*, Egypt No. 7 (1883), C. 3554, p. 21 (Appendix).

[61] P. Gelat, *Répertoire de la législation et de l'administration Egyptienne*, vol. 1, part 2, Alexandria, 1889, p. 249.

[62] Gelat, 1 (2):253; and 3 (A, 1), Alexandria, 1897, p. 686.

[63] Cf. "Décret relatif aux réquisitions pour destruction des sauterelles, 16 Juin 1891," in U. Pace, *Répertoire permanent de législation Egyptienne*, Alexandria, 1934, no. 165.

[64] H. H.-Ayrout, s.J., *Fellahs*, Cairo, 1942, p. 111.

keinerlei Gemeindeversammlung. Es gibt deshalb auch keinen Versammlungsplatz aller . . . im Dorfe.[65]

. . . À aucun moment de notre enquête, nous n'avons jusqu'ici trouvé la vie communale organisée. Pas même les rudiments municipaux. . . .[66]

Another question to be asked is why the three attributes of the Egyptian village community dealt with in this article disappeared during the nineteenth century and not before. The main factor, it seems, was the profound economic revolution which Egypt was undergoing during that time, namely, the transition from basin irrigation to perennial irrigation. As a result of this development Egyptian agriculture was able to change gradually from a subsistence economy into a producer of cash crops for the market, especially cotton. Closer connection with the market and dependence upon its fluctuations brought on economic and social differentiation among the village population, or at least the opportunity for certain rural groups to enrich themselves and to climb up the social ladder. Such a differentiation and such opportunities for the rural population had never before existed in Muslim Egypt. The natural result was a growing tendency toward the introduction of full private property in land, toward private individualistic economy and enterprise. During the reigns of Saʿīd and Ismāʿīl this tendency corresponded to growing European influence on Egyptian finances and administration; and this was the time when private property in land and individual responsibility for the payment of taxes were introduced. If individual responsibility did not apply, at that time, to the supply of labor for the *corvée*, this is to be explained by the weakness of the administrative machine: organizing the recruitment of each individual for the labor service would have been too much for the government of Saʿīd or Ismāʿīl. It should be remembered, in this connection, that a cadastral survey had already been undertaken in Muḥammad ʿAlī's days, whereas the first real population census was not carried out until the end of the century.

To conclude: The Ottoman conquest resulted in no fundamental economic transformation that could explain the dissolution of the Egyptian village community, had it taken place at that time. As against this, the disappearance of the tangible attributes of a village community in nineteenth-century Egypt can be accounted for by an important economic and social transformation. In Syria, where no such change took place at that time, the village community remained intact until the beginning of the twentieth century.

[65] H. A. Winkler, *Bauern zwischen Wasser und Wüste*, Stuttgart, 1934, pp. 136, 140.

[66] J. Berque, "Sur la structure sociale de quelques villages égyptiens," *Annales Economies—Sociétés—Civilisations*, 1955, p. 214.

3

The Village Shaykh, 1800–1950

It is not too much to say that the whole life of the village turns upon the Omdeh.—
LORD CROMER

Lord Cromer's statement of 1905 may be said to hold true for the whole period between 1800 and 1950 which we are here considering. Nevertheless, basic changes did take place within this space of time in the functions, socio-economic status, and political power of the Egyptian village shaykh. These changes, their causes, and their interaction are the subject of this study.

It will be necessary first of all to explain some of the terms associated with the office of village headman in the literature on nineteenth-century Egypt: *shaykh*, *shaykh al-balad*, and *ʿumda*. The evidence is often contradictory: according to the French savants and sources dependent on them, most Egyptian villages at the time had several shaykhs, each of whom stood at the head of a family or clan. By the end of the eighteenth century a head shaykh called shaykh al-balad was appointed in each village.[1] According to the historian al-Jabartī, it was the French who introduced this innovation during the period of their rule over Egypt after Napoleon's expedition. However, Jabartī himself tells us about ordinary village shaykhs called shaykh al-balad in the parts of his chronicle dealing with the early eighteenth century, and Evliya Çelebi, in his description of Egypt at the

Originally published as "The Village Shaykh in Modern Egypt, 1800–1950," in U. Heyd (ed.), *Studies in Islamic History and Civilization*, Scripta Hierosolymitana, vol. 9 (Jerusalem, The Magnes Press, 1961), pp. 121–53. (Here somewhat expanded, with many additional references.)

[1] Le Comte Estève, "Mémoire sur les finances de l'Egypte," in *Description de l'Egypte, état moderne*, 1, Paris, 1809, p. 310; Michel-Ange Lancret, "Mémoire sur le système d'imposition territorial et sur l'administration des provinces de l'Egypte," in *Description de l'Egypte, état moderne*, 1:241, 244; General Reynier, *State of Egypt after the Battle of Heliopolis*, London, 1802, pp. 61–62; N. W. Senior, *Conversations and Journals in Egypt and Malta 1855–1856*, London, 1882, 1:279; S. J. Shaw, *The Financial and Administrative Organization and Development of Ottoman Egypt 1517–1798*, Princeton, 1962, p. 54.

end of the seventeenth century, has a shaykh al-balad, explained by him as *köylerde fellâhlar hâkimi.*[2] From the middle of the nineteenth century on, an additional name appears—*ʿumda* (*ʿumad* in the plural; the term generally employed in European literature is *omdeh*, in keeping with the pronunciation of the word in spoken Egyptian Arabic). Throughout the second half of the nineteenth century we find the two terms used indiscriminately. Attempts to distinguish definitively between them have yielded nothing conclusive. There are those who maintain that the ʿumda was in charge of several villages, while the shaykh al-balad invariably headed only one;[3] but in his geographic-biographic encyclopedia Mubārak lists dozens of villages, including small ones, each of which was headed by an ʿumda—or even two ʿumdas in a substantial number of cases.[4] It appears that the British Agent was closer to the truth when he wrote, in his Report for 1906: "The title 'Omdeh' (Mayor) has now generally taken the place of 'Shaikh el-Beled' which was commonly used at the time Lord Dufferin wrote his Report (1883)."[5] An order issued in 1887 and dealing with the recruitment of manpower for public works specifies that the lists of recruits are to be drawn up by the shaykh al-balad, while an amendment to this same order, published in 1895, employs the word ʿumda instead.[6] The Agent's statement should, however, be accepted with the reservation that the change began not toward the end of the century but as early as the 1850's.

The office of ʿumda was legally defined in the ʿUmda Law of 1895[7] and in the law of 1947 on ʿumdas and shaykhs.[8] These provide that the ʿumda administers the village while the shaykh, his subordinate, heads part of the village (*ḥiṣṣa*) or a smaller locality (*ʿizba, nagʿ, kafr*, or *nazla*) which is actually the dependency of a village. The Minister of Interior may, however, issue a special ruling appointing two ʿumdas in one village or, temporarily, a single ʿumda over two or more villages. This is the practice in Egypt to this day.[9]

[2] Jabartī, 4:106. Cf. 1:180, 190; Evliya Çelebi, *Seyahatname*, vol. 10, Istanbul, 1938, p. 159 (cf. also pp. 753, 803, etc.)

[3] Hekekyan Papers, vol. 7, B.M. Add. 37454, f. 220; D. Mackenzie Wallace, *Egypt and the Egyptian Question*, London, 1883, pp. 209–10.

[4] Mubārak, 12:12; 13:62; 16:65; etc.

[5] Egypt No. 1 (1907), Cd. 3394, p. 28 n.

[6] Philippe Gelat, *Répertoire (annoté) de la législation et de l'administration egyptienne*, 1 (2), Alexandria, 1889, p. 253; 3, (A, 2), Alexandria, 1897, p. 686.

[7] "Décret réglementant la nomination des omdehs et des cheikhs—16 mars, 1895," in Gelat, 3 (A, 2):367–71.

[8] Law No. 141 of August 29, 1947, *al-Waqāʾiʿ al-Miṣriyya* (*Official Gazette*) of November 30, 1947.

[9] Cf. H. Habib-Ayrout s.J., *Fellahs*, Cairo, 1942, p. 41; J. Berque, *Histoire sociale d'un village égyptien au XX ième siècle*, Paris-La Haye, 1957, pp. 47, 65; Sayyid Quṭb, *Ṭifl min al-qarya*, Cairo, 1945, pp. 152–53; H. A. Winkler, *Bauern zwischen Wasser und Wüste*, Stuttgart, 1934, p. 137.

Appointment of the ʿUmda and the Shaykh

Like the village headmen in other Middle Eastern countries, the shaykh al-balad or ʿumda in Egypt represented the authorities to the villagers rather than the villagers before the authorities. "Al-ʿumad wa'l-mashāyikh hum nuwwāb al-ḥukūma," said a circular letter of the Ministry of the Interior to the *mudīrs* in 1884.[10] It was therefore natural that throughout the period under discussion holders of this office were appointed by the authorities and not elected by the villagers. Under the *iltizām* the shaykh was appointed by the *multazim*, generally in a special ceremony in which he was invested with a cloak;[11] during the period of Muḥammad ʿAlī, according to Bowring, the shaykh al-balad was frequently displaced and replaced by the government.[12] An English traveler who visited Egypt under ʿAbbās (1848–54) also noted that the shaykh al-balad was appointed by the central government, either directly or by the top administrative officials—the *mudīr* (governor of a province) or the *nāẓir* (inspector of a district).[13] This also applies to the reign of Saʿīd (1854–63).[14] Under Ismāʿīl (1863–79), the period when the village notables reached the peak of their economic, social, and political power, the government's appointment of village headmen became nothing more than a formal stamp of approval on what constituted, according to the impression of contemporary observers, virtual election by their fellow villagers;[15] but even then the government succeeded in retaining the power of decision as to who would be village shaykh in newly established settlements.[16]

After the British occupation the government won back its authority in the selection of the ʿumda, the procedure for whose appointment was set in detail in the law of 1895. Under this legislation[17] the *mudīriyya* prepared the list of candidates for the positions of ʿumda and shaykh, the final selection being in the hands of a commission headed by the *mudīr* himself or his authorized representative. The other members were a representative of the Ministry of Interior, the local prosecutor, and four notables or ʿumdas appointed for the purpose by the *mudīr*. Further, even this appointment, though made by a body in which the authorities exerted such overwhelming

[10] *Majmūʿat al-manshūrāt wa'l-qarārāt wa'l-muʿāhadāt*, Cairo-Būlāq, 1884, pp. 94f.

[11] Lancret, p. 241; Reynier, pp. 61–62, 138–39.

[12] J. Bowring, *Report on Egypt and Candia*, London, 1840, p. 121.

[13] Bayle St. John, *Village Life in Egypt*, London, 1852, 1:75.

[14] Cf. Senior, 1:279.

[15] J. C. McCoan, *Egypt as It Is*, London, 1877, p. 115; Wallace, pp. 208–9, 215 (Wallace describes such an election in detail).

[16] Mubārak, 14:48, says in connection with the new village of ʿIzbat Shalaqān, which came into being when public works were undertaken in the vicinity: "warattabnā lahā mashāyikh" ("we"—i.e., the Minister of Public Works).

[17] Décret of March 16, 1895, Clauses 2, 3, and 5.

influence, did not go into effect until the Ministry of Interior approved it. In addition, the Ministry might decide to appoint two ʿumdas in one village or one ʿumda for several villages, and it also decided how many shaykhs there would be in each village (the *maʾmūr*, the administrative official of the *markaz* (district), divided up the village population into the *ḥiṣaṣ* of the various shaykhs). The Ministry of Interior could dismiss ʿumdas and shaykhs.

The law of 1895 remained in force, with very minor amendments, almost throughout the first half of the twentieth century, and successive governments made full use of their authority to discharge ʿumdas and to return them to office. In 1925, Ismāʿīl Ṣidqī Pasha, Minister of Interior in the anti-Wafdist Zīwar government, reappointed twenty-two ʿumdas who had been dismissed a year earlier by the Zaghlūl government.[18] At the end of the same year the Zīwar government dismissed ten ʿumdas in the province of Minūfiyya and thirty-one more resigned in protest;[19] less than a year later the government of ʿAdlī Yeghen, which depended for support on a Wafdist majority in Parliament, restored all the ʿumdas to office.[20] The broadest sweep of all was made at the beginning of 1935, when the government of Tawfīq Nasīm relieved from their posts some six hundred ʿumdas appointed by the preceding government.[21] The lighter side of these appointments and dismissals was depicted by the Egyptian writer, Tawfīq al-Ḥakīm: the change of régime in the village is marked by a solemn procession accompanied by wails of lament on one side and shouts of joy on the other, while the telephone is borne from the residence of the dismissed ʿumda to the house of the villager appointed to take his place.[22]

In various Egyptian quarters this situation led to the demand that the ʿumda be elected by the villagers rather than designated by the authorities. Motions to this effect were frequently submitted to the General and Legislative Assemblies in the years 1912 to 1914.[23] A repeated plea to substitute direct elections for government appointment was voiced mainly by the Wafd during the period between the two world wars. Inasmuch as the

[18] Lord Lloyd, *Egypt since Cromer*, London, 1934, 2:110; *Oriente Moderno* (henceforth *OM*), 5 (1925):38.

[19] *OM*, 6 (1926):48–49; ʿAbd al-Raḥmān al-Rāfiʿī, *Fī Aʿqāb al-thawra al-miṣriyya*, Cairo, 1947, 1:247–48.

[20] *OM*, 6 (1926):491.

[21] *OM*, 15 (1935):25, quoting *The Times* (London), January 5, 1935.

[22] Tawfīq al-Ḥakīm, *Yawmiyyāt nāʾib fī l-aryāf*, Cairo-Maktabat al-Ādāb, n.d., pp. 100–102.

[23] *Journal Officiel*, Supplement to No. 65 of 1912, p. 8; Supplement to No. 93 of 1912, pp. 9–12; Supplement to No. 59, May 16, 1914. Cf. also J. Alexander, *The Truth about Egypt*, London, 1911, pp. 126–27. Some notables retorted by proposing to deny the inhabitants of the villages any say in the choice of ʿumdas and appointing them only from families which traditionally had supplied them ("les familles ayant toujours joui de ce privilège"). Muḥammad Shurayʿī in the Legislative Council, *Journal Officiel*, Supplement to Nos. 27 and 44 of 1912. For the Shurayʿīs and other traditional ʿumda families, see below.

Wafd enjoyed a large measure of popular support, this proposal was apparently designed to prevent the party's opponents from forging a base of popular support for themselves through the administrative dismissal of the ʿumdas, most of whom backed the Wafd, and their replacement by others. In the summer of 1926 the Parliamentary Commission on Interior Affairs drafted a bill providing for the election of the ʿumdas and shaykhs for a period of seven years by an electorate consisting of every villager with the right to vote. However, the Prime Minister, ʿAdlī Yeghen, who was not himself a Wafdist although his government leaned on the Wafd majority in Parliament, opposed the bill, and Saʿd Zaghlūl, who was not willing to risk the government's defeat, dropped the proposal.[24] It was revived during the short term of office of Muṣṭafā al-Naḥḥās as Prime Minister in 1928,[25] but the Cabinet fell before it could be passed. When the Wafd returned to power in 1936–37, it again failed in its effort to put the proposal through Parliament. The Speech from the Throne read by Naḥḥās Pasha on November 18, 1937 announced that the ʿUmda Law of 1895 would be amended to provide for the direct election of ʿumdas and shaykhs,[26] and on November 30 of that year a commission established to draft legislation concerning the village councils (*majālis qarawiyya*) submitted to the Prime Minister a plan under which ʿumdas and shaykhs would be elected by the population of their villages.[27] The Wafd government was, however, dismissed exactly one month later.

Dr. Muḥammad ʿAbd-Allāh al-ʿArabī, a jurist who was long in charge of the Ministry of Interior section supervising the appointment and dismissal of ʿumdas, had since the 1940's been one of the outstanding fighters for a change in the method of their appointment. In a lecture delivered early in 1942, he proposed that every village elect a village council (*majlis qarawī*) which in turn would select the ʿumda from among its members. The few village councils that did come into being in the course of twenty years (in eighty-four out of 4,200 villages) were, according to al-ʿArabī, lifeless bodies, being, in practice, government institutions rather than representatives of the villagers.[28]

[24] *OM*, 6 (1926):499, quoting *The Times* (London), August 27, 1926; Lloyd, 2:180–81. Lord Lloyd says that such a measure would have had disastrous consequences in the system of the administration. He disregards the disastrous consequences of the very frequent political dismissals of ʿumdas.

[25] Lloyd, 2:257.

[26] *OM*, 17 (1937):632.

[27] *OM*, 18 (1938), 48, quoting *al-Ahrām*, December 1, 1937.

[28] M. Z. ʿAbd al-Qādir, "Ikhtiyār al-ʿumad", *al-Ahrām*, April 9, 1942. Village councils had been established according to a law of February 9, 1918, but apparently without much *élan* from the beginning. See M. Delcroix, "L'Institution municipale en Egypte," *L'Egypte contemporaine*, 13 (1922):299. For text of the 1918 law, see U. Pace, *Répertoire permanent de législation égyptienne*, Alexandria, 1934, s.v. "Conseils de village."

In 1947, as has been noted, the Law of 1895 regarding ʿUmdas and Shaykhs was replaced by new legislation.[29] Notwithstanding a number of far-reaching modifications and amendments, the Law of 1947 did not affect the basic fact that the authorities retained the final say in the ʿumda's appointment. This law provided for the ʿumda's election by a public body consisting of the candidates themselves, the shaykhs, anyone qualified to be a candidate for shaykh, and anyone paying £E 3 a year in taxes (Article 7). However, the ʿumda was appointed by a commission called the *lajnat al-shiyākhāt*, made up of the *mudīr* or his deputy, a representative of the Ministry of Interior, the district attorney, and four notables chosen by the district ʿumdas and appointed to their posts by the Minister of Interior. This commission might refuse to confirm the ʿumda's election; moreover, approval by the Minister of Interior was also required. The ʿumda could be dismissed by the Minister or the *mudīr*.[30]

Notwithstanding everything that has been said above about the government's decisive power over the appointment of the ʿumda, local considerations always played an important role in the selection of the man for the position, inasmuch as the government would derive no benefit from the appointment of someone who had no influence over the villagers. Foremost among these local considerations was the candidate's socio-economic status; and indeed, from the time that the office of shaykh al-balad or ʿumda came into existence, an affluent man, if not the most affluent in the village, was always appointed to the post. This fact was already noted by some of the French observers who accompanied Napoleon's expedition.[31] There is no evidence to the effect that Muḥammad ʿAlī behaved differently; on the contrary, there are accounts which indicate that under his rule, too, the village shaykhs belonged to wealthy families.[32] On the period of ʿAbbās and Saʿīd, W. N. Senior quotes Hekekyan, the Armenian engineer who was a shrewd observer of the Egypt of his day: "After him [the saint] come the sheykhs or great landed proprietors. The most eminent of these, taking property and personal qualities into consideration, is generally appointed by the Government Sheykh al-Beled. . . ."[33]

[29]See note 8, above.

[30]The Law of 1947 recognized, however, the right of big landowners (the five or fewer who owned four-fifths or more of the village lands) to designate half of the candidates for the office of ʿumda (Article 5). Although no evidence has been found by the present writer, one may assume that even prior to the Law of 1947 large landowners had a say in the election of ʿumdas in villages which formed a part of their estates. However, in modern Egypt the ʿumda was never officially the representative of the landowner—in contrast with the *kadkhudā* in Persia (see A. K. S. Lambton, *Landlord and Peasant in Persia*, London, 1953, pp. 190–91, 338).

[31]Lancret, pp. 241, 259; Estève, p. 310; Reynier, pp. 61–62.

[32]Cf., e.g., J. A. St. John, *Egypt and Nubia*, London, 1845, p. 194; Bowring, p. 45; Mubārak, 17:21.

[33]Senior, 1:279.

The correspondent of the *Times* of London, D. Mackenzie Wallace, says the same of Ismāʿīl's period: "By traditional custom and in accordance with practical convenience the office devolves on the largest landowner. . . ."[34] ʿAlī Pasha Mubārak's geographic-biographic encyclopedia affords for the same period dozens of examples of ʿumdas belonging to their villages' wealthiest and most respected families.[35]

As we shall see, the socio-economic standing of the shaykh and ʿumda deteriorated substantially after the British occupation. Nevertheless, in this period, too, Egypt's successive governments sought to maintain the principle that ʿumdas and shaykhs should be recruited from among the affluent and the large property owners. A circular dispatched by the Ministry of Interior to the mudīrs of Egypt's provinces on March 23, 1890 is most enlightening in this respect. It instructed mudīrs not to appoint as shaykh anyone without landed property: His parents' ownership of land could not make him eligible. It was essential that the shaykh al-balad be himself a landowner and a man of standing in his village, the circular pointed out.[36] This principle was embodied in the Law of 1895, which required every candidate for the office of ʿumda to be the owner of at least ten feddans and every shaykh to own at least five feddans (except in villages where all the land was owned by proprietors not residing in the village.) If fewer than five persons in the village fulfilled the above requirements, the ʿumda was to be selected from among those who paid the highest taxes.[37] The Law of 1947 retained this principle, with some minor alterations dictated by the times. It stated (Article 3 [3]) that a candidate for the post of ʿumda must pay a land tax of at least £E 10 a year, and a candidate for the office of shaykh at least £E 5 a year. Article 4 stipulated that if not enough villagers had these qualifications, those who paid the next highest taxes were to be co-opted to the list until the required number of candidates was secured.

This principle—that the ʿumda and the shaykhs be chosen from among

[34]Wallace, p. 208 (see also p. 191); Baron de Malortie, *Egypt: Native Rulers and Foreign Interference*, London, 1882, p. 214 n: "In practice . . . we find generally the richest man also the sheikh."

[35]Mubārak, 8:82, 102; 9:7; 10:56, 65; 11:16, 70; 12:127, 129, 137; 14:4, 5; 15:47, 79; 17:7, 22; etc.

[36]Fīlīb Jallād, *Qāmūs al-Idāra wa-'l-qaḍā'*, Alexandria, n.d., 5:770. A similar circular of a few years earlier had required the mudīrs to appoint ʿumdas from among "*al-buyūt al-shahīra arbāb al-aṭyān.*" *Majmūʿat al-manshūrāt wa'l-qarārāt*, 1884, pp. 94f.

[37]Décret of March 16, 1895, Clause 1. It is interesting to note that in one circular to mudīrs at about the same time they were requested to see to it that positions of village shaykhs which had become vacant be filled with *ʿumdat al-muzāriʿīn* (*Majmūʿat al-qarārāt*, 1887, pp. 169–70). The *ʿumdat al-muzāriʿīn* has been defined as "the chief cultivator; he is not an official but is the recognized wise man on all questions of agriculture. . . ." (Sir Thomas Russell Pasha, *Egyptian Service 1902–1946*, London, 1949, p. 45.)

the village's largest proprietors—was, accordingly, adhered to for over 150 years. The inevitable result was that in practice these offices were in many cases handed down from father to son, or at least remained within the same families in each village. Almost every writer dealing with the Egyptian village since the eighteenth century has pointed out that, generally, the office of shaykh al-balad or ʿumda was inherited.[38] Among the families which retained the office of shaykh al-balad or ʿumda for generations in the nineteenth century were the al-Sharīfs of Ibyār village (Gharbiyya), the al-Hawārīs of Tirsā (Fayyūm), the al-Jiyārs of Khirbitā (Buḥayra), the ʿAbd al-Ḥaqqs of Duwayna (Asyūṭ), the Shaʿīrs of ʿAshmā (Minūfiyya), the al-ʿUqālīs of al-ʿUqāl (Asyūṭ), the Siyāghs of Luxor, and others.[39] Among the ʿumdas whose names I have seen mentioned in the mid-twentieth-century Egyptian press and whose ancestors held this office back in the nineteenth century are al-Wakīl in Sumukhrāṭ (Buḥayra), Atrabī in Ikhṭāb (Daqahliyya), al-Shurayʿī in Samālūṭ (Minyā), and others.[40] There were some villages with two rival leading families between which the office of ʿumda passed back and forth.[41] In a great many cases, however, when the ʿumda was dismissed, his post was given to his brother or to a relative.[42] Another result of choosing the ʿumda from the richest family in the village was that in many villages the ʿumda and at least one of the shaykhs were from the same family.[43]

The Functions of the Village Shaykh

The functions of the shaykh al-balad or ʿumda underwent basic changes between the end of the eighteenth century and the middle of the twentieth. As the *multazim*'s representative among the village folk, the shaykh al-balad exercised both political and economic functions. He passed the *multazim*'s instructions on to the fellahs, adjudicated disputes, and saw to the execution of his commands and verdicts through his armed auxiliaries, the *khafir*s or

[38] Cf. Lancret, p. 259; Estève, p. 310; Bowring, p. 121; Bayle St. John, p. 75; de Malortie, p. 214 n.; Wallace, p. 191; Mubārak, 8:13; 10:98, 99; 13:52; 17:22; *Reports by Mr. Villiers Stuart respecting Reorganization in Egypt*, Egypt No. 7 (1883), C. 3554, p. 29; Berque, p. 65; I. Lichtenstadter, "An Arab Egyptian Family," *Middle East Journal*, vol. 6, Autumn, 1952, p. 381; H. Ammar, *Growing Up in an Egyptian Village*, London, 1954, p. 64; etc.

[39] Cf. ʿAbd al-Raḥmān al-Rāfiʿī, *ʿAṣr Ismāʿīl*, 2d ed., Cairo, 1948, 2:82–84, 110ff., 149ff.; idem, *al-Thawra al-ʿUrābiyya*, Cairo, 1937, pp. 176ff.; Mubārak, 10:32, 93; 11:70; 14:51, 53; G. Legrain, *Une Famille copte de Haute-Egypte*, Brussels, 1945, p. 32.

[40] Cf. al-Rāfiʿī, *ʿAṣr Ismāʿīl*, 2:83, 84, 110, and *al-Ahrām*, June 28, 1943, March 20, 1944, September 19, 1952, and February 28, 1954 (obituaries).

[41] Cf. Lancret, p. 244; Mubārak, 9:86; Tawfīq al-Ḥakīm, pp. 101–2.

[42] Cf. Wallace, p. 209; see also example in *al-Ahrām*, April 14, 1955.

[43] See, e.g., *al-Qarārāt waʾl-manshūrāt*, Būlāq, 1888, pp. 504, 737–78; 1890, pp. 231, 649; 1891, pp. 105 (ʿumda and two shaykhs), 128; 1898, pp. 163, 183, 323, 389, 418, 444 (ʿumda and two shaykhs); 1899, p. 437; 1900, pp. 75, 179, etc.

ghafirs. For this purpose he had the power to arrest fellahs and to have them flogged. He was responsible for the village's land, supervised its cultivation, and saw to the collection of the *multazim*'s due.[44] Further, in Upper Egypt (and apparently also in Middle Egypt), where all the village land was redivided each year, it was the shaykh's task to carry out this reallocation.[45] Even in Lower Egypt, where this annual redivision was not the custom, the shaykh al-balad was responsible for providing the *multazim* with new fellahs in place of those who could not pay the taxes imposed on them.[46]

When the *iltizām* was abolished, the village shaykh was transformed from a representative of the *multazim* to that of the government, but otherwise there were no radical changes in his functions. He continued to be "political chief of his village . . . [he] settles quarrels and terminates disputes amiably, is Chief of the Police. . . ."[47] For instance, it was the mashāyikh al-balad who were charged with searching for, and returning to their homes, fellahs who had fled their villages in consequence of the growing taxes and man-power levies. They were also supposed to hand over criminals who had taken refuge in their villages, and if, fearing revenge, they hesitated to do so, a detachment of Albanian soldiers might be sent to give them a beating until they changed their mind.[48] Shaykhs were held responsible for thefts occurring in their villages and were forced to make compensation for stolen goods.[49] Frequently they led contingents of fellahs of their villages which had been recruited for public works.[50] They also retained the functions associated with allocating land and collecting taxes: "They superintend sowing, planting, harvest, transport of produce. . . ."[51]

Since under Muḥammad ʿAlī the fellahs' holdings were not yet inheritable, it was up to the shaykh al-balad to decide who would get the land of the villagers who died. When title to the lands was registered, in 1814, the shaykhs furnished the required data to Muḥammad ʿAlī's officials, and

[44]Jabartī, 4:207–8; Lancret, pp. 241, 244; Estève, pp. 311–12; Reynier, p. 64. "Souvent les *cheykhs el-beled* vous vexent, vous font payer des avanies qu'ils partagent avec les moultezimes. . . ." (Menou, aux habitans de l'Egypte, Le Kaire, 6 Brumaire an IX, *Courier de l'Egypte*, No. 87, 15 Brumaire an IX, p. 2).

[45]Lancret, p. 247; P. S. Girard, "Mémoire sur l'agriculture, l'industrie et le commerce de l'Egypte," in *Description de l'Egypte, état moderne*, 2 (1), Paris, 1812, p. 586.

[46]De Chabrol, "Essai sur les moeurs des habitans modernes de l'Egypte," in *Description de l'Egypte, état moderne*, 2 (1):480.

[47]Campbell Report, FO 78/408B.

[48]Order of Muḥammad ʿAlī dated February 10, 1844, in FO 141/11; N. Hamont, *L'Egypte sous Méhémet-Ali*, Paris, 1843, 1:66; Wallace, pp. 260–62.

[49]Order of the Dīwān al-Māliyya dated 8 Jumādā II 1260 A.H./June 25, 1844, art. 121 of *Qānūn al-Muntakhabāt*, Jallād, 3:369.

[50]Cf. H. Rivlin, *The Agricultural Policy of Muḥammad ʿAlī in Egypt*, Cambridge, Mass., 1961, pp. 219–20, 244–45.

[51]Campbell Report.

certificates to those who sought to establish land claims. They also gave evidence with regard to what the former *multazim*'s income from the village had been (for purposes of calculating the indemnity due him from his expropriated lands).[52] At registration time they assessed the land of every village for taxes: it is said that for this purpose the shaykhs of Upper Egypt were brought to appraise land in Lower Egypt, and vice versa.[53] Their functions, however, extended not only to valuation but to collection:

> H. H. [Muḥammad ʿAlī], as a measure of finance, lately assembled all the sheiks of districts, 126 in number and submitted to them . . . the necessity of obliging the cultivators to pay up their arrears amounting to . . . 25,000,000 piasters. . . . A great part of these arrears are said to be in the hands of the sheiks of the villages, the native secretaries and Coptic writers.[54]

Various observers point out another function of the shaykh al-balad in the days of Muḥammad ʿAlī: the duty of extending hospitality to wayfarers: "Travellers, with Firman from the Pasha, are lodged . . . by the Cheik el Beled and provided by him with . . . animals, guides and provisions."[55] We may assume this to have been a function of the village shaykhs before Muḥammad ʿAlī as well; the fact that accounts of the period do not mention this may be ascribed to two reasons. In the first place, before Muḥammad ʿAlī travel had been insecure and the Europeans had journeyed much less frequently in the countryside (on their inland voyages they had generally sailed the Nile on hired boats, spending the night on board; when they did require hospitality, they preferred, for reasons of security, that of the Mamluk kāshif, the Bey's provincial officer).[56] Secondly, there are very few Arabic sources on the eighteenth-century village, and their writers must have considered hospitality something so self-evident that it did not require mentioning. Still, we find in al-Jabartī the story of Shaykh ʿĀrif of Sūhāj, whose house had been open to travelers of all classes for generations. Like many other hosts, he met the travelers' needs and equipped them for the road out of the income of the *rizaq aḥbāsiyya* (*waqf* lands), and he and others claimed before the agents of Muḥammad ʿAlī that they would be

[52] Y. Artin-Bey, *La Propriété foncière en Egypte*, Cairo, 1883, pp. 101, 276; Jabartī, 4:209, 257–58.

[53] Hekekyan Papers, vol. 3, British Museum Add. 37450, f. 169.

[54] Reports on Egypt by Henry Salt, British Consul General, March 10, 1827, PRO, FO 78/160. Cf. also Campbell to Palmerston, October 26, 1833, FO 78/228; Jabartī, 4:256, 273; von Kremer, 1:255. Muḥammad ʿAlī's *Lāʾiḥat zirāʿat al-fallāḥ*, published December, 1829–January, 1830, enumerates, in addition to some of the above mentioned functions, responsibility for the irrigation system and providing people for the *corvée* and the army. Its provisions were, however, theoretical to a large extent. See Rivlin, pp. 95–97.

[55] Campbell Report; cf. also von Kremer, 1:255, and J. A. St. John, *Egypt and Nubia*, pp. 96, 194 (describing the unpleasant side of this hospitality).

[56] Cf., e.g., M. Savary, *Lettres sur l'Egypte*, Paris, 1785–86; C. S. Sonnini, *Voyage dans la Haute et la Basse Egypte*, Paris, an VII, etc.

unable to continue this practice if the *waqf* lands were expropriated.[57]

Under ʿAbbās an important additional function fell to the village shaykhs: recruiting fellahs for the army and public works. In the days of Muḥammad ʿAlī this draft had been carried out rather arbitrarily: sometimes all the able-bodied men of a village were taken by military forces without the intermediary of any civil authority.[58] On the other hand, ʿAbbās who did not need so many draftees—both because he reduced the scale of public works and because he conducted no wars—imposed manpower quotas on all villages in proportion to their population. The village shaykhs were responsible for filling the quotas:

> On the present occasion, the duty of carrying out the conscription, instead of devolving on the Nizam, or regular troops, was entrusted entirely to the sheiks of the villages, with power to call in the assistance, when necessary, of that estimable rural police, the Arnaout cavalry. Perhaps these officials were never engaged in an operation at once so invidious and so profitable.[59]

As against this expansion of the village shaykhs' function in the period of ʿAbbās, their authority in land and tax matters was substantially reduced under Saʿīd. A law of January 27, 1855 already provided that, from then on, land transfers would be based on official documents issued by the *mudīr* and no longer on the evidence of the shaykh al-balad. The same law also set out inheritance rights with respect to *kharājiyya* lands, thus depriving the shaykhs of the authority to reallocate lands upon the holder's death (the rights of fellahs to transmit their holdings in inheritance were further expanded in Saʿīd's Land Law of August 5, 1858).[60]

As for taxes, under Saʿīd's tenure collective responsibility of the village for the payment of taxes was abolished, thus taking away from the village shaykhs the power to allocate taxes among the villagers—a function they had fulfilled until the first years of Saʿīd's rule: "Les cotes étant établies par avance et personnelles à chaque cultivateur, l'intermédiaire du chef de village est devenue inutile."[61]

This does not mean that the shaykh al-balad or ʿumda was shorn of all his tax-collecting functions. On the contrary, once it was no longer his job to divide up a fixed village assessment among the landholders, a diversification of his duties in this domain seems to have taken place under Ismāʿīl.

57 Jabartī, 4:183–84. On *waqf* see chapter 5, below.

58 J. A. St. John, *Egypt and Mohammed Ali*, London, 1834, 2:176.

59 Bayle St. John, *Village Life in Egypt*, 2:84. Amīn Sāmī, *Taqwīm al-Nīl*, part 3, Cairo, 1936, 1:239–40; Hekekyan Papers, vol. 7, British Museum Add. 37454, ff. 365a–66a. See also chapter 2, above.

60 Artin, pp. 101–4. In other Oriental countries, too, the duties of village officials shrank with the development of private property. Cf. K. A. Wittfogel, *Oriental Despotism*, New Haven, 1957, p. 119.

61 P. Merruau, *L'Egypte contemporaine 1840–1857*, Paris, 1858, p. 63.

This was a time when lands were periodically reclassified for tax purposes, and it was on the basis of the shaykhs' and ʿumdas' evidence that the lands were assigned to the various categories, or even assessed for tax purposes.[62] The duty of village shaykhs to collect the taxes of his village and transmit the yield to the *ṣarrāf*s (tax collectors) was expressly reiterated in Article 28 of the decree of September, 1871, providing for the establishment of village councils.[63] Moreover, as late as 1878 the village shaykhs of Upper Egypt allocated the professional tax among the artisans of their villages.[64] At the same time, the village shaykhs retained others of their previous functions: they continued to be responsible for the provision and selection of manpower for the *corvée* and for military service;[65] they continued to be in charge of public security in the village and to arbitrate disputes;[66] and in this period too, they had to extend hospitality to passing travelers:

> Without being exactly an innkeeper, he is bound to receive strangers, he has almost every day to entertain various kinds of officials, providing food for them and their beasts, and he is not allowed to ask anything for so doing. However, he takes care afterwards to repay himself with the moneys that his servants often receive from the guests (the officials as a rule give nothing), and takes what meat, fowls, eggs, &c., he requires now from one member of his village flock now from another, and thus prudently shares the burden of quartering strangers.[67]

In addition, it was during this period that the village shaykhs were charged with a number of tasks connected with the introduction of sanitary supervision into the villages.[68] However, it is difficult to tell whether the relevant regulations of the Sanitary Board were carried into effect.

The village shaykhs' functions were radically altered after Ismāʿīl's deposition and the imposition of Dual Control over Egypt's finances, and then under the British occupation. In the first place, some of the functions that had constituted the basis of the village shaykh's socio-economic and political power in earlier periods were abolished or restricted. The most

[62] Artin, pp. 144–49, 166, 202, 208 n. Egypt No. 14 (1885), C. 4421, p. 93.

[63] See Sāmī, part 3, 2:945.

[64] Cf. G. Baer, *Egyptian Guilds in Modern Times*, Jerusalem, 1964, p. 90. See also *Majmūʿat al-dakrītāt waʾl-qarārāt*, 1876–80, p. 148.

[65] McCoan, pp. 115, 186; Wallace, pp. 208, 215; Stuart Reports, p. 21; Earl of Cromer, *Modern Egypt*, London, 1908, 2:190.

[66] McCoan, p. 115; Wallace, p. 215; Stuart Reports, pp. 5, 25. In August, 1871, Ismāʿīl created special "Judicial Councils" in towns and large villages to take over the judicial functions of the shaykhs (Jallād, 4:58–67; see also *Reformen im Verwaltungs- und Finanzwesen Egyptens*, Wien, 1872). However, according to Mubārak's work, published about twenty years later, less than forty villages had such councils.

[67] C. B. Klunzinger, *Upper Egypt: Its People and Its Products*, London, 1878, pp. 119–120.

[68] Intendance Générale Sanitaire d'Egypte, *Règlements sanitaires autorisés par le gouvernement de S.A. Le Vice-Roi d'Egypte. En vigueur au 1er janvier 1866 et publié sous la présidence de M. Colucci-Bey*, Alexandria, 1866, pp. 127–28.

important of these was recruitment for the *corvée*. Under foreign control and British administration manpower levies were gradually restricted to a few emergencies, such as fighting pests or manning the dikes at floodtime. What is more, the duty of reporting for such service now devolved on the individual fellah and not on the village as a unit, in which latter case the shaykh al-balad had the opportunity to exercise his power of selection arbitrarily. The only function which the village shaykh retained in this respect was the preparation of a list of the villagers liable to recruitment for labor, and submission of it to the *mudīriyya*.[69] Parallel with this, he was deprived of the function of drafting the villagers for military service, and left only with the duty of compiling an annual list of those within draft age.[70] However, he was responsible, together with the shaykh of the *khafirs* (village guards), for arresting all deserters from the army who might have taken refuge in the village.[71]

Another extremely important function which was entirely taken out of the village shaykhs' hands was tax assessment and collection; in 1884 detailed regulations were published which strictly defined the functions of the tax collectors (*ṣarrāf*) and the relations between them and the village shaykhs in this respect.[72] In addition, the ʿumda's adjudicative authority was restricted and specifically defined: under the Law of 1895 he was forbidden to impose fines of over fifteen piastres or to detain anyone for more than twenty-four hours; and a special decree of April 28, 1898 stipulated that no ʿumda could try cases unless he was specifically empowered to do so by the Minister of Justice. Even then, he could not try cases involving real property, and in money matters his authority was limited to disputes involving sums no larger than a hundred piastres.[73]

[69]Gelat, 1 (2):249, 253; 3 (A, 2):686. Cf. Cromer, 2:190; Stuart Reports, p. 21; However, apparently ʿumdas were frequently held responsible for the actual recruiting of their villagers for emergency works (Orders of January 25, 1886, July 14, 1887, June 29, 1899—*al-Awāmir al-ʿaliyya waʾl-dakrītāt*, Būlāq, 1886, p. 35; 1887, pp. 501–2; 1899, pp. 205–8).

[70]Cromer, 2:190; Egypt No. 6 (1888), C. 5430, p. 10; Gelat, 1 (2):336, 344; for Law of November 4, 1902, Article 53, see M. R. Basyūnī, *al-Majmūʿa al-dāʾima li-ʾl-qawānīn wa-ʾl-qarārāt al-miṣriyya*, Cairo ("Jaysh"). It seems however, that during World War I the recruiting of the labor corps was carried out by the ʿumdas and that their power thus increased considerably. Cf. Sir Valentine Chirol, *The Egyptian Problem*, London, 1920, pp. 138, 161–62; Russell, p. 191; Sayyid Quṭb, p. 155; Lloyd, 1:240; ʿAbd al-Raḥmān al-Rāfiʿī, *Thawrat Sanat 1919*, Cairo, 1946, p. 31.

[71]*Majmūʿat al-manshūrāt waʾl-qarārāt*, 1883, p. 15.

[72]Cromer, 2:190; *Majmūʿat al-manshūrāt waʾl-qarārāt*, 1884, pp. 108–9. Nevertheless, as late as 1889 the *mudīr* of Banī Suwayf made a speech to his ʿumdas in which he told them that one of their tasks was to collect taxes of all kinds (*al-Qarārāt waʾl-manshūrāt*, 1889, pp. 511–22).

[73]Décret of March 16, 1895, Article 9; H. Lamba, *Code administratif égyptien*, Paris, 1911, pp. 432–34; R. de Chamberet, *Enquête sur la condition du fellah égyptien*, Paris, 1909, pp. 58–59. In accordance with the 1898 decree, 418 ʿumdas were appointed by the Ministry of Justice as local judges (*al-Qarārāt waʾl-manshūrāt*, 1898, pp. 362–83; 425).

On the other hand, in this same period the village shaykh was assigned a large number of new functions that had to do with the reorganization of Egypt's administration and with the economic and legal changes in the country during the last quarter of the nineteenth century. He was in charge of carrying out the census in his village; he had to keep the register of births, deaths, and vaccinations; to report animal epidemics and to supervise health conditions generally, including the purity of the water supply and the cleaning of canals and ditches, streets, mosques, bathhouses, and so on; to compile the electoral roll; to safeguard postal, telegraphic, telephone, and rail communications; to see to it that public roads, dikes, and canals were in good condition; to lease out state lands and to give any information required by surveyors regarding state lands in the village; to report any illegal cultivation of hashish or tobacco to the authorities; to attach the land of state debtors; and to carry out orders of the *mudīr* regarding the confiscation of crops for the benefit of landowners whose tenants had not paid their rent.[74] In addition, the village shaykh retained a number of the functions he had fulfilled in earlier periods. Under Article Four of the Law of 1895 the ʿumda was responsible for public security in the village and saw to the implementation of government laws and decrees and ministerial regulations; under Article 11 he was charged with intervening as arbitrator to prevent land disputes between villagers whose plots adjoined each other. He was in charge of the *khafīrs*, whom he appointed, and he was supposed to report vagabonds and deserters from the army.[75] Lord Cromer himself felt that all these responsibilities represented a heavy burden that was actually beyond the ʿumda's capacities: ". . . The Omdeh has a great deal more to do than heretofore. He is at the beck and call of the inspectors of every Department. He is responsible for the execution of a number of regulations, which he often fails to understand thoroughly. . . ."[76]

Indeed, quite a few of these new functions were reduced in scope or even transferred entirely to various government departments upon their more rational reorganization during the first half of the twentieth century, and particularly after Egypt had won her independence. Further, this period was also marked by the liquidation in theory of the ʿumda's remaining

[74]Gelat, 1 (1):70–71, 258; 1 (2):331–32, 386, 407; 1 (suppl.):107, 201; *al-Manshūrāt*, 1876 81, p. 89; *al-Awāmir al-ʿaliyya waʾl-dakrītāt*, 1884, pp. 164–67. Egypt No. 2 (1890), C. 6135, p. 131; U. Pace, *Répertoire permanent de législation égyptienne*, Alexandria, 1934, "Routes agricoles," p. 3; Chamberet, pp. 41–42.

[75]Décret of March 16, 1895, Articles 4 and 11; Jallād, *Qāmūs al-Idāra*, 2:470–71; Gelat, *Répertoire*, 1 (1):97; Chamberet, pp. 41–42. In 1888 many village shaykhs were dismissed because they had neglected those of their tasks which were connected with public security. See *al-Qarārāt waʾl-manshūrāt*, 1888, pp. 531–32, and 1890, *passim*.

[76]Egypt No. 1 (1905), Cd. 2409, p. 51.

adjudicative and economic functions. Demands to this effect had been presented by villagers and merchants to the Legislative Assembly as early as March, 1914.[77] The Law of July 3, 1930 abolished the ʿumda's power to impose fines and to make arrests—power that had been conferred on him, within certain limitations, by the Law of 1895; it also abrogated the decree of 1898 that had defined and therefore recognized his adjudicative authority.[78] Even functions such as the arbitration of land disputes between the villagers are no longer mentioned in the ʿUmda Law of 1947.[79] The village shaykh was also deprived of the power to lease out state property and of all other functions with regard to these lands, which were placed under a unified central administration in 1913; moreover, the authority to attach the land of state debtors was taken away from him.[80]

The scope of a number of the ʿumda's administrative functions was reduced in this same period. Under Laws of 1912 and 1946, the registers of births and deaths are kept at the local sanitation office (*maktab al-ṣiḥḥa*); where there is no such office the *ṣarrāf* keeps the register, and the ʿumda has a duplicate copy. The Law of 1946 requires that the entries themselves be made by authorized officials.[81] Preparation of the list of villagers liable to military service has not been taken entirely out of the ʿumda's hands, but the difference in the wording of the relevant article between the Laws of 1902 and 1947 is worth noting. While the former provided that the list was to be made up by the ʿumda and the shaykhs together with the *ṣarrāf*, the latter specified that it was to be compiled by the *ṣarrāf*, in collaboration with the ʿumda and the shaykhs.[82]

While the Election Law of 1883 entrusted the village shaykhs with drafting local voters' rolls, the Election Laws of 1925, 1930, and 1935 (Article 7 in each case) provided for a commission, headed, it is true, by the ʿumda but including two other members, one of whom was to be appointed by the *maʾmūr* (District Officer).[83] The ʿumda's duty to report reputed

[77] *Journal Officiel*, Supplement to No. 45 of April 11, 1914.

[78] Pace, "Omdeh," p. 2.

[79] Nevertheless, in everyday life the ʿumda seems to have been called upon frequently to settle disputes. See, for instance, Ammar, *Growing Up in an Egyptian Village*, p. 61, and also Ayrout, *Fellahs*, p. 41. (Ayrout, however, erroneously ascribes to him legal authority to fine and imprison, which had already been abolished by the time his book was written).

[80] See Pace, "Saisie-Gagerie," Laws of 1928 and 1929.

[81] Basyūnī, *al-Majmūʿa al-dāʾima*, "al-Mawālīd wa'l-wafayāt," Laws of August 11, 1912 and September 11, 1946. Actually many ʿumdas retained this function, together with the *ṣarrāf*, since few villages have sanitation bureaus.

[82] Basyūnī, "Jaysh," Law of November 4, 1902, Article 53; and Order of September 3, 1947, Article 2.

[83] Cf. Gelat, 1 (1):258 and *OM*, 6 (1926):68; Pace, "Loi Electorale," p. 2; H. M. Davis, *Constitutions, Electoral Laws, Treaties of States in the Near and Middle East*, Durham, N.C., 1953, pp. 48–49.

vagrants was restricted by a law of 1923 to giving evidence in the legal prosecution of persons suspected of vagabondage.[84] A law promulgated in 1944 and dealing with the ban on hashish no longer mentions the ʿumda, but only the gendarmerie and officials of the Ministry of Agriculture.[85] The village shaykh's functions relating to health and sanitation were also restricted and partly transferred to officials of the Ministry of Health.

Still, even in the middle of the twentieth century the ʿumda had retained quite a number of administrative functions. He received, passed on, and was responsible for implementing government regulations—hence the village telephone- and post-office were in his house; he certified documents and other evidence; he was the government's representative in census taking; he had to report all livestock epidemics; he continued to compile the list of villagers who must man the dikes or fight insect pests in case of

TABLE 1

Village Shaykhs' Functions, End of Eighteenth Century to Middle of Twentieth Century

	End of 18th Century	Muḥammad ʿAlī	ʿAbbās	Saʿīd	Ismāʿīl	1880–1922	1922–1950
Security	+	+	+	+	+	+	+
Passing on government instructions; giving evidence	+	+	+	+	+	+	+
Hospitality	+	+	+	+	+	+	>
Arbitrating villagers' disputes	+	+	+	+	+	+	>
Trying cases; imposing punishments	+	+	+	+	+	>	–
Ensuring payment of taxes; tax collection	+	+	+	+	+	–	–
Division of land and of tax burden among villagers	+	+	+	–	–	–	–
Tax assessment		+	+	+	<	–	–
Draft of fellahs for public works and army service			+	+	+	>	>
Leasing of state lands; attachment of debtors' property						+	–
Registry of births, deaths; electoral roll; supervising sanitation; reporting violations						+	>
Census taking; post office and telephone						+	+

+ Part of village shaykh's functions (sign first appears at the time the shaykh originally took on function).
– No longer part of village shaykh's functions.
> Function restricted in scope.
< Function broadened in scope.

[84] Pace, "Vagabondage," Law of June 29, 1923, Article 7.
[85] Basyūnī, "Ḥashīsh," Law of May 10, 1944.

need.[86] He was also still expected to extend hospitality to government officials and travelers going through the village, although he could not perform this function on the same scale as in the past.[87]

Concern for village security, however, remained the ʿumda's main responsibility. Article 7 of the Law of 1895, which we mentioned earlier, was replaced by Article 19 of the Law of 1947, but this involved no changes in content. Unnatural deaths and murders were still among the ʿumda's main worries and often, being connected with village politics and with various means of pressure employed to influence him (witness various descriptions of village life published in modern Egypt), these made him stray from the straight and narrow path.[88]

The evolution of the functions of the village shaykh in Egypt from the eighteenth century to the middle of the twentieth is summed up in table 1.

Socio-economic Position

It has been noted above that throughout the period under discussion the village shaykh or ʿumda was appointed from among the richest families in the village. The extent of the village shaykhs' wealth varied, however, from period to period, and there were pronounced changes in the kind of property they owned. At the end of the eighteenth century their wealth came mainly from three sources. In the first place, they held large tracts of land. These were then of three main kinds: the *rizaq aḥbāsiyya* (*waqf*), part of the revenues from which was devoted to providing for guests; lands whose existence was kept from the knowledge of the *multazims*; and lastly, a special category called *masmūḥ* or *masmūḥa*, the exact character of which in the eighteeenth century is not clear.[89] Al-Jabartī tells of one village shaykh whose family held at least a thousand feddans before Muḥammad ʿAlī came to power.[90] In addition, the village shaykh would rent from the *multazim ūsya* lands, that is, part of the latter's demesne.[91]

A second reason for the village shaykhs' wealth at the time was the exemption from certain taxes granted them. They paid no tax on the

[86] Cf. Basyūnī, "Taʿdād," Law of September 12, 1936; Pace, "Maladies Epizootiques," "Irrigations," etc.; Ayrout, p. 41 (Ayrout's list of the functions of the village shaykh does not seem to be very accurate).

[87] Ammar, p. 61; Tawfīq al-Ḥakīm, pp. 47–48; *al-Jumhūriyya*, August 19, 1958; and see below.

[88] Cf. Quṭb, pp. 83, 143, 147; al-Ḥakīm, pp. 7–8.

[89] Jabartī, 4:61, 183–84, 209–10; Lancret, p. 247.

[90] Jabartī, 4:210. A. N. Poliak's generalization that "their (the village shaykhs) holdings amounted to 1,000 faddāns and more" (*Feudalism in Egypt, Syria, Palestine and the Lebanon*, London, 1939, p. 70) seems to be based on an erroneous reading of the passage cited from Jabartī, since no additional documentation is given.

[91] Lancret, p. 243.

masmūḥa lands that we have just mentioned, and some of their other lands were exempt from the *barrānī*—the new taxes introduced by the beys and *multazims* in the course of the eighteenth century. According to Comte Estève, the village shaykhs of Upper Egypt were entirely exempt from these tax increases.[92]

The third source of wealth was various payments received by the shaykhs under various heads, but consisting mainly of gifts from the *multazims* in token of appreciation for the shaykh's services. Lancret calls these *el mesâha meta el-mechâykh.*[93] Very interesting data about these payments are furnished in Comte Estève's detailed figures on the taxes paid by the villages of al-Anbūṭayn (Gharbiyya) in Lower Egypt and Ṭahṭā (Asyūṭ) in Upper Egypt in 1798–99.[94] Tabulation of the figures in his lists shows that in the villages of Anbūṭayn the shaykhs received 31,020 *medins*[95] out of a total of 686,044 *medins* in old and new taxes, that is, 4.5 per cent, and in the villages of Ṭahṭā they received 183,153 *medins* out of a total of 1,902,690, or 9.6 per cent, plus 32.1 per cent of all payments in kind. It is not likely that the difference in the shaykhs' share as between the districts of Lower and Upper Egypt investigated by Estève was an accident. It can be explained, in the first place, by the fact that Upper Egypt was farther away from Cairo, the seat of government and administration, making the *multazims* more dependent on local elements for the maintenance of their rule.[96] It is likely, however, that the difference also had something to do with the fact that in Upper Egypt it was the shaykhs' function to reallocate lands among the villagers every year, while in Lower Egypt this was not the practice. It seems that the great power of village headmen in regions where communally held land is periodically redistributed was not peculiar to Egypt.[97]

It is clear that Muḥammad ʿAlī's rise to power at first dealt a blow to the village shaykhs' economic position. A tax was imposed on their *masmūḥa* lands as early as 1807.[98] *Iltizāms* were confiscated between the years 1808 and 1814 until the whole *iltizām* system was finally abolished, eliminating the source of most of the payments from which the village shaykhs had benefited. From then on to the present day, village shaykhs have not

[92]Jabartī, 4:61; Lancret, pp. 245, 247; Estève, p. 324.

[93]Estève, p. 318; Lancret, p. 245.

[94]Estève, pp. 314–17, 324–29.

[95]"*Medin*" is the European form of the coin called "*mu'ayyadī*" and pronounced *mīdī* in colloquial Egyptian Arabic. In 1798 the official rate was 150 *medins* to the Thaler. Cf. H. A. R. Gibb and H. Bowen, *Islamic Society and the West*, vol. 1, part 2, London, 1957, pp. 39 n, 57 n, and see note 104 below.

[96]Cf. Estève, p. 324.

[97]Cf. Wittfogel, *Oriental Despotism*, p. 118. For Persia, see Lambton, p. 301.

[98]Jabartī, 4:61.

received a salary or any other direct payment from the government.[99] Along with this the *rizaq aḥbāsiyya* lands were confiscated in the years 1812 to 1814, depriving the village shaykhs of an important source of income, apparently used mainly to meet the expense of entertaining and lodging guests.[100] There is, however, no way of determining the exact extent to which their property and income were affected by these measures; and in any case one has the impression that during the course of Muḥammad ʿAlī's rule their economic condition improved again. Dealing with the events of the year 1820, al-Jabartī notes that when lands were surveyed the shaykhs were given *masmūḥ*—5 per cent of all of the village's lands, to cover the expenses of their guest houses. Artin adds that these lands allotted to the shaykhs, which were called *masmūḥ al-mashāyikh* or *masmūḥ al-maṣṭaba*, were exempt from taxes.[101] It also appears that the village shaykhs succeeded in taking over a considerable part of the lands of fellahs who were drafted by Muḥammad ʿAlī for labor or the army and did not return to their villages. This was made possible by the absence, at the time, of legislation governing the inheritance of lands held by fellahs.[102] Similarly, the village shaykhs seem to have frequently deprived fellahs of their property, such as houses, trees, irrigation wheels, and so on—to judge by articles of Muḥammad ʿAlī's *Qānūn al-filāḥa* which expressly prohibited such actions.[103] On the other hand, they were officially authorized to keep for themselves a certain proportion of the taxes which they collected from their villages—first only in Lower Egypt and later (from 1835 onward) also in Upper Egypt. The minimum which they were allowed for poor villages amounted to one *mīdī* for each *para* of taxes collected, that is, not more than 1.1 per cent.[104] Toward the end of Muḥammad ʿAlī's rule the shaykhs apparently succeeded in collecting taxes from the villagers and not passing

[99] Artin's assertion that in the 1820's the ʿumda or shaykh received a salary (*Essai sur les causes du renchérissement de la vie matérielle au Caire 1800–1907*, Cairo, 1907, p. 89) is the result of a misinterpretation: the shaykh al-mashāyikh who was, according to his source, the recipient of a salary, is rendered by Artin *Omdeh ou Cheikh*. Cf. Sir John Gardner Wilkinson, *Topography of Thebes and General View of Egypt*, London, 1835, pp. 277–78. Wilkinson makes it quite clear that the shaykh al-balad was not paid by the government. For the situation in other countries of the Middle East, see G. Baer, *Population and Society in the Arab East*, New York, 1964, p. 166.

[100] Jabartī, 4:183–84, 210.

[101] Jabartī, 4:311; von Kremer, 1:255; Artin, pp. 89–90.

[102] Cf. Artin, p. 280.

[103] Articles 50 and 52 of the *Qānūn al-filāḥa* of 1245 A.H./1830. See F. Jallād, *Qāmūs al-idāra wa'l-qaḍā'*, Alexandria, 1890, 3:356. Article 40 deals with shaykhs who use the fellahs' camels without permission or payment, and Article 31 with those who try to force fellahs to give them their daughters in marriage (pp. 354–55). For more details about this law see chapter 7, below.

[104] Order of Rabīʿ II 1250 A.H./August 23, 1834, Sāmī, vol. 2, Cairo, 1928, p. 426. For Egyptian currencies, see C. Issawi (ed.), *The Economic History of the Middle East, 1800–1914*, Chicago, 1966, pp. 522–23.

them on to the authorities, or in turning tax collection to their profit in other ways.[105] According to Hekekyan, a Turkish *mudīr* complained: "They [the shaykhs] have become as fat as pigs. Many of them are enormously rich, by plundering the poor fellahs. If we allow them to go on amassing money they will summon courage to drive us out of the land altogether."[106]

The shaykhs' self-enrichment gathered impetus under ʿAbbās. According to contemporary observers, the new authority which the Pasha had delegated to the village shaykhs—authority to draft the fellahs for labor and army duty—greatly increased their moneymaking potentialities.[107] It appears that in this same period the shaykhs' power and the fellahs' misery resulted in the villagers' contracting debts to the shaykhs and sinking deeper and deeper into debt until the shaykhs seized their property.[108]

The period of Saʿīd's rule, on the other hand, was marked by a decline in the village shaykhs' socio-economic standing. This can be attributed to the breakup of the village community as a landholding entity, a process which was going through its decisive stages at that time: in Upper Egypt the village lands were no longer reallocated each year, inheritance and private property rights were set for the fellahs' lands and tax payments ceased to be the collective responsibility of the village.[109] The village shaykhs thus lost the functions of distributing the land among the fellahs and allocating the tax burden among them. There were, furthermore, laws promulgated by Saʿīd for the purpose of limiting the wealth of the village shaykhs. On September 14, 1857, a tax was imposed on the *masmūḥ al-mashāyikh* lands. It was to be applied at the highest rate obtaining in the village. A few months later, on June 17, 1858, Saʿīd expropriated these lands entirely, assigning their usufruct to the fellahs. Further, his Land Law of August 5, 1858 contained specific provisions (Article 28 of the original law) for measures to be taken against any shaykh al-balad or ʿumda who failed to report to the authorities cases of landowning villagers dying without heirs and who took over their lands or allowed others to do so.[110]

We do not know to what extent all these factors influenced the shaykhs' economic position under Saʿīd. It is evident that even if they did, it was for

[105] Bowring, pp. 45–46; Hekekyan Papers, vol. 3, B.M. Add. 37450, ff. 153, 164.

[106] Hekekyan Papers, vol. 3, f. 166 (written in Sharqiyya province in 1846). For additional testimony to the wealth of the village shaykhs' families during the later part of Muḥammad ʿAlī's rule, see note 32, above.

[107] Bayle St. John, *Village Life in Egypt*, 2:84.

[108] Hekekyan Papers, vol. 7, B.M. Add. 37454, f. 367a (written 1854 in Manṣūriyya, Gīza province). See also vol. 5, B.M. Add. 37452, f. 477b.

[109] For details, see chapter 2, above; and cf. note 97.

[110] Artin, pp. 102–3, 77, 293.

a short time only; for under Ismāʿīl the village shaykhs attained the apogee of their socio-economic power in modern times. This rise stemmed from the combination of a number of factors. In the first place, the part they were given in classifying the lands and assessing them for tax purposes enabled them to derive great economic advantages for themselves. Secondly, they made loans to the fellahs, who were in increasingly greater need of cash as a result of the transition to market crops, and of the collection of taxes in cash rather than in kind. In consequence, fellahs who could not pay their debts forfeited their property to the village shaykhs.[111] Thirdly, the shaykhs' rule in the village enabled them to gain great economic benefits in that period of intensified agricultural development: they rented out their holdings, which were much more extensive than what they themselves could cultivate; they saw to it that their lands got priority in irrigation and were the first to be cultivated by the villagers—not always for pay. By applying various kinds of pressure, they took over many lands that had previously belonged to fellahs.[112] Finally, in an expanding market for labor and goods they took advantage of the villagers' ignorance: often serving as intermediaries in marketing the produce of the fellahs or in hiring them out to plantations and sugar mills, they kept a good part of the prices or wages for themselves.[113]

As a result of all these factors, many village shaykhs attained very substantial landed wealth in the period of Ismāʿīl. Among the waqfs that they established at the time and that remained in existence until the middle of the twentieth century several extended over eight hundred and a thousand feddans, and Mubārak tells of ʿumdas who had private estates of that size or even larger. There were, of course, many shaykhs whose landholdings were smaller, but they, too, owned a substantial part of the village land.[114] Artin believes that it was the pressure of the village shaykhs which in 1869 brought about the decision not to apply Moslem inheritance law to *kharājiyya* lands, since the headmen derived their power from their landed property and wanted to preclude its parcellation.[115]

The hundreds of entries dealing with villages in Mubārak's encyclopedia attest to the ʿumda's high socio-economic status in that period. In almost every village he dwelt in the most luxurious house (*qaṣr*, *dawwār*) larger than

[111] Cf. Stuart Reports, p. 25; G. Legrain, *Fellah de Karnak*, Paris, 1902, p. 312.

[112] See Wallace, pp. 222–23, 227.

[113] Cf. Egypt No. 1 (1880) C. 2549, p. 118; Stuart Reports, p. 45.

[114] For details, see G. Baer, *A History of Landownership in Modern Egypt, 1800–1950*, London, 1962, pp. 50–56.

[115] Artin, pp. 108–9. One should add, however, that another class, the Turco-Egyptian officials, surpassed the ʿumdas as owners of large estates.

others and built of better materials; in most places he owned the guest house (*manzil ḍiyāfa*, *maḍyafa*, etc.); in many localities he had a garden (*junayna*, *ḥadīqa*); if a village had an irrigation pump (*wābūr*), it generally belonged to the ʿumda. Some ʿumdas set up olive- and sugar-presses, small silk spinneries, and cotton ginneries.[116] Many of them built mosques or *sabīls* (public fountains) in their villages, and some sent their sons to Cairo to study at al-Azhar.[117] Their commercial and other ties sent them on frequent trips to the cities, where they picked up some European fashions, particularly in building and furnishing their houses.[118] This development widened the gap between them and the village masses, the bulk of whom remained at the same economic and social level as before. To this and to the political development with which we shall deal below may be ascribed the fact that from the days of Ismāʿīl on, many village shaykhs moved to the city.

The departure of many of the former ʿumdas from the village was one of the reasons for the changed socio-economic position of the men who filled this post after the British occupation. The departure of ʿumdas is often mentioned in circulars sent to the *mudīrs* by the Ministry of Interior in this period: one of these, dated September 5, 1884, states specifically that in various places the authorities had been compeled to appoint as ʿumdas persons whose standing in the village, landed property, and so forth were unsuitable.[119]

No less important a factor in the ʿumdas' socio-economic decline was the restriction of their authority under the British occupation, particularly when it came to those functions that involved material profit, such as assessment and collection of taxes and drafting villagers for public works and military service.[120] To this must be added the fact that, from 1881 on, Muslim inheritance laws were again applied to the land categories held by the village shaykhs, bringing about the beginning of the disintegration of their landed property.[121] It was also at this time that the regulation prohibiting them from acting at one and the same time as ʿumdas and inspectors of agricultural lands (*nāẓir zirāʿa*) began to be enforced.[122]

Of course all these factors did not do away overnight with the economic

[116] Mubārak, *passim*. Cf. also Wallace, p. 211. However, at that time most industrial establishments were owned by Europeans.

[117] See also W. S. Blunt, *Secret History of the British Occupation of Egypt*, New York, 1922, p. 99.

[118] See Wallace's vivid description of Ali Bey, the Omdeh—pp. 211–13.

[119] Jallād, *Qāmūs al-idāra*, 3:146–47. Not all of them, of course, went to towns; many established new *kafrs* or *ʿizbas* (see Gelat, *Répertoire*, 2 (1):620–21).

[120] Cf. Cromer, *Modern Egypt*, 2:190.

[121] Artin, p. 111.

[122] Jallād, 3:146.

power of the village shaykhs. As late as 1885 and 1887 British consular representatives reported cases of fellahs engaged in forced labor on the lands of ʿumdas and shaykhs,[123] and a report written in 1889 mentions instances of village shaykhs who "had appropriated land belonging to peasants who had left the village."[124] In 1895 Villiers Stuart came across ʿumdas who owned several hundred feddans.[125] Such cases, however, increasingly came to be exceptions rather than the rule, as was demonstrated by the fact that the ʿUmdas' Law promulgated in 1895 set the lower limit of the landed property required of ʿumdas at only ten feddans, and of shaykhs at as little as five feddans. Further, in a decree of the same date as the law, the legislators saw fit to exempt the ʿumda from taxes on five feddans of his land.[126] While until the British occupation all observers had depicted village shaykhs as a class of large landowners, the British Agent's Reports for 1902 and 1904 noted that there were small landowners and even poor men among them, and that in some districts it was difficult to find candidates for the post of ʿumda meeting the requirements of ownership of at least ten feddans.[127] In 1922, too, Dr. Saleh found many village shaykhs who, not owning the number of feddans required of them by law, had to resort to fictitious land transfers by their relatives.[128]

This decline in the ʿumda's socio-economic position continued throughout the first half of the twentieth century. The reasons were the same: the removal of rich village families to the cities, the restriction of the ʿumda's functions, and the disintegration of his landed property. Yet there continued to be rich village shaykhs throughout the period under discussion, and most of the ʿumdas stood out among the rest of the villagers in their income and way of living (the ʿumda's house was generally located just outside the village).[129] However, in relation to the past, an incontestable change had taken place. Hamed Ammar describes it in Silwa, the village of Upper Egypt which he studied in the forties:

> . . . with the decrease of the wealth of the village Omda, and consequently with his inability to provide hospitality in the traditional way, or to represent the village properly without extending his hands for help from the village, his

[123] Egypt No. 4 (1886) C. 4768, p. 41; Egypt No. 2 (1888) C. 5316, p. 35.

[124] Egypt No. 2 (1890) C. 6135, pp. 5–6.

[125] *Reports by Mr. Villiers Stuart respecting Progress of Reorganization in Egypt since the British Occupation in 1882*, Egypt No. 2 (1895), C. 7712, p. 27.

[126] Pace, "Omdehs," p. 3. The law of 1947 replaced the minimum of ten feddans by a land tax of at least £E 10 per year. Since in 1948 the average tax amounted to £E 1 per feddan, this did not make any difference.

[127] Egypt No. 1 (1903), Cd. 1529, p. 43; Egypt No. 1 (1905), Cd. 2409, p. 51.

[128] M. Saleh, *La petite propriété rurale en Egypte*, Grenoble, 1922, p. 47.

[129] Cf. Quṭb, p. 53; Russell, p. 44.

> authority has been flouted. . . . They [the people] complain that the Omda is not what he used to be in the good old days. . . . In a conversation between the writer and the Omda, the latter answered the villagers' allegation by saying, "If the Omda or any other man in his position would stick to what these people expect from his generosity, he would run the risk of complete bankruptcy." The decrease of the headman's authority reveals itself in the local remarks such as "We have an Omda without lands." . . .[130]

The large landowning ʿumda, so frequent in the days of Ismāʿīl, became a rare sight in mid-twentieth-century Egypt.

Political Power

There is little real evidence on the political standing of the village shaykh in the eighteenth century. Gibb and Bowen say, in a very general manner, that "it was he who kept the village together, and his position was respected not only by the villagers but also by the *multazims*."[131] It should also be noted that he was more influential and powerful in Upper Egypt than in Lower Egypt, as Estève brings out in the study we summarized above.

Opinions are divided with regard to the changes wrought in the village shaykhs' power by the rise of Muḥammad ʿAlī and by developments during the first years of his rule. While Michaud and Poujoulat claim that the end of the *multazims*' rule and the expansion of the functions of the mashāyikh al-balad raised the position of the latter,[132] the British Consul asserted in 1817 that the shaykhs no longer had much importance now that the Pasha saw to everything himself and the fellahs could address themselves directly to the central government.[133] The latter opinion is borne out to a certain extent by the description in ʿAlī Mubārak's autobiography of the pressure and control to which the shaykhs were subjected about the year 1830.[134] It may well be that the situation varied from region to region and from year to year, and that there were two factors at work simultaneously: strong, direct, central rule restricting the shaykh's power while his widening functions, mainly in the field of tax assessment, enlarged it.

Be this as it may, it is evident that in the second half of Muḥammad ʿAlī's tenure the power and political influence of the village shaykhs and their families increased considerably. Muḥammad ʿAlī appears to have arrived

[130] Ammar, *Growing Up in an Egyptian Village*, p. 80.

[131] Gibb and Bowen, 1 (1):263.

[132] M. Michaud and M. Poujoulat, *Correspondence d'Orient*, Paris, 1834, 7, lettre 166, Avril 1831, p. 51.

[133] Report by Henry Salt, April 18, 1817, PRO, FO 78/89.

[134] Mubārak, 9:37–38.

by the end of the 1820's at the decision to replace part of the Ottoman officialdom by Egyptians; the most likely candidates for this new class were largely village shaykhs. It is true that the French Consul's suggestion to this effect was turned down in 1826, but by 1829 Ibrāhīm Pasha had begun to consult with shaykhs in affairs of state.[135] The decisive step came in 1833, when Muḥammad ʿAlī dismissed a number of his Ottoman officials and appointed village shaykhs (and beduin shaykhs) to be *maʾmūr*s and *nuẓẓār qism*.[136] Mubārak's encyclopedia tells of a large number of village shaykhs who were appointed officials in the days of Muḥammad ʿAlī.[137] There was a reaction in 1841, when Ottomans were again appointed—mainly in the rank of *mudīr*.[138] Still, the village shaykhs continued in their administrative posts, at least below the rank of *mudīr*.

These changes, the instability they produced, the weakening of central rule, and the enrichment of the shaykhs may well have been at the root of the rebellious mood that manifested itself among shaykhs in some districts of Egypt toward the end of Muḥammad ʿAlī's rule. It is significant that in the different penal codes issued by Muḥammad ʿAlī or compiled during his rule and issued by ʿAbbās the insubordination of village shaykhs occupied a prominent place: provisions for such cases were included at least in five articles of these laws.[139] However, there is also more direct evidence for this mood of the village shaykhs at that time. In 1846 Hekekyan noted in his diary that the shaykhs of Sharqiyya province were refusing to pay taxes and to send men for "government services." As we have noted earlier, according to Hekekyan a Turkish *mudīr* cited the shaykhs' wealth in explanation of their behavior and expressed the apprehension—surely exaggerated—that they would soon be running the country.[140] This insubordination on the part of some of the shaykhs appears to have continued into the time of ʿAbbās: Hekekyan recorded another instance of refusal to supply fellahs for forced labor in 1851.[141] Against this insubordination ʿAbbās tried, according to Hekekyan's interesting explanation, to maintain a political equilibrium among Egypt's various social forces:

[135] Report by Henry Salt, April 1826, PRO, FO 78/147; Barker to Malcolm, July 8, 1829; Barker to Sir Robert Gordon, August 1, 1829 and September 22, 1829, FO 78/184.

[136] Campbell to Palmerston, June 13, 1833, FO 78/227; October 26, 1833, Inclosure No. 2, FO 78/228; Mubārak, 14:38; Lane, *Manners and Customs*, p. 129; Hamont, 1:87; F. Mengin, *Histoire sommaire de l'Egypte sous le gouvernment de Mohammed-Aly 1823–1838*, Paris, 1839, pp. 56–57.

[137] Mubārak, 8:105; 9:7, 14, 86; 12:44, 129; 13:40; etc.

[138] Sir John Gardner Wilkinson, *Modern Egypt and Thebes*, London, 1845, 1:438–39.

[139] *Qānūn al-Muntakhabāt*, arts. 8–9, 23–24, 27, 53, Jallād, 3:352–56; *Code d'Abbas*, arts. 9, 11, 14, 54, 79. See FO 78/875 (also 141/95). For details about these codes, see chapter 7, below.

[140] Hekekyan Papers, vol. 3, B.M. Add. 37450, ff. 153, 164–66.

[141] Hekekyan Papers, vol. 5, B.M. Add. 37452 f. 59a.

> We govern the mass of the population by means of these sheikhs, aiding them to keep down the rising tendency of the people who, since the establishment of schools, manufactories, fleets and armies, formed and maintained after the European model, are now no longer what they used to be. To keep the sheikhs in order we maintain a kind of balance between them and the people. The hostile desert tribes, whose privileges we respect, are a powerful instrument at our disposal to prevent any serious coalition between the sheikhs and the fellahs.[142]

At the same time, these symptoms of insubordination attest to the great power then wielded by the shaykhs—not only against high Ottoman officials but mainly over the villagers. In illustration of their "great power over the community" Hekekyan gives a description of the rule of the shaykhs of the Ṭahāwī family over the village of Manṣūriyya (Gīza), where the fellahs virtually "belonged" to them and were subjected to their despotism when it came to their livelihood, to the *corvée*, and even to women.[143] There were observers who accounted for the rise of the shaykhs under ʿAbbās, politically as well as economically, by the fact that they had been placed in charge of drafting villagers for public works and military service.[144] Be that as it may, the village shaykhs retained most pleasant memories from the period of ʿAbbās.[145]

The decline in the village shaykhs' political power under Saʿīd grew from, among other things, government legislation specifically directed to that end. It is not fully clear just what drove Saʿīd to break the shaykhs' political hold, and there must have been something arbitrary about this decision, for in everything he undertook Saʿīd appears to have been governed by the principle of reversing whatever his predecessor ʿAbbās had done. Perhaps his intention was to eliminate every political force which he did not fully control—his resolute operations against the beduins are a case in point; perhaps it was either the wish to gain the sympathy of the Europeans or the influence of the Tanzimat that drove him to "root out corruption," to "establish order," and to "organize the administration," in the words of sympathetic foreign observers, as reported by N. W. Senior,[146] or as the Pasha himself said: "I am resolved that all my people shall bear the same burdens and perform the same services. I will not pet one class—Sheykh, Bedouin, Copt, Cairene or Fellah—at the expense of the others. All shall be equal."[147]

142 Hekekyan Papers, vol. 6, B.M. Add. 37453, ff. 29b–30a (written June 1, 1854).

143 Hekekyan Papers, vol. 7, B.M. Add. 37454, ff. 366a–367a.

144 Bayle St. John, 2:84.

145 See the story of Abdu, the Village Shaykh, Wallace, pp. 266–67.

146 Senior, *passim*. Senior's journals in Egypt, covering the period from November, 1855, to March, 1856, contain excellent descriptions of Egyptian society under Saʿīd.

147 Senior, 2:86–87.

Whatever his motives, Saʿīd's reforms were designed to break not only the economic power of the village shaykhs but also their political might. As soon as he came to power, he issued a decree extending conscription to the sons of village shaykhs, who had been exempt from it till then.[148] When many of the shaykhs and their sons demurred, he warned them that instead of the shaykhs' sons he would enlist Albanians, who would then be quartered in the villages at the residents' expense. A shaykh's son who attempted to elude the draft was sent off to work as a fellah in one of the villages, a punishment that deterred many other would-be shirkers; and a shaykh who sent someone else for military service in place of his son was hanged in public in the town of Ṭanṭā.[149] According to one official, Saʿīd explained these measures as follows:

> The Sheykhs and their families were the most ignorant, ragged and useless aristocracy that ever were seen. They would not work, they could not read; they passed their lives in smoking and contriving how to oppress the Fellahs, and to defraud the Government. They owe forty years' arrears of conscription; I take from them arrears of only twenty years and I shall return their sons in a year or two educated and civilised, with more knowledge of men and of things than they would have acquired in ten years squatting before the gates of their village. . . .[150]

The criminal code of 1855 forbade village shaykhs to force fellahs to work without compensation and imposed heavy punishments on this and other transgressions committed by the shaykhs.[151] As late as 1861 Saʿīd had a shaykh al-balad executed in Minūf for illegally oppressing villagers.[152] No wonder, therefore, that a generation later village shaykhs did not speak of Saʿīd—unlike ʿAbbās—"in very sympathetic terms."[153]

The various economic and social developments with which we have dealt earlier played a part, along with the official measures, in the decline of the village shaykhs' political power. Foremost among these developments was the disintegration of the village community, as it was expressed in the discontinuation of the annual reassignment of the village land among the fellahs and the abolition of collective liability for taxes.

Under Ismāʿīl, the village shaykhs' political power rose along with their

[148]Von Kremer, 1:256; Senior, 1:261, 293. One of the sons of village shaykhs who entered the army at that time was ʿUrābī—see his autobiography, *Kashf al-sitār ʿan sirr al-asrār fī l-nahḍa al-miṣriyya* . . ., Cairo, n.d., 1:12; also Blunt, *Secret History*, pp. 99, 367.

[149]Von Kremer, 1:256; Senior, 1:261–62, 294–95; 2:10, 85; Merruau, p. 27.

[150]Senior, 2:55–56.

[151]See von Kremer, 2:61–63; see also chapter 7, below.

[152]Von Kremer, 1:256.

[153]See Wallace, pp. 267–68.

economic standing. This rise was given institutional expression in the Assembly of Delegates (*Majlis Shūrā al-Nuwwāb*) which Ismāʿīl set up in 1866. The members of this body were chosen mainly by village shaykhs,[154] and of the seventy-four or seventy-five delegates who attended its three sessions (in 1866, 1870, and 1876), between fifty-eight and sixty-four were ʿumdas.[155] Again, we have no authoritative explanation for Ismāʿīl's step in setting up the Assembly: one opinion has it that he assembled the shaykhs in order to control them effectively, but another explanation was "that he created the Chamber of Notables as a counterpoise to the influence of the *Dhawāt*" (the high Turco-Egyptian officials).[156] Opinions are also divided on the extent of the influence exerted by the Assembly, which many European observers regarded with derision and contempt. It is true that in theory it was merely a consultative body, but it seems that the government paid increasingly greater heed to it. The most striking example was the reinstatement of the Muqābala Law on November 18, 1876 after the Assembly had voiced its opposition to its repeal on May 7 of the same year.[157] The Assembly also decided that village shaykhs should be designated only in keeping with the wishes of the residents and should not be removed unless it was proved that they had committed a crime.[158] Whatever its actual influence, it was noted that as the years went by, the Assembly developed an ever increasing spirit of "self-assertion."[159]

Ismāʿīl also began once more to appoint village shaykhs to the office of *mudīr*, in addition to a number of other administrative posts they held.[160] The shaykhs' power in the villages greatly increased under his rule. In 1879 the British Vice-Consul reported from the province of Qalyūbiyya, near Cairo: ". . . I hear from different sources that the oppression received at their [the shaykhs'] hands is such that the fellaheen often abandon their small holds and become laborers to the Zawâts and Europeans in the hope of obtaining protection against their Sheikhs."[161] In districts that were further removed from the center the shaykhs' rule was absolute.[162] The general impression of contemporary observers was that the village shaykhs

[154]See its "*Lā'iḥa Asāsiyya*," Article 6, Rāfiʿī, *ʿAṣr Ismāʿīl*, 2:79, and text on p. 289. Stuart claims that they were virtually appointed by the *mudīrs* (Stuart Reports, pp. 22, 23, 25).

[155]Rāfiʿī, *ʿAṣr Ismāʿīl*, 2:82–84, 109–11, 149–51.

[156]J. M. Landau, *Parliaments and Parties in Egypt*, Tel-Aviv, 1953, p. 8; Wallace, p. 214.

[157]Rāfiʿī, 2:151–52; McCoan, pp. 117–18; Artin, p. 110.

[158]Rāfiʿī, 2:108.

[159]Rāfiʿī, 2:152; cf. Landau, pp. 20, 22.

[160]Rāfiʿī, 2:280; Wallace, pp. 148, 152. Cf. Mubārak, 9:34, 97, 99; 10:54, 84; 11:2, 5; 12:59, 148; 13:27, 40; 15:34, etc.; Sāmī, part 3, 2:862–63.

[161]Egypt No. 1 (1880), C. 2549, p. 49.

[162]Cf. Wallace, pp. 18–23.

were practically uncontrolled, virtually masters of the country.[163] ʿUrābī's rebellion, which the village shaykhs supported, increased their insubordination to the authorities, and they felt that the time had come to get rid of the Turco-Egyptian Pashas.[164]

However, the situation was reversed when the revolt was suppressed and the British occupied the country: "After Tel-el-Kebir the ancient submissiveness to Pashadom returned."[165] At a later stage the British occupation weakened the position of the Turco-Egyptians as well, but this did not revive the power lost by the shaykhs upon the deposition of Ismāʿīl and the suppression of ʿUrābī's revolt. Considerable prestige still attached to the office of ʿumda, especially in Upper Egypt, and Lord Dufferin's plan to free the population from the tyranny of the village shaykhs by broadening the franchise for the election of a Council and an Assembly failed, for the villages generally continued to elect their ʿumdas as their delegates.[166] Nevertheless the authority of the ʿumda had been much undermined, and the fellahs were freed to a certain extent from the oppression of their village shaykhs; and people even began to feel pity for the ʿumda: "The Omdeh has come to need protection. He is the servant of all and master of none. . . ."[167]

It is not difficult to establish the causes of this development. Many were the functions which had constituted the foundation of the village shaykh's power and rule in the past and of which he found himself shorn in that period; as against this, burdensome new administrative duties were piled on him; the organization of justice deprived him of the discretionary power of which he had made free use with regard to the peasants; his authority suffered particularly from the interdiction on resorting to the *kurbāj*; and finally, in certain areas the increasing enlightenment of the entire population may have played a certain part in the process.[168]

This development continued through the second quarter of the twentieth century. Among the causes of the decline in the ʿumda's prestige, Ammar lists, along with the reduction of his wealth and his ability to extend hospitality, the fact that ". . . with the establishment of a police station, with the availability of more people who can write out complaints . . . people

[163] Cromer, 2:190; Wallace, p. 17.

[164] Cromer, 2:187–88; cf. Egypt No. 7 (1882), C. 3249, p. 43.

[165] Cromer, 2, 187–88.

[166] Egypt No. 1 (1905), Cd. 2409, p. 51; Egypt No. 1 (1907), Cd. 3394, pp. 28, 72.

[167] Egypt No. 2 (1888), C. 5316, p. 35; Egypt No. 1 (1906), Cd. 2817, p. 61.

[168] For the restriction in the scope of the village shaykhs' functions, see above; for the other factors mentioned, see Egypt No. 1 (1885), C. 4278, pp. 37, 42; Egypt No. 3 (1887), C. 4942, p. 63; Egypt No. 3 (1891), C. 6321, p. 23; Egypt No. 1 (1906), Cd. 2817, p. 61.

tend to send their complaints and disputes directly to the police station or to the provincial authorities."[169]

At the same time, there appeared in the second quarter of the twentieth century a new element that imparted a measure of renewed importance to the ʿumda: the Egyptian parliamentary system. Since the village had no local democratic institutions and there were no public organizations of any kind among the fellahs, the ʿumda became the parties' main channel of influence over the villagers and the focus of all activity at election time.[170] The frequent dismissals of ʿumdas for political reasons show not only that the central regime had the decisive say in appointment for this office but also that it attached great importance to the post. ʿUmdas who had no influential rivals in their villages could derive a good many advantages and strengthen their own position by exploiting the contest of parties and political personalities for the votes of the ignorant fellahs. The ʿumdas were aware of this renewed importance and began, as in similar circumstances in the past, to show signs of insubordination: under the constitutional monarchy in modern Egypt, village shaykhs refused at least twice—in 1925–26 and in 1930–31—to cooperate with the government in holding elections.[171] Moreover, changes in electoral legislation in this period somewhat strengthened the ʿumdas politically: while they were denied the right of being elected to Parliament or to the Senate under the Election Law of 1925 (Article 73), the ʿumdas and shaykhs were accorded it in the election laws of 1930 (Article 30) and 1935 (Article 26), which even permitted them to seek seats in the district in which they held office.[172]

Thus the Egyptian parliamentary system seems once more to have raised the political power and prestige of the ʿumda in some degree. While the reports of the British Consuls at the end of the last century and the beginning of the present one cannot but create the impression that at that time the office of ʿumda was losing its importance,[173] all the sources dealing with the constitutional monarchy attest to the fact that during that period this office was eagerly contested, making for bitter struggles and feuds in many Egyptian villages.[174] No small number of these feuds, which frequently

[169] Ammar, p. 80.

[170] Cf. Dr. M. ʿA. al-ʿArabī, "al-Qarya al-miṣriyya fī'l-ʿahd al-jadīd," *al-Ahrām*, December 4, 1952; Tawfīq al-Ḥakīm, pp. 112–13.

[171] *OM*, 6 (1926):48–49; 11 (1931):109; al-Rāfiʿī, *Fī aʿqāb al-thawra*, 1:247–48; 2 (Cairo, 1949):143.

[172] *OM*, 6 (1926):76; Pace, "Loi Electorale," p. 5; Rāfiʿī, *Fī aʿqāb al-thawra*, 2:138; Davis, *Constitutions*, p. 53.

[173] See notes 167 and 168, above; de Chamberet (*Enquête*, p. 43) differs, but factual errors in the paragraph on this subject make his authority in this respect doubtful.

[174] Cf. Ayrout, p. 110; Ammar, p. 64; al-ʿArabī, in *al-Ahrām*, December 4, 1952; *al-Ahrām*, May 26, 1953, etc.

resulted in murder, were connected with party politics.[175]

Conclusion

An analysis of the development of the office of village shaykh in Egypt between 1800 and 1950 leads us to the following conclusions:

1. The function of the village shaykh, his socio-economic position, and his political power seem to have developed along virtually parallel lines: a decline after Muḥammad ʿAlī came to power (except where the shaykhs' functions were concerned, while as regards their political power no clear-cut conclusions can be drawn); a rise during the second half of the period of his rule; a marked rise under ʿAbbās; an evident decline under Saʿīd; a tremendous rise under Ismāʿīl; a decline during the British occupation (the expansion of the shaykhs' purely administrative function in this period weighed them down with work without strengthening their position); and a further decline under the constitutional monarchy (except for the shaykhs' political power, which was bolstered by the parliamentary system).

2. This development in the position of the shaykh is due fundamentally to socio-economic and legislative-political factors which tended to operate in the same direction. The transition from the *iltizām* to a monopolistic economy and the expropriation of the *rizaq* went together with the establishment of a centralistic regime at the beginning of Muḥammad ʿAlī's rule; and the abolition of the monopolies, together with the appointment of village shaykhs as high officials in the later stages of his rule; the breakup of the village community and the emergence of private property in land, together with legislation reducing the village shaykhs' position under Saʿīd; the development of agriculture and the transition to cash crops, together with the express policy of strengthening the class of village notables, followed by Ismāʿīl; and the migration of rich village notables to the cities and the parcellation of the village residents' land, together with the restriction of the functions of the village headmen entailed by the establishment of modern administration from the British occupation until today. The parliamentarism of the constitutional monarchy constitutes an exception to this parallelism between the two sets of factors.

3. On the whole, it may be said that the village shaykhs' position waxed when centralized government waned. The outstanding examples are the period of ʿAbbās, when the function of drafting the fellahs for military

[175] *OM*, 11 (1931):552; Ayrout, pp. 42–43; *al-Ahrām*, April 14, 1955 (reporting a case of murder connected with competition for the office of ʿumda against a background of party politics prior to the military *coup d'état*). There were also, of course, many cases of murder connected with the office of the ʿumda but apparently not with party politics—e.g., *al-Ahrām*, June 27, 1953, May 25, 1954, June 17, 1954, July 11, 1954, December 4, 1954, etc.

service and the *corvée*, exercised until then by the army, was delegated to the village shaykhs; the chaotic days of the ʿUrābī revolt; the period of instability during World War I, when the shaykhs' power increased; and finally, the period of modern parliamentarism, which weakened the central autocratic regime without at the same time developing democratic institutions of local government.

4. The fact that central government in Upper Egypt was far weaker than in Lower Egypt was also one of the important reasons why the position of the village shaykh was much stronger in the Ṣaʿīd, at least until the middle of the nineteenth century. Another important reason for this phenomenon was the annual reallocation of the village community's land among the fellahs, practiced in Upper Egypt but not in Lower Egypt.

4

The Development of Private Ownership of Land

In the Ottoman Empire and after its disintegration in the Arab countries of the Fertile Crescent, private ownership of land developed during the nineteenth and twentieth centuries as it did in Egypt in the nineteenth century. There were, however, fundamental differences between the two developments with regard to both their pace and character. The analysis of these differences is essential for understanding the differences between the agrarian structure of these two areas, as well as between the conditions under which land reform measures today are to be implemented in the various states of the Middle East.

The Abolition of Feudalism

The agrarian system of the Ottoman Empire in the eighteenth century was not uniform as it was in Egypt. As in Egypt, in remote and isolated districts of the empire, the *iltizām* prevailed, by which the land, theoretically owned by the state, was made over to tax farmers for the collection of its revenue. In the adjacent vicinity of Turkey, however, the remnants of a system of military feudalism survived, by which feudal estates (*timar*) were granted to the *sipahis*, the Ottoman cavalry. At the beginning of the nineteenth century, feudalism was abolished in the Ottoman Empire and *iltizām* in Egypt, and an attempt was made to introduce ownership by the farmers over their lands and direct collection of taxes by the state. But many factors

Originally published as "The Evolution of Private Landownership in Egypt and the Fertile Crescent," in Charles Issawi (ed.), *The Economic History of the Middle East, 1800–1914* (Chicago: University of Chicago Press, 1966), pp. 80–90.

caused this development to be quicker and more thorough in Egypt than in the Fertile Crescent. The following are among the most important:

1. The government in Egypt was of a centralist character, stemming from its importance to the economy as a regulator of irrigation by the waters of the Nile.

2. The Nile enabled every government in Egypt to reach the most remote parts of the state with comparative ease, while the communications of the Ottoman Empire were rather deficient, not enabling the state to control efficiently all its territory. Without such an efficient control over every acre of state land, it was impossible fully to abolish feudalism and to introduce a system of private individual ownership, since such a system requires registration of land and rights of ownership, the effective protection of these rights, systematic collection of taxes from every farmer, and so on.

3. The population of the Fertile Crescent was much more variegated than that of Egypt: it included beduins in ʿIrāq and the Syrian Desert, tribes in the mountains of Syria, Lebanon, Palestine, and Kurdistan, as well as ethnic and religious minorities. Of all these problems, only that of the beduin tribes existed in Egypt, but conditions were much more favorable for its solution than in the countries of the Fertile Crescent; indeed, Egypt preceded the Fertile Crescent in its solution by about a century. It was thus much easier for the rulers of Egypt to introduce a new uniform system of private ownership of land than it was for the Ottoman government to do so.

4. From Muḥammad ʿAlī's time onward, Egypt's irrigation network developed tremendously, and summer crops, especially cotton and sugar-cane, became more and more important. Thus the changeover to cash crops took place much earlier in Egypt than in the countries of the Fertile Crescent. This gave a strong impetus to the acquisition of lands. Simultaneously, extensive ownership rights were granted to the new owners by Egypt's rulers as an incentive to agricultural development in which they were interested in order to increase the income of the state. Therefore land transactions and the development of mortgage credit, requiring a modern system of legislation, made much progress as early as the middle of the nineteenth century, while in the Fertile Crescent these did not evolve before the second quarter of the twentieth.

5. Political conditions in the Ottoman Empire during the Tanzimat period, both external (especially the wars with Russia) and internal (for instance, the Balkan and Lebanon problems), were not conducive to the efficient introduction of reforms even when Mahmud II and Abdülmecid actually wished to bring them about. If similar problems existed in Egypt, they were much easier to overcome.

Muḥammad ʿAlī carried out his "agrarian reform" in a very short time: between 1811 and 1814 he destroyed the Mamluks, abolished the *iltizām* system, and appropriated all land held as *iltizām*. He seized all agricultural *waqf* land (called in Egypt *rizaq aḥbāsiyya*), that is, land not subject to normal transactions, the income of which was assigned by the founder of the endowment to his offspring, to a family guest house, to a mosque, or to any other beneficiary in order to prevent its being confiscated by the ruler or its being split up among a large number of heirs. After having become the actual owner of almost all agricultural land in Egypt, Muḥammad ʿAlī carried out a cadastral survey and registered all land in the name of the villages to which it belonged.[1]

As against this, during the thirty-two years between the destruction of the Janissaries in 1826 and the Ottoman Land Law of 1858, Mahmud II and Abdülmecid introduced only a part of these reforms in theory and even less in practice. A few days after the destruction of the Janissaries (or, according to others, in 1831), Mahmud II ordered the reunification of lands held in the past by the *sipahis* as military feudal estates with those of the state.[2] The order was carried out in stages, first in the central districts and then in the more distant ones, until finally all feudal estates were abolished.[3] At the time of the Egyptian occupation, the revenue of the former *timars* of *sipahis* in the districts of Aleppo, Damascus, and Jaffa was apparently collected by the government.[4]

Compensation was paid to the former owners of *timars* throughout the nineteenth century, reaching very substantial proportions: the sum assigned for pensions to former timariots amounted to 120,000 purses.[5] At the same time, payment of the *fāʾiẓ*, the *multazim's* profit commuted into an annual pension, to the former *multazims* of Egypt never constituted a serious problem for the treasury. There were two reasons for this: first, in Upper Egypt lands were seized from the Mamluk *multazims* (who offered resistance) without compensation; second, the *fāʾiẓ* of the *multazims* in Lower Egypt was reduced at frequent intervals and paid only in part. Moreover, the *multazims* had in general contrived to reduce payments to the state by declaring a smaller income than they had had in fact. As a result, the compensation they received, based on their own assessments, was

[1] For a detailed treatment of this development, see G. Baer, *A History of Landownership in Modern Egypt 1800–1950*, London, 1962, pp. 1–7.

[2] M. Belin, "Du Régime des fiefs militaires dans l'Islamisme," *Journal Asiatique*, March–April, 1870, pp. 293–94; B. Lewis, *The Emergence of Modern Turkey*, London, 1961, pp. 89–90. On 17 Rabīʿ al-awwal 1247 A.H./August 26, 1831 ʿAbdallāh Pasha, the *wālī* of Sidon and Tripoli, transmitted to the *mutasallim* of the sanjaq of Jerusalem the imperial decree about the dissolution of the *timars* (numbering 82 in that sanjaq) and ordered him to collect their revenue retroactively, beginning with 1829, for the imperial treasury. See A. Rustum, *Al-uṣūl al-ʿarabiyya li-taʾrīkh Sūrya fī ʿahd Muḥammad ʿAlī Bāshā*, vol. 1, Beirut, 1930, pp. 36–37. For this and some other references in this section, I am grateful to Mr. Ori Standel, who permitted me to use his unpublished seminar paper "Agrarian Relations in Syria and Palestine in the Nineteenth Century."

[3] According to Belin, in 1837; according to E. Engelhardt, *La Turquie et le Tanzimat*, Paris, 1882, 1:37 (note) and 92, as late as in 1851.

[4] J. Bowring, *Report on the Commercial Statistics of Syria*, London, 1840, p. 22.

[5] Belin, p. 295; Lewis, p. 90; A. Granott, *The Land System in Palestine*, London, 1952, p. 31. (One purse = 500 piastres.)

extremely small. It amounted to 6,000 purses in 1821, to 3,500 in 1833, and to 2,500 in 1835. Thereafter it became part of the general pension, until at the end of the century (1889–94) it was abolished in favor of a single, once-for-all payment.[6]

There was, however, a much more fundamental difference between Egypt and the Ottoman Empire in this respect. The Ottoman feudal estates taken away from the *sipahis* were made over, in the first instance, to tax farmers (*multazims* or *muḥaṣṣils*), which was exactly the system that had been abolished by Muḥammad ʿAlī in Egypt.[7] *Iltizām*, called in Syria *muqāṭaʿa*, thus became the prevailing way of tax collection in the Fertile Crescent. When Ibrāhīm Pasha conquered Syria he tried to do away with *iltizām* there as his father had done in Egypt, but these experiments turned out to be among the causes for the uprising against him.[8] At the same time, in 1839, *iltizām* was officially abolished in the Ottoman Empire by the *Hatt-i Şerif* of Gülhane.[9] However, financial difficulties led to the reintroduction of the *iltizām* system in the Ottoman Empire in 1842,[10] to be again "finally" abolished in 1856 by the *Hatt-i Humayun.*[11]

Actually the system survived much longer.[12] In Lebanon, a fellah rebellion against the *muqāṭaʿajiyya* broke out in 1858, the rebels demanding the abolition of feudal privileges, and it was found necessary to abolish once again all feudal privileges by the Regulation for the Administration of Lebanon of June 9, 1861.[13] In Palestine and Syria, the *aʿshār* or tithes were farmed out to the highest bidder as late as in the 1890's, and, in some places, even at the beginning of the twentieth century. The following was written in 1891:

> From all the produce of the farming lands of the empire a tithe is taken in kind. As, however, it would be a complicated and difficult process for the Government to collect these taxes directly, they are accustomed to let them out to tax farmers

[6]F. Mengin, *Histoire de l'Egypte sous le gouvernement de Mohammed-Aly*, Paris, 1823, 2:338, 389; *Histoire sommaire de l'Egypte sous le gouvernement de Mohammed-Aly* . . ., Paris, 1839, p. 153; Col. Campbell, *Report on Egypt*, PRO, FO 78/408 B; Egypt No. 2 (1879), C. 2233, pp. 252–53; P. Gelat, *Répertoire de la législation et de l'administration égyptienne*, 2ᵉ période, Alexandria, 1893, 1:7–8; 3ᵉ période, Alexandria, 1897, 1:645–46.

[7]Lewis, p. 442.

[8]See A.D. al-ʿAqīqī, *Thawra wa-fitna fī lubnān*, Beirut, 1936, pp. 26 ff.; F. Perrier, *La Syrie sous le gouvernement de Méhémet-Ali*, Paris, 1842, pp. 358 ff.

[9]Cf. W. Padel and L. Steeg, *De la Législation foncière ottomane*, Paris, 1904, pp. 17, 23; Lewis, p. 379.

[10]Engelhardt, 1:50–51; 2:52 (where the year 1841 is given). Cf. Lewis, p. 380.

[11]Engelhardt, 1:268–69.

[12]Engelhardt 1:52; Granott, p. 58.

[13]al-ʿAqīqī, pp. 84, 161–63, 178, and *passim*. For text of the Regulation, see J. C. Hurewitz, *Diplomacy in the Near and Middle East*, Princeton, 1956, 1:165–68.

> (*multazamin*), for a sum agreed upon by both parties. . . . The Government supplies them with soldiers to assist them in the collection of the taxes. . . . He has the power to quarter his horsemen and other animals without compensation on the poor villagers, who are glad to buy him off and get rid of him by paying two tenths or more.[14]

Moreover, in the Fertile Crescent the power of the local dynasties (to be compared, to a certain extent, to the Turkish *derebeys*, whose power had been broken at the beginning of the century) survived much longer than elsewhere in the Middle East. Throughout the first half of the nineteenth century, local families of shaykhs virtually ruled large parts of Palestine and continued to do so even later in the century, though their power had been reduced during Ibrāhīm Pasha's rule.[15] In the Syrian Jabal Drūz (Ḥawrān) the leading families exercised semi-feudal rights which were partly broken in the wake of a peasant revolt in 1886–87.[16] The strongholds of the remnants of feudalism and *iltizām* were the hilly areas of Lebanon, Palestine, and northern Iraq, as well as the tribal marsh areas of southern Iraq. There were no provinces or areas in Egypt geographically or socially equivalent to these. This was certainly the main reason why the abolition of feudalism and *iltizām* in the Ottoman Empire took so much longer than in Egypt and why, even after their abolition, vestiges of the old agrarian system survived in the Fertile Crescent.

The Laws of 1858

After Muḥammad ʿAlī's reforms, the next important stage in the evolution of the rights of private landowners in Egypt was Saʿīd's Land Law of 24 Dhū al-Ḥijja, 1274 A.H./August 5, 1858. The fact that Egypt was at that time part of the Ottoman Empire and that Saʿīd's law was promulgated only four months after the well-known Ottoman Land Law of the same year (7 Ramaḍān, 1274 A.H./April 21, 1858) has misled a number of authors to believe that the former was no more than the application of the latter to Egyptian conditions. Thus Gatteschi wrote:

[14] G. E. Post, "Essays on the Sects and Nationalities of Syria and Palestine. Essay 2: Land Tenure," *Quarterly Statement of the Palestine Exploration Fund (QPEF)*, 1891, pp. 106–7; cf. S. Bergheim "Land Tenure in Palestine," *QPEF*, 1894, pp. 197–98; A. Ruppin, *Syrien als Wirtschaftsgebiet*, Berlin, 1920, p. 149.

[15] J. Finn, *Stirring Times*, London, 1878, 1:228–32, 240–41; L. Oliphant, *Haifa or Life in Modern Palestine*, 2d ed., London, 1887, p. 198; R. A. S. Macalister and E. W. G. Masterman, "Occasional Papers on the Modern Inhabitants of Palestine," *QPEF*, 1905, pp. 344, 352–56.

[16] M. von Oppenheim, *Vom Mittelmeer zum persischen Golf*, Berlin, 1899, pp. 169–70, 175; A. Latron, *La vie rurale en Syrie et au Liban*, Beirut, 1936, p. 212.

> The order of the Viceroy of 1274 [Saʿīd's Land Law] applied the imperial law of 1858 [to the conditions of Egypt]. . . . It was impossible to accept simply the laws of Constantinople for Egypt, where there did not exist a system parallel to that of Turkey. . . . It was therefore necessary to make special arrangements, which in taking into account these differences, would carry out in Egypt the broad and liberal reforms of the imperial laws.[17]

This view seems to us to be completely mistaken. There certainly were some sections of the two laws which were partly or even entirely identical. Both draw a distinction between two kinds of land: one type over which the persons holding it have full ownership (in Egypt *ibʿādiyya*, in the Ottoman Empire *mulk*), and a second type whose *raqaba* (ownership without usufruct) is in the hand of the state and whose holders possess rights of usufruct only (in Egypt—*athariyya* or *kharājiyya* lands; in the Ottoman Empire—*mīrī*). Both laws regulate the prescription of *kharājiyya* (*mīrī*) lands; Article 5 of the Egyptian law states that whoever has tilled a parcel of land for five years in succession cannot be deprived of his right of prescription, and Article 20 of the Ottoman law states: "Actions concerning *mīrī* lands the occupation of which has continued without dispute for a period of ten years shall not be maintainable."[18] Both laws grant preferential rights in acquiring the holding of an heirless holder of *kharājiyya* (*mīrī*) lands to the inhabitants of his village (Article 3 in the Egyptian law; Article 59 in the Ottoman law).[19] Both laws (Article 9 in both) allow holders of *kharājiyya* (*mīrī*) land to rent it out (although this right is limited differently in each of them).

However, in these common provisions no rights were granted that did not exist before that time. These were no more than a codification of the traditional rights of *kharājiyya* (*mīrī*) landholders. In all other respects the two laws were completely different from one another not only in form but also in their intentions. In the Ottoman Empire, vestiges of feudalism still survived, the state was weak, and, as we have seen, its rights over its lands were still challenged by local powers. Therefore, the Ottoman law aimed at consolidating these rights of the state, mainly by imposing severe restrictions on holders of *mīrī* lands and by listing exactly and in detail all rights held by

[17] D. Gatteschi, *Des Lois sur la propriété foncière dans l'empire ottoman*, Paris, 1857, p. 28.

[18] For the Ottoman Land Law, see, for instance, the English translation by F. Ongley (London, 1892). In addition, the Arabic translation of Duʿaybis al-Murr in his *Kitāb aḥkām al-arāḍī* (in later references: Murr), Jerusalem, 1923, part 2, and the Hebrew translation in the appendix of M. Doukhan, *Dinei qarqaʿot b'eretz yisrael*, Jerusalem, 1925, have been consulted. Saʿīd's Land Law has been published separately in *Loi sur la propriété territoriale*, Alexandria, 1875. See also Y. Artin-Bey, *La Propriété foncière en Egypte*, Cairo, 1883, *passim*.

[19] In the Ottoman law the inhabitants of the village share the preference rights with other groups.

them before its enactment which could not be denied them.[20] In Egypt, on the other hand, the state had already gained satisfactory control over its lands long before. Private agricultural enterprise began to develop rapidly after the abolition of Muḥammad ʿAlī's monopolies, and a need was felt to facilitate land transactions in order to encourage the development of agriculture. Thus the principal purpose of Saʿīd's law was to expand the ownership rights of Egyptian landholders and to give their property security and stability.[21] Unlike the Ottoman Land Law, Saʿīd's Land Law was a far-reaching change in relation to the conditions of the past.

The different spirit permeating the two laws finds a very clear expression in the provisions concerning the erection of buildings and the planting of trees on *kharājiyya* (*mīrī*) land. Article 11 of Saʿīd's law granted full ownership rights to holders of *kharājiyya* land who had erected buildings or set up a *sāqiya* (water-raising apparatus for irrigation) or planted trees on it. In contrast, the Ottoman Land Law states: "Without the permission of the official, new buildings cannot be erected on *mīrī* land. If they have been erected the government can have them demolished." Article 25 states: "Without the permission of the official a person cannot make into a garden or vineyard the land he possesses by planting vines and different kinds of fruit trees. Even if he has done so without permission the government has the power during three years to make him pull them up." The purpose of the Egyptian law obviously was to encourage the development of agriculture. The Ottoman law, on the other hand, reflected the government's intention not to let out of its grasp any right or part of a right over *mīrī* land, for buildings and plantations were *mulk* property, and if they belonged to a person who was not the owner of the land on which they were established, they invested this person with the right of preemption over the land.[22]

However, the differences between the two laws are not confined to provisions regarding buildings and plantations. The Egyptian law granted a number of new rights, while the Ottoman law imposed many restrictions on holders of *mīrī* land. Saʿīd's law provided for *kharājiyya* lands to be inherited according to the Muslim laws of inheritance (like land in full ownership), and authorized their sale (without the necessity of obtaining prior permission from the state) and their mortgage. As against this, the

[20] Englehardt, 1:209; Granott, p. 87—as against Gatteschi, pp. 20, 28, and N. H. Chiha, *Traité de la propriété immobilière en droit ottoman*, Cairo, 1906, p. 18.

[21] Artin, p. 105; A. Crouchley, *The Economic Development of Modern Egypt*, London, 1938, p. 127.

[22] Article 44 of the Ottoman Land Law. This is Doukhan's explanation, which looks much more convincing than that given by Padel and Steeg.

Ottoman law stated that leaving *mīrī* land fallow for three years was sufficient cause for confiscation by the state (Article 68–71); prohibited the holder of *mīrī* land from using its soil for making bricks (Article 12); made its sale conditional on official consent (Article 36), and did not recognize preemption rights (*shufʿa*) over *mīrī* land (Article 46). Whoever cultivated *miri* land over which he had no right of usage and paid the taxes to the state was not required to pay an indemnity or rent to the owner but just to return it to him (Article 21). *Mīrī* land held in partnership might be divided only with the permission of the government (Article 17). The Ottoman law prohibited the mortgaging of *mīrī* land, although the owner was allowed, after having obtained a special permission from the authorities, to "alienate it to his creditor . . . on condition that at the time he settles his debt the creditor will return the land to him," or to sell it in "a returnable sale (*farāgh al-wafāʾ*) on condition that whenever he returns the cost of the sale he has the right to claim the restitution of the land from the buyer" (Article 116). This last right had already been granted to Egyptian *kharājiyya* holders in 1846 without the stipulation of a special permit from the authorities.[23]

There was only one point in which the Ottoman law was more "liberal" than the Egyptian one: the 1858 Land Law, and Ottoman legislation relating to immovable property in general,[24] did not draw the same distinction between *mīrī* and *mulk* land as the Egyptian law did between *kharājiyya* and *ibʿādiyya* lands with regard to rights of compensation in case of confiscation for public purposes. Thus the Ottoman law granted rights of compensation to holders of *mīrī* land confiscated for public use, while Egypt's rulers did not undertake such an obligation. The reason for this difference was the importance of public land in Egypt as a result of the extensive irrigation network. Saʿīd, and Egypt's rulers after him, did not wish to jeopardize the plans for development of irrigation and other works by placing obligations on the treasury, so long as they could prevent this by arguing that the *raqaba* of *kharājiyya* lands belonged to the state. That Egypt differed fundamentally from the Fertile Crescent countries in this respect is shown by figures on the area of public domain (*matrūka*)[25] in proportion to the total area: In Egypt this proportion rose from 7.9 per

[23]There is, however, a difference between *farāgh al-wafāʾ* and *rahn ḥiyāzī* or *ghārūqa* which was practiced in Egypt: *farāgh al-wafāʾ* transfers the ownership to the creditor, while *rahn ḥiyāzī* transfers only cultivation rights. From this stems the provision in the Ottoman law which makes *farāgh al-wafāʾ* conditional on permission from the authorities.

[24]Cf. G. Young, *Corps de droit ottoman*, Oxford, 1906, 6:127–31.

[25]"Public domain" is land marked for special purposes, such as roads, irrigation canals, etc., which cannot be sold by the state.

cent in 1922 to 10.8 per cent in 1949, while in Iraq it amounted to only 3.4 per cent in 1951 and in Transjordan to only 1.5 per cent in 1950.[26]

1858–1950: Mīrī and Mulk; Land Registration

The year 1858 had been a landmark in the history of landownership in the Middle East, after which the property rights of landowners continued to grow. They did so, however, with the same difference in pace and character between Egypt and the Fertile Crescent as before. In Egypt cash crops, especially cotton, became ever more important, land transactions multiplied, and foreign capital became interested in Egypt's landed property. Nothing comparable took place in the Fertile Crescent; only in the second quarter of this century did a slight changeover to cash crops begin to manifest itself, but it never attained the importance it did in Egypt. This difference in economic development was fully reflected in land legislation.

Throughout the second half of the nineteenth century the proportion of *mulk* land in Egypt, that is, land held as full private property, grew steadily. From less than one-seventh of the total area in the 1850's, it increased to more than one-quarter in 1875, and it was approaching one-third in the 1890's. By that time, however (to be exact, in 1896),[27] *kharājiyya* land was fully assimilated to *mulk*, so that in the twentieth century all agricultural land in Egypt was the full private property of its owners (except, of course, *waqf* land).

In the Ottoman Empire and the countries of the Fertile Crescent the proportion of agricultural *mulk* land did not increase at all. But here, too, ownership rights over *mīrī* were extended. This was done, however, much later than in Egypt: the first main group of laws in this direction was issued in 1913, and the second phase took place, in Syria and Iraq, in 1930 and 1932. Moreover, in the Fertile Crescent *mīrī* land was never entirely assimilated to *mulk*, and some restrictions on *mīrī* land have remained in force to this day.

Although the state's right to demolish buildings erected on *mīrī* land without its permission was abolished by a special order in 1890,[28] the need for special authorization to erect buildings and to plant trees on *mīrī* land remained in force for another twenty years. It was abolished on 5 Jumādā al-ūlā, 1331 A.H./April 12, 1913 by Article 5 of the Law of Transfer of

[26] The International Bank for Reconstruction and Development (IBRD), *The Economic Development of Iraq,* Baltimore, 1952, p. 179; al-Mamlaka al-Urdunniyya al-Hāshimiyya, *al-Nashra al-iḥṣā'iyya al-urdunniyya 1950* (*Jordan Statistical Yearbook*).

[27] For details, see Baer, *A History of Landownership*, pp. 10–12.

[28] Doukhan, p. 53.

Immovable Property,[29] which also permitted the transfer and sale of *mīrī* lands. Article 7 of the same law abolished the prohibition on the use of *mīrī* land for making bricks. Article 14 required persons who cultivated other people's *mīrī* land to pay the owner rent, though not compensation for the depreciation of the land (the 1858 law required no payment of either kind). Mortgaging of *mīrī* land was permitted by the Law of Mortgages of 16 Rabīʿ al-thānī, 1331 A.H./March 25, 1913.[30] The need to obtain official permission for the division of *mīrī* land held in partnership was abolished by the Law of Division of Immovable Property of 4 Muḥarram, 1332 A.H./ December 13, 1913, which made such a division much easier.[31] All these rights, which were granted in the Ottoman Empire in 1913, had been granted for *kharājiyya* lands in Egypt by Saʿīd in 1858 and partly even before that. Moreover, preemption rights in relation to *mīrī* land were not granted as long as the Ottoman Empire existed. They were granted in Syria and Lebanon in 1931,[32] but never in Palestine and Israel.[33] Another restriction which remained in force in all Fertile Crescent countries (more often than not in theory only) is the regulation that after a certain period of lying fallow *mīrī* land passes into the possession of the state: in Palestine (like the original provision of Ottoman times) after three years,[34] in Syria and Lebanon after five years,[35] and in Iraq after three to four years, according to different kinds of *mīrī* land.[36]

While these last-mentioned restrictions were of little practical importance, others had quite substantial influence on the development of landownership in the Fertile Crescent and its divergence from the course in which this development proceeded in Egypt. Originally the tilling of *kharājiyya* lands in Egypt (formerly called *athariyya*) passed from father to son; in 1855 the right of inheritance was established for male heirs, and in 1858 Saʿīd ordered that *kharājiyya* lands were to be inherited like *mulk* according to the Muslim law of inheritance. This provision remained in force except for the short period 1869 to 1881, during which only the income from the land, but not the land itself, was divided in accordance with the Muslim inheritance law.[37] In the Ottoman Empire, too, the tilling of the peasants' land

[29] For text, see Murr, 2:119–23; Doukhan, pp. 232–35.
[30] For text, see Murr, 2:86–92; Doukhan, pp. 240–42.
[31] For text, see Murr, 2:97–101; Doukhan pp. 243–45.
[32] L. Cardon, *Le Régime de la propriété foncière en Syrie et au Liban*, Paris, 1932, pp. 160–61.
[33] M. Doukhan, *Dinei qarqa'ot bimdinat yisrael* (Doukhan, *Israel*, in later references), Jerusalem, 1953, p. 164.
[34] Doukhan, *Israel*, p. 475; Granott, p. 20.
[35] Cardon, p. 150.
[36] IBRD, *Iraq*, p. 139.
[37] See Baer, *A History of Landownership*, pp. 38–39.

originally passed from father to son, but later other relations were included in the list of potential heirs, though their number was very small.[38] Subsequent enactments gradually expanded the number of potential heirs but never assimilated *mīrī* land to *mulk* in this respect. The laws containing such provisions were the Ottoman Land Law of 1858 (Articles 54–59), the Law on Expansion of Inheritance Rights in *mīrī* and *mawqūfa* lands of May 21, 1867,[39] and the Law on Inheritance of Immovable Property of March 12, 1913.[40] This last-mentioned law is still in force in the Fertile Crescent countries, where *mīrī* land is not subject to the Muslim law of inheritance.

The right to bequeath *kharājiyya* lands by will was granted in Egypt in 1866.[41] From the 1890's onward, when they became *mulk*, they also could be endowed as *waqf* without prior permission from the Khedive. These two rights were never granted to owners of *mīrī* land in the Ottoman Empire, and as late as 1913, in the Law of Transfer of Immovable Property, it was explicitly stated (Article 8) that "the holder of *mīrī* land is not permitted to endow it as a true *waqf*[42] and not to bequeath it by will except if the government had transferred the land to him as his own absolute property (*mulk*) by special order of the Sultan in accordance with the religious law."[43] This law remained partly in force in several of the Fertile Crescent countries. In Syria and Lebanon permission was granted to bequeath *mīrī* land by will in 1930,[44] and in Iraq in 1932.[45] Palestine and the State of Israel retained the Ottoman provision in its entirety.[46] The prohibition on endowing *mīrī* land as *waqf* without special authority (i.e., without having it turned into *mulk* by the government) remained in force throughout the Fertile Crescent. *Mīrī lazma* land in Iraq cannot be endowed as *waqf* under any circumstance.[47]

To appreciate the significance of all these laws governing *mīrī*, one has to take into account the fact that practically all agricultural land in the Fertile

[38] See Padel and Steeg, pp. 213–14.

[39] Murr, 2:113–15; Doukhan, pp. 228–29.

[40] Murr, 2:109–12; Doukhan, pp. 230–31.

[41] For text, see *Loi sur la propriété territoriale*, p. 41.

[42] Called *waqf ṣaḥīḥ*. The ruler may endow as *waqf* the taxes from the land, or the rent may be assigned as a *waqf*, to a specified beneficiary. Such a waqf is called *waqf ghayr ṣaḥīḥ* or *takhṣīṣāt*.

[43] Doukhan, p. 233.

[44] Cardon, p. 151.

[45] *Qānūn taswiyat ḥuqūq al-arāḍī*, no. 50, 1932. See S. Himadeh, *al-Niẓām al-iqtiṣādī fī'l-ʿirāq*, Beirut, 1938, p. 127.

[46] Doukhan, *Israel*, p. 250.

[47] Doukhan, *Israel*, p. 63; S. Himadeh, *Economic Organization of Syria*, Beirut, 1936, p. 53; Himadeh, *Iraq*, pp. 127, 130. *Mīrī lazma* is land held by tribes which may not be transferred to anyone outside the tribe.

Crescent is *mīrī* and that *mulk* land amounts to a negligible quantity. Statistics distinguishing between these two categories are rather inadequate. The only exact figures are those pertaining to Iraq, which reveal that only 0.3 per cent of the area that had been registered up to February, 1951 (one-half of the total), was *mulk*.[48] The area of *mīrī* land in Syria is not known, but "actually all agricultural land in Syria is *mīrī*."[49] Doukhan estimated *mīrī* land in Palestine to amount to "95 per cent of all cultivated lands."[50] Lebanon is the only exception: the greater part of its land is *mulk*. This seems to be the result of the autonomous status enjoyed by Lebanon in the Ottoman Empire for many centuries.[51]

There was, finally, another important difference between the development of landownership in Egypt and in the Ottoman Empire. Muḥammad ʿAlī and Saʿīd had already carried out a full, though primitive, cadastral survey in Egypt; and by 1907, a full modern land registration had been completed.[52] As against this, in the Ottoman Empire absolute confusion and anarchy reigned in the survey of lands and registration of ownership up to its disintegration. Instructions for the registration of lands issued in the wake of the Ottoman Land Law on February 29, 1860[53] were carried out only sporadically and most inaccurately because of administrative incompetence and because the major part of the agricultural land was held collectively by the villages in so-called *mushāʿ* tenure to be periodically redistributed among the villagers; as long as the villagers were not ready to forgo the security of the village community or driven to do so by economic differentiation among its members, *mushāʿ* prevented registration of individual ownership rights. In this respect too Egyptian practices differed completely. In Lower Egypt, village lands apparently were never periodically redistributed among the villagers, while in Upper Egypt, this custom had been abandoned by the middle of the nineteenth century.[54] To this day *mushāʿ* tenure in the Fertile Crescent still constitutes a severe impediment to registration of land and, for that matter, to economic development in general. A third reason for the failure of registration in the Fertile

[48] IBRD, *Iraq*, p. 179.

[49] Himadeh, *Syria*, p. 53.

[50] Doukhan, p. 26.

[51] See *Rapport général sur les études foncières . . .*, Beirut, 1921, pp. 72–73. According to this, apparently official, publication, nearly all immovable property in Mount Lebanon is *mulk*. According to *Lubnān fī ʿahd al-istiqlāl*, Beirut, 1947, p. 58, about 65 percent of the land of the republic of Lebanon is *mulk*.

[52] Cf. H. G. Lyons, *The Cadrastral Survey of Egypt 1892–1907*, Cairo, 1908.

[53] Doukhan, pp. 223–37.

[54] Chapter 2, above.

Crescent was the tribal character of a substantial part of its population.[55]

In the 1920's, the mandatory government in each of the Fertile Crescent countries set up an administration for the survey and registration of land, and in the 1930's registration was undertaken again, this time by modern methods. But the mandatory authorities too encountered part of the basic difficulties mentioned above, and new political ones on top of them. Nevertheless, land registration continued slowly under both mandatory rule and independence, but by the middle of this century not one of these countries had reached the position attained by Egypt at the beginning of it. The greatest progress was made in Transjordan, where, up to 1950, two-thirds of the total area had been registered—6,279,850 dunums out of 9,428,835.[56] In Iraq about half had been registered by 1951—50,447,034 Iraqi dunums out of 107,032,725,[57] and in Syria in 1950 little more than 40 per cent—3,430,407 hectares out of 8,339,028.[58] The lack of a complete and exact registration of land is certainly one of the main difficulties encountered by Syria and Iraq in their efforts to implement reforms of their agrarian structure.

The Effect of Unlike Development on the Agrarian Structure in the 1950's

We have dwelt at length on the legal development of landownership in Egypt and the Fertile Crescent, and we must now ask the question: to what extent is this development relevant to the present structure of land tenure in these two areas of the Middle East, or rather to the structure of land tenure prior to the land reforms which are carried out today, and therefore to the problems which these land reforms intend to solve? Before answering these questions, one point must be stressed: as we have seen, differences in land laws reflected differences in geographical and social conditions as well as in economic development. It would be a grave mistake not to take these basic conditions into account as direct causes for different structures of land tenure; but it is our contention that the legal development had an important influence on shaping these different structures.

[55] For the failure of nineteenth-century land registration in Iraq see S. H. Longrigg, *Four Centuries of Modern Iraq*, Oxford, 1925, p. 307; for Palestine, L. French, *Reports on Agricultural Development and Land Settlement in Palestine*, Jerusalem, 1931, p. 13; for Lebanon, T. al-Shidyāq, *Akhbār al-aʿyān fī jabal lubnān*, Beirut, 1858, pp. 701, 718; A. Ismail, *Histoire du Liban, tome iv: Redressement et déclin du féodalisme libanais*, Beirut, 1958, pp. 303–7. On the situation of land registration in the various countries of the Fertile Crescent at the end of World War I, see, for Palestine, Doukhan, pp. 86–87, 166; for Syria and Lebanon, *Rapport géneral sur les études foncières*, pp. 136–43 and *passim*; for Iraq, Himadeh, *Iraq*, pp. 159–60, and E. Dowson, *An Inquiry into Land Tenure and Related Questions*, Letchworth, 1932, p. 19 and *passim*.

[56] *Jordan Statistical Yearbook, 1950.*

[57] IBRD, *Iraq*, p. 179.

[58] Government of Syria, *Statistical Abstract of Syria, 1950*, p. 178.

In the first place, the fact that for almost a century Egypt's landed property was subdivided, generation after generation, according to the Muslim law of inheritance, while agricultural land in the Fertile Crescent, being *mīrī*, was not, was certainly of major significance. Under Muslim inheritance law an extremely large number of persons of varying degrees of kinship are entitled to share an estate, and not more than one-third of a person's property may be transferred by will. The result was extreme fragmentation of landownership in Egypt, hundreds of thousands of fellah families owning tiny plots, too little to make their living out of them. There were, of course, ways to circumvent the law, but these were used mainly by big landowners and very seldom by small or medium ones. It is very difficult to compare the fragmentation of landownership in Egypt with that in the Fertile Crescent, since no adequate statistics exist for any of the Fertile Crescent countries. But there can be no doubt that this problem is much more severe in Egypt than in any of the other Arab countries. That it has troubled Egypt and continues to do so is evident from the fact that Egyptian governments have tried twice to solve it by special legislation (while none of the Fertile Crescent countries has ever deemed it necessary to enact such legislation). The first attempt was the Five Feddan Law of 1912, according to which agricultural holdings of farmers who did not own more than five feddans could not be seized for debt. The second attempt was the Land Reform of 1952 which prohibited the splitting up of a unit of land, by sale, transfer, inheritance, or attachment, below the size of five feddans. The Five Feddan Law, which tackled only the problem of indebtedness, failed because fellahs and moneylenders found ways to evade it. According to Sayyid Marʿī, former Minister of Land Reform, the provisions of the land reform in this respect have also not been carried out.[59]

Secondly, since from the end of the past century all land in Egypt was *mulk* it could freely be endowed as *waqf*, while most agricultural land in the Fertile Crescent, being *mīrī*, could not. Egyptian landowners, particularly big ones, made ample use of this freedom in order to prevent the splitting up of large estates and to keep them in the family and thus to maintain the family's power and social status. During the first half of the twentieth century the area of *waqf* land in Egypt doubled, reaching about 10 per cent of the total area (as against 1.2 per cent in Iraq at midcentury and less than 0.1 per cent in Transjordan). There seem to exist quite extensive areas of *waqf* land in Lebanon (where land was *mulk* as in Egypt) and in Palestine (although there *waqf* was of the "untrue" kind, the so-called *waqf ghayr ṣaḥīḥ*), but there are no statistics to show how large these areas were. Thus a

[59] Sayyid Marʿī, *al-Iṣlāḥ al-zirāʿī fī miṣr*, Cairo, 1957, pp. 183–84, 191.

strange situation was created: although she had lifted the burden of *waqf* from her lands at the beginning of the nineteenth century, Egypt found it a more acute problem in this century than did any other successor state of the Ottoman Empire (which had not radically confiscated all agricultural *waqf* land at an earlier stage). In this respect, however, the radical cure of the recent Egyptian land reform seems to have been successful.[60]

Thirdly, Egypt's more extensive ownership rights, her greater simplicity in classification of land, and her more exact and more complete registration of lands contributed decisively to another important distinction: foreign capital became interested in purchasing land in Egypt, and estates owned by non-Egyptians soon reached much larger dimensions than those of foreigners in any Arab country of the Middle East. Moreover, since Muḥammad ʿAlī's time Egypt's rulers had ignored Muslim law, according to which strangers are not allowed to own landed property in the Muslim state, and Egypt's agricultural development in the nineteenth century and after induced foreigners to acquire lands in Egypt rather than in other parts of the Middle East. By the 1920's foreign-owned land amounted to about 10 per cent of the total area; later, however, foreigners either sold much of their landed property for political reasons or acquired Egyptian nationality, so that by 1950 the percentage had dropped to 3.6. Therefore, insofar as the land reform dealt with foreign-owned land, it was rather the land owned by the ruling Muḥammad ʿAlī family (of "Turkish" origin), extending as it did over a much larger area than the estates of foreigners of European origin. In any case, although no figures are known, it is evident that neither of these two kinds of foreigners owned nearly so much land in the Arab Fertile Crescent countries as they did in Egypt.

The activity of land companies was another feature of the agrarian structure which distinguished Egypt from other Arab countries of the Middle East. Though joint stock companies bought, sold, and cultivated land in a number of Middle Eastern countries, they never attained such importance as they did in Egypt. During the peak period of the foundation of land companies in Egypt, that is, the last decade of the nineteenth and the first decade of the twentieth century, no company was entitled to hold land in the Ottoman Empire—a right that was granted only in 1913.[61] But there were also economic and social reasons: land reclamation, a typical field of activity for companies, was carried out on a much larger scale in Egypt than in the countries of the Fertile Crescent, and nowhere in the Middle East except in Egypt did there exist large plantations, especially sugarcane

[60] See chapter 5, below.
[61] Doukhan, pp. 69–70; Murr, 2:94.

plantations, a type of economic activity undertaken in many countries by companies. In this connection it is interesting to note that Egyptian land companies which operated in other countries of the Middle East bought mainly urban land and property, not agricultural estates, even if their main concern in Egypt was agricultural land.

Earlier survey and registration of land in Egypt brought with it yet another important difference between its system of landownership and that of the Fertile Crescent countries: the much lower proportion of state land. While Egypt was already busy transferring cultivated and cultivable state lands into private hands, the Syrian and Iraqi governments, for instance, were still claiming and recovering lands illegally occupied and appropriated by various persons (the most prominent among them being beduin shaykhs). In addition, in the Fertile Crescent there are much larger cultivable but not yet cultivated reserves of land (which form the main part of lands registered in the name of the state), and therefore a lower density of population in relation to the cultivated and cultivable area. Thus pressure on the government to dispose of its lands was much higher in Egypt than in the other countries. Finally, the earlier development of cash crops as well as land reclamation by land companies accelerated the pace of transfer of state lands into private hands. The result was that in the early 1950's state land covered in Egypt only about 17 per cent of all registered land, as against 30 per cent in Transjordan, more than 40 per cent in Syria, and as much as 62 per cent in Iraq.[62] It should therefore be much easier in the Fertile Crescent to carry out a policy of creating a new class of small landowners by granting them state land than to do so in Egypt. Indeed, in the legislation of recent years in Syria and Iraq the distribution of state lands has always figured as a major item, while it did so in Egypt before the revolution mainly as an argument against the necessity to redistribute privately owned estates. In fact state land in Egypt was sold, generally by auction, to big landowners or to rich urban merchants who thus became big landowners.

This leads us to our final observation. Reserves of uncultivated state land granted or sold by the ruler or the government to officials, village notables, or urban merchants were the primary source for the formation of Egypt's large estates during the past 150 years. Big landownership in Egypt derived from the state, and Egypt's big landowners concentrated in Cairo. In the Fertile Crescent, on the other hand, many of the large estates evolved because of the weakness of the state: fellahs asked powerful notables for protection and paid for it in land; land registration being vague, socially

[62] Cf. G. Baer, "Land Tenure in the Hashemite Kingdom of Jordan," *Land Economics*, 33 (August, 1957):188–89.

influential families managed to have the land registered in their name; beduin shaykhs with power over their tribes succeeded, when title deeds were made out, to appropriate the tribal *dīra* (area fixed for the pasture and agricultural activity of a tribe). This does not mean that other factors for the concentration of land in a few hands, as, for instance, peasant indebtedness, have not been operative in both areas, in Egypt as well as in the Fertile Crescent. But local power based on the control of vast tracts of land always was and has remained much stronger in Syria or Iraq than in centralized Egypt. This is certainly a factor which makes the implementation of any reform in the Fertile Crescent much more difficult than in Egypt.

5

Waqf Reform

The Problem

In 1812, on the eve of Muḥammad ʿAlī's agrarian reform, waqf lands (or *rizaq aḥbāsiyya*, as their main category was then called) amounted, in Upper Egypt and the Cairo region alone, to 600,000 feddans.[1] In the fall of that year Muḥammad ʿAlī confiscated all waqf lands and promised to provide for those persons and institutions to whom the income from these lands had been dedicated.[2] But while Muḥammad ʿAlī definitely brought the *iltizām* system to an end, he only confiscated waqf lands without abolishing waqf as an institution. Throughout the nineteenth and, with even greater impetus in the twentieth, century, new waqfs were created by landowners in order to perpetuate their family's name and to consolidate its influence, to guard the property against confiscation by the ruler and splitting up through inheritance, and particularly against seizure for nonpayment of debts. According to various estimates, the area of waqf lands had again reached 300,000 feddans by 1900, 350,000 by 1914, and 400,000 by the end of World War I;[3] but the main years of creation of new waqfs seem to have been the twenties, and by 1927 the area of waqfs in Egypt amounted to as much as 611,203 feddans.[4] Official statistics on waqf lands, which have been published regularly since 1935, show a further steady increase up till 1942, when

Originally published as "Waqf Reform in Egypt," *Middle Eastern Affairs, Number One*, St. Antony's Papers, no. 4 (London, 1958), pp. 61–76.

[1] Jabartī, 4:141 (31–32). Until Muḥammad ʿAlī's reforms the feddan was almost 1.5 acres.

[2] Jabartī, 4:147 (2); 148 (8); 153 (27); 154 (2); 183 (30–31); 184 (19–21); 210 (14–15).

[3] *al-Ahrām*, March 23, 1944; Fahmi Abdel Latif, *La Loi des 5 feddans*, Paris, 1914, p. 134; Sami Gabra, *Esquisse de l'histoire économique et politique de la propriété foncière en Egypte*, Bordeaux, 1919, p. 111.

[4] A. Sékaly, *Le Problème des wakfs en Egypte*, Paris, 1929, pp. 94, 448.

waqfs covered an area of 677,555 feddans, that is, more than 11.5 per cent of all owned lands (except state domain). Since then a certain decline in the area of waqf land has taken place, but on the eve of the reform it was still about 600,000 feddans. Although waqfs also consisted of urban real estate, and recently even of shares in joint-stock companies, agricultural lands seem to have become the predominant component of waqf property in the twentieth century. For instance, the Waqf Ministry's revenue from agricultural lands was, at the beginning of the present century, twice as large as that from urban property, and by the middle of the century it had become more than three and a half times as large.

As the waqf turned more and more into an agrarian problem, it had a growing share in bringing about the ills of Egypt's agrarian structure. For reasons to be explained later on, many Egyptian writers and politicians tended to put the blame for these ills on the *waqf ahlī* system alone, while maintaining that the *waqf khayrī* had no harmful economic and social influence whatsoever.[5] This claim, however, has very little basis in reality. To begin with, no clearcut line can be drawn between these two kinds of waqf, either from the point of view of Muslim law[6] or, what matters more in this respect, from the social and economic point of view. Upon the establishment of either kind the property endowed is no longer subject to normal transactions, that is, it cannot be transferred, mortgaged, or the like. It is handed over to a *nāẓir*, an administrator nominated by the founder of the waqf, who receives about 10 per cent of the income and whose duty it is to maintain the property and to distribute its income according to provisions laid down by the founder in his *waqfiyya* (endowment deed of a waqf). The difference between the so-called *waqf khayrī* and the so-called *waqf ahlī* is that, upon the creation of a waqf of the former kind, the income goes immediately to some religious, cultural, or charitable institution, while the income from the latter, though being ultimately devoted to such an institution as well, is first assigned to a person specified in the *waqfiyya* (generally the male offspring of the founder). But even this distinction is not a very definite one, since many waqfs had part of their income dedicated to a religious or charitable purpose, while another part was assigned to members of the founder's family (such waqfs were known as *awqāf mushtaraka*).[7]

[5] See, e.g., Sékaly, pp. 407–12, 450–51, 627–29; and Muḥammad ʿAlī ʿAllūba Pasha, *Mabādiʾ fiʾl-siyāsa al-miṣriyya*, Cairo, 1942, pp. 300–2.

[6] Cf. J. N. D. Anderson, "The Religious Element in Waqf Endowments," *Royal Central Asian Journal*, 38, part 4, (October, 1951), pp. 292–99.

[7] Particulars of such waqfs have been published, for instance, in *al-Ahrām*, May 12 and 24, 1943; August 4, 1952; September 7, 1952; October 16, 1952; November 2, 1952; July 13, 1953; November 3, 1953; December 8, 1953; April 9, 1954; June 22, 1954.

Others provided for allocations to the poor members of the founder's family or to the family's guest house (in Egypt the term *awqāf khayriyya khāṣṣa*, i.e., "private charitable waqfs," has been invented for such cases).[8] Moreover, the income from some of the so-called *khayrī* waqfs was spent on the maintenance of noble families in Egypt, especially princes of the royal family.[9] Indeed, this institution, that is, the *waqf khayrī*, once the material basis of the golden age of Muslim learning, has become an anachronism in a modern state with an education and health budget and with cultural needs which are no longer compatible with the sometimes bizarre and capricious provisions of the founders of *awqāf khayriyya*. The beneficiaries of a large *khayrī* waqf founded in Ṭanṭā, for instance, were the stray dogs of that town. *Sabīls* (public fountains), a favorite purpose for endowments, have been prohibited by the Health Ministry, the education system has been unified, and the specified conditions regarding staff and curriculum as laid down in many *waqfiyyāt* have become a nuisance; and the numerous provisions for institutions in Turkey to be found in *waqfiyyāt* of the nineteenth century collide with considerations of policy and currency regulations. *Waqf khayrī*, therefore, has not been at all such a meritorious and harmless institution as some writers like to have it.

However that may be, the main economic and social ills resulting from the waqf system were not connected with any special kind of waqf but with the essential characteristics of the institution as such. It has been generally agreed that waqf lands have always been neglected and that their yields have been lower than those of other lands. Although no statistical proof can be furnished for such an allegation, this is what has been observed by all writers of the nineteenth and twentieth centuries, and none of them has held the opposite view.[10] There are two principal reasons for the bad condition of waqf lands. First, since they are inalienable, they cannot serve as security for a loan to be invested in their development, nor can a part of the land be sold so that the proceeds might be invested in the development of the other part (they must be used, according to waqf law, for acquisition of other waqf property). Secondly, waqf lands were neglected because they were administered by *nāẓirs*, who generally had no interest in investing part of the proceeds, since they received a certain percentage of the net income, and they were never sure how long their "nāẓirship" would last. The class of waqf *nāẓirs* has become notorious for neglect and for embezzlement of waqf

[8] See *al-Ahrām*, August 11, 1952; March 17, 1954; November 22, 1955.

[9] See *al-Ahrām*, May 10, 1953; June 17, 1953; November 4, 10, 12, 16, 19, and 22, 1953; December 2 and 7, 1953; March 26, 1954.

[10] Cf., e.g., Jabartī, 4:124 (3); 184 (17–20); Mubārak, 9:52–53; Gabra, p. 111; Sékaly, pp. 412, 451; ʿAllūba, p. 302; *al-Ahrām*, March 23, 1944; November 11, 1952.

funds—a well-known feature of the waqf system which found its expression in hundreds and thousands of cases brought before the law courts.[11] The recurrent attempts of the governments of Egypt during the past hundred years to put an end to this situation by imposing control upon the *nāẓirs* failed completely because the provisions laid down in the *waqfiyyāt* were frequently so ambiguous as to leave to the *nāẓirs* freedom of action even within the bounds of the law.

Not less harmful was the fact that the waqf system resulted in the preservation of large estates—one of the main ills of Egypt's agrarian structure—and in the concentration of wealth, or of the control over wealth, in few hands. One of the main aims of landowners who constituted their property as waqf was to evade its splitting up through inheritance, since a waqf was statutorily indivisible.[12] Thus about 80 per cent of all waqf lands were large estates of more than fifty feddans, covering almost a quarter of the total area of such large estates. A further concentration of wealth in few hands was brought about by the fact that some of the *nāẓirs* controlled numerous waqfs and vast areas of waqf lands. In 1953 there were thirty-two waqfs in Egypt whose nāẓirship had been vested in the Shaykh al-Azhar; the average yearly income from their administration (10 per cent of the proceeds) amounted, between the years 1929 and 1951, to £E 2,400 (of which the Shaykh al-Azhar received £E 1,200 yearly since he left the actual administration to the Ministry of Awqāf).[13] The private waqf administration of the King, *dīwān al-awqāf al-khuṣūṣiyya al-malakiyya*, had, by 1952, taken over the nāẓirship of more than 100,000 feddans of waqf lands.[14]

Thus, by preserving large estates and by leading to the concentration of property in few hands—as well as by making a considerable part of the lands inalienable—the waqf system aggravated the most serious problem of Egypt's agrarian structure, namely, high rents and high prices of land, partly the result of the monopolistic power of a few large landlords. It is interesting to note, in this connection, that one of the arguments adduced by Shaykh Bakhīt (in the twenties) against the abolition of waqf was that such an act would cause the collapse of the prices of real estate![15] Furthermore, all waqf lands were let and none worked by their "owners," contri-

[11] See, e.g., the cases involving matters of principle, which alone occupy sixty pages in U. Pace and V. Sisto, *Code annoté du Wakf*, Alexandria, 1946, pp. 63–123.

[12] Muḥammad Qadrī Pasha, *Qānūn al-ʿadl waʾl-inṣāf liʾl-qaḍāʾ ʿalā mushkilāt al-awqāf*, 5th ed., Cairo, 1928, art. 76.

[13] *al-Ahrām*, September 11, 1952; July 13, 1953.

[14] *al-Ahrām*, August 11, 1952; October 19, 1952; February 27, 1954; August 5, 1954. The figure given varies between 120,000 and 130,000 feddans. It was mainly *khayrī* waqfs whose control was concentrated in a few hands.

[15] See Shaykh Bakhīt's lecture on the waqf problem in Sékaly, p. 613.

buting thereby to another of Egypt's agrarian defects, absenteeism. It was these undesirable consequences of the waqf system which made its reform overdue, rather than the splitting up of income from *waqf ahlī* by the "alarming increase in the number of its beneficiaries," as has been claimed by so many writers, all of them supporting their argument by the same one or two examples.[16]

Controversy and Legislation in the Nineteenth and Twentieth Centuries

The harmful effects of the waqf system began to acquire disturbing proportions only in the early twenties. From the beginning of the nineteenth century up till that time the waqf problem of Egypt was mainly a struggle for the administration of the *awqāf*, which we will review in short as a background for one of the aspects of the recent reform.[17] This struggle can be divided into three main periods. In the first period, from Muḥammad ʿAlī to the British occupation of Egypt, Egypt's rulers tried to gain some kind of authority over private *nāẓirs* through a central department of waqfs. Ismāʿīl, for the first time, established a Waqf Ministry, whose task was to take over those *khayrī* waqfs whose *nāẓirs* had been deposed, and many unlawfully administered waqfs passed into its hands.[18] In the second period, from the British occupation till the end of World War I, the power of private *nāẓirs* was further reduced, especially by the Regulation of Waqf Administration of July, 1895, which remained in force, with minor amendments, during the first half of the present century. But at the same time a new conflict arose over the administration of waqfs between the British

[16] See Sékaly, pp. 95, 408–9, 449; ʿAllūba, p. 301; two articles in *Journal du Commerce et de la Marine* (Alexandria), August 22, 1952 and April 29, 1954; and also C. Issawi, *Egypt: An Economic and Social Analysis*, London, 1947, pp. 78–79, and *Egypt at Mid-Century*, London, 1954, p. 132. The first to advance this thesis was ʿAllūba, the others repeating his argument and examples almost word for word. It is not convincing for the simple reason that if the properties in question had not been endowed as waqf, they would have been split up at least to the same extent as the income from the waqf and probably to an even greater extent, since the creation of a waqf generally involved the exclusion of some of the legal heirs from participation in the income. In 1952 the number of beneficiaries of *awqāf ahliyya* administered by the Ministry totaled some 16,000 and the area of waqf lands under the Ministry's management amounted to 160,000 feddans (*al-Ahrām*, September 21, 1952; August 13, 1954). Half of this area, at the most, consisted of *awqāf khayriyya*, but, on the other hand, part of the beneficiaries were entitled to income from urban real estate and not from agricultural lands. The average share of each beneficiary, therefore, works out at a much higher figure than the average area owned by each of Egypt's landowners.

[17] Further particulars will be found in Sékaly, *passim*. Coptic waqfs constituted a special problem with which the writer has dealt elsewhere. See G. Baer, "The Conflict over the Administration of Coptic Waqfs in Egypt," in *Hamizrah Hehadash* (*The New East*), 6, no. 4 (1955) (in Hebrew with English summary).

[18] Cf., Mubārak, 9:52–53.

representative and Egypt's Khedive. In order to prevent British interference in waqf affairs, Tawfīq abolished, in 1884, the Waqf Ministry and established in its place a General Administration directly responsible to him. The British representatives did not acquiesce in this state of affairs. Many irregularities in waqf administration were reported, and the blame was put by Cromer and, later by Kitchener, on ʿAbbās II personally. After a fierce public controversy a compromise was arrived at: Kitchener's demand to restore the Waqf Ministry was complied with, but the Ministry retained financial and administrative autonomy; moreover, the Minister of Awqāf was to be appointed directly by the Khedive and authorized "to represent the Khedive in the matter of waqfs administered by him." Thus not only was the traditional procedure preserved—that is, the transfer of authority to administer waqfs without *nāẓirs* from the Khalīfa to the Chief Qāḍī of Egypt and from him to the Khedive (who was represented by a department or a ministry)[19]—but the Khedive also retained actual power over these waqfs. This was the background for the main struggle of the third period, the period of the Constitutional Monarchy (1923–52), in which the King tried, against constitutionalist tendencies, to maintain the traditional right of the ruler to administer the waqfs. Section 153 of the 1923 Constitution provided for the enactment of a special law that was to regulate the way in which the King should exercise his authority regarding religious institutions (including the waqf). Such a law was enacted in fact in 1927 in respect of all religious institutions—except the administration of waqfs. The King, therefore, continued to consider the Waqf Ministry, in contrast with other ministries, as his personal agency. Thus, for instance, in August, 1948, the Minister of Awqāf (at that time ʿAlī ʿAbd al-Rāziq) received an order from the Royal Cabinet that he should transfer the administration of a waqf founded by the Khedive Ismāʿīl (ten thousand feddans, for the upkeep of mosques and schools) from the Ministry to the Dīwān of Private Royal Awqāf. Constitutional arguments brought by ʿAbd al-Rāziq before his Prime Minister were of no avail, and the waqf had to be delivered—like many other waqfs in the years 1945 to 1949.[20]

In the meantime, however, discussion about the waqf became less concerned with its administration and began to concentrate rather on the problems of the institution of waqf itself. In the first instance, this was the result of the menacing increase in the number and area of waqfs, which grew in the early twenties by an average of twenty thousand feddans yearly, and some people saw the time coming when most of Egypt's lands would

[19] Cf. J. Schacht, "Šarīʿa und Qānūn im modernen Ägypten," *Der Islam*, 20, no. 3, 1932.

[20] *al-Ahrām*, August 3 and 7, 1952; August 13, 1954, and especially August 6, 1952, where the documents of the case were reproduced in full.

have turned into waqf. Then came the radical reforms of the waqf system in Turkey, which were hailed by some Egyptian reformers from the parliamentary tribune. At the same time, Egypt witnessed a growing intellectual activity of the "modernists," who attempted to prove that Islam in its original form was not incompatible with liberal Western ideas and that only later corruptions had resulted in beliefs and practices which are harmful from the modern point of view. Many of the writings on waqf in the twenties and thirties correspond to this trend; their authors advanced the thesis that waqf, or at least *waqf ahlī*, had no religious basis whatever, and can therefore be reformed according to modern requirements.[21]

In the ensuing public controversy three basic positions can be discerned: (1) the conservative orthodox attitude of opposition to any change in the waqf system; (2) the modernist demand for reform of the laws governing waqf; and (3) the opinion of some more radical intellectuals that *waqf ahlī* should be abolished. The most prominent of the orthodox group was Shaykh Muḥammad Bakhīt, formerly Muftī of Egypt. In two lectures, delivered in reply to those of ʿAllūba,[22] he tried to refute the claim that the waqf had no religious basis and that it was economically harmful, as well as to establish its vital importance for the existence of charitable, educational, and health institutions and for the maintenance of noble families. Were it not for being waqf, he said, many properties would have fallen into the hands of foreign moneylenders. But not only *ʿulamāʾ*[23] voiced opposition to any change in the waqf system. A second important conservative group was that of the royal family and the royalists. In 1943, when the drafts of the law for reform of the waqf system had become known, Prince ʿUmar Ṭusūn wrote an open letter to the Prime Minister, expressing his strong opposition to the proposed law because, he said, it imposed restrictions on the liberty of proprietors to do with their property whatever they liked, and because the spirit of the law was one of disregard for the property of the great families.[24] In the Senate debate royalists such as Muḥammad Zakī al-Ibrāshī and Muḥammad Ḥilmī ʿĪsā opposed some of the most important reforms and praised the usefulness of *waqf ahlī*.[25]

The principal exponent of the modernist view was Muḥammad ʿAlī ʿAllūba Pasha of the Liberal Constitutionalist party, sometime Minister of Waqfs, who elaborately explained his arguments in two lectures given in

[21] For the influence of "modernism" on the waqf controversy, see Schacht.

[22] The lectures have been published, together with ʿAllūba's, in the appendix to Sékaly.

[23] There were also *ʿulamāʾ* who favored the reform of the waqf system. A number of them have been quoted by ʿAllūba.

[24] *al-Ahrām*, March 28, 1943.

[25] *al-Ahrām*, March 23 and 29, 1944; May 25, 1944; *al-Miṣrī*, May 30, 1944.

1926 and 1927 and published in full in *L'Egypte Contemporaine*, and in his book *Mabādī' fī l-siyāsa al-miṣriyya*, published in 1942. ʿAllūba also submitted to the Egyptian Parliament in 1927 a draft law including a rule that any *waqf ahlī* to be created in future must be a temporary one, for thirty years at most. In his above mentioned lectures he denied the religious basis of *waqf ahlī* and tried to expose its economic and social harm; and in his book he suggested prohibiting the deprivation of legal heirs by creating a waqf, annulling *ahlī* waqfs which had been founded prior to a certain date, and allowing beneficiaries to divide waqf property between them into separate waqfs according to the share of each in the income. Many of these views have been adopted by other Egyptian politicians, and some of the suggestions were incorporated in the Waqf Law of 1946.

The complete abolition of *waqf ahlī* has been advocated by a variety of politicians and intellectuals of different shades with no common denominator; even the vague "radical" seems to be too definite and too extreme to characterize them. They include a group of intellectuals who propagated, in the forties, a moderate agrarian reform of which the abolition of *waqf ahlī* was thought to constitute one element. This group consisted of Muḥammad Khaṭṭāb, Ibrāhīm Bayūmī Madkūr, and Mirrīt Ghālī.[26] Similar views were propagated by the formerly Wafdist politician ʿAbd al-Ḥamīd ʿAbd al-Ḥaqq, who for years was a fervent advocate of the abolition of *waqf ahlī*. A draft law with this aim was submitted by him to Parliament in 1936, and after he had left the Wafd in the forties he founded the Egyptian Workers' party, whose main slogan was the abolition of *waqf ahlī*.[27] But there were also the Liberal Constitutionalist Aḥmad Ramzī,[28] and the fascist group Miṣr al-Fatāt, which in its program of 1940 demanded the prohibition of creating *ahlī* waqfs in the future if not the dissolution of existing ones.[29]

Two further aspects of this discussion must be mentioned here. First, all those who took part in it, whatever opinion they held on the waqf as such, unanimously agreed that the institution of private *nāẓirs* had to be reformed. Indeed, those who opposed the reform of the waqf system were the most eager to put all the blame on the bad administration and corruption of the *nāẓirs*.[30] But none of them expressed the view that the state or some official agency should take over all *khayrī* waqfs and do without the private *nāẓirs* of such waqfs. Probably nobody was prepared to come into conflict with the

[26] For their view on the waqf problem, see *al-Ahrām*, March 22 and 23, 1944, and Mirrīt Ghālī: *al-Iṣlāḥ al-zirāʿī*, Cairo, 1945, pp. 30–32.

[27] See Sékaly, pp. 286–87; *al-Ahrām*, August 4 and 25, 1952, and November 11, 1952.

[28] Sékaly, pp. 618–49; *al-Ahrām*, March 22, 1944.

[29] *OM*, 20, no. 4 (April, 1940): 184–85. The editor's note to the effect that this meant the abolition of *waqf ahlī* is misleading.

[30] Thus, e.g., Shaykh Bakhīt; see Sékaly, pp. 434–35.

important vested interests involved in the administration of *khayrī* waqfs. (Naḥḥās Pasha, for instance, was *nāẓir* of a large *waqf khayrī* whenever he was in office.) For the same reason, nobody ever mentioned the Royal Waqfs except for some eulogies in the Senate debate on the draft waqf law.[31] This leads us to the second point: nobody ever demanded the abolition of *waqf khayrī* or even its reform, as, for example, spending its income according to the needs of a modern state and not according to what seemed to people in the nineteenth century to be a worthy aim. The reason was, again, that in *khayrī* waqfs the vested interests of, for example, religious dignitaries, "noble families" (especially the royal family), and politicians were involved. While to every *ahlī* waqf there were not only beneficiaries but also deprived heirs, sometimes of important families, the reform of *khayrī* waqfs would have hurt some of the most influential families and groups and benefited only the general public.

Nevertheless, the awakening of interest in the waqf problem was not fruitless, even if the ripening of the fruits took some twenty years. Already in 1926 the parliamentary waqf committee remarked that the abolition of *waqf ahlī* should be studied, and in 1927 two draft laws were laid before the legislature, one for a reform of the waqf system submitted by ʿAllūba, and one for the abolition of *waqf ahlī* submitted by Ramzī and Jundī. The latter was transferred to the waqf committee, but, as Ramzī remarked seventeen years later in the Senate debate on the waqf law, "*al-ḥallu adraka'l-majlisa qabla an yudrika'l-waqf*" (i.e., dissolution was the fate of the Parliament before being the fate of the waqf).[32] In 1936 and 1937 the parliamentary waqf committee again suggested abolishing *waqf ahlī*, but in the meantime (1936) the commission for reform of the personal-status legislation (including waqf legislation) had been appointed.[33] The draft of the waqf law was ready by 1941, but only after another five years of debates, amendments, and so on, was the new law enacted.[34] The law attempted (Articles 23–30) to prevent circumvention of the laws of inheritance through the creation of waqfs by restricting the creation of new waqfs in a similar way to that in which bequests by will are restricted, thus limiting, to a large extent, the motive for turning property into waqf. Article 5 states that a *waqf ahlī* must be for a set term (for two generations or sixty years at the most), whereas a *waqf khayrī* can be either for a set term or in perpetuity, but an endowment

[31] *al-Ahrām*, March 29, 1944.

[32] *al-Ahrām*, March 22, 1944.

[33] See *OM*, 17 (1937): 51–52; 19 (1939): 137.

[34] Law No. 48 of 1946. An excellent analysis of this law will be found in J. N. D. Anderson, "Recent Developments in Shariʿa Law, IX—the Waqf System," *The Muslim World*, 42, no. 4 (October, 1952).

in favor of a mosque must be in perpetuity. In contrast with traditional practice in Egypt, the law allowed beneficiaries to divide their waqf into separate waqfs—according to their shares in the income. Other provisions were concerned with tightening the control over the *nāẓirs*. But since only a few of the provisions of the law were retroactive, that is, applied to existing waqfs, its influence would have been felt only many years later. Furthermore, royal waqfs were excluded from almost all its provisions.

The Recent Reforms

However, not more than six years later this law was superseded by much more radical reforms of the waqf system. These were the direct result of the establishment of the military régime whose agrarian reform was one of the main pillars of its socio-economic policy. The abolition of all kinds of mortmain, entail, and other forms of tying up property has been a corollary of agrarian reforms in many countries, and the Egyptian agrarian reform too would have forfeited many of its potential gains had it left the waqf untouched.

The law abolishing *waqf ahlī* was enacted not more than five days after the coming into force of the Agrarian Reform Law.[35] According to this law, all waqfs for other than charitable purposes are considered null and void, existing ones as well as those to be created in future (Articles 1–2). The property of existing *ahlī* waqfs is to be divided among the beneficiaries according to their shares in the income, or reverts to the founder if he is still alive and if he had reserved to himself the right to revoke his waqf—unless a beneficiary received his share as compensation for claims on the founder: in this case, property rights go to the beneficiary and usufruct rights to the founder for his lifetime (Articles 3–4). The same provisions apply to *amwāl al-badal* (the proceeds of sales of waqf property which have not been reinvested and which are deposited at the *Sharīʿa* courts) (Article 5). The remaining sections of the law deal with *ḥikr* (perpetual lease of waqf property) and with matters of procedure.

The abolition of *waqf ahlī* met with very little opposition, which is not astonishing in view of the sharp criticism of this institution voiced for the past thirty years. The only opponents were deprived legal heirs (*al-maḥrūmūna min al-awqāf*), who formed an association to contest the provision in the law that assigns the property to the present beneficiaries. They demanded that the property be distributed in accordance with the *sharīʿa* (that is to say, the Muslim laws of inheritance) and referred the issue to the courts but lost their

[35] Décret-loi n. 180 de 1952, *Journal Officiel* n. 132 bis, September 14, 1952.

case. But they also stressed their claim to have been for many years the most fervent enemies of the *waqf ahlī* system as such (which one would expect).[36]

The execution of the law, however, met with some difficulties. Beneficiaries showed very little initiative in taking the necessary measures for the transfer of the property into their hands—probably because they had got used to receiving income without doing anything.[37] Then there was the problem of some *ahlī* waqfs with a larger number of beneficiaries each of whom was entitled to a very small income from the waqf; their division would have resulted in each beneficiary receiving less than five feddans—which would have been contrary to the Agrarian Reform Law.[38] Another serious complication was caused by *awqāf mushtaraka*. According to the law, that part of the waqf the income of which is devoted to a charitable purpose is not to be abolished. To fix this part was the subject of many conflicts and hundreds of lawsuits.[39] For all these reasons the division of *awqāf ahliyya* and *awqāf mushtaraka* proceeded very slowly. This fact is illustrated by the estimated revenue of the Waqf Ministry from these kinds of waqfs, which exceeded in the years 1954–55 and 1955–56 £E 2 million, an even higher amount than their estimated revenue prior to the law abolishing *waqf ahlī*. To break this deadlock the Waqf Ministry was authorized, late in 1954, to requisition *ahlī* waqf property administered by it, and to compensate beneficiaries out of *amwāl al-badal* of *khayrī* waqfs to which the property would be attached.[40] Reports in the press seem to indicate that this was carried out.[41] But this concerns the Ministry's waqfs only, and there was no intention of applying this procedure to waqfs with private *nāẓirs* as well.

The necessity of dealing with *khayrī* waqfs arose a few days after the *coup d'état* as King Fārūq, who was *nāẓir* of *khayrī* waqfs extending over more than a hundred thousand feddans, went into exile on July 26, 1952. The Waqf Ministry had no difficulty in convincing the *qāḍī* that, since the *nāẓir* of these waqfs was absent from the country and was therefore unable to execute his duties as *nāẓir*, the Ministry should be appointed *nāẓir* over these waqfs. But there was no legal way of deposing other *nāẓirs* of large *khayrī* waqfs, some of whom were also prominent figures of the old régime. In May, 1953,

[36] See, for this episode, *al-Ahrām*, September 16–26, 1952; November 17 and 23, 1952; January 9, 1953; February 1, 1953; March 15, 1953; June 11, 1954.

[37] *al-Ahrām*, December 27, 1954.

[38] *al-Ahrām*, September 12 and 30, 1954, December 27, 1954.

[39] *al-Ahrām*, October 28, 1955; November 3 and 9, 1955. On December 5, 1955 *al-Ahrām* put the number of lawsuits of this kind at 1,900!

[40] Law No. 525 of 1954. See *al-Ahrām*, September 30, 1954; November 28, 1954.

[41] See, e.g., *al-Ahrām*, February 4, 1955, where it was reported that 177 waqfs had been dealt with in this way; and also *al-Ahrām*, November 15, 1955.

therefore, a law governing *khayrī* waqfs was enacted,[42] according to which (Article 2) the Ministry of Awqāf was given the right to administer all *khayrī* waqfs except those whose *nāẓirs* were their founders. The Ministry might decline the nāẓirship of waqfs with a very small revenue and of those dedicated to a private charitable purpose (a family guest house, the poor of the founder's family, etc.). The former *nāẓirs* were required (Article 4) to inform the Ministry immediately of the particulars of each waqf and to deliver its property within six months. Detailed regulations were worked out according to which the Ministry decided to take over a waqf or to decline its administration.[43]

The resistance to this law was much stronger than the opposition to the *waqf ahlī* law. This may have had two reasons: first, *nāẓirs* of *ahlī* waqfs generally were also beneficiaries, and as such they now received a part of the property, while many *nāẓirs* of *khayrī* waqfs lost a sinecure without getting any compensation. Secondly, by the transfer of a number of *khayrī* waqfs and their documents to the Ministry, irregularities in their former administration were discovered and published. In any case, some of the former *nāẓirs* filed a suit with the State Council, claiming that the law was: (a) unconstitutional since the revolutionary constitution had guaranteed property rights; (b) contrary to the *sharīʿa*, because an important Islamic principle was "*sharṭ al-wāqif kanaṣṣ al-shāriʿ*" (i.e., the provision laid down by a founder of a waqf is as binding as the text of the *sharīʿa*).[44] Other *nāẓirs* simply ignored the law and refrained from handing over the waqf, some of them even after they had been personally ordered to do so.[45] Nevertheless, the transfer was gradually carried out, and before long most private *nāẓirs* of waqfs in Egypt had handed over their waqfs.

The same law (Article 1) introduced another very important innovation into the *waqf khayrī* system: the Minister of Waqfs was given authority to spend, with the sanction of the Higher Waqf Council and the *Sharīʿa* Court, the revenue of any *waqf khayrī*, or part of it, on a purpose to be designed by him without being bound to execute the provisions laid down by the founder of the waqf—if that purpose was more deserving of support than the founder's one. This authority has since been exercised by the Minister of Waqfs in many cases. Among the waqfs whose revenue has been diverted to other purposes were those dedicated to stray dogs, tombs, *sabīls*, the Turkish

[42] Law No. 247 of 1953. See *al-Ahrām*, May 21, 1953; November 14, 1953.

[43] See *al-Ahrām*, April 2, 1954, and, e.g., *al-Ahrām*, December 3, 1955.

[44] *al-Ahrām*, June 21, 1954; for similar cases see, e.g., *al-Ahrām*, July 8, 1954; November 22, 1955. It is perhaps interesting to note that the Waqf Ministry answered the latter claim with the modernist argument that in matters concerning the relations between human beings the *maṣlaḥa*, i.e., the interest of the community, must prevail.

[45] *al-Ahrām*, January 4, 1955; February 22, 1955.

Army,[46] and the Ḥanafi *ʿulamāʾ* of the Azhar (who receive a salary like the *ʿulamāʾ* of the other schools). The latter appealed to the Supreme *Sharīʿa* Court, but their appeal was set aside.[47] Thus, *khayrī* waqfs have in fact been nationalized: they are managed by a government department which has authority to spend their revenue according to its needs.

However, the managing of these large additional areas of *khayrī* waqfs by the Waqf Ministry apparently involved certain difficulties. One of the main problems seems to have been that the way in which the Ministry disposed of them through lease or sale has been inconsistent with the social and agricultural policy of the Land Reform Ministry, whose lands were in many instances adjacent to the large waqf areas.[48] This gap has been filled by a third law enacted on July 18, 1957.[49] According to its provisions, all agricultural lands appertaining to public *khayrī* waqfs were to be transferred, in three equal annual installments, to the Land Reform Committee and to be distributed according to the Land Reform Law. Their former *nāẓirs* (i.e., in the case of the majority of the lands, the Waqf Ministry) were to receive Land Reform bonds, but on their redemption the capital is to be transferred to the Economic Organisation of the Government (established in January, 1957) to be invested in development projects. The former *nāẓirs* will receive, on behalf of their waqfs, interest due on the bonds and later profits from the invested capital.

There seems to be no doubt that the changes brought about in the waqf system of Egypt in the past fifteen years have led to some important socio-economic results. The abolition of *waqf ahlī* has made some of the largest estates in Egypt liable to expropriation (one of the landowners had endowed 7,300 feddans as waqf in favor of his wife and sons as late as 1950), and it has facilitated the confiscation of estates of the royal family, whose *ahlī* waqfs covered tens of thousands of feddans. Moreover, in a certain way the *Waqf Ahlī* Law has been extended the scope of the agrarian reform, which provided for expropriation of properties larger than two hundred (or, in some cases, three hundred) feddans only. Yet a property of one hundred, or even fifty feddans is still quite a large estate in Egypt and, so far as such properties were *waqf ahlī*, they were divided among the beneficiaries. The merits of the *Waqf Khayrī* Law are obvious: the administration of this kind of waqf will

[46]The fact that many of the waqfs were dedicated to objects in Turkey was given great publicity; see *al-Ahrām*, November 30, 1953; December 4, 1953.

[47]See *al-Ahrām*, September 23, 1953; November 12, 1953; April 9, 1954; September 22, 1954; October 10, 1954; December 12, 1954; January 24, 1955; October 15, 1955.

[48]Cf. *al-Ahrām*, July 14, 1957. See also S. M. Gadalla, *Land Reform in Relation to Social Development, Egypt*, University of Missouri Press, Columbia, 1962, *passim*.

[49]See *al-Ahrām*, July 19, 1957.

serve no longer, as it served in the past, as a stronghold of economic and social power, in many cases of persons holding a certain religious or political office or appertaining to influential families or groups. Also, the income from these extensive properties will no longer be spent on purposes some of which are anachronistic curiosities and on other objects opposed to the interests of the state. And by the latest step taken in 1957, capital buried in land was made available for productive investment and a considerable additional area of land was made available for distribution among fellahs according to the provisions of the Land Reform Law (the area of public *khayrī* waqfs managed by the Ministry alone has been estimated at 160,000 feddans). Thus a grievance voiced in the beginning will be mitigated: waqf lands sold by the Ministry in 1954 and 1955 were put up for sale by auction, and fellahs from Upper Egypt protested against this way of selling the land, because they could not compete with wealthier landowners, to whom the land went in the end.[50] It should be remembered that the Land Reform program will provide land for only about 10 percent of the landless peasants and owners of less than a viable plot; therefore, an addition of more than 25 percent to the land available for distribution is a very important factor indeed.

The main importance, however, of the three waqf laws has been that they have cured Egypt of the harmful consequences of the waqf system in general. This has been achieved both by almost liquidating that part of waqf property which consisted of agricultural lands and by making the creation of new waqfs out of agricultural lands improbable. When all *ahlī* waqfs have been divided and all lands of public *khayrī* waqfs transferred to the Land Reform, only an inconsiderable area of private *khayrī* waqfs will remain. In the future, few waqfs will be created; the endowments made in the present century were mainly *ahlī* waqfs, which cannot be created any longer, and it is extremely improbable that proprietors would in the future create *khayrī* waqfs which would be transferred, after the death of the founder, to the management of the Waqf Ministry, their revenue spent according to the Minister's decision, and their agricultural lands exchanged for shares in government development projects. Thus waqf reform has been perhaps the most successful part of the Egyptian land reform.

[50] *al-Ahrām*, September 22 and 29, 1954.

6

Submissiveness and Revolt of the Fellah

There have been many writers, and these include not only passing travelers but also scholars, who have found one of Egypt's fundamental social phenomena to be the submissiveness of the fellah, a psychological trait expressed by his acquiescence with fate, his humility before those in power over him, and his lack of rebelliousness. From the many who have stated this opinion we shall quote three here: Dr. John Bowring, the English statesman who prepared a classic report on the Egypt of Muḥammad ʿAlī's time; Piot Bey, the director of the veterinary service of the government estates and secretary of the Institut Egyptien for many years toward the end of the nineteenth century; and H. H. Ayrout, the priest who wrote the well-known work on the Egyptian fellah which first appeared about thirty years ago and has since had several editions.

In his report, Bowring emphasizes the "habit of submission" of the Egyptian fellah and claims that this habit is so deeply enrooted in him that "he will rather die than revolt."[1] "Hundreds of years of oppression and suffering," Piot Bey writes, "have made him very suspicious. . . . He mercilessly tyrannizes over those below him in station, he is arrogant towards those equal to him, while towards those above him he is submissive and humiliates himself to the very limit of abasement."[2] And in Ayrout's book we read that

Originally published as "The Submissiveness of the Egyptian Peasant," *Hamizrah Hehadash*, 12, nos. 1–2 (1962): 55–63 (in Hebrew); and in *New Outlook* (Tel Aviv), November–December, 1962, pp. 15–25. (Here considerably expanded.)

[1] John Bowring, *Report on Egypt and Candia*, London, 1840, p. 7.
[2] Piot Bey, *Causerie ethnographique sur le fellah*, Cairo, 1900, p. 34.

"murder and revenge among the fellahin arise more from a quick temper and wounded pride than from ill nature; they are signs of hot blood. . . . Their outbursts do not last for long, and are succeeded by resignation, which, being habitual, is a much more noticeable characteristic.

Further on, the author cites the following *ḥadīth* (tradition):

"When God created all things," says Kaʿb al-Akhbār, the traditionist, according to Maqrīzī, "He gave to each a companion." "I shall go to Syria," said Reason. "And I shall go with you," said Rebellion. Poverty said, "I am going to the desert." "I'll come along too," said Health. Abundance said, "I am going to Egypt," and "I will accompany you," said Resignation. [And Ayrout adds:] Such is the fellah's resignation, but it is carried to the extent of servility and degradation, imposed not so much by poverty as by the unceasing pressure of his master and his society. . . . It is often claimed by that class that the fellahin cannot understand an authority which is humane and appeals to their better instincts. That is true, but it is true because in the past they have been brought up to nothing but blows, fines, curses, insults and intimidation, which have finally rendered them insensible.[3]

These remarks also contain some of the reasons used to explain the submissiveness of the fellah: hundreds of years of harsh oppression, they say, left this psychological trait and made it part of his nature. By means of the *ḥadīth* which he quotes from Maqrīzī, Ayrout emphasizes that this trait distinguishes the Egyptian peasant from the rebellious Syrian peasant. This difference is generally explained by the completely different natural, ethnical, and political conditions prevalent in the two regions—Egypt and the Fertile Crescent. While Egypt is a flat land, Syria is broken up by ranges of mountains. Where the Nile forms an easy channel of communication connecting all the parts of Egypt, the Fertile Crescent had no such convenience until roads and railroads were built in the second quarter of the twentieth century. As a result, Egypt's armed forces were able relatively easily to reach every part of the country and to crush any possible rebellion at the beginning, while the Fertile Crescent's geographical structure did not make this possible. What is more, the Egyptian fellah's livelihood depended on irrigation by the Nile water and the system of canals, dikes, and dams for whose maintenance the organization and planning of a central government were needed. His life and living therefore were in the government's hands. The situation was not the same for the Syrian fellah, most of whose farming was unirrigated. In addition, the Fertile Crescent, unlike Egypt, had whole regions inhabited by minorities, a fact which often encouraged revolt. As a result of all these factors the central government in Egypt was always stronger than in the Fertile Crescent.

[3] H. H. Ayrout, *The Egyptian Peasant*, translated by J. A. Williams, Boston, 1963, pp. 145–46.

We shall return again to the differences between Egypt and Syria; but let us try first to examine the facts for Egypt herself. First of all, however, we must point out that as far as we know there is no proof for the claim that a trait of a whole people, or even of a whole class, can be passed from one generation to the next by heredity. It can, of course, be argued that Egypt's fundamental conditions re-created the same trait of the fellahs in every generation, and that it has remained therefore in effect during the course of history. The only trouble with this argument is that the facts prove the opposite. It is true that Egypt's conditions—her flatness, the relative ease of communications, the peasants' dependence on the central government, and so on—made it harder for the fellah to revolt. But for that very reason even a small number of peasant revolts would prove that it was not a natural trait imbedded in their psychology which prevented them from rebelling. Since the number is not small at all it seems that there are no grounds for the theory concerning the "submissiveness of the Egyptian fellah." The following is a survey of rebellions in the course of two centuries.[4]

Peasant Revolts in Egypt from 1778 to 1951

In 1778 a French naval officer by the name of Sonnini traveled through Egypt. In the summer of that year he reached Upper Egypt. Here are his comments concerning the Ṭahṭā district:

> This district was far from being in a state of tranquility. The *fellahs* of the surrounding country had risen in a body, and refused the imposts. Some Arabs also, from whom tribute had been exacted, joined themselves to the malecontents. The several *Kiaschefs* [Mamluk district officers] had united their forces to march against the insurgents, and had just sustained a complete defeat. A victory over authority, or rather over the most detestable despotism, had rendered this country a scene of riot and confusion. The fields were abandoned or laid waste; the husbandman forsook his plough to fly to arms; the flocks were carried off, or destroyed, and every sort of provision became the prey of the enemy or of robbers. The highways, lined with banditti, were shut against communications and intelligence of every kind.[5]

[4] On peasant revolts during the period of the Mamluk regime, see A. N. Poliak, "Les révoltes populaires à l'époque des Mamelouks et leurs causes économiques," *Revue des Etudes Islamiques*, 3 (1934):260–62. Gibb and Bowen made the following note with regard to that period: "It is historically false to regard the *fellâhîn* of the Delta and a large part of Middle Egypt as lineally descended from the ancient Egyptians and inured to tyranny. The population of these districts was completely recreated by a continuous process of Arab settlement from the middle of the seventh century, and from that time almost down to the Ottoman conquest there was no lack of agrarian revolts." H. A. R. Gibb and H. Bowen, *Islamic Society and the West*, vol. 1, part 1, Oxford University Press, 1950, p. 264, n. 1. A study of this subject for Ottoman Egypt has still to be made.

[5] C. S. Sonnini, *Travels in Upper and Lower Egypt*, English translation, London, 1807, 3:273.

We have some information concerning the unrest of the fellahs of the Delta during the 1790's. In 1794–95 the inhabitants of one village in the district of Bilbays (Sharqiyya) appeared in Cairo and demanded of Shaykh ʿAbdallāh al-Sharqāwī, who held an *iltizām* over part of this village, that he cancel the taxes and imposts that had been imposed at that time. After some disturbances and councils these impositions were temporarily abolished.[6] Revolts in the Fuwwa (Gharbiyya) district, during the French invasion in 1798, which were put down by the French expeditionary forces, are described by V. Denon, one of the scholars who accompanied the French expedition.[7] Many additional peasant rebellions against the French are mentioned in the memoirs of Niqūlā Turk. At the end of that same year, 1798, the fellahs of Fāriskūr and Manzala revolted against the French who were concentrated in Damietta, and threatened to slaughter them and all the Christians in the city. The fellahs also participated in the other revolts in the Delta against the French, and the peasants of Upper Egypt took part in the religious revolt of the Meccan Muḥammad al-Jīlānī against the French.[8]

The end of the eighteenth century was a period of disintegration of central government in Egypt. He who does not presuppose that the mentality of the Egyptian peasant restrained him from rebelling will therefore find no cause for surprise in the information about revolts at that time. What is more surprising is the fact that there were a number of very serious peasant revolts even after Muḥammad ʿAlī established his centralistic regime in Egypt.

In 1236 A.H./1820–21 a man by the name of Shaykh Aḥmad, who was called al-Ṣalāḥ, appeared in the village of al-Salīmiyya (Qenā province) and succeeded in mobilizing many of the villagers of the district—according to one story, 40,000 men. He revolted against the government, appointed governors from among his followers, and imposed taxes on the district under his control. His revolt held out for two months, until Muḥammad ʿAlī succeeded, with the aid of a military expedition, in dispersing the rebels.[9] Even larger and more dangerous for the régime, apparently, was the revolt that broke out two years later, in 1238 A.H./1822–23, in the same area, also headed by a man named Aḥmad who called himself al-Mahdī (or al-Wazīr). The center of the rebellion was in the village of al-Baʿīrāt near Luxor and it grew out of the complaints against the régime of Muḥammad ʿAlī, whose deposition was one of its leader's declared aims. He did not achieve this, but

[6] Mubārak, 4:34.
[7] V. Denon, *Voyage dans la Basse et la Haute Egypte*, London, 1819, pp. 50–52.
[8] *Mudhakkirāt Niqūlā Turk*, Cairo, 1950, pp. 21–22, 25–28, 32–33.
[9] Mubārak, 12:44.

he did succeed, with the support he obtained from all the villages in the area, in driving out the officials of the central government, in taking control of the government warehouses, and in establishing a kind of independent régime. One eyewitness to this revolt was the English traveler J. A. St. John, who described it in detail in his book on Egypt and Nubia. When he passed through the region of Luxor the revolt was in full force. After the government army had destroyed and burned the village of al-Baʿīrāt, the villagers of Qurna (about 10 km further north, where he stayed at the home of a Greek trader) joined the spreading revolt despite promises that they would be freed of taxes that year if they remained quiet. Gradually the whole neighborhood joined the insurrection. After the revolt of Qurna, the "prophet" collected about a thousand of his followers and conquered Qamūlā (10 km to the north) from its garrison. More fellahs joined the rebels after their villages had been destroyed by government troops. The rebel leader, the "Mahdī," succeeded in mobilizing several thousand villagers and in threatening the gates of the city of Qenā. However, the arrival of an infantry force from the south and a sudden sortie by the forces of the governor of the city decided the issue. The surrender was not complete, however, and additional measures of repression were required: from time to time and for periods of a number of days, signs of revolts would appear in one village or another. In order to cow the peasants some of the prisoners were bound to the mouths of the guns and killed by cannon fire. Aḥmad Pasha Ṭāhir, the governor of Upper Egypt at the time, ordered hundreds of peasants slaughtered. According to one source, the number of fellahs killed in the revolt reached one thousand.[10]

This was not, however, the last of the peasant revolts during Muḥammad ʿAlī's reign. Less than a year had elapsed after the great revolt in Upper Egypt when a revolt broke out in Minūfiyya, near Cairo, against extortions of Muḥammad ʿAlī's officials and against conscription into the army. Muḥammad ʿAlī himself, with his military advisers, went to the site to prevent chaos and to punish the rebels. The revolt was speedily crushed.[11] However, only a few months later, at the beginning of 1824, a man named Aḥmad, who had become involved with the customs at Quṣayr on his way back from Mecca, succeeded in raising some of the local inhabitants. He then went to Qenā and Isnā, where there was a great deal of grumbling against conscription. Aḥmad put himself at the head of the rebels and set

[10] J. A. St. John, *Egypt and Nubia*, London, 1845, pp. 378–86; R. Cattaui, *Le règne de Mohamed Aly d'après les archives russes en Egypte*, vol. 1, Cairo, 1931, p. 51; Mubārak, 14:76.

[11] Cattaui, p. 45; H. Rivlin, *The Agricultural Policy of Muḥammad ʿAlī in Egypt*, Cambridge, Mass., 1961, p. 201.

out with a large number of followers for Farshūṭ (in the north of Qenā province). Here a number of engagements took place between the army and the rebels before the latter were dispersed. But only in June of that year did the British Consul, Henry Salt, report that the revolt had been completely crushed.[12] Two years later the same consul reported to London concerning a new revolt of villages in Sharqiyya district against unbearable new taxes. An army was also sent to put this revolt down.[13] Indeed, peasant revolts at that time seem to have been so frequent that one eyewitness account describes this period as one of "des perpétuelles rébellions d'une natione profondément irritée."[14]

As a result of the numerous peasant revolts during the 1820's, a law which was promulgated in 1830 (*qānūn al-filāḥa*) dealt with this problem in particular. Paragraph 26 of that law deals with the case of villagers attacking a government official or their shaykh because he demanded taxes, and details the punishments and the procedures of paying indemnities in the event they killed him. Paragraph 27 states:

> In the event of an armed revolt by a whole village where the village does not obey the representative of the *ma'mur* or the *ḥākim*, the *ma'mur* is required to proceed to the village himself. If he is also not obeyed, he is required to lay siege to the village, to capture its head shaykhs and to send the chief instigator of the revolt to Fayzoğlu [a place of exile in the Sudan] for five years. The other instigators will be sent to hard labor for the same period. The other shaykhs and the fellahs will be punished by 400 stripes of the *kurbāj* [whip] each. If some one from a neighboring village comes to the aid of the rebellious village, he will be conscripted into the army if he is a young man; if he is an older person he will be sent to hard labor in the port of Alexandria for three years. If shots were fired and there were wounded or killed, the punishments listed in paragraph 26 would go into effect."[15]

There were apparently some more peasant revolts during Muḥammad ʿAlī's reign.[16] Details of several revolts in 1846 are given in the diary of Hekekyan, noted for his sharp eye and excellent analyses of the Egyptian society of his time. In August of that year he wrote that hatred of the govern-

[12] F. Mengin, *Histoire sommaire de l'Egypte sous le gouvernement de Mohammed-Aly*, Paris, 1839, pp. 5–6; A.B. Clot-Bey, *Aperçu général sur l'Egypte*, Paris, 1840, 2:107; PRO, FO 78/126, *passim*; Rivlin, pp. 201–2. See also G. Douin, *Une Mission militaire française auprès de Mohamed Aly*, Cairo, 1923, pp. xv–xvi; Le Général Weygand, *Histoire militaire de Mohammed Aly et de ses fils*, Paris, 1936, 1:143. (I am grateful to Mr. D. Farhi for these two references.)

[13] Report by Henry Salt, Alexandria, August 12, 1826, FO 78/147.

[14] P. and H., "Egypte sous la domination de Méhémet Aly," *L'Univers, ou histoire et description de tous les peuples*, Paris, 1877, p. 132.

[15] Filīb Jallād, *Qāmūs al-idāra wa'l-qaḍā'*, Alexandria, 1890, 3:354.

[16] Cf. Rivlin, pp. 113, 207.

ment was growing because of the Pasha's orders to increase the area grown to rice. Because of these orders the peasants did not have enough manpower to cultivate their fields. Their response was to take to arms and to disregard the government's orders. In Qurayn (Sharqiyya) seventy of the 180 peasants who were conscripted for labor in the rice mills fled. The shaykhs of the villages led the armed revolts in some of the districts of Sharqiyya. In the same year the peasants of Minyā province also revolted against the *corvée*. They took to arms and murdered some of the village shaykhs.[17]

There is not much information about peasant revolts during the reigns of ʿAbbās and Saʿīd, but apparently a number of the villages in Gīza district revolted in the period between the death of ʿAbbās and Saʿīd's ascension to the throne.[18] In the criminal-administrative law promulgated immediately after Saʿīd's ascension we once more find special clauses fixing punishments in the event of peasant revolts or disobedience. One of these clauses states:

> In the event of a *shaykh al-balad* conspiring with the fellahs or of one fellah conspiring with the others against the *nāẓir* [inspector] of the village or the shaykh and attacking him with clubs or arms: in the case of blows alone without the use of firearms, the shaykh or the fellah at the head of the rebels is to be punished by 200 stripes and each of the fellahs by 100 stripes. If they used firearms the set punishments for such cases would go into effect.[19]

It is interesting to note that no other social groups' possible rebelliousness was mentioned in this law.

During the early years of Ismāʿīl's reign (1863–65) there was a great deal of unrest among the fellahs of Upper Egypt in general and a large-scale outbreak in the district of Abū Tīg (Asyūṭ) which was very like the revolts of the 1820's. The factors behind the revolt were once again the *corvée* and in addition, this time, the fact that Ismāʿīl compelled the peasants to work on his tremendous estates at less than customary wages. This revolt was once again headed by a man called Aḥmad who claimed that he was one of the descendents of the Prophet and was considered a saint by the peasants. Thousands of soldiers and cannons were sent to surround the region, and Ismāʿīl himself traveled to Upper Egypt in order to put down the revolt. Shaykh Aḥmad was finally killed, the army destroyed a number of villages, and the villagers were deported or fled.[20]

17 Hekekyan Papers, vol. 3, B.M. Add. 37450, ff. 152–53; vol. 4, Add. 37451, f. 44a.

18 Hekekyan Papers, vol. 7, B.M. Add. 37454, f. 67b.

19 Jallād, 2:98 and A. von Kremer, *Aegypten*, Leipzig 1863, 2:62.

20 Hekekyan Papers, vol. 14, B.M. Add. 37461, f. 300–2; O. Audouard, *Les Mystères de l'Egypte dévoilés*, Paris, 1865, pp. 185–86; FO 78/1871, nos. 27, 32, 41; Mubārak, 11:82; 14:53, 95.

It may well be that religious resentment was one of the important reasons for a later revolt, that of 1919. However, in view of what has been related above about revolts under Muḥammad ʿAlī and Ismāʿīl, this cannot be proved by a claim that Egyptian fellahs revolted only against non-Muslim rulers. Such a theory has been advanced by one scholar, as follows:

> The fellahin had been exposed only recently to worse oppression under Muslim rulers, such as Muḥammad ʿAlī and Ismāʿīl, and were to suffer no less in the depression of the early thirties and in World War II and after, but they did not revolt. Only if the factor of the latent religious resentment against the oppressor is taken into account does the uprising [of 1919] become understandable.[21]

We have seen that fellahs did in fact revolt against Muslim rulers, but we have also seen that this does not exclude religious motives for their revolts: many of the leaders apparently succeeded in arousing the fellahs because of their claim to holiness. Moreover, the above cited author himself, in another place in his book, defined Ismāʿīl's rule as a régime that "had radically diverged from the traditional belief-system" and that "had lost any claim to the allegiance of the people."[22]

Like the first years of Ismāʿīl's reign, his last years were also marked by agrarian unrest, a fermentation that actually continued until the British occupation of Egypt. These were years of disintegration of Egypt's government and economy, of unrest in the army, of foreign intervention which undermined the ruler's prestige, and of growing indebtedness, not only of the Egyptian state but also of the peasants. They were also years of natural afflictions like the drought (1877–78, 1881), livestock epidemics, and the like. In 1877–79, peasant unrest was felt mainly in the district between Sūhāg and Girgā, and was caused chiefly by the drought and the nefarious taxes. At first this was reflected in robberies and murders, but in 1879 it took on much larger dimensions: the tax collectors and soldiers sent to the region were met by resistance, and peasants fled to the hills and formed armed bands.[23] In 1880 the unrest moved to the rice-growing region. The reasons were the same as those which led to the revolt in this region in 1846: it was customary for the rice cultivators to be freed of the *corvée*, and in the busy seasons they had even been sent additional manpower from the adjoining areas. This custom was broken in 1880, and as a result the shaykhs began to disobey government orders. When the government yielded and retracted its order, this encouraged other regions to protest against the *corvée*. Many

[21] N. Safran, *Egypt in Search of Political Community*, Cambridge, Mass., 1961, p. 105.
[22] Safran, p. 50.
[23] FO 141/112, 141/119, 141/128, *passim*.

were arrested, released, and arrested again when they continued their revolt.[24] In 1882 the British consuls reported a general state of rebelliousness among the peasants. In the spring of the same year there broke out a strike of the tenants of the Khedive's estates in four villages in the district of Zankalūn (Sharqiyya). The strike was sparked when the manager of the estate leased part of the lands to a large renter, while the peasants claimed that they had prior rights over them in exchange for cultivating the private lands of the Khedive. They declared that they would not work for the new landlord and would oppose him and the government by force, and the renter eventually gave up his lease as a result. This victory encouraged the peasants, and rebelliousness continued a few months more.[25] The disobedience of the peasants on the "Turkish" estates was stimulated further by ʿUrabī's revolt.[26]

The period of the British occupation—until World War I—was apparently the longest period during the past two hundred years in which Egypt was free of peasant revolts. In any case, this writer does not know of any peasant revolts during that period. (The Danshawāy affair in 1906 cannot be considered a revolt since the peasants attacked the officers who came to hunt in the village and not the government and its officials or the landlords.)

However, immediately after World War I, in the revolt of 1919, the Egyptian peasants participated for the first (and only) time in modern Egyptian history in a revolutionary movement of national dimensions. The factors that incited the peasants more than any other were the expropriation of their animals and their conscription into labor battalions during the war, and their bitterness found an opportune time to break out during the national revolution centered in Cairo. The peasants' participation in the revolt consisted mainly in acts of sabotage against the means of communication, and these led to conflicts and engagements with the army in many villages throughout Egypt.[27] But the accumulated anger of the fellahs was not directed only against the British. In Asyūṭ, for example, the peasants attacked the home of Maḥmūd Sulaymān, one of the largest of the landowners of Upper Egypt, whose son, Muḥammad Maḥmūd, had been exiled to Malta together with Saʿd Zaghlūl. The writer Fikrī Abāẓa, who was present, tried to stop them, and, as he related it, received the answer: "Has

[24]Borg to Malet, May 25, 1880, FO 141/138.

[25]*Further Correspondence respecting the Affairs of Egypt*, Egypt No. 7 (1882), C. 3249, *passim*.

[26]Cf. D. Mackenzie Wallace, *Egypt and the Egyptian Question*, London, 1883, pp. 228–29.

[27]Sir Valentine Chirol, *The Egyptian Problem*, London, 1920, pp. 134–41, 168, 179, 247; P. G. Elgood, *Egypt and the Army*, London, 1924, p. 349; cf. ʿAbd al-Raḥmān al-Rāfiʿī, *Thawrat 1919*, Cairo, 1946, 1:165–72, etc.

Maḥmūd Pasha Sulaymān distributed bread to the hungry? We want bread!"[28]

No instances of fellah revolts during the relatively prosperous years of the 1920's are known to us. In the 1930's, however, after the crisis, tension apparently rose. The holdings of fellahs were often seized because the landowner, who had mortgaged his land, did not pay his debts. Ayrout relates the following incident which happened on April 23, 1936. A great bank foreclosed the *ʿizba* [here: estate] of a notable of Shubrā Rīs in Kafr al-Zayyāt district, which was rented to fellahs. When the officials arrived to execute the order, they met with the opposition of the villagers. The police intervened and sent an armed force, which was attacked by the inhabitants of the *ʿizba*. A few shots were fired by the police, whereupon the fellahs cut the telephone wires and burned the government cars. Two more police detachments had to be sent before order could be restored. "Voilà une histoire qui n'est pas extraordinaire," concludes Ayrout.[29]

The end of World War II, like that of the first, brought Egypt a wave of social unrest, which, this time too, did not pass over the peasants. A number of peasant revolts broke out in 1951, when, in addition to the general social and political instability, rents increased suddenly because of the cotton prosperity. The sharpest dispute over rising rent rates took place on the estates of the Badrāwī-ʿĀshūr family in the village of Buhūt (Gharbiyya) in June of that year. The main facts concerning the Buhūt events, distilled from various contradictory descriptions, are the following. An argument between the *nāẓir* (manager) of the estate and some of the tenants over rentals led to the peasants congregating and marching on the house of the Badrāwī family in the village. A number of shots were fired on them from the house, but they were reinforced by additional peasants from the village. Security forces called to help the estate owners entered into conflict with the peasants, and there were a number of killed and wounded.[30]

Similar events took place during that same year also in Kufūr Nijm (Sharqiyya) on the estates of Prince Muḥammad ʿAlī Tawfīq, the then Crown Prince and the Averoff estate near Dikirnis (Daqahliyya).[31] In October, 1951, peasants who rented government land in al-Sirū

[28] Fikrī Abāẓa, *al-Ḍāḥik al-bākī*, Cairo, 1933, pp. 74–76. See also Safran, pp. 197–98.

[29] H. H. Ayrout, *Fellahs*, Cairo, 1942, pp. 34–35. These details have been omitted in the English translation quoted above, which summarizes them in the following words: "Occasionally it was necessary to put the ordinarily passive and obedient peasants down with police force," (p. 18).

[30] *al-Ahrām*, June 24, 1951; December 30, 1953; January 18, 1954.

[31] Rāshid al-Barāwī, *Ḥaqīqat al-inqilāb al-akhīr fī miṣr*, Cairo, 1952, pp. 92, 189; *al-Ahrām*, May 18, 1954; Gabriel Saab, *The Egyptian Agrarian Reform 1952–1962*, London, 1967, p. 13 (note).

(Daqahliyya) carried out a sitdown strike on the lands they had formerly rented and demanded that the government fulfill its promise to sell them the land instead of offering it at a public auction, as has been decided. Their statement declared that "public auctions inevitably benefit the capitalists and despite all the government's need for money it cannot ignore the rights of those struggling for their piece of bread".[32] Sayyid Marʿī, formerly Minister of Land Reform in Egypt, probably had these events in mind when he wrote in 1954:

> We all remember the days preceding the revolution of July 1952; we remember how the Egyptian village became restless as a result of dangerous agitation; we remember the events which led to bloodshed and destruction of property—for the first time in the history of the Egyptian village. Would the large landowners have preferred to be left exposed to the wind blowing through this unrest, exploiting want and poverty, until it became a tempest uprooting everything . . . and endangering, perhaps, the peace of our entire fatherland?[33]

Conclusions

This history of peasant revolts in Egypt since the end of the eighteenth century is certainly not complete, and we can assume that there were others which we do not know about. We might summarize by saying that during the past two hundred years there were many peasant revolts in Egypt against the *corvée*, taxes, expropriation of land and animals, decline of wages, and rise in rents. Some of these revolts were of such dimensions that only considerable military efforts on the part of the government were able to suppress them. It is true that more than a few of the revolts occurred in Upper Egypt, that is to say, in a region further removed from the center of government. But the same is true for peasant revolts in all countries and at all times. At the same time we also found signs of fermentation at certain periods in districts as close to Cairo as Gīza and Minūfiyya. Some of the revolts took place in areas which might be considered to be under beduin influence. But first, that is not the general rule, as shown by revolts in the rice-growing areas, the revolt of 1919, the unrest of 1951, and some of the other examples which we mentioned. Second, it is very doubtful whether there was any beduin influence on the peasants who revolted in various parts of Upper Egypt and Sharqiyya. In any case it was the peasants who revolted. (We have not discussed the very numerous beduin outbreaks.)

[32] *al-Miṣrī*, October 25, 1951.

[33] *al-Ahrām*, August 4, 1954 (erroneously referred to *al-Ahrām* of September 4, 1954 in G. Baer, *A History of Land Ownership in Modern Egypt 1800–1950*, London, 1962, p. 222). Sayyid Marʿī was wrong to think that it was for the first time in Egyptian history that such things happened.

sometimes these revolts took on a religious-messianic character, a phenomenon which is not uncommon among peasant revolts throughout the world, and which is certainly quite natural in a Muslim country and especially in Egypt, where the cult of saints is so popular. It is true that except for 1919 the peasant revolts in Egypt were local in character and did not take on national dimensions. But peasant revolts going beyond limited areas have been very uncommon in human history in general and in all the various parts of the Middle East in particular. The reason certainly does not lie in any psychological trait of the Egyptian peasants but rather in the lack of contact between farmers of one region and those of another. In the most famous peasant revolt of the Middle East in modern times, that of the Kisrawān peasants in 1858–61,[34] the longest distance between rebelling villages was shorter than the distance between Fāriskūr and Manzala in Egypt, both of which revolted in 1798 against the French, or between Qurna and Qenā—the extent of the peasant revolt against Muḥammad ʿAlī in 1822–23. The area of the part of Kisrawān whose villages revolted in 1858–61 was smaller than the present area of the Cairo Governorate or, for that matter, of almost any of the more than eighty rural districts (*markāz*) of Egypt.

The question remains why, despite all this, the conception of the Egyptian peasant's submissiveness is so widespread. It seems to us that the answer is a simple one. As in other countries, the peasants in Egypt were not always in revolt, and there were periods, sometimes long ones, when they accepted their lot. European observers who witnessed the terrible exploitation and humiliation suffered by the Egyptian peasants or the subhuman conditions under which they lived (so unlike anything known in Europe of their time) could not conceive of individuals being able to suffer such a situation even for a short period of time without revolting, unless there was some natural trait which restrainted them from doing so.

It should be noted that very similar things have been said by European observers about the Turkish peasant. Here are two examples.

> The Turkish peasant is a good, quiet, and submissive subject, who refuses neither to furnish his Sultan with troops nor to pay his taxes, so far as in him lies; but he is poor, ignorant, helpless, and improvident to an almost incredible degree. At the time of recruiting he will complain bitterly of his hard lot, but go all the same to serve his time; he groans under the heavy load of taxation, gets imprisoned, and is not released until he manages to pay his dues. He is generally discontent with his government, of which he openly complains, and still more with its

[34]For a detailed study of this revolt, see Y. Porath, "The Peasant Revolt of 1858–61 in Kisrawān," *Asian and African Studies* (Jerusalem), 2 (1966): 77–157.

agents, with whom he is brought into closer contact; but still the idea of rebelling against either, giving any signs of disaffection, or attempting to resist the law, never gets any hold upon him.[35]

... The Turkish peasantry ... are sluggish, docile people, unready to take violent action on their own initiative, but capable of perpetrating any enormity on the suggestion of those they are accustomed to obey.[36]

However, not only Western observers are to be blamed for such generalizations.

The assumption of the peasant's passivity . . . is based on a surprising ignorance about his life, even among his fellow-countrymen. . . . Most landlords who speak readily about the attitudes of peasants are absentees living in cities. . . . Since almost no one speaks for the peasant, it has been possible for Middle Eastern governments dominated by landowners, and also for a number of foreign observers, to take comfort in the thought that the peasant has long ago learned to accept misery, and that his passivity and conservatism will not let him revolt.[37]

One of the first who put such thoughts into writing was al-Jabartī, who said that the fellahs despised weak *multazims* who did not know how to squeeze taxes out of them, called them by women's names, and hoped for their substitution by others who knew how to oppress them.[38] This story, which has been frequently adduced as a proof for the submissiveness of the Egyptian fellah, is highly improbable. Perhaps Jabartī had heard such views from his fellow *ʿulamāʾ*, who were themselves *multazims* and tried to justify their own tyranny. It may well be that fellahs despised weak *multazims*, but it seems to be unreasonable that they longed to be oppressed.

Thus, both Western and Middle Eastern observers seem to have made the very common and widespread mistake of generalizing, without asking themselves the crucial question, whether changing conditions would not very soon bring about changing attitudes as well.[39] If "essence" is "that which can persist through change,"[40] then submissiveness certainly was not

[35] *The People of Turkey: Twenty years' Residence among Bulgarians, Greeks, Albanians, Turks and Armenians*. By a Consul's Daughter and Wife [Mrs. Blunt]. Edited by Stanley Lane Poole. London, 1878, 1:89–90.

[36] A. Toynbee, *The Treatment of Armenians in the Ottoman Empire*, London, 1916, p. 652.

[37] M. Halpern, *The Politics of Social Change in the Middle East and North Africa*, Princeton, 1963, pp. 87–88.

[38] Jabartī, 4:208.

[39] A very interesting illustration is the case of the Lebanese Christian peasants at the beginning of the nineteenth century. Prior to the rule of Bashīr II they had been considered as being submissive, bashful, and soft-spoken by nature, but the Druze lords who returned after an exile of less than two decades found that they had changed into the opposite. See H., Y., and A. Abū-Shaqrā, *al-Ḥarakāt fī Lubnān*, Beirut, n.d., p. 33.

[40] Aristotle's definition as quoted, in a similar context, by Halpern, p. 351.

an essential trait of the Egyptian fellah. It is interesting to point out that the three authors we quoted at the beginning of this chapter wrote in relatively quiet periods during which there were either no large revolts or no revolts at all. But other observers who wrote in more stormy periods or remembered such times held completely different opinions. Thus, for example, two such observers who witnessed the events at the end of the eighteenth century wrote:

> . . . the stubbornness of these peasants revealed in acts of hatred and revenge, in their lust for blood during wars between one village and another . . . prove that when we do find them possessing energy in certain spheres, it only requires some guidance to become tremendous courage. The revolts and rebellions breaking out from time to time when their patience comes to an end, especially in the province of Sharqiyya, point to a flickering flame that only has to be fanned in order to break out into a conflagration.
>
> This almost continual state of warfare [of the fellahs], these alliances, and general confederacies, accustom the fellahs to resist the oppression of their proprietors [the *multazims*], and even of the government, when exigencies do not permit them to keep up a sufficient force to overawe the villages; and hence revolts are very frequent in certain provinces, and especially where the Arabs are numerous.[41]

In 1852 the following was written by Bayle St. John, the author of one of the best descriptions of Egypt at that time—apparently under the impression of the unrest in the 1840's:

> In the Saïd [Upper Egypt] these people, fellâhs by birth and position, are distinguished from the serfs of the Delta, and other low provinces, by many peculiarities, some of which they possess in common with the Bedawins, whilst others are probably derived from very ancient times. Among these peculiarities is one which, no doubt, depends principally on their distance from the seat of government. This is their love of arms and their independent disposition. In spite of the attempt, made frequently, to disarm them, warlike weapons are constantly to be seen in their hands—spears, swords, and even guns. . . . It ought to be mentioned, that there is no tendency among them to become banditti; whilst in Middle Egypt this tendency is strongly marked, and has required several very energetic demonstrations on the part of the Government. . . . The few formidable insurrections that have taken place among the Egyptian peasants have been above Siout.[42]

[41] C. F. Volney, *Voyage en Egypte et en Syrie pendant les années 1783, 1784 et 1785*, Paris, 1864, pp. 155–56. General Reynier, *State of Egypt after the Battle of Heliopolis*, English translation, London, 1802, p. 67.

[42] Bayle St. John, *Village Life in Egypt*, London, 1852, 1:294–95.

In the middle of the nineteenth century, Egypt was visited by the famous English economist Nassau William Senior. His diary, which was published after his death, consists of conversations which he had conducted with the people he met. Here is an exchange he had with the Armenian engineer Hekekyan, whose diary we quoted earlier:

> *Senior.*—Mr. Bruce [the British consul] ridicules the notion of a revolution in Egypt. He says that the Fellahs are too submissive, too abject for revolt.
> *Hekekyan.*—I think him utterly wrong. About 1823, in the height of Mehemet Ali's power, a half-mad saint roused the people against him, and was put down with great difficulty.
> *Senior.*—But for a popular revolution you must have a popular cry.
> *Hekekyan.*—The popular cry would be "cheap bread and no conscription."[43]

Finally, a British eyewitness of the 1919 revolt made the following remarks:

> An agrarian movement, if once started under the pressure of economic distress, might easily assume against the landlords the same disorderly character of violence as the anti-British rising last year.[44]

It thus becomes clear that the generalization about the "submissiveness of the Egyptian fellah" is based on fleeting impressions which are valid only for the moment and which are completely subjective. What is more, not one of those who have held this opinion have told us how to measure a trait of this kind or what would have to be the degree of oppression and humiliation under the objective conditions of Egypt and in a specific situation which would make it possible to determine that the fellah was "submissive" if he did not revolt against them.

Is there then no difference between Egypt and the countries of the Fertile Crescent in this matter? An answer is made difficult by the fact that the revolts in the Fertile Crescent have been investigated almost as little as those in Egypt. It may very well be that when such an investigation is made it will become clear that the revolts in the Fertile Crescent were more numerous and generally more persistent. This would only prove that because of the different geographic, social, and economic conditions in the two regions, central government was weaker in the Fertile Crescent than in Egypt and it was therefore more difficult for it to put down revolts or to prevent them from breaking out. But this is no proof of any supposed difference between the psychological traits of the fellahs in the two regions—the rebelliousness of the Syrian fellah and the submissiveness of the Egyptian. How can we

[43] N. W. Senior, *Conservations and Journals in Egypt and Malta*, London, 1882, 2:222–23.
[44] Chirol, p. 163.

compare the psychological traits of rebelliousness or submissiveness among peasants in two regions under completely different conditions? We migh be able to do so if they reacted differently to the same measure of exploita tion, oppression, and degradation and under the same geographic, social economic, and political conditions. If there were such difference in "mentality," in addition to the differences in geographic, social, economic and political conditions, it would be hard to understand how the Egyptian peasants revolted at all, and even more so how it happened that during the past two hundred years there were peasant revolts in Egypt in every generation (except, perhaps, for a little more than a generation after the British occupation), and that Egypt had the only countrywide revolt in the Middle East in which peasants from all parts of the country participated actively—in 1919.

In conclusion, it is worth remarking that it is not at all our intention to prove that the Egyptian peasant is naturally rebellious; on the contrary, it is our intention to show how misleading the generalizations concerning the "mentality" of any people or group of people can be and on what shaky grounds such generalizations sometimes stand.

7

Tanzimat in Egypt: The Penal Code

In the new activity of *qānūn* making at the beginning of the nineteenth century, Egypt preceded Turkey, especially with regard to criminal law. Although Egypt was still part of the Ottoman Empire, Muḥammad ʿAlī framed new laws based on Egyptian conditions and valid in Egypt only, while the Ottoman laws of the Tanzimat did not come into force in Egypt before Saʿīd's days. The purpose of this chapter is to trace the development of Egyptian penal laws in the nineteenth century, to analyze their relation to Ottoman laws, and to relate the story of the Ottoman Sultan's attempt to introduce into Egypt the "Tanzimat"—meaning mainly the Ottoman penal code.

Muḥammad ʿAlī's Penal Legislation

The first Egyptian penal code of the nineteenth century was the so-called *qānūn al-filāḥa* of Muḥammad ʿAlī. Its provisions were at first part of a booklet called *lāʾiḥat zirāʿat al-fallāḥ* published at Būlāq in Rajab 1245 A.H./December, 1829–January, 1830. This *lāʾiḥa* contains detailed instructions concerning agricultural work with regard to different crops and districts and the functions of various officials in the provinces and the villages.[1] From page 61 to the end, the *lāʾiḥa* lists penalties for crimes and offenses

Originally published as "Tanzimat in Egypt—The Penal Code," *Bulletin of the School of Oriental and African Studies* (University of London), 26, part 1 (1963): 29–49.

[1] For extensive quotations from these instructions, see Helen Rivlin, *The Agricultural Policy of Muḥammad ʿAlī in Egypt*, Cambridge, Mass., 1961, pp. 89–101, 139, 167, 192–94, 241–42. In Ottoman use *lāʾiḥa* was a draft law; in Egypt it acquired, in the nineteenth century, the meaning of law in general.

most of which, though not all, have to do with fellahs and agriculture. The *lā'iḥa* is written in an interesting mixture of colloquial and ungrammatical literary Arabic. A month after its publication, in Shaʿbān 1245 A.H./January–February, 1830, the part dealing with crimes and offenses was republished in literary Arabic, but otherwise with few changes, under the title of *qānūn al-filāḥa*.[2] This *qānūn* consisted of fifty-five articles dealing with village theft, the neglect of duties in connection with taxes, public works, and the army, offenses by village shaykhs, injury to persons and damage to property, murder and rebellion in the countryside, and a number of other crimes and offenses. The main penalties were the *kurbāj* (flogging), banishment, and hard labor. In many cases it was explicitly stated that *sharīʿa* law applied; the *qānūn* did not diverge from the *sharīʿa* except in its provisions for punishment of theft—but this was no novelty.

In agricultural Egypt, where control of the provinces was the main economic and administrative problem, it was only natural that the first new penal code should deal mainly with the village. The next step was the codification of penal laws dealing with offenses and crimes by officials. This was done by the *qānūn al-siyāsa al-malakiyya* printed in Rabīʿ al-ākhar 1253 A.H./July–August, 1837. Its twenty penal clauses laid down the kinds of punishment to be inflicted on officials who embezzled state funds or damaged state property, took bribes, deprived others of their property, broke laws, disobeyed orders, or neglected their work. Except for major crimes, which were punished by banishment and hard labor, most of the officials' offenses were punished by dismissal from office, deprivation of part of the salary, or imprisonment at the place of the official's work or in the *qalʿa*—the citadel of Cairo.[4]

[2] See Fīlīb Jallād, *Qāmūs al-idāra wa'l-qaḍā'*, Alexandria, 1890, 3:351. The most important differences between the *lā'iḥa* and the *qānūn* were the following: hard labor in Alexandria harbor as punishment for some offenses was replaced by banishment to the penal settlement Fayzoğlu (Fāzūghlī) in the Sudan; in some cases one hundred strokes of the *kurbāj* were augmented to two hundred, and from two hundred to three hundred to five hundred; a small number of clauses was omitted; and in some others the provision for making inquiries before inflicting punishment was added. It should be noted that a few provisions for punishment of village shaykhs and other officials scattered over the *lā'iḥa* on pp. 40, 41, 45, 47, and 54, were not included in the *qānūn al-filāḥa*.

[3] Jallād, 3:357. *Siyāsa*, in connection with penal law (as against its meaning of politics), apparently had in Egypt a more comprehensive meaning than the Ottoman *siyaset*, which included only severe corporal and capital punishment; see U. Heyd, *Ottoman Documents on Palestine*, Oxford, 1960, p. 59. Cf. also H. A. R. Gibb and H. Bowen, *Islamic Society and the West*, vol. 1, part 2, London, 1957, p. 119.

[4] It is interesting to note that when an official committed murder the *dīya* (blood money) was accepted, while when an official was killed and his murderers known they were put to death without asking the official's relatives whether they accepted blood money. See Jallād, 3:353–54, 357 (Articles 26 and 60). See below for later development.

This was the situation of Egyptian penal legislation when on December 6, 1839 the *Hatt-i Şerif* of Gülhane was sent to Muḥammad ʿAlī.[5] On January 5, 1840 he replied that he had had the firman read before the Grand Assembly of Cairo and sent it to the provinces under his rule, that for some years past he had already implemented the main provisions of the *hatt* by a number of laws regulating capital punishment and prohibiting the law of talion, and that he would supplement these means by the introduction of further reforms.[6] On May 3, 1840 the first Ottoman penal code was published,[7] and a year later, on May 23, 1941, Muḥammad ʿAlī was sent the famous firman which confirmed that the government of Egypt would be vested hereditarily within his family (known in Egypt as *farmān al-wirātha*). This firman stated explicitly that all laws of the Empire should be applied in Egypt.[8] As we shall see, this order was not carried out for another fifteen years. The Ottoman penal code of 1840 was never applied in Egypt; moreover, in a letter to the Grand Vezir, some years later, ʿAbbās Pasha, M. ʿAlī's successor, went so far as to claim that not only had the "Tanzimat" not been carried out in Egypt, but they had never even been published in that province.[9] After 1840 M. ʿAlī continued to enact a large number of penal laws year after year, but there was no relation whatsoever between these laws and the Ottoman penal code: even the provisions common to both completely differed in their formulation.

Between 1842 and 1845 M. ʿAlī issued the following laws: in Rajab 1258 A.H./August–September, 1842 he published the *lāʾiḥat al-jusūr* dealing with offenses connected with the maintenance of dikes; neglect by officials and their punishment was dealt with by a law of Shawwāl the same year (November–December, 1842); a further law laying down the duties of engineers and other officials in connection with public works, especially dikes, was published in Dhū al-Ḥijja 1258 A.H./January, 1843; a new *qānūn-nāmeh siyāsiyya*, containing offenses of *multazims* (farmers of revenue) and their punishment, was enacted in Shawwāl 1259 A.H./October–November, 1843; punishment for some kinds of administrative misdemeanor was provided for by regulations published in Rabīʿ al-ākhar 1260

[5] *Recueil de firmans impériaux ottomans addressés aux Valis et aux Khédives d'Egypte*, Cairo, 1934, p. 219.

[6] *Recueil de firmans*, pp. 224–26.

[7] See Bernard Lewis, *The Emergence of Modern Turkey*, London, 1961, p. 107. For text, see Ahmed Lûtfi, *Mirat-i adalet*, Istanbul, 1304 A.H./1886–87, pp. 127–46. I am greatly indebted to my friend and colleague the late Professor Uriel Heyd for having drawn my attention to this text as well as for advice and help with a number of problems and Turkish texts in connection with this study.

[8] *Recueil de firmans*, pp. 233–34.

[9] ʿAbbās to Grand Vezir, January 23, 1852, inclosure in Canning to Granville, February 18, 1852, PRO, FO 78/890.

A.H./April–May, 1944; and on 9 Shaʿbān, 1260 A.H./August 24, 1844 the Jamʿiyya Ḥaqqāniyya[10] enacted a supplementary penal code of seventy-three articles regulating the execution of punishments and dealing with counterfeiting of coins, falsification of seals or their opening without authority, vagrancy, murder and manslaughter, theft and robbery, fraud and perjury, and a large number of other crimes and offenses. Besides being the penal law with the widest scope issued under Muḥammad ʿAlī, it is of interest for two special reasons: first, it tried for the first time to guard the rights of the citizen *vis-à-vis* the government and to prevent arbitrary punishment by defining the right of a prisoner to his property, by fixing the penalties of juveniles and aged people, by prohibiting unlawful arrest, and so on. Secondly, it went further than former laws in encroaching on *sharīʿa* law: for instance, while the *qānūn al-filāḥa* of 1830 explicitly stated that violation of honor (*ta addin ʿalā ʿirḍ*) was a crime to be tried by the *qāḍī* according to *sharīʿa* law and whatever he decided should be carried out by the secular authorities, the new law of 1844 did not mention the *qāḍī* or *sharīʿa* law in this respect at all and fixed the penalty (imprisonment in the *qalʿa* or hard labor in Alexandria harbor).[11]

All the above mentioned penal laws of Muḥammad ʿAlī, from the *qānūn al-filāḥa* to the law of August, 1844, together with sporadic legislation of the Jamʿiyya Ḥaqqāniyya during the years 1843 and 1844, were published in a booklet on 1 Muḥarram, 1261 A.H./January 10, 1845 at Būlāq as *al-qānūn al-muntakhab*.[12] Among Europeans in Egypt this code, composed of penal laws enacted between 1830 and 1844, was known as "Code de Mehemet Ali."[13] Some additions (*dhayl al-qānūn al-muntakhab*) were published in October and December of the same year.[14] Besides, in 1843 Muḥammad ʿAlī had issued a code of instructions for officials on his private estates (*jafālik* or *shafālik*) which included a number of penal clauses.[15] Altogether

[10] A special administrative court established on 3 Muḥarram 1258 A.H./February 14, 1842. See Jean Deny, *Sommaire des archives turques du Caire*, Cairo, 1930, pp. 121–22.

[11] Compare Jallād, 3:353 (Article 16) with 371–72 (Articles 156 and 165).

[12] The booklet has no title on the cover. At the head of the first page: "*fihrist qānūn al-muntakhabāt*." At the end: "*kamula ṭabʿ ʿtarjamat al-qānūn al-muntakhab al-jadīd fī ghurrat Muḥarram al-ḥarām ifitāḥ sanat 1261. . . .*" The booklet has 20+115 pages. The articles are arranged in numbers running from 1 to 203. The *qānūn al-muntakhabāt* has been reprinted in full by Jallād, 3:351–78.

[13] For the manuscript of a French translation, see FO 141/96. Except for a few articles which he omitted (146–51, 165, 167, 170–71, 187–88, and 201–3 of the Arabic original), the translator rendered each article separately, but in some places he gave a shortened and summarized version only.

[14] Amīn Sāmī, *Taqwīm al-Nīl*, pt. 2, Cairo, 1928, pp. 535–36.

[15] *Qānūn al-shafālik*, Būlāq, Ṣafar 1259 A.H./March 1843. The main delicts dealt with in this law were neglect, theft, and embezzlement; the penalties were the bastinado, dismissal from office, imprisonment, and hard labor.

one cannot but agree with the argument advanced by Egypt's rulers when they were pressed to introduce the Ottoman penal code into Egypt, namely, that their own legislation had already developed much further than the Ottoman.

Meanwhile, at the end of 1259 A.H./the beginning of 1844 Muḥammad ʿAlī issued a so-called General Law (*qānūn ʿāmm*) which was a popular summary of his penal legislation. Apparently this was not published during his rule but only in Rajab 1265 A.H./May–June, 1849, half a year after ʿAbbās's accession to the throne.[16] Therefore it became known, among Europeans, as "Code d'Abbas."[17] Its first twenty-six articles deal with agricultural crimes and offenses, mainly in accordance with the *qānūn al-filāḥa*; the next chapter, of twenty-six articles, is called *siyāsa* and includes various crimes and offenses mentioned in the *qānūn al-siyāsa al-malakiyya* and the law of August, 1844; a special section of eleven articles is concerned with crimes to be punished according to *sharīʿa* law (*fīmā yuḥkam fīhi biʾl-sharīʿa*); the next ten articles deal with military offenses and those connected with dikes; then follow fifteen (or sixteen?) articles on theft and robbery; and, finally, eleven (or twelve?) articles on forgery of seals and counterfeiting of coins. There are in this code only one or two unimportant articles not to be found in the *qānūn al-muntakhab*, but as regards penalties the differences between the two are quire substantial (see below). Since the *qānūn ʿāmm* ("Code d'Abbas") was written prior to the law of August, 1844, it still was more conservative with respect to *sharīʿa* law: violation of honor was still tried and punished according to the *sharīʿa* (Article 44), and so was beating and wounding (Article 43), while the law of August, 1844, fixed for these crimes punishment by flogging and imprisonment without any reference to *sharīʿa* law (Article 166). During the year 1844 the attitude to *sharīʿa* law must have undergone a certain change.

ʿAbbās and the Tanzimat

On 15 Rabīʿ al-ākhar 1267 A.H./February 17, 1851 the second Ottoman penal code (*kanun-i cedid*) was published.[18] It differed from the first one in its arrangement and in that it dealt with certain additional crimes and offenses such as manslaughter, kidnapping of girls, falsification of docu-

[16] Sāmī, pt. 2, vol. 1, Cairo, 1936, p. 22. According to Sāmī, it was published in the colloquial language. I have not seen the Arabic original and in the following the French translation (see below) has been used.

[17] For the manuscript of a French translation, see FO 141/95. There are small differences of arrangement between the Arabic original as described in detail by Sāmī and the French translation and a difference of two in the number of articles.

[18] For text, see Lûtfi, pp. 150–76.

ments, and offenses connected with agriculture and taxes; also, it laid down procedure of imprisonment and punishment of officials, slaves, murderesses, and so on. It did not constitute, however, a fundamental departure from traditional Ottoman legislation with regard to penalties and comprehensiveness of codification. The difference between this code and Muḥammad ʿAlī's legislation will be examined further on; as a background for the following account it will suffice to point out that the Egyptians laws, particularly the law of August, 1844, were much more comprehensive (even with regard to protection of the citizen against arbitrary treatment by officials); that, generally speaking, their measures of punishment were much more severe than those of the Ottoman law; and that the Ottoman law did not contain any important provisions not dealt with by Muḥammad ʿAlī's laws—except on one subject, that is, murder. On this subject it laid down details of procedure and, most important, it established the rule that all over the Empire no murderer should be executed without the Sultan's confirmation of his death sentence. It was this rule, indeed, which became the main bone of contention between Cairo and the Sublime Porte in the early fifties of the past century.

Shortly after the publication of the new penal code a combined effort was made by the Sublime Porte and the British government to achieve its introduction into Egypt. Although on February 20, 1851 the Grand Vezir still told Sir Stratford Canning that there was no intention of forcing Egypt to accept the new code "which gradually, and quietly, as opportunities offered, would be extended over the whole Empire,"[19] less than one month later Canning reported that the Sultan intended to require that the principles of the Tanzimat, adapted to the local requirements of Egypt, should be carried into effect by the Viceroy, and that the Ottoman Minister to Egypt had remarked that, though some parts of the code were not applicable to Egypt, the basis and principles of it were perfectly so.[20] At the same time, both Palmerston and Canning insisted on Charles Murray, the British Consul-General in Egypt, inducing ʿAbbās to apply the Tanzimat to Egypt: ". . . the Porte demands no more than what the Firman [of May, 1841] warrants, and what the Viceroy admits; namely, that the principles of the Reform code should be introduced into Egypt with such modifications as the local peculiarities of that country may be found to require."[21]

The reaction to this demand in Egypt seems to have been very unfavorable. The Egyptian argument, reiterated again and again, was that, should

[19] Canning to Palmerston, February 20, 1851, FO 78/853.

[20] Canning to Palmerston, March 19, 1851, FO 78/853.

[21] Canning to Murray, March 20, 1851, FO 78/853. For Murray's correspondence with Palmerston, see FO 78/875, *passim.*

the wālī of Egypt be deprived of his powers to punish criminals severely according to the Egyptian laws and forced to delay executions by submitting the sentence to the Sultan, the beduins of Upper Egypt and the Eastern Desert would return to their unruliness of pre-Muḥammad ʿAlī times. This is what the Egyptian representatives claimed during the subsequent negotiations,[22] but it seems that this was also the general feeling of Egyptian officialdom. Shortly after the publication of the new code, Hekekyan Bey wrote in a letter to the British merchant S. Briggs:

> I sincerely hope that he [the Viceroy] will succeed in baffling the endeavours of his enemies in Constantinople to introduce disorder and anarchy into his hereditary dominion. The introduction of the tanzimat would be a great evil. The bedoween of Upper Egypt would be taught to despise the prince who should no longer possess the power of chastening them promptly and summarily. . . .

Egypt, he wrote, would return to the days of the Beys and the Hawara and robbers would paralyze shipping and commerce on the Nile. In another letter Hekekyan said that the Ottoman Empire should be interested in a strong vassal, that his powers should be augmented, not reduced. ʿAbbās should oppose the introduction of the Tanzimat into Egypt with all his powers.[23] This he did, in fact, claiming that he had his own code, the "Code d'Abbas," which promptly was forwarded by Murray to Lord Palmerston.[24] Furthermore, ʿAbbās claimed that Muḥammad ʿAlī used to execute murderers without referring the matter to the Sultan, and that to deprive him, ʿAbbās, of this power would be understood by Egypt's population as meaning that he had lost the favor of the Sultan.[25] Murray fervently supported ʿAbbās, stressing the argument that the introduction of the Tanzimat into Egypt would be contrary to the firman of 1841, and that the rumor about their introduction into Egypt had already threatened security in that country.[26]

In view of this opposition the Sublime Porte modified its position. In a communication to ʿAbbās, the Grand Vezir reiterated the demand that the Tanzimat should be carried into execution in Egypt, but he agreed that

[22] See Memorandum by Edhem Pasha and Hayreddin Pasha, inclosure in Canning to Palmerston, June 18, 1851, FO 78/856.

[23] Hekekyan Papers, vol. 5, B.M. Add. 37452, ff. 5b–7a (written between February 22 and 26, 1851). It appears, however, from rumors mentioned by Hekekyan, that Egyptian officials at that time had not yet a clear idea what the "introduction of the Tanzimat into Egypt" really meant. See f. 8b.

[24] Inclosure in Murray to Palmerston, March 24, 1851, FO 78/875.

[25] ʿAbbās to Grand Vezir, January 23, 1852, inclosure in Canning to Granville, February 18, 1852, FO 78/890.

[26] Murray to Canning, May 1, 1851, FO 78/875.

"there should be no great haste with reference to the details, and that further communications should be had with Your Highness and the necessary measures gradually looked into."[27] Thereupon ʿAbbās decided to enter into negotiations with the Sublime Porte, and on May 12 he replied to the Grand Vezir that "Edhem Pasha and Hayreddin Pasha have been selected with a view to arranging the adaptation of details of the Tanzimat to local exigencies, and to completing a code of regulations to be held as a basis for action, by the addition of such articles from the Egyptian regulations as may be necessary."[28]

ʿAbbās's mission arrived in Istanbul on May 24, 1851 and started negotiations with the Sublime Porte which lasted for more than one year. The Egyptian point of view was made clear from the beginning in a detailed note submitted by Edhem and Hayreddin to the commission of negotiations.[29] First and foremost, they opposed the rule of the *kanun-i cedid* requiring the Sultan's sanction for the execution of death sentences in Egypt. They pointed out that in recent years Egyptian procedure of examining and confirming death sentences had been regulated and made to conform to the new requirements of the *kanun-i cedid*. Accordingly they demanded the replacement of the Ottoman institutions and authorities mentioned in connexion with capital punishment in Articles 2, 3, 4, 6, 7, 8, and 12 of the *kanun-i cedid* by the parallel Egyptian ones. As to the remaining articles of chapter I, only light modifications would be necessary in order to harmonize them with the Egyptian code. For a number of crimes they demanded more severe penalties than those provided for by the *kanun-i cedid*, and in some cases of parallel legislation they would prefer the Egyptian law.[30] Finally, they demanded the addition of thirty-one articles from the Egyptian code dealing with crimes and offenses peculiar to the character of Egypt and its inhabitants.

During the negotiations the Egyptian mission received instructions from ʿAbbās, whose arguments were transmitted, at the same time, by his friend

[27] Inclosure in Canning to Palmerston, April 4, 1851; see also Canning to Murray, April 3, 1851, FO 78/854.

[28] Translation of letter from ʿAbbās Pasha to the Grand Vezir dated May 12, 1851, inclosure in Canning to Palmerston, June 4, 1851, FO 78/856. Edhem Pasha was ʿAbbās's Minister of Commerce and Hayreddin Pasha his Director of Transit (i.e., of communications between Cairo and Suez).

[29] For text of the note, see inclosure in Canning to Palmerston, June 18, 1851, FO 78/856.

[30] For example, embezzlement of state funds: *kanun-i cedid*, part 3, Article 2; *Muntakhab*, Articles 56, 64–65; "Code d'Abbas," Article 65. Also: sedition and rebellion against the government (*kanun-i cedid*, part 1, Articles 5–6; *Muntakhab* and "Code d'Abbas," Article 29); see letter from ʿAbbās to the Egyptian commissioners, 17 Shaʿbān 1267 A.H./June 17, 1851, loose leaf (in Turkish), FO 141/96.

and supporter Murray, the British Consul-General in Egypt, to Canning. The Egyptian commissioners were instructed to apply to Canning in case of difficulties.[31]

Apparently the Sublime Porte was not much interested in the secondary questions raised by the Egyptian delegation. As early as June, 1851, the British Ambassador got the impression that the Sublime Porte would be willing to make far-reaching concessions with regard to secondary demands, provided ʿAbbās conceded the Sultan's rights in the matter of capital punishment. To press its view the Porte declared, at a certain point of the negotiations, "that all other questions must remain in abeyance until the question of capital punishment should be settled agreeably to the Sultan's view," and only Canning's intervention prevented the breakdown of the negotiations.[32] In a reply to the note of the Egyptian commissioners dated June 26, 1851,[33] the Ottoman Privy Council did not touch the minor questions at all. It explained that execution of *qiṣāṣ* (talion; in this context: death sentence for a murderer) was "one of the special rights of the High Caliphate vested in the person of His most gracious Majesty." Egypt was autonomous only in administrative matters, and the laws of the Empire must be carried out. The question of *qiṣāṣ* was a basic principle concerning the Sultan's rights. As to the claim that this would create anarchy in Egypt, the reply stated that in the Empire the introduction of the Tanzimat had not undermined security. The population of Baghdad, Kurdistan, Hijaz, and Tripoli lived under conditions similar to those of Egypt and farther away from the central government. Since the *qiṣāṣ* did not apply to insurrections, the Egyptian claims were groundless.[34]

At the end of August, 1851 (or the beginning of September), the conference on the introduction of the Tanzimat into Egypt was suspended because another conflict between the Sublime Porte and ʿAbbās had become acute: the construction of a railway in Egypt.[35] Hayreddin was sent back to Egypt with a message from the Sublime Porte. However, as the result of Palmerston's intervention, this new conflict was soon settled, ʿAbbās asked for

[31] ʿAbbās to Egyptian commissioners, June 17, 1851, FO 141/96.

[32] Canning to Palmerston, June 18 and July 4, 1851, FO 78/856.

[33] Inclosure in Canning to Murray, June 26, 1851, inclosed in Canning to Palmerston, July 4, 1851, FO 78/856.

[34] Generally speaking, the Egyptian argument that there were beduin tribes in Egypt was of course ridiculous, since the problem of unruly nomads was much more difficult in other parts of the empire. But the years of ʿAbbās's rule were a period of acute unrest in Egypt, and this may explain, to a certain extent, the Egyptian apprehensiveness.

[35] Canning to Palmerston, September 4, 1851, FO 78/858. For details on the railway affair, see Helen Rivlin, "The Railway Question in the Ottoman-Egyptian Crisis of 1850–1852," *Middle East Journal*, 15, no. 4 (1961): 365–88.

permission to build the railway, and in the second half of October, 1851, the Sultan issued a firman with his formal sanction.[36] In November the Tanzimat negotiations were resumed. The commission dealt now with the secondary questions, on which it reached agreement in a short time. A number of articles were modified to meet the wishes of ʿAbbās—mainly by referring to the wālī of Egypt, in addition to the Sultan, wherever the government was mentioned in the code. On December 4, 1851 the work of the commission was finished.[37] On the main point, however, no progress was made at all: "With regard to the question of capital punishment . . . the Pashas [Egyptian commissioners] were made clearly to understand that no hope should be entertained on this point."[38]

At this juncture Canning tried to find a way out by suggesting to the Grand Vezir that the right to confirm death sentences should be left, in principle, to the Sultan, but the Sultan should delegate it temporarily, for the period of ten years, to ʿAbbās.[39] The first reaction of the Sultan was negative.[40] However, great pressure was brought to bear on the Sultan to change his mind: European ambassadors in Constantinople, consuls in Egypt, and even British merchants sent petitions and memoranda to the Sublime Porte asking it to grant ʿAbbās the temporary power of *qiṣāṣ*, claiming that otherwise Egypt's security would be jeopardized.[41] At last the Sultan made a small concession. In March, 1852, Fuad Pasha was sent to Egypt and reached an agreement with ʿAbbās, which was ratified by the Sublime Porte after further pressure (the British Foreign Minister had enlisted the aid of the four powers for this purpose).[42] According to the terms of the settlement, ʿAbbās was granted, for a period of seven years, the right to confirm death sentences in certain cases only (for details, see below). The price for this concession was an increase in the yearly tribute of Egypt to the Sublime Porte to £400,000.[43]

[36] Canning to Palmerston, October 15, 17, and 24, 1851 and November 4, 1851 (inclosing text of firman), FO 78/858. For text of firman, see also *Recueil de firmans*, pp. 255–56; Rivlin, "Railway Question . . .," pp. 377–78.

[37] See note by ʿAbd al-Raḥmān Rushdī (secretary of the Egyptian mission) to Canning, December 5, 1851, inclosure in Canning to Palmerston, December 6, 1851, FO 78/861. For details of the modified code, see below.

[38] Rushdī to Canning, inclosure in Canning to Palmerston, December 6, 1851, FO 78/861.

[39] Canning to Pisani, December 14, 1851, FO 78/861. For an earlier suggestion by Canning in the same spirit, see Canning to Murray, inclosure in Canning to Palmerston, July 4, 1851, FO 78/856.

[40] Canning to Palmerston, December 31, 1851, FO 78/861.

[41] Canning to Granville, February 18 and 26, 1852, FO 78/890.

[42] Canning to Malmesbury, March 12, 1852, FO 78/891; May 4, 5, 6, and 12, 1852, FO 78/892.

[43] De Redcliffe to Malmesbury, June 17, 1852, FO 78/892.

In May, 1852, when the question of the *qiṣāṣ* had been settled, the Egyptian commissioners resumed their work and began the definite composition of the Tanzimat code to be applied in Egypt.[44] In mid-July, 1852, the Sultan issued a firman to ʿAbbās containing the details of the settlement.[45] In this firman he demands that ʿAbbās should henceforth apply the new code to Egypt. He reiterates that execution of criminals depends absolutely on the Sultan's orders. Thus, if an heirless person is murdered, the files of the case should be sent to Istanbul for confirmation of the verdict before the murderer's execution. However, ʿAbbās is given permission, for a period of seven years, that is, until the end of 1275 A.H., to execute murderers whose victims have heirs, if these heirs so demand. Nevertheless, ʿAbbās will be obliged to send the *iʿlām* (the judge's notification of the verdict to the authorities) of such cases to the Sublime Porte (after execution). Death sentences according to administrative laws[46] should be commuted, during the period of seven years, from ten to fifteen years of hard labor. These orders should be published in Egypt.

It is not quite clear what happened to this firman and the new code during the remaining years of the reign of ʿAbbās. According to one author, ʿAbbās had the firman read in public;[47] however, the new code was not introduced into Egypt by ʿAbbās. This becomes clear from the following order of Saʿīd issued to the *majlis al-aḥkām* (Judicial Council) on July 25, 1854, a few days after he ascended the throne:

> Since the Tanzimat law, the sublime firman, and the exalted letters sent by a special official in the reign of our late predecessor, have never been submitted to the *majlis*, we order that they should be implemented henceforth, their provisions carried out immediately and their clauses applied carefully and literally; we have therefore sent you a copy of these documents.[48]

About half a year later the new Egyptian code, based on the Ottoman Penal Code of 1851, was published in Egypt under the name *qānūn-nāmeh al-sulṭānī*.[49]

[44] De Redcliffe to Malmesbury, May 19, 1852, FO 78/892; Rose to Gilbert, July 6, 1852, FO 78/893.

[45] For a full French translation of the firman, see inclosure in Rose to Malmesbury, August 23, 1852, FO 78/893. The shortened version in *Recueil de firmans*, p. 257, has a number of mistakes.

[46] That is, not according to the *sharīʿa* law of talion—for instance, in cases of rebellion.

[47] G. Rosen, *Geschichte der Türkei*, 2, Leipzig, 1867, p. 137.

[48] Sāmī, pt. 3, 1:79.

[49] For Arabic text, see Jallād, 2:90 ff. According to Alfred von Kremer, *Aegypten*, Leipzig, 1863, 2:52–53, it was published on 5 Jumādā al-ūlā 1271 A.H./January 24, 1855. I have not seen any other source giving the exact date. Since it was published in Arabic together with the *Hatt-i Şerif* of Gülhane, Jallād gives as its date 26 Shaʿbān 1255 A.H./November 3, 1839, which is of course absurd.

The Egyptian and the Ottoman Tanzimat Codes

The Ottoman Penal Code of 1851 has an introduction and three chapters (*fasıl*) consisting of seventeen, seven, and twenty-two articles (*madde*) respectively.[50] These three chapters, without changes in subjects or arrangement, form the nucleus of the Egyptian *qānūn-nāmeh al-sulṭānī* published in 1855.[51] But they constitute less than half of it. The additions are of several kinds. First of all, Saʿīd's Code opens with the Arabic version of the *Hatt-i Şerif* of Gülhane, which apparently had not been published in Egypt before. Then follows the introduction, which is completely different from the introduction to the Ottoman code: the latter explains the necessity of the "New Law" and its division into three subjects, life, honor, and property, according to the principles of the *Hatt-i Şerif.* This is summarized in a few lines in the Egyptian introduction, which goes on to explain the particular conditions of Egypt and the structure of the Egyptian law resulting therefrom.

The next important addition to be found in Saʿīd's Code is a note (*ḥāshiya*) to Chapter 1, Article 2, which deals with murder and with the execution of murderers after confirmation of the verdict by the Sultan. This, the note explains, was the prevalent procedure until the recently issued firman,[52] which introduced a change for a period of seven years, until 1275 A.H. The change, according to the Arabic text as published by Jallād, consists in that the wālī of Egypt has been granted the permission to execute murderers of heirless persons, and to send the *iʿlām* afterward to Istanbul. This is the opposite of what was said in the firman and must be an error of translation.[53] But since Saʿīd apparently did not carry out the provisions of the firman (see below), the discrepancy evidently had no practical consequences.

[50] In Lûtfi's edition the third chapter has only nineteen numbered articles, but this must be a printing error, since Article 19 is exceptionally long and includes all the various subjects which are subdivided in the Egyptian version into Articles 19–22.

[51] Henceforth in short Saʿīd's Code, or the Tanzimat Code. It has been connected with Saʿīd's name because it was published in his reign, although it had been worked out under ʿAbbās. Similarly, the "Code d'Abbas" had been composed in Muḥammad ʿAlī's time (see above).

[52] *Sic.* We have seen that ʿAbbās and his negotiators had claimed that the opposite was the case, as a precedent for their demands. One may assume that they were right with regard to Muḥammad ʿAlī's rule.

[53] It cannot be a printing error since the wording *al-qaṭīl alladhī lā walīya lahu walā wāritha* appears twice in the note, and because in the opposite case a completely different formulation would have been necessary and something would have had to be said about the heirs' wishes. There can be no doubt that the firman granted the right to execute assassins whose victims had heirs without prior confirmation by the Sultan. First, this is confirmed by two independent translations, as well as by the Foreign Office records on Fuad's mission to Egypt. Moreover, it is logical, since in this case the wālī of Egypt acted as a quasi-agent of the victim's heirs. There is another grave error of translation in the Arabic version of chapter 3, Article 22.

It will be remembered that the addition of parts from the Egyptian *qānūns* was one of the demands of the Egyptian side at the negotiations on the introduction of the Tanzimat into Egypt. The fact that Saʿīd's Code is so much larger than the Ottoman code from which it was adapted is mainly the result of two additional chapters and a number of administrative regulations which have been incorporated in it. Chapter IV consists of twenty-seven articles taken from Muḥammad ʿAlī's *qānūn al-filāḥa* and *lā'iḥat al-jusūr*, partly through the "Code d'Abbas" and partly directly.[54] Chapter V is a medley of eleven unconnected articles from various laws of Muḥammad ʿAlī. Then follow eleven administrative regulations dealing with officials in general (eleven articles), rules for conduct of officials (twenty-three articles), other employees of the councils and their functions (fifteen articles), agricultural offices (four articles), *mudīrs* (sixteen articles), police (two articles), *waqf* (one article), contracts (ten articles), and building regulations (one article). These regulations have nothing to do with the penal code, but the fact that they are mentioned in the introduction shows that they were published together with it. Moreover, it seems that they too were adapted partly from Ottoman regulations, since the Egyptian mission for the negotiation on the introduction of the Tanzimat into Egypt dealt with them and suggested changes in accordance with Egyptian conditions.[55]

We have seen that in the negotiations the Egyptians insisted on reference to the wālī of Egypt together with the Sultan wherever the government was mentioned in the code. To this the Ottoman side agreed. The Egyptian version of Chapter I, Article 1, where rebellion against the Ottoman government is dealt with, runs as follows: ". . . against the Sublime [Ottoman] Government or the local government vested in the wālīs of Egypt according to the exalted firman which granted them heredity, or against the hereditary wālī, or against one of the officials." Similarly, the wālī of Egypt, the heredity of his office, and the "*farmān al-wirātha*" are mentioned in Chapter I, Article 5, and Chapter III, Articles 1, 5, and 7. In many cases Egyptian institutions replace Ottoman ones in the Egyptian version of the code: *majlis al-aḥkām al-miṣriyya* comes instead of *meclis-i ahkâm-i adliye* (I, 7, and III, 5); the *dīwān* of the wālī of Egypt instead of the *müşür* (I, 8); *mudīr al-jiha* or *mudīr al-maḥall* instead of *mahallin meclisi* (II, 2

[54] Articles 1–13 and 14–18 appear in the same sequence as in the "Code d'Abbas." Articles 19–27 have been taken directly from the *qānūn al-filāḥa*—they do not appear at all in the "Code d'Abbas." The penalties stipulated in Saʿīd's Code differ from those fixed in the original laws; see below.

[55] See note from ʿAbd al-Raḥmān Rushdī, December 5, 1851, inclosure in Canning to Palmerston, December 6, 1851, FO 78/861.

and 6); "*shaykh* or *faqīh* or *maḥkama*" instead of *mahkeme* alone (II, 6); *umarā'* instead of *vükelâ* (III, 5); *al-maqṭū'iyya al-maḍrūba 'alā'l-arāḍī lijānib al-mīrī* instead of *üşür* (III, 14), and so on. "Cairo" replaces "Istanbul" (I, 2, and 7; II, 2), and where cases have to be brought before the *şeyhülislâm* Egyptian judicial institutions act as an intermediate stage (I, 2 and 3).

In accordance with the demand of the Egyptian mission, the article dealing with embezzlement of state funds (Chapter II, Article 2) was taken from the "Code d'Abbas." This, however, seems to be the only case in which a whole article of the Ottoman Code was replaced, in the Egyptian version, by an article from Egyptian legislation. The mission's demand to replace Article 5 of Chapter III by Article 20 of the "Code d'Abbas" was based on a misunderstanding of its contents and was rejected—the result being that the Egyptian version emerged in a somewhat mutilated form. Similarly, the efforts of 'Abbās and his commissioners to replace the articles on sedition and rebellion (I, 5–6) by Article 29 of the "Code d'Abbas" were not successful—but then they themselves were aware of the fact that they did not deal exactly with the same offenses.[56]

On the other hand, the Egyptian commissioners succeeded in convincing their Ottoman counterparts that Articles 3, 6, and 14 of Chapter III deal with matters pertaining to the financial administration which was organized in Egypt in a different manner. These articles are formulated differently in the two codes; in one case at least (Article 14) this involved far-reaching changes: whereas in the Ottoman code a peasant hiding his crop to evade payment of taxes was treated as if he evaded payment of custom duties and punished by double payment, in the Egyptian version he was treated as if he evaded the payment of taxes and punished with imprisonment. Another "success" of the Egyptian mission was that they convinced the Ottomans that theft of seed committed by agricultural laborers (III, 18) was considered in Egypt to be as severe a delict as robbery; as a result it is punished, according to Sa'īd's Code, with the bastinado and not just by deducting the price of the stolen goods from their wages, as stipulated by the Ottoman code. These two examples show that agricultural offenses were considered more serious in Egypt than in Turkey.[57]

[56] See above, notes 29 and 30. In the following paragraphs, specification of the demands of the Egyptian commissioners refers to their memorandum mentioned in note 29.

[57] A curious difference exists between the Egyptian and Ottoman version of chapter III, Article 9, dealing with bribery. In the Ottoman law customary gifts (*bazı teatisi mûtad olan hedaya-yi resmiye ve aleniye*) or friendly presents without compensation (*dostane itası mesnun olan hedaya muhabbetten gayri garaz ve ıwazdan âri . . .*) are explicitly allowed. Apparently such gifts had been institutionalized in Turkey for centuries: see, for instance, R. Tschudi, *Das Aṣafnâme des Lutfî Pascha*, Berlin, 1910, pp. ١٣-١٤ (13). In Egypt apparently no such institution existed, and the second half of this article has been omitted in the Egyptian version of the code. This does not mean, of course, that no such gifts existed in Egypt or that they were prohibited.

In a few other cases too the penalties provided for by the Egyptian version are more severe than those of the Ottoman code: for instance, according to Chapter III, Article 11, an Egyptian thief is to be sent into exile to the Sudan after his third offense, but no such punishment is mentioned in the Ottoman code. However, generally speaking the attempt of the Egyptian negotiators to introduce into the Egyptian version some of the more severe penalties of former Egyptian codes failed. A case in point exists in Articles 5 and 7 of Chapter II, dealing with drunkards, gamblers, and troublemakers and with hitting with blunt instruments (*bimā laysa min al-ālāt al-jariḥa*). The penalty laid down for these offenses is the bastinado, up to seventy-nine strokes, "according to the *sharīʿa*," or imprisonment up to three months. To this the Egyptian commissioners objected, claiming that Egyptian troublemakers (the *falātiyya* and *ḥashshāshīn*—loiterers, vagabonds, and addicts of hashish) would not be deterred by such a light punishment and demanding a more severe one. Apparently their demand was rejected: the final Egyptian version does not differ from the Ottoman original.

As against this, the Ottoman code stipulates the death penalty for instigators of rebellion (I, 6), while in the Egyptian version the punishment is only exile or from ten to fifteen years hard labor. A special note states that this lighter penalty has been fixed for the period of seven years, after which a more severe punishment will be introduced. As we have seen, this was one of the provisions of the firman of mid-July, 1852, and it may have had two reasons. First, according to former Egyptian legislation, similar crimes had been punished by exile or hard labor only; second, ʿAbbās may have been interested in prompt punishment of rebels without the need to wait for the Sultan's confirmation, even if the penalty was not so severe, and the Sultan would not have made another exception to his right with regard to capital punishment over and above the exception he made in cases of victims of murder with heirs. However that may be, since Saʿīd did not at all refrain from executing offenders against the authorities, this difference too was a theoretical one only.

So far we have examined the relation between the Ottoman Penal Code of 1851 and its Egyptian version, Saʿīd's Code. We shall now try to compare Saʿīd's Code with earlier Egyptian legislation of the nineteenth century. As we have said, its main novelty was that it specified procedure in various cases of murder (I, 2–3, 11–12, 14–15, and III, 21–2). In all other respects it did not add much to the *Muntakhab* and the "Code d'Abbas." Crimes and offenses treated in Saʿīd's Code which had not been mentioned in former Egyptian laws are unruliness of drunkards, gamblers, and other troublemakers (II, 5); kidnapping of girls (II, 6); imposition of fines (III, 10);

and crimes and offenses of male and female slaves (III, 20). Resistance against authority, rebellion, and revolt are dealt with in Saʿīd's Code in a general manner, in accordance with the Ottoman code (I, 1, 5–8, 16), while earlier Egyptian legislation dealt only with rebellion and revolt of peasants and villages.[58] A number of other crimes too are formulated in a different way in Saʿīd's Code, on the one hand, and in the *Muntakhab* and the "Code d'Abbas," on the other.

As against this, a very large number of provisions of Muḥammad ʿAlī's penal legislation have not been adopted by the Egyptian Tanzimat Code, not even in Chapters IV and V (the Egyptian additions to the original Ottoman code). These include[59] part of the penal regulations connected with canals and dikes, evasion of military duty, flight of peasants, causing damage to flocks and herds, nonpayment of debts, hiding of criminals, some offenses connected with tax farming, breaking of seals, organizing bands, fraud, killing in self-defense, sale of adulterated or harmful drinks, kidnapping of children, fradulent bankruptcy, escape of prisoners, perjury, defamation of governors and judges, begging, as well as many regulations connected with offenses of officials and the procedure of punishment. It is interesting to note that part of these regulations were included in the "Code d'Abbas," the last penal legislation before the Tanzimat Code. We have been unable to find out which principle, if there was any, guided the Egyptian legislators in choosing the articles from earlier Egyptian legislation to be included in the additional chapters, IV and V, of Saʿīd's Code.

In general, the penalties laid down by the Tanzimat Code were much lighter than those for the same crimes and offenses stipulated by Muḥammad ʿAlī's legislation (including the "Code d'Abbas"). In a large number of articles the number of strokes of the *kurbāj* was reduced, the maximum being fixed at seventy-nine in the first three chapters which had been adapted from the Ottoman code, and at two hundred in the two chapters taken from the Egyptian laws, while the same crimes were punished according to Muḥammad ʿAlī's laws with up to five hundred strokes. Similarly, in many cases the duration of imprisonment or exile or hard labor was reduced, for some offenses from hard labor for life to between four and five years. Highway robbers (who were not convicted of killing) and forgers, for whom the penalty of hard labor for life was laid down in the *Muntakhab* and the "Code d'Abbas," were to be punished, according to Saʿīd's Code, with a few years' imprisonment only. Beduins who intentionally let their flocks and herds graze on cultivated land forfeited their animals, according to the *Muntakhab*, and also had to pay a heavy fine. The Tanzimat Code retained the fine

[58] *Muntakhab*, Articles 24, 26–27; "Code d'Abbas," Articles 11, 14, 47.
[59] The following list is arranged according to the order of articles in the *Muntakhab*.

only, fixed at twice the damage done. Peasants who stole animals or changed boundaries were no longer imprisoned because, as the law explained (IV, 7), this would harm agricultural work, but were to be punished with from fifty to one hundred and fifty strokes of the *kurbāj* (instead of from one hundred to five hundred in the *Muntakhab* and "Code d'Abbas"). This was not only due to the fact that penalties in Ottoman laws were lighter than in Egyptian ones and that Saʿīd's Code was based on an Ottoman law: the relaxation of penalties is also found throughout the two chapters taken from earlier Egyptian laws. Its main reasons probably were the greater security achieved in Egypt during the rule of Muḥammad ʿAlī and European pressure to abolish the cruelty of former Egyptian penalties.

There are, however, a few articles of Saʿīd's Code stipulating heavier penalties than did former Egyptian legislation for the same crimes. A case in point is murder committed by an official of the state. This was punished according to the *Muntakhab* and the "Code d'Abbas" by the payment of blood money or exile for life; the Tanzimat Code categorically imposes the death sentence. Other cases in which heavier penalties were introduced concern offenses against the security of land tenure. Property rights of peasants to the land they tilled were not yet legally defined during Muḥammad ʿAlī's rule. Their land was transferred by custom from father to son (*athariyya* land). If somebody seized such land his only duty, according to the *qānūn al-filāḥa* (Article 1) was to pay its taxes and to return it after a year. Later the "Code d'Abbas" laid down that he should return it immediately, pay a compensation, and be punished. Under Saʿīd property rights consolidated[60] and punishment for their violation became heavier: to that of the "Code d'Abbas" the payment of rent and imprisonment or the bastinado were added (IV, 1). Similarly, a village shaykh who did not respect the *athariyya* rights of peasants (i.e., who did not respect the priority of the son when his father's land was allocated on his death) was reprimanded; on committing the offense the second time he received three hundred strokes of the *kurbāj* (*Muntakhab*, 45). According to Saʿīd's Code (IV, 26), he received seventy-nine strokes of the *kurbāj* for the first offense and was liable to be dismissed from his office the second time.

A few years after it had been published, Alfred von Kremer commented upon Saʿīd's Code in the following words:

> Dieses Gesetz in Strafsachen ist insofern von Bedeutung, als es in Ägypten der erste vom streng mohammedanischen Rechtsprincip der Alleingültigkeit des Korangesetzes abweichende und eine selbständige Gesetzgebung anbahnende Schritt war.[61]

[60] See chapter 4, above.
[61] Von Kremer, 2:52–53.

For two reasons we cannot agree with this appreciation. First, the exclusive validity of the Qur'anic law had been infringed already extensively by Muḥammad ʿAlī's *qānūn* making. Secondly, one cannot even say that Saʿīd's Code diverged from the *sharīʿa* to a larger degree than did Muḥammad ʿAlī's laws. True, in cases of infanticide and when the heirs of victims of murder were satisfied with the *dīya* (blood money), additional penalties to those fixed by the *sharīʿa* were stipulated in Saʿīd's Code (I, 11; V, 4). But except for these two cases, all provisions concerning murder in Saʿīd's Code are expressly in accordance with the *sharīʿa* and deal mainly with procedure. On the other hand, Muḥammad ʿAlī's laws not only dealt with a large number of crimes that had been provided for by *sharīʿa* law, but in one case at least their divergence from the *sharīʿa* was greater than that of Saʿīd's Code: as we have seen, the law of 1844 deprived the *qāḍī* of his right to try violation of honor according to the *sharīʿa*; in Saʿīd's Code the validity of *sharīʿa* law with regard to this crime was reestablished (II, 1). One may add that the number of strokes of the *kurbāj* as stipulated in Saʿīd's Code are much more in accordance with the *sharīʿa* than those fixed by Muḥammad ʿAlī's legislation.

To sum up: "the introduction of the Tanzimat into Egypt" was of no great consequence so far as the penal code is concerned. With regard to comprehensiveness, it was rather a regression, and its provision for more humane penalties than those prevalent under Muḥammad ʿAlī were largely disregarded, as we shall see below. Both Egyptian arguments against, and Ottoman arguments in favor of, its introduction into Egypt were virtually irrelevant, the only real issue being the struggle for authority in Egypt which ended with the victory of the Sultan signified by the reestablishment of his right of *qiṣāṣ*. Even this, however, was apparently disregarded in practice.

Penal Law under Saʿīd and Ismāʿīl

There are many indications that under Saʿīd penalties were imposed quite arbitrarily and not according to the Tanzimat Code. The Code did not provide for punishment of evasion of military duty, but the *Muntakhab* of Muḥammad ʿAlī (Article 9) fixed a maximum penalty of five hundred strokes of the *kurbāj* for a shaykh who refrained from sending the required peasants to the army. When, however, early in 1856 a shaykh sent someone else for military service instead of his son, he was hanged in public in the town of Ṭanṭā.[62] Village shaykhs who forced fellahs to work without compensation were to be punished, according to Saʿīd's Code (IV, 6), with

[62] Nassau W. Senior, *Conversations and Journals in Egypt and Malta*, London, 1882, 1:261–62, 294–95.

up to forty-five days' imprisonment or up to fifty strokes of the *kurbāj*. But Saʿīd did not refrain from executing, in 1861, a *shaykh al-balad* in Minūf for such a crime.[63] His arbitrary punishments and executions were frequently the subject of reports of foreign consuls.[64] Saʿīd's officials, too, apparently did not care much about the provisions of the Code. On April 23, 1858 Saʿīd wrote to his Office for Home Affairs (*Dākhiliyya*) that he had heard that it was the custom to punish offenders with more strokes of the *kurbāj* than fixed by law, and he gave orders not to exceed two hundred strokes at the utmost.[65] In July, 1861, Saʿīd prohibited the bastinado completely and replaced it by imprisonment, claiming that people were not deterred from crime by the bastinado and needed a more severe punishment.[66] This order, however, was not carried out in the countryside,[67] and in January, 1863, a few days after he ascended the throne Ismāʿīl reversed it under the pretext that he had decided to carry out the "Imperial Code" (*al-qānūn al-humāyūnī*) word for word.[68]

Furthermore, Saʿīd introduced a number of changes into the Code in order to reestablish the more severe Egyptian penalties. Two such changes were promulgated in September, 1858. First, for hitting with blunt instruments (II, 7) the penalty was increased from up to three months' to up to three years' imprisonment (it will be remembered that the Egyptian mission to the Tanzimat negotiations had objected, without success, to the lighter punishment laid down by the Code). Secondly, calumny was to be punished, in the provinces, by up to forty-five days' imprisonment (II, 2). Saʿīd now reestablished Muḥammad ʿAlī's rule (*Muntakhab*, 69) that if an accusation proved to be false, the accuser would undergo the same penalty that would have been inflicted on the accused had he committed the crime. A false accusation of murder should be punished with up to five years' hard labor.[69]

On the whole, however, the Tanzimat Code was in force throughout Saʿīd's rule, and when he reorganized his judicial administration at the end of June, 1862, half a year before his death, the first thing each of the new provincial councils was ordered to do was to acquire a copy of the "Imperial Code."[70] This is remarkable because four years before, on August 9, 1858, a new, third, penal code, which followed French law, had been promulgated

[63]Von Kremer, 1:256.
[64]See, for instance, Bruce to Clarendon, July 21, 1856, FO 78/1222.
[65]Sāmī, part 3, 1:279–80.
[66]Sāmī, part 3, 1:375–76.
[67]Von Kremer, 2:67.
[68]Sāmī, part 3, 2:450.
[69]Sāmī, part 3, 1:296–97.
[70]Sāmī, part 3, 1:414. There can be no doubt that the Tanzimat Code of 1855 was meant.

in the Ottoman Empire.[71] Saʿīd did not take cognizance of this new code. But Ismāʿīl visited Istanbul shortly after he ascended the throne (January 18, 1863) and on returning to Egypt he brought back with him a copy of the *Düstur*, the Turkish collection of laws. In the first volume of this collection the text of the new penal code had been published, and on July 5, 1863 Ismāʿīl issued an order that henceforth the new code should be applied to Egypt and the old one, the Tanzimat Code, should be abrogated—as soon as a sufficient number of copies for all concerned should arrive in Egypt.[72] Soon afterward, however, he had second thoughts, and on September 15, 1863 he ordered that the chapters and articles peculiar to Egypt which had been appended to the Tanzimat Code should remain in force, be added to the new *düstur*, and published together with it.[73]

It took exactly twelve years to edit this new Egyptian code.[74] At last, by a decree of September 16, 1875, the new Egyptian criminal code was promulgated.[75] The result shows that what the Egyptian legislators did was hardly what Ismāʿīl had in mind in 1863. Essentially the Egyptian Penal Code of 1875 is based on the Ottoman code of 1858. They have the same division into subjects and chapters, if not the same subdivision into articles: the Egyptian code has 341 articles, while the original Ottoman code had only 264 (a few articles had been added to the Ottoman code in the meantime).[76] The majority of the articles are the same word for word.[77] So are the penalties fixed for the different crimes, although local conditions, like currency, places of exile, and so on, as well as differences in procedure, were taken into account. Minor differences are that in the Egyptian code public exposing of a convict does not exist as a penalty while in the Ottoman code it does,[78] and, curiously enough, that in the Ottoman code (Article 213) calumny is now punished with the penalty that applies to the crime with which the calumniator charges his victim (the rule of Muḥammad ʿAlī reintroduced into Egypt by Saʿīd), while in the Egyptian code (Articles 268 ff.) fixed penalties are laid down.

[71] See Lewis, p. 116 and n. 79. The text used in the following is the translation of Aristarchi Bey, *Legislation ottomane*, vol. 2, Constantinople, 1874, pp. 212 ff.

[72] Sāmī, part 3, 2:499.

[73] Sāmī, part 3, 2:513.

[74] Meanwhile, however, penal laws in Egypt underwent some changes. For instance, on October 23, 1865 Ismāʿīl ordered that crimes and offences of state officials should be tried in the future according to French law. See Sāmī, part 3, 2:624.

[75] See Borg to Lascelles, September 8, 1879, FO 141/129. For text, see *Codes égyptiens*, Cairo, 1883, pp. 427 ff.

[76] See Aristarchi, 2:268–73.

[77] Again, one of the exceptions is the rule with regard to customary gifts (Ottoman code, Article 67), which does not exist in Egypt. See above, note 57.

[78] See also Borg to Lascelles, September 8, 1879, FO 141/129.

There are, however, some more important differences. First, the Egyptian code is more comprehensive: here and there clauses have been added, for instance, concerning offenses with regard to bankruptcy and fraud (Ottoman code, Articles 231–33; Egyptian code, Articles 293–302). In the chapter on destruction and damage a special article on damage to dikes has been added in the Egyptian code (Article 324)—perhaps the only vestige of the so-called articles peculiar to Egypt. Secondly, in the Egyptian code there is no reference whatsoever to the Sultan and the Ottoman Empire: wherever they were mentioned in the Ottoman code, they had been replaced by the "Khedive" and the "State." This includes the case of capital punishment: according to the Ottoman code (Article 16), death sentences must be confirmed by a firman of the Sultan; in the relevant article of the Egyptian code (Article 25), it is said that the documents should be sent to the Khedive, who may decide to reprieve the person condemned to death.[79] I have been unable to find out whether the Sultan ever officially relinquished his right of *qiṣāṣ* with regard to Egypt. To judge by the development of a similar question (see appendix to this chapter), it is very probable that he did not, but just tacitly recognized a *fait accompli*.

Another difference between the Ottoman Penal Code of 1858 and the Egyptian Penal Code of 1875 exists in their attitude to *sharīʿa* law. To be sure, both codes constitute the first radical departure from the *sharīʿa* in criminal matters in their respective countries. In neither is blood money any longer an alternative to execution for murder (OC, Article 170; EC, Article 204); and both contain a number of articles dealing with adultery, in which provisions for penalties and evidence are completely contrary to *sharīʿa* law (OC, addition of 1864 to Article 201; EC, Articles 242–46). The Egyptian code, however, went further than the Ottoman one. The latter says in the introduction (Article 1) that the state has the right to punish crimes committed against individuals as well as those committed against the state, but that the penalties it imposes do not prejudice individual rights as laid down by the *sharīʿa*. Accordingly, the death sentence for homicide does not prevent the victim's heirs from demanding their right before the *sharīʿa* court (Article 171); unintentional homicide, not caused by negligence, is punished by payment of the *dīya* according to the *sharīʿa* (Article 182); the same penalty is imposed for unintentional wounding (Article 183) and for causing abortion by violence (Article 192). In the Egyptian code, all these provisions have been omitted and no reference whatsoever to *sharīʿa* law is made in criminal matters. It should be mentioned, however, that some of

[79] This of course solved the problem of punishment of revolt (see above). As in Turkey, revolt was now to be punished in Egypt too with death (Egyptian code, Articles 83 ff.).

these provisions, including the general explanation in the introduction, were reintroduced into later Egyptian penal codes.[80]

The Egyptian Penal Code of 1875 was also the first code to break away from traditional *qānūn* making with regard to comprehensiveness and arrangement: it was based on the Ottoman Penal Code of 1858, which had been modeled after the French code. It was the first Egyptian code that did not include flogging among its penalties. It was of historical importance, if not of much practical use: apparently by 1879 it had not yet been applied in Egypt,[81] and in 1883, after the British occupation, it was superseded by a new penal code, based on the French code, after which a number of modern penal codes were enacted in later years.

Appendix: The Appointment of the Qāḍī of Cairo

We have seen that the right of *qiṣāṣ* in cases of murder committed in Egypt was one of the prerogatives of the Sultan as a sign of his sovereign power. Similarly, the right to appoint the *qāḍī* of Cairo was held to be a prerogative of the Ottoman Sultan. During the nineteenth century this latter prerogative underwent changes not unlike those we have traced with regard to the right of *qiṣāṣ*, until it became extinct in the days of Ismāʿīl. Since both rights lay in the sphere of the administration of justice, it is of interest to compare their respective developments.

Until the middle of the nineteenth century, the *qāḍī* of Cairo was appointed yearly by Imperial firman, and, in general, the office was held for the period of one year only. It was sold in Istanbul to the highest bidder, whose income, while occupying the post, came from court fees, not from any fixed salary. His position was a privileged one: it was he who appointed the other *qāḍī*s of the country, whose duty it was to transmit to the Sublime Porte a substantial part of the fees they collected.[82] An exception was the office of the *qāḍī* of Alexandria, which was sold by its holder to his successor.[83] To judge by Amīn Sāmī's *Taqwīm al-Nīl*, it appears that during certain periods of Muḥammad ʿAlī's rule, especially in the years of his war against the Sultan, the latter was unable to carry out his right to appoint the *qāḍī* of Cairo. It will be remembered that there were very strong grounds for the assumption that in those years he could not implement his right of *qiṣāṣ* either.

[80] See J. Grandmoulin, *Le Droit pénal égyptien indigène*, Cairo, 1908, pp. 39–41; and, for text of the penal code of 1904, J. A. Wathelet and R. G. Brunton, *Codes égyptiens et lois usuelles en vigeur en Egypte*, Brussels, 1919, 1:542 (Article 7) and 574 (Article 216).

[81] Borg to Lascelles, September 8, 1879, FO 141/129.

[82] See von Kremer, 2:73.

[83] Sāmī, part 3, 1:118.

The first to introduce a change into this system was Saʿīd. In an order to the governor of Alexandria dated 5 Shawwāl, 1271 A.H./July 21, 1855 he proclaimed his intention to buy the office of the Alexandria *qāḍī* on behalf of the state for a period of three years and to appoint a *qāḍī* with a fixed salary, to be chosen by an assembly of Alexandria's notables, *ʿulamāʾ*, and honorable merchants. The salary of the *qāḍī* and the budget of the Alexandria *sharīʿa* court should also be fixed by this assembly. This was done and approved by Saʿīd on September 20 of the same year.[84] Shortly afterward, in February, 1856, Saʿīd reached an agreement with the Sublime Porte, according to which all *qāḍī*s of Egypt, except the *qāḍī* of Cairo, were to be appointed by the Egyptian government and paid a fixed salary. They would be obliged to transmit all fees to the government of Egypt, which undertook to transfer to Istanbul the share of the Sublime Porte.[85]

The *qāḍī* of Cairo, however, was appointed by firman of the Sultan for two more decades. Still, in the early 1870's Ismāʿīl reached an agreement with the Sublime Porte according to which he undertook to pay 250 Ottoman pounds monthly to the person appointed as *qāḍī* of Cairo, who would not occupy his post but remain in Istanbul. Instead, a *nāʾib* (judge substitute) would be chosen by the Khedive and officially appointed by Imperial firman.[86] The terms of this agreement were either changed shortly afterward or simply ignored by Ismāʿīl: all indications point to the latter possibility.[87] On 5 Muḥarram, 1293 A.H./February 1, 1876 he appointed ʿAbd al-Raḥmān Nāfidh as *qāḍī* (not *nāʾib*) of Cairo for a period of five years, reserving the right to extend the appointment after that period. As a matter of fact, Nāfidh remained in office for more than fifteen years. At the same time it was laid down that he should receive a fixed salary from the government, and that in the future a committee of *akābir al-ʿulamāʾ al-afāḍil* should recommend the candidate for office.[88] Article 4 of the new Regulations for Sharīʿa Courts of June 17, 1880 explicitly stated that the *qāḍī*s, including the *qāḍī* of Cairo, were to be appointed by the Khedive.[89]

[84] Sāmī, part 3, 1:118–19, 131.

[85] Sāmī, part 3, 1:154; von Kremer, 2:73; Senior, 2:182.

[86] See discourse by Buṭrus Pasha Ghālī, Egyptian Foreign Minister, *al-Qarārāt waʾl-manshūrāt*, Būlāq, 1899, p. 189. Ghālī does not give the date of the quoted telegram which included the terms of this agreement, nor have I found it in other sources.

[87] There seems to be no record of another agreement with new terms. Ghālī, the Foreign Minister, who would have been only too happy to cite such an agreement in order to prove his case (namely, that it was the Khedive's right to appoint the *qāḍī* of Cairo), merely says: "*walākin al-ẓāhir annahu ṣāra taʿdīluhu. . . .*" See also the report by Ibrāhīm Fu'ād, Minister of Justice (quoted below), who does not mention the existence of another agreement, although he tries to prove the same case.

[88] Sāmī, part 3, 3:1294; Report by Ibrāhīm Fu'ād, Minister of Justice, on the Draft Decree on the Supreme Sharīʿa Court, May 7, 1899, *al-Qarārāt waʾl-manshūrāt*, 1899, p. 180.

[89] For text, see *al-Qarārāt waʾl-maushūrāt*, 1876–80, pp. 260–99.

It was probably no coincidence that the appointment of Nāfidh by the Khedive took place only one year after the promulgation of the Egyptian Penal Code of 1875, by which the Sultan's right of *qiṣāṣ* with regard to murder committed in Egypt was formally abolished.

Apparently the Sublime Porte tacitly relinquished the Sultan's prerogative. No protest against the appointment by the Khedives has become known; on the contrary, from the day Nāfidh was appointed by Ismāʿīl the Ottoman government ceased to issue the yearly firman of appointment to this office. A further sign of the Sultan's tacit resignation is the fact that, while the firman of 1873 to Ismāʿīl by which many of his rights were increased speaks of the "civil and financial administration of the country," the firman of investiture sent to Tawfīq in 1879 puts into his hands the "civil, financial and judiciary administration of the country." Yet the appointment of the *qāḍī* of Cairo is not explicitly mentioned.[90] In order to retain a vestige of the principle, Egypt paid for a "*qāḍī* of Cairo" to remain in Istanbul and continued to do so throughout the nineteenth century.[91] This situation—the adherence in theory to a prerogative which had been abolished long ago in practice—enabled the Muftī of Egypt to raise the question again as late as in 1899, but by then the practice had become so firmly entrenched by precedent that the civil authorities had no difficulty in defeating the Muftī's case.[92]

[90] Cf. texts of firmans as translated in *Recueil de firmans*, pp. 318 and 330.

[91] Ghālī, pp. 187–88.

[92] Ghālī's discourse and Fu'ād's report quoted above were published in connection with this renewed discussion.

8

The Beginnings of Urbanization

Urbanization and modernization are closely connected with each other. Modernization of the rural and urban economy generally starts a movement of part of the population into towns, and as a result of urbanization profound changes occur in the society: old groupings and ties are disrupted and more modern loyalties are created. The greater the relative number of town dwellers, the greater the chances to raise the level of education. The history of urbanization is therefore an important aspect of the history of modernization of any country.

As with so many other questions concerning the social history of modern Egypt, the primary difficulty of the study of urbanization is the lack of reliable data. In table 2 we have assembled all figures for the population of Egyptian towns between the years 1821 and 1907 which we found in sources known to us. We then added up the figures for all towns with more than twenty thousand inhabitants (and for nine important towns for which data relating to the first half of the nineteenth century were available). The changes in the proportion of the town population in the total population, as well as a comparison between the rate of growth of the town population and that of the total population of Egypt, should indicate the extent of urbanization from the beginning of the nineteenth to the beginning of the twentieth century, as well as during each period shown in the table.

The principal defect of table 2 is that the figures for the total population of Egypt cannot possibly be correct, a fact which has been pointed out by

Originally published as "Urbanization in Egypt, 1820–1907," in W. R. Polk and R. L. Chambers (eds.), *The Beginnings of Modernization in the Middle East. The Nineteenth Century* (Chicago: University of Chicago Press, 1968), pp. 155–69.

TABLE 2

TOWNS OF OVER 20,000 INHABITANTS AND SELECTED OTHER IMPORTANT TOWNS

	1821–26	1846	% of 18
Lower Egypt—inland			
Cairo	218,560	256,679	+
Ṭanṭā	10,000	19,500	+
al-Maḥalla al-Kubrā	17,000	20,000	+
Manṣūra	8,500	9,886	+
Damanhūr		8,000	
Zaqāzīq			
Bilqās			
Minūf			
Shibīn al-Kawm		4,500	
Lower Egypt—maritime			
Alexandria	12,528	164,359	+1
Damietta	13,600	37,089	+
Rosetta	13,400	18,300	+
Suez	2,900	4,160	+
Port Said			
Middle Egypt			
Madīnat al-Fayyūm			
Minyā			
Banī Suwayf			
Mallawī			
Upper Egypt			
Asyūṭ	17,000	20,000	+
Akhmīm			
Qenā			
Girgā		7,500	
Aswān			
Nine important towns	304,988	549,973	+
Towns of over 20,000 inhabitants—total	218,560	498, 127	+
% of total population	8.6	11.1	
Total Population	2,536,400	4,476,439	+

SOURCES for 1821 and 1846: A. Boinet, "L'Acroissement de la population en Egypte", *Bulletin de l'Institut E* no. 7 (1886), p. 278 (according to housing censuses carried out under Muḥammad ʿAlī); E. W. Lane, "D Egypt," vol. 1, British Museum Add. MS. 24080, pp. 124–25; A. von Kremer, *Aegypten* (Leipzig, 1863), 2:109

demographers long ago.[1] According to these figures, the average annual rate of increase of Egypt's population was 3.0 per cent between 1821 and

[1] Cf. C. C. Lowis, Director General of the Census Department, in his introduction to *The Census of Egypt Taken in 1907*, Cairo, 1909, pp. 24–25, and other authorities quoted there. (It should be noted that we do not agree with many of the other statements made in this introduction).

% of Growth 1846–82	1897 (Census)	% of Growth 1882–97	1907 (Census)	% of Growth 1897–1907
+ 46.0	570,062	+ 52.0	654,476	+14.8
+ 80.3	57,289	+ 69.7	54,437	− 5.0
+ 39.1	31,100	+ 11.8	33,547	+ 7.9
+172.5	36,131	+ 34.1	40,279	+11.5
+145.1	32,122	+ 63.6	38,752	+20.7
	35,715	+ 80.3	34,999	− 2.0
	19,469		25,473	+30.8
	19,726	+ 21.1	22,316	+14.7
+360.0	20,512	+ 16.2	21,567	+ 5.1
+ 40.8	319,766	+ 38.2	332,247	+ 3.9
− 8.2	31,515	− 7.4	29,354	− 6.9
− 8.9	14,286	− 14.3	16,810	+17.7
+153.5	17,173	+ 62.7	18,347	+ 6.8
	42,095	+157.5	49,884	+18.5
	31,262	+ 21.2	37,320	+19.4
	20,404	+ 28.3	27,221	+33.5
	15,297	+ 51.7	23,357	+52.7
	15,471	+ 43.6	20,249	+31.0
+ 56.8	42,012	+ 33.4	39,442	− 6.1
	27,953	+ 48.7	23,795	−14.9
	24,364	+ 58.2	20,069	−17.7
+ 97.2	17,271	+ 16.5	19,893	+15.2
	13,005		12,618	− 3.0
+ 43.2				
+ 57.7	1,322,302	+ 68.0	1,528,793	+15.6
	13.6		13.7	
+ 52.0	9,717,228	+ 42.7	11,189,978	+15.2

3, British Museum Add. MS. 37450, ff. 199, 247; and vol. 19, Add. MS. 37466, f. 100; M. Gisquet, *L'Egypte, Arabes* (Paris, n.d. [1848], 1:107; 2:217, 222.

1846 and 2.8 per cent between 1882 and 1897. Because of the high mortality rate in nineteenth-century Egypt, population increase was certainly much lower. In order to arrive at a more realistic estimate, we assumed that Egypt's population increased by 22.5 per cent between 1882 and 1897 (an average of 1.5 per cent per annum), by 50 per cent between 1846 and 1882 (1.4 per cent per annum), and by 25 per cent between 1821 and 1846 (1 per cent per annum). Working backward from the 1897 census, the first in Egypt with more or less reliable results, we thus arrived at the estimated population figures shown in table 3. Data for the town population, on the other hand, are probably much more accurate than those for rural areas, an assumption borne out by many indications. We therefore assumed the figures for towns in table 2 to be more or less correct. In order to arrive at comparable figures, we estimated, on the basis of various indications, the population of those of the twenty-three towns specified in the table for which no definite data were available in our sources with regard to the years 1821, 1846, and 1882. The results are shown in table 3.

TABLE 3

REVISED ESTIMATE OF URBAN AND TOTAL POPULATION OF EGYPT, 1821–1907

Total Population of Egypt		Population 23 Towns Specified in Table 2		Percentage of of Increase	
		Absolute Figures	Percent of Total Population	of Total Population	of Urban Population
1821 (est.)	4,230,000	400,000	9.5		
1821–46				25.0	68.7
1846 (est.)	5,290,000	675,000	12.7		
1846–82				50.0	50.4
1882 (est.)	7,930,000	1,015,000	12.8		
1882–97				22.5	43.2
1897 (census)	9,717,228	1,454,000	15.0		
1897–1907				15.2	9.8
1907 (census)	11,190,000	1,596,453	14.3		

Before trying to analyze the general trend of urbanization in Egypt between 1821 and 1907, I think it worthwhile to find out which of Egypt's towns, or which kind of towns, grew or stagnated in each of the different periods, and what were the reasons for growth or stagnation.

Period I: 1821–46

Urbanization in Egypt during the first half of the nineteenth century consisted almost exclusively in the tremendous growth of Alexandria. Before the digging of the Maḥmūdiyya Canal (completed in 1820) Rosetta was the principal harbor of the western Delta serving Egypt's foreign trade; it was this town where European companies maintained their factories. The diversion of the foreign trade to Alexandria, as well as Muḥammad ʿAlī's industrial and maritime enterprises, gave an enormous impetus to Alexandria's growth. Between 1822 and 1838 the number of European firms carrying on business in Alexandria increased from sixteen to forty-four;

between 1833 and 1846–47 the income from the Alexandria customs increased from 6,000 to 54,710 *kīs*.[2] Thus Alexandria developed, during a relatively short time, from a small fishing village to the second largest town in Egypt.

The growth of Alexandria was the main reason, if not the only one, for the great difference between the increase in the population of towns and that of the total population of Egypt during that period. Most of the other important towns increased much more slowly or even experienced a relative decline. Cairo, by far the largest of all, relatively declined at that time, for two reasons. First, during the whole of that period Cairo's commerce suffered severely from the competition of emerging Alexandria, and many people left the old capital for the new port. Secondly, the terrible plague of 1835 wrought havoc among Cairo's population more than anywhere else: the number of victims in this city alone was estimated as between fifty thousand and eighty thousand, more than one-third of the total number of victims in Egypt, and about one-third of Cairo's total population.[3]

The growth of other towns too was impeded by the development of Alexandria. We have mentioned the transfer of foreign trade from Rosetta to Alexandria. Already in the early 1820's, Rosetta was "falling to decay; a great number of the merchants and shop-keepers . . . having removed to Fooweh and other places." In Rosetta there were "long streets of deserted shops," and "many large houses empty and falling to ruin."[4] About twenty years later another observer wrote: "The population [of Rosetta] is so much diminished, that a great proportion of its houses are completely deserted, and falling, if not already fallen, to ruins."[5] Damietta seems to have suffered less because at that time it was the only port of the eastern Delta.[6]

[2]F. Mengin, *Histoire sommaire de l'Egypte sous le gouvernement de Mohammed-Aly*, Paris, 1839, pp. 150–53, 225–26; Murray to Palmerston, inclosure 1 in No. 11, March 17, 1848; PRO, FO 757. (One *kīs* = 500 piastres.)

[3]Mengin, p. 227; E. W. Lane, *The Manners and Customs of the Modern Egyptians*, Everyman's Library, London, 1944, p. 3, n. 1; Campbell to Palmerston, Alexandria, June 25, 1835, FO 78/257.

[4]E. W. Lane, *Description of Egypt*, vol. 1, B.M. MS. Add. 34080, pp. 98–99.

[5]Sir Gardner Wilkinson, *Modern Egypt and Thebes*, London, 1843, 1:194. The figures in table 2 do not concur with these conclusions. The reason seems to be that the figure for 1846, derived from Boinet's article in *BIE*, probably is too high: in 1844 the population of Rosetta was estimated, according to "official documents," at fifteen thousand (see inclosures 7 and 8 in Barnett to Aberdeen, December 12, 1844, FO 78/583). This would mean an increase of only 12 per cent between 1821 and 1844, about half the rate of increase of the total population as assumed by us in table 3 and much less according to the official figures.

[6]The figure for Damietta's population in table 2 is that given in Boinet's article in *BIE*. Other sources have considerably lower figures: according to the British Consul at Damietta, the result of the 1846 census for Damietta was 29,848 (Surur to Murray, Damietta, May 30, 1847, FO 141/13). Cf. Wilkinson, 1:452–53. Still, there remains a discrepancy between the figures and the descriptions.

Yet the influence of Alexandria's growth was felt even there: "Damietta . . . once famous as the principal emporium on this side of the Delta, has sunk in importance, in proportion as Alexandria has increased, and now only carries on a little commerce with Greece and Syria."[7]

A further reason for the relative decline of some of the smaller towns was Muḥammad ʿAlī's fiscal policy. In Manṣūra, for instance, the weaving industry was ruined, the weavers became destitute, and the houses were deserted because of the government monopoly introduced by Muḥammad ʿAlī.[8] Similar factors probably caused the relative decline of such towns as al-Maḥalla al-Kubrā and Asyūṭ during that period. The very small absolute increase in the population of Suez was mainly the result of lack of drinking water, which was brought to Suez, until the 1860's, by beduins in water skins or by train from Cairo. Were it not for this reason, Suez probably would have grown considerably because of the overland route to India established during the rule of Muḥammad ʿAlī.[9]

Period II: 1846–82

During the third quarter of the nineteenth century, towns did not grow faster than the total population of Egypt. This is clearly shown by the figures in table 2 as well as by the revised estimate in table 3. There were two main reasons for the lack of significant urbanization during this period. First, this was a period of tremendous agricultural development, but there was no parallel growth of specifically urban branches of the economy, such as industry. The towns that expanded most at that time were relatively small mercantile centers of agricultural areas. Secondly, the digging of the Suez Canal in the 1860's brought about, on the one hand, the growth of Suez and the creation of Port Said, but, on the other hand, it severely hit not only other maritime towns but also Cairo, the traditional center of the overland transit trade.

Mercantile centers of agricultural areas which grew considerably during this period were Ṭanṭā, Manṣūra, Damanhūr, and the newly created town of Zaqāzīq. Ṭanṭā became the principle market of a large area of cotton plantations. The area of the town itself grew from 73 feddan in 1854–55 to 180 feddan in 1875, mainly by making *waqf* land available for *ḥikr*, permission for which was given at the time of Ismāʿīl's rule. In 1856 Ṭanṭā was connected to the railway network. The number of visitors to the annual fair, the *mawlid al-Sayyid al-Badawī*, was estimated in the 1860's and 1870's

[7] Wilkinson, 1:452–53. Cf. Mengin, p. 228; Hekekyan Papers, vol. 3, B.M., Add. 37450, f. 220.

[8] Hekekyan Papers, vol. 3, B.M., Add. 37450, f. 173a (Persian text, written in 1846).

[9] A. von Kremer, *Aegypten*, Leipzig, 1863, 2:173–74.

at half a million, as against from 100,000 to 150,000 in the first half of the century. Finally, Ṭanṭā became the capital of Gharbiyya province, a position occupied in the days of Muḥammad ʿAlī by al-Maḥalla al-Ḳubrā. This was certainly one reason for the further relative decline of al-Maḥalla at that time (another reason being the stagnation or even decline of its industries).[10]

Manṣūra too profited by the railway connection which was established in 1865.[11] "Seit die Eisenbahn regelmässige Fahrten bis Sammanut macht ist es [Mansura] zugleich der Centralpunkt für die Handelsoperationen der umliegenden Provinzen geworden." In the 1860's the sales of cotton, wool, flax, fruit, rice and oilseed in Manṣūra amounted to about a quarter of the yield of Lower Egypt.[12] As a result of these developments foreign merchants settled in Manṣūra and it became the seat of a Mixed Court; moreover, Manṣūra was the first town in Egypt, except Alexandria and Cairo, in which a municipal commission was established (in 1881).[13]

Like Ṭanṭā in Gharbiyya province and Manṣūra in Daqahliyya, Damanhūr became an agricultural center in Buḥayra. Its development may be demonstrated by a comparison between descriptions of the 1840's and and 1850's, stressing the misery of its houses and their inhabitants, and those of the 1870's and 1880's, which specially mentioned its fine buildings and the three fairs annually held at this place.[14] Shibīn al-Kawm, which had become the capital of Minūfiyya instead of Minūf at the time of Muḥammad ʿAlī, remained a center of weaving; in 1866 it was connected to the railway system.[15]

The most impressive development, however, was that of Zaqāzīq, which, after having been founded by Muḥammad ʿAlī in 1836–37,[16] soon became the capital of Sharqiyya province, comprising all administrative institutions of a provincial capital. It grew out of a small group of huts erected by workers brought there to build irrigation works on the Baḥr Muways Canal. Later, beduin shaykhs, notables from neighboring villages, and numerous Christians and foreigners settled at this place (the percentage of

[10] Von Kremer, 2:221; Mubārak, 13:46; Muḥammad Amīn Fikrī, *Jughrāfiyyat Miṣr*, Cairo, 1879, p. 53.

[11] Amīn Sāmī, *Taqwīm al-Nīl*, part 3, vol. 2, Cairo, 1936, p. 642.

[12] Von Kremer, 2:219.

[13] *Majmūʿat al-awāmir al-ʿaliyya wa'l-dakrītāt*, Cairo, 1881, pp. 104–5, and see chapter 11, below.

[14] Cf. M. Gisquet, *L'Egypte, les Turcs et les Arabes*, Paris, n.d. [1848], 1:107; von Kremer, 2:241; Mubārak, 11:23 (especially lines 16–17); H. Stephan, *Das heutige Aegypten*, Leipzig, 1872, p. 421.

[15] Mubārak, 12:147; Hekekyan Papers, vol. 3, B.M., Add. 37450, f. 199; Sāmī, part 3, 2:694; Fikrī, pp. 73–74.

[16] Cf. Sāmī, part 2, Cairo, 1928, p. 465.

Christians in Zaqāzīq remained for a long time higher than in Egypt as a whole). The foreigners established cotton gins and other workshops, and the place became an important center of the cotton trade. In the early 1860's the railway connection was established.[17]

However, it should be pointed out that, though all these mercantile centers of agricultural areas experienced a great relative expansion, the absolute number of their population remained quite low: none of them exceeded thirty-five thousand, and most of them kept in the neighborhood of twenty thousand. Therefore, their growth had little influence on the rate of urbanization in Egypt as a whole.

The most important development among maritime towns was the founding of Port Said in 1859. By 1869, when the Suez Canal was opened, its population had grown to about eight thousand, and during the next thirteen years it had doubled. Suez too profited by the digging of the canal. There was an influx of foreigners into the town, commercial agencies were established, and a brisk building activity was going on.[18] In 1857 the railway connection with Cairo was established; in 1864 the canal supplying Suez with sweet water was completed; and by 1869 a company with a concession for distribution of fresh water had established its works.[19] Another reason for the growth of Suez was the diversion of the *ḥajj*, the pilgrimage to Mecca, from Quṣayr to Suez: a definite order to this effect was issued by Saʿīd in 1859, and in 1861 the *maḥmal* (litter) passed through Suez for the first time after a long interval.[20] However, after the Canal had been opened, this development seems to have come to an end. By 1871 the population of Suez had already increased to 13,625[21] and the figure for 1882 on table 2, if it is correct, expresses a decline of Suez during the 1870's. In fact there are some indications that such a decline set in. With the opening of the Canal the works connected with its building stopped and many of the European shopkeepers and artisans seem to have left the town. In addition, as a result of the suppression of the slave trade, Suez lost a lucrative branch of its economy.[22]

[17] For a detailed description of Zaqāzīq's development, see Mubārak, 11:93–94. Cf. also Wallis to Vivian, Cairo, March 29, 1877, FO 141/110.

[18] Mubārak, 12:75, 93–94.

[19] Von Kremer, 2:243; H. de Vaujany, *Alexandrie et la basse Egypte*, Paris, 1885, p. 242; Consul West, Suez, 1872, *Commercial Reports*, 1873, 64:238, 244.

[20] Sāmī, part 3, 1:329–30; von Kremer, 2:194–95, 208.

[21] E. de Régny, *Statistique de l'Egypte*, 3ᵉ Année, 1872, Alexandria, 1872, p. 132. Estimates for the late 1860's were as high as sixteen thousand.

[22] Consul West, pp. 239, 267–68; West to Clarendon, Suez, September 25, 1869, FO 84/1305.

The digging of the Suez Canal granted Damietta a respite of three years in the early 1860's, when the offices of the company had been located in that town;[23] afterward its decline continued, even in the absolute number of inhabitants, the main reason being the competition of Alexandria and the ruin of the traditional handicrafts.[24] Rosetta too declined in absolute numbers and for the same reason; by the 1860's its harbor was used merely by fishing boats, and in 1870 a grand total of five sailing vessels with a combined tonnage of 72.5 entered it.[25]

The opening of the Canal had, however, another much more decisive influence on urban development in Egypt. After the Alexandria-Cairo-Suez railway had been completed in the years 1856–58, Cairo's position as a center of the trade with the East, as well as Alexandria's prosperity, had experienced an enormous rise. The opening of the Canal put an end to this development, since, from then on, the overland transit route was superseded by the maritime way.[26] Throughout the 1870's British consuls, in their commercial reports, complained about the decline in the commerce of Cairo because trade took the route of the Canal.[27] Alexandria probably suffered less since Egypt's imports and exports increased during that time and Alexandria's share in Egyptian foreign trade rose in relation to that of other ports. In any case, if we are to believe the population figures for 1871 published by Régny[28] (Cairo, 353,851; Alexandria, 219,602), the annual growth of these two largest towns of Egypt averaged 1.5 per cent between the years 1846 and 1871 (probably a little more than the total population), but only 0.5 per cent between the years 1871 and 1882 (certainly less than the total population).

Concerning the development of Upper Egyptian towns during this period, we have data only for Asyūṭ and Girgā. Those for Girgā are doubtful: it may well be that the estimate for 1846 was too low.[29] True, in Ismāʿīl's days works were undertaken to prevent the inundation of Girgā by the Nile flood, which may have helped its progress, but, on the other hand, Girgā

[23]Le Docteur Stacquez, *L'Egypte, la basse Nubie et le Sinai*, Liège, 1865, pp. 265–66; de Vaujany, p. 204.

[24]Cf. von Kremer, 1:167; 2:166.

[25]Consul Stanley, Alexandria, 1866, *Commercial Reports*, 1867, 67:607; Régny, 2e Année, 1871, Alexandria, 1871, pp. 20–38. Cf. also de Vaujany, p. 211.

[26]Cf. A. von Fircks, *Aegypten 1894*, Berlin, 1895, 2:197–98.

[27]See, for instance, Consul Rogers, Cairo, 1872, *Commercial Reports*, 1873, 64:217; Consul Cookson, Alexandria, 1879, *Commercial Reports*, 1880, 73:559; etc. However, if figures for Cairo's population in 1882 published later are correct, the rate of increase during the period 1846–82 would be higher (see below, table 4). Perhaps even at that time Cairo's position as the capital made up for the loss of its overland trade.

[28]See note 21.

[29]It is based on Gisquet, 2:222.

certainly was reversely affected by the transfer of the provincial capital to nearby Sūhāg by Saʿīd and by the diversion of the *ḥajj* from Upper Egypt to Suez.[30] As against this, the figures for Asyūṭ probably express a real increase in its population at a higher rate than general population increase. The definite impression gained by all visitors to Asyūṭ during the whole of this period was one of a flourishing and prosperous town. The principal source of its prosperity was trade with the Sudan, including the slave trade (even as late as 1880). From the 1850's onward an extensive building activity went on, and the railway line which reached Asyūṭ in 1874 gave the development of the town a further impetus. Many people from other places in Upper Egypt settled there, and especially in times of famine fellahs from its vicinity flocked into it.[31] Nevertheless, one should not forget that by 1882 the number of its inhabitants barely exceeded thirty thousand.

Period III: 1882–97

In contrast with the third quarter of the nineteenth century, figures for the years 1882 to 1897, in both table 2 and table 3, show a significant difference between the growth of towns and the rate of increase of the total population as well as a considerable rise in the percentage of urban population in Egypt. There seems to be no doubt that at that time there was a notable movement from country to town.

By far the most important part of this movement was the growth of Cairo. While Cairo's population increased by 52 per cent in the course of fifteen years, all other towns together grew by 38 per cent. Cairo's share in the increase of the urban population was 44.4 per cent, while its inhabitants amounted, in 1882, to 37 per cent of the urban population. The average annual increase of Cairo's population during this period was 3.5 per cent as against 0.7 per cent in Period I, 1.3 per cent in Period II, and 1.5 per cent in Period IV.

The reasons for this trend are at all not obvious. The detrimental effect of the opening of the Suez Canal on Cairo's position as a center of trade between East and West probably continued to be felt; moreover, the revolt of the Mahdi and the resulting disruption of the Sudanese trade must have further hit Cairo's commerce. In addition, by the end of the century many branches of local crafts which had flourished in former times had declined and succumbed to European competition,[32] and no modern industry had

[30] Cf. Mubārak, 10:53; Fikrī, pp. 150–52; and see above.

[31] See Mubārak, 12:103; Fikrī, pp. 133–34; von Kremer, 2:223–24; Stacquez, pp. 135–36; Samī, part 3, 3:1201; Report by Mr. Beaman on the state of the Nile villages, Cairo, March 15, 1879, FO 141/131; etc.

[32] Cf. G. Baer, *Egyptian Guilds in Modern Times*, Jerusalem, 1964, p. 138, and sources mentioned there. See also chapter 9, below.

been established to take their place at that time. Nor can the growth of Cairo be explained by the immigration of foreigners: if we deduct their number, the rate of growth remains about the same (the main influx of foreigners into Cairo occurred in the following decade; see below). In fact, if figures published later are correct, the growth of Cairo may have been slower than shown in table 2.

Table 4

Population of Cairo and Alexandria, 1882–1907

	Cairo	Alexandria
1882	398,683	232,636
% 1882–97	47.9	35.8
1897	589,573	315,844
% 1897–1907	15.1	12.0
1907	678,433	353,807

Source: *Population Census of Egypt, 1927* (Cairo, 1931), p. 28.

There seems to be only one explanation for the relative growth of Cairo at that time: its development as the center of the new administration established after the British occupation of Egypt. The growing administrative machinery was in need of numerous services, which attracted rural immigrants into Cairo from nearby villages as well as from distant Upper Egypt. Thus the number of officials, servants, building and transport workers, petty traders, and members of similar occupations rose considerably. Moreover, so far as official initiative was concerned, building and other development activities were concentrated mainly in Cairo. In 1891 Lord Cromer wrote in his annual report: "I conceive that there is already a tendency . . . to devote an undue proportion of the money available to the improvement of the capital, to the detriment of the provincial towns, whose interest, though equally deserving, are brought somewhat less prominently to the notice of the Government."[33] Private initiative, no doubt, tended even more to concentrate its activities in the capital.

The mercantile centers of the Delta—Ṭanṭā, Damanhūr, Zaqāzīq, and, to a much smaller extent, Manṣūra—continued to expand at a higher rate than the total population or even than the average increase of the urban population as a whole. Among the coastal towns, Port Said continued to grow fast and Alexandria seems to have had recovered from the first shock of the opening of the Canal, while Damietta and Rosetta more and more lost the position they had occupied at the beginning of the century. Suez

[33] *Report on the Administration and Condition of Egypt and the Progress of Reforms, March 29, 1891*, Egypt No. 3 (1891), C. 6321, p. 33.

grew again because it served as a coaling station for ships from the East which did not pass through the Canal. As to Middle and Upper Egypt, one should note the relative growth of two towns: Banī Suwayf, which became an important administrative center and the place where the most important annual fair south of Cairo was held; and Qenā, a town with a flourishing traditional industry (pottery and baskets) and a commercial center of an extensive agricultural area, which was described as a prosperous town as late as the 1880's.[34]

Period IV: 1897–1907

The first decade of the twentieth century was the only period in modern Egyptian history during which the twenty-three Egyptian towns listed in table 2 grew to a smaller extent than Egypt's total population, and therefore the proportion of the number of their inhabitants in the total population declined. (The slightly higher rate of increase of the population of towns with more than twenty thousand inhabitants, as shown in table 2, is merely the result of the fact that four towns passed the twenty-thousand limit during that period and therefore their populations were not included in the figure of 1897.)

This lack of urbanization, or even deurbanization, was probably caused by the same factor which retarded urbanization during the third quarter of the nineteenth century (Period II): a tremendous development of agriculture, which in the first years of our century grew into a veritable boom, together with a simultaneous lack of industrial development. Various other reasons too contributed to the considerable relative decline, or even the absolute, in the population of some towns. As in Period II, the towns that expanded significantly were a few small provincial towns which profited by their situation in areas specifically favored by the agricultural development of that time.

In Lower Egypt, such agricultural centers were Damanhūr and Bilqās, situated in Buḥayra and northern Gharbiyya, respectively; the latter was an area which at that time was brought into the orbit of agricultural expansion, while in the former development was intensified. All other towns in Lower Egypt declined either relatively or even in absolute numbers of inhabitants.

Cairo would have grown less than indicated by the figures in table 2 and table 4 were it not for the considerable influx of foreigners: the number of Ottoman subjects (Syrians, Armenians, and others), Greeks, and Italians in Cairo doubled between 1897 and 1907 (from 31,543 to 62,005). In fact,

[34] *Majmūʿat al-qarārāt waʾl-manshūrāt*, Cairo, 1889, pp. 551–52; von Fircks, 2:220; Mubārak, 14:121.

"it is believed that in portions of many urban areas the native residents have actually been replaced by foreigners. . . . The result has been to actually drive a portion of the indigenous community, not to other quarters of the same town, but altogether out of the urban area."[35] Ṭanṭā seems to have suffered by the decline in the importance of its *mawlid* (fair) as a result of the suppression of the slave trade and the development of communications and thereby other channels of commerce. In most of the years under review the *mawlid* was not held at all, for sanitary and other reasons;[36] and "apart from its fairs and markets, [the trade of Tanta] is comparatively small."[37]

Among the maritime towns of Lower Egypt, Port Said maintained its position as the one with the highest rate of increase, a rate higher than that of the total population. By 1907 there lived in Port Said a greater proportion of people born elsewhere than in any other Egyptian town—29,756 out of 49,884, that is, 59.5 per cent. Among them, 8,804 were born in Damietta, which explains the continuous decline of that town. Many came from Upper Egypt, especially Luxor and other places in Qenā province.[38] All other coastal towns declined either relatively or in absolute numbers—except Rosetta, for whose revival we have not found any other indication or explanation, but in any case the absolute number of inhabitants involved was extremely small. The rate of increase of Alexandria's population may perhaps not have been as low as 3.9 per cent (as in table 2); according to later figures (see table 4), it was 12.0 per cent. But even this latter figure is lower than the rate of increase of the total population, and there can be no doubt that Alexandria's growth had slowed down considerably.

> Der Handel hat nicht mehr die Lebhaftigkeit von früher. . . . Zudem ist Alexandrien von der Konkurrenz Port Saids bedroht. Sobald eine direkte Eisenbahnverbindung zwischen Port Said und Kairo hergestellt sein wird . . . muss Alexandrien einen bedeutenden Teil seiner kommerziellen Wichtigkeit verlieren.[39]

This direct railway connection between Port Said and Cairo was established in the early years of our century. But even more than Alexandria, it hit the development of Suez.[40] Local trade declined to such a degree that people began to leave the town for the villages of the interior, and the government

[35] Lowis, p. 28.

[36] See A. Cunningham, *Today in Egypt*, London, 1912, p. 226.

[37] A. Wright and H. A. Cartwright, *Twentieth Century Impressions of Egypt*, London, 1909, p. 477.

[38] For a description of this migration from Luxor to Port Said, see G. Legrain, *Fellah de Karnak*, Paris, 1902, pp. 317–18.

[39] T. Neumann, *Das moderne Ägypten*, Leipzig, 1893, p. 236.

[40] Wright and Cartwright, p. 474.

even granted the inhabitants of Suez agricultural land for cultivation.[41]

The most conspicuous phenomenon of this period is the extraordinary expansion of the Middle Egyptian towns, which had never before reached comparable proportions. As a result of the changeover from basin to perennial irrigation made possible by the completion of the Aswān Dam in 1902, the increase in privately owned land, the growth of large estates, and agricultural development in Middle Egypt in general reached a peak at the beginning of our century.[42] Middle Egyptian towns, particularly Minyā and Banī Suwayf, served as administrative and commercial centers of this development and attracted immigrants from other parts of Egypt, especially from Upper Egypt.

The decline of the towns of Upper Egypt during this period was indeed almost general; in most of them even the absolute number of inhabitants decreased. In Asyūṭ, the largest town of Upper Egypt, a relative decline had already set in, mainly as a result of the loss of the Sudanese trade at the time of the Mahdi revolt and the suppression of the slave trade, an important branch of Asyūṭ's economy. At the beginning of our century there followed the almost complete ruin of Asyūṭ's traditional industries, especially weaving and the manufacture of red leather, as the result of the competition of European goods.[43] Similar conditions affected Akhmīm and Qenā. Aswān's decline may have been the result of the completion of the dam in 1902 and the consequent move of workers and their families to Isnā, where the new barrage was being built (completed in 1909). In fact, Isnā (which is not included in table 2) grew during this decade from 13,564 to 19,102 inhabitants, that is, by 40.8 per cent, more than any other town in Egypt except Banī Suwayf.

Conclusion

As we have said, the primary difficulty of the study of urbanization in nineteenth-century Egypt is the lack of reliable data, and it should be stressed again that we do not claim that the figures in tables 2, 3, and 4 are accurate. Nevertheless, it would be wrong to dismiss them as useless. We contend that we have shown that in the overwhelming majority of cases they express trends which may be corroborated by other contemporary evidence. It remains to summarise these trends of urban development during the century in which Egypt began to modernize.

[41] Cf. Baer, p. 141, and sources mentioned there.

[42] Cf. G. Baer, *A History of Landownership in Modern Egypt, 1800–1950*, London, 1962, pp. 93–94, 226, and sources mentioned there.

[43] See chapter 9, below.

Between the years 1821 and 1907 the number of towns in Egypt with more than twenty thousand inhabitants increased from one to nineteen (and a few others came very near this limit). Their inhabitants constituted, according to official figures, 8.6 per cent of the total population at the beginning of this period and 13.7 per cent at its end. The picture emerging from our revised estimate is not very different: the population of the twenty-three towns listed in table 2 grew from 9.5 per cent of the total population to 14.3 per cent. The conclusion to be drawn from these figures is that there was some urbanization in Egypt before World War I, but that the result was scanty indeed.

Obviously the main reason for the small extent of urbanization in Egypt before World War I was the lack of modern industrial development.[44] Yet at the same time traditional industries succumbed to European competition, the traditional trade with the Sudan, especially the slave trade, was suppressed and cut off, and the overland route of trade between Europe and Asia, which flourished during the third quarter of the nineteenth century, was superseded by the Suez Canal.

Under these conditions, intensive agricultural development generally slowed down the development of Egypt's main towns. This was the case in Periods II and IV. True, it contributed to the growth of mercantile centers of agricultural areas: Ṭanṭā, Manṣūra, Damanhūr in Lower Egypt (Period II), Damanhūr and Bilqās in the northern Delta and the towns of Middle Egypt (Period IV). But these were only relatively small towns, whose growth did not make up for the stagnation or relative decline of other towns. Moreover, the relative increase of the population of these centers was only temporary; it was preceded and followed by periods of stagnation or relative decline.

It was indeed the two periods of slower agricultural development, Periods I and III, during which the proportion of the urban population grew to a notable extent. In each of these two periods one of Egypt's two largest towns, its capital and administrative center and its principal port, experienced its great leap forward. One may indeed say that urbanization in Egypt before World War I was the story of the growth of Cairo and Alexandria. Since the population of Cairo and Alexandria together constituted during the whole period about 60 per cent of the inhabitants of the twenty-three towns listed in table 2, this is not astonishing. In fact, no other large town emerged before World War I, the largest (Ṭanṭā) having grown to little more than fifty thousand inhabitants.

[44] For a short analysis of the reasons for the lack of industrial development in Egypt before World War I, see Baer, *Egyptian Guilds*, pp. 136–37.

Even these two large towns sometimes grew one at the expense of the other (e.g., Alexandria at the expense of Cairo in Period I). The same happened with regard to most other towns too. Al-Maḥalla al-Kubrā lost its position to Ṭanṭā, the maritime towns were first overshadowed by Alexandria and later by Port Said, Aswān was superseded by Isnā, and so on. This was a further reason why even extraordinary growth, in certain periods, of Cairo and Alexandria and also of smaller towns, had so little influence on the general process of urbanization before World War I.

9

Decline and Disappearance of the Guilds

In earlier parts of this work we have analyzed the dissolution of the traditional social units of the beduins and the rural population—the tribe and the village community, respectively. A parallel development took place with regard to the most important unit in which the urban population was organized, the guilds.[1] It may perhaps be said that "modernization" was the common factor which brought about this parallel development in all the three environments of the Egyptian population. However, this common factor expressed itself in a different way in each of the three spheres. The most important factor in the disruption of the tribe was the socio-economic differentiation among its members as a result of the development of agriculture which led to sedentarization; the village community dissolved mainly because of the transition from basin irrigation to perennial irrigation and from a subsistence economy to the production of cash crops, accompanied by the development of full private property in land; and the urban guild disappeared as a result of the influx of European goods and of Europeans settling in Egypt, the change of its commercial system, the growth of its towns, and the reorganization of its administration.

It has been the assumption of most writers who touched on this subject that the creation of a large industry by Muḥammad ʿAlī was responsible for the guilds' decline or even for their disappearance. By completely transforming the way of production, so they said, he did away with all restrictions

Originally "Egyptian Guilds in Modern Times," paper submitted to the 26th International Congress of Orientalists, New Delhi, January 4–10, 1964. (Here modified, with substantial additions of text and references.)

[1] On the historical background of Egyptian guilds, their number, organization, structure, and functions, see G. Baer, *Egyptian Guilds in Modern Times*, Jerusalem, 1964.

on industrial liberty, and the craft guilds were suppressed. The masters and artisans became wage earners, and the organization of corporations disappeared. Muḥammad ʿAlī's industry had the same influence on the Egyptian corporative system as Colbertism had on that of France, the main difference being that the change was abrupt in Egypt while in Europe it developed gradually. We find this theory, for the first time, in Germain Martin's book *Les bazars du Caire* published in 1910, and since then in many books and articles, among them a very recent one published in *Studia Islamica*. In none of these books and articles is this assumption based on serious research into the matter.[2]

The obvious proof of the fallacy of this theory is the fact that until the 1880's a ramified system of guilds existed in Cairo and in many other towns of Egypt, comprising almost the whole indigenous gainfully occupied population. Details about the number of these guilds and of their members, their organization according to locality, community, and sex, their social and administrative classification, their internal structure, and their administrative, economic, and social functions, are found in a large variety of sources. Most important among these sources are, first, the collections of official decrees and instructions issued by government departments, such as Amīn Sāmī's *Taqwīm al-Nīl* and a collection of more than thirty volumes called *Majmūʿat al-qarārāt wa'l-manshūrāt* and *Majmūʿat al-awāmir al-ʿaliyya wa'l-dakrītāt*. Another group of important sources consists of the documents at the Public Record Office in London; it includes the correspondence between the British consuls in Egypt and the Foreign Office and the British consular archives of Cairo and other towns. In the latter we have found, for instance, a long and detailed account of the Cairo guilds and another of those of Suez, both written in 1870.[3]

These and other sources prove beyond doubt not only that the guilds existed in the second half of the nineteenth century but also that they fulfilled important public functions. Thus throughout the century the shaykhs of the guilds controlled and supervised the guilds' members' activities and ensured that the instructions of the government were carried out; they were made responsible for misdemeanor of their guilds' members; they supplied

[2]Germain Martin, *Les Bazars du Caire et les petits metiers arabes*, Cairo–Paris, 1910; N. Tomiche, "La Situation des artisans et petits commerçants en Egypte de la fin du XVIIIe siècle jusqu'au milieu du XIXe," *Studia Islamica*, 12 (1960). For other protagonists of this theory, see Baer, *Egyptian Guilds*, pp. 127–30, and the discussion in *Middle Eastern Studies*, 2, no. 3, (April, 1966):272–76, and 3, no. 1, (October, 1966):106–7.

[3]Raphael Borg, "Report upon the Native Guilds, and on the Work, Wages and Cost of Living of Working Classes at Cairo," in Borg to Stanton, No. 47, Cairo, October 14, 1870, Arch. No. 495, FO 141/73; Report by Consul West to Col. Stanton, No. 35, Suez, July 13, 1870, FO 141/72.

labour and service to the government and private employers; and they arbitrated disputes among the members of the guilds. Until the last quarter of the century the shaykhs were responsible for the payment of taxes by the guilds' members, collected these taxes, and their advice was sought with regard to the assessment of the taxes to be paid by the guilds; until 1880 they fixed maximum wages for the guilds' members; and until the late 1860's they assisted the authorities in fixing prices of comestibles. It was the function of the guilds to restrict the number of persons exercising a certain trade, and in many occupations the guilds kept a monopoly of their trades until the last decades of the nineteenth century.[4]

The question arises, therefore, how it happened that the establishment of a large industry employing wage earners by Muḥammad ʿAlī did not do away with the old guild system. The answer seems to us to be obvious. First of all, the number of the guilds' members remained by far greater than that of workers engaged in the factory system. Moreover, most of the large industry of Muḥammad ʿAlī consisted of new branches of production which had not existed previously in Egypt and therefore did not compete with the crafts exercised by the members of the guilds. In some cases artisans were recruited for work in the new factories, but apparently not so many that the guilds incurred fatal losses; many artisans of the bazaars had to be rejected because of their working habits, even when they applied for being accepted into the factories. (This, at least, is what we are told by an anonymous contemporary who published in 1838 an excellent account of Egyptian guilds in the German journal *Das Ausland.*)[5] Even the builders' guilds, which suffered severely from frequent recruitment for government works, emerged intact and became one of the groups of guilds best known and most often described in sources of the second half of the century.

There was one possible exception: the weavers' guild. In Jabartī's chronicle and in other sources we find evidence that this guild was abolished by Muḥammad ʿAlī, who monopolized the weaving industry.[6] Nevertheless, in his geographical and biographical encyclopedia *al-Khiṭaṭ al-tawfīqiyya*, ʿAlī Pasha Mubārak lists a guild of weavers in Cairo in the 1870's, with a membership of 585.[7] It may well be that the case of this branch induced many authors to generalize about the effect of Muḥammad ʿAlī's industry on the guilds.

[4] For details and documentation, see Baer, *Egyptian Guilds*, pp. 77–112.

[5] Anon., "Aegyptens industrielle Corporationen," *Das Ausland* (Stuttgart-Tübingen) 11, nos. 121 and 122 (May 1–2, 1838): 486.

[6] Jabartī, 4:257; Sāmī, part 2, p. 290; *Lāʾiḥat zirāʿat al-fallāḥ*, Cairo–Būlāq, 1829–30, pp. 44, 49–50.

[7] Mubārak, 1:99.

A further important reason for the fallacy of these generalizations is the fact that, in Egypt of the eighteenth and the nineteenth centuries, artisan guilds never amounted to more than half the total number of guilds; the number of their members was about a third of the total membership of guilds, the remainder being made up by merchant guilds and guilds of persons engaged in transport and services. (These figures are based on three complete lists of guilds, one each for Cairo, Alexandria, and Suez.)[8] Therefore, the establishment of Muḥammad ʿAlī's industries could not have affected the overwhelming majority of the guilds' members.

Finally, Muḥammad ʿAlī's industrial experiment was too short-lived to bring about a transformation of urban society, as it did not last longer than ten years. That he did not suppress the guilds administratively is borne out by contemporary evidence.[9] Nor were they suppressed by Muḥammad ʿAlī's heirs. Until the last quarter of the nineteenth century the government was unable to replace them by a new administrative system and was therefore forced to keep them intact. Moreover, in many cases new administrative functions were added to the old ones of the guilds' shaykhs. In 1867, for instance, the shaykh of the Cairo slave dealers (*shaykh al-yasīrjiyya*) was charged by the government with lodging and feeding liberated slaves; in 1891 the Ministry of Public Works issued an order to the shaykh of the Alexandria boatmen to assign night duties and to organize the queue of boats for transporting passengers from the ships to the shore; and as late as in 1896 the shaykhs of the fishermen and boatmen at Lake Manzala were ordered to assist in making an inventory (*jard*) and a numeration (*tanmīr*) of the boats in that area.[10] These are only some examples out of many.

Furthermore, since the guild system survived and fulfilled important functions, new occupations which emerged in the course of the nineteenth century were incorporated in it. A guild of domestic servants, for instance, did not exist at the time of the French occupation but was formed in the days of Muḥammad ʿAlī; when Port Said was founded, the coal heavers at that town organized as a guild; in 1873 the Egyptian government established a guild of pilots in Alexandria; and as late as in 1900 the guides at the Pyramids were incorporated as a guild by government order.[11]

[8] A. Raymond, "Une Liste des corporations de métiers au Caire en 1801," *Arabica*, 4, fasc. 2, (1957):154–62; E. Régny, *Statistique de l'Egypte*, Alexandria, 1870, pp. 69–72; Mubārak, 12:95.

[9] Cf., e.g., *Das Ausland*, p. 481: "Mehemet ʿAli war zu klug, um diesen Zustand der Dinge nicht erhalten zu wollen."

[10] Cherif Pacha to Reade, Alexandria, August 18, 1867, FO 84/1277 (not Reade to Charif, as in Baer, *Egyptian Guilds*, p. 134, n. 24); *al-Qarārāt wa'l-manshūrāt*, 1891, pp. 139–40 (Articles 6 and 11); 1896, p. 518 (Article 4).

[11] For details and documentation, see Baer, *Egyptian Guilds*, pp. 135–36.

The interest of the government in maintaining the guild system was not the only reason for its long survival. Not less important was the fact that the guilds did not disintegrate as a result of class struggle among the various strata of its members. There was no rigid system of apprenticeship, no clear cut distinction between apprentice and journeyman, and it was relatively easy for an apprentice or a journeyman to become master. No associations of journeymen evolved in Egypt, and no sharp economic or social differentiation developed between the guilds' masters and the shaykhs, whose economic and social position did not rise much above that of other members of the guilds, but rather depended upon the position of the guild as a whole.[12] With one or two exceptions, shaykhs did not become contractors, and no such transformation occurred in artisan guilds.[13] This was mainly due to the fact that, after the failure of Muḥammad ʿAlī's industrial experiment, no serious industrial development took place in Egypt for decades.[14] Therefore, the emergence of new kinds of economic organization, which perhaps would have superseded the traditional guilds if it had occurred, was delayed for a long time. Indigenous merchants did not form chambers of commerce and industry before the second decade of the twentieth century. The first labor trade union was established in 1899, and by 1911 there were no more than eleven unions, some of them with exclusively foreign membership.

Thus Egyptian guilds were neither suppressed by law nor did they disintegrate as a result of internal differentiation, nor were they superseded by the emergence of a modern industrial society. Their decline and disappearance were mainly the result of the impact of Europe: of the influx of European goods and of Europeans settling in Egypt. This process took place during the second half of the nineteenth century. By the end of the century many branches of Cairo's local crafts had succumbed to European competition, such as the production of copper vessels, work in ivory, engraving in wood or metal, indigo dyeing, and so on.[15] Asyūṭ's weaving industry declined to such an extent on account of competition with European fabrics that by 1910 no more than seventy looms were left, while only a few years earlier their number had amounted to three hundred. In the 1870's the manufacture of red leather in that town employed more than three thousand men, but by 1909 there remained no more than twelve shops in this

[12] Baer, *Egyptian Guilds*, pp. 57–76.

[13] Baer, *Egyptian Guilds*, pp. 97–100.

[14] See chapter 12, below.

[15] A Métin, *La Transformation de l'Egypte*, Paris, 1903, pp. 247, 292; A. Wright and H. A. Cartwright, *Twentieth Century Impressions of Egypt*, London, 1909, p. 230; al-Ḥukūma al-Miṣriyya, *Taqrīr lajnat al-tijāra waʾl-ṣināʿa*, Cairo, 1919, pp. 133–34.

branch.[16] The same story has been told about other centers of traditional crafts, such as Damietta, Suez, and Banī Suwayf.

Merchant guilds were equally hit by a complete change of Egypt's commercial system at that time. On the one hand, the traditional organization of the *sūq* gradually dissolved, retail trade spreading all over the town and foreigners infiltrating into branches which previously had been monopolized by Egyptian merchants. Thus the control of the guilds' shaykhs was made impossible. The following account of this process, written in 1870 by Consul West with regard to Suez, seems to have given a typical example of what happened in most Egyptian towns:

> The butchers have also become disseminated about the town since the trade has been engaged in by Europeans. A few native butchers still congregate near together and constitute what is called the meat market under the supervision of their shiek [*sic*]. There is nominally a fish market—some dealers setting up their stalls during the forenoon daily on the shady side of a building. Europeans as well as natives have stalls. There should be a sheikh or Chief of their market, but he could not exercise supervision over European stalls.[17]

On the other hand, foreign trade was completely transformed: in the past it dealt mainly in Sudanese, Arabian, and Oriental goods, Cairo being one of the most important centers of this trade and Egyptian, Syrian, and Turkish merchants being engaged in it. During the nineteenth century the export of cotton to Europe and the import of European industrial goods into Egypt became the main business of foreign trade, and Greeks and other Europeans became the principal importers and exporters. Moreover, like the artisans, Egyptian merchants suffered from a large variety of oppressive taxes and duties, from which foreign merchants were exempted by the capitulations.

The heaviest blow, however, was dealt to the guilds by Europeans towards the end of the century, when they began to disregard the shaykhs of the guilds as suppliers of labor.

> Les résidents occidentaux se défient des *cheikh* des domestiques, des portiers, des cochers, des cuisiniers: ils choisissent leurs serviteurs par l'intermédiaire de leurs amis ou de placeurs européens. Pour toutes ces raisons, les corps de métiers, bien qu'ils ressemblent encore superficiellement à ce qu'ils étaient un siècle auparavant, perdent peu à peu leur solidité et leur vie.[18]

[16] W. V. Shearer, "Report on the Weaving Industry in Assiout," and N. L. Ablett, "Notes on the Industries of Assiout," *L'Egypte Contemporaine*, vol. 1, 1910, pp. 185, 333.

[17] Report by Consul West to Col. Stanton, No. 35, Suez, July, 1870, FO 141/72.

[18] Métin, p. 292.

But restrictions and monopolies of the guilds were undermined not only by Europeans. An important additional factor was the growth of Egyptian towns, especially during the last quarter of the century.[19] The influx of people into towns considerably increased the number of those who were not members of guilds and thus made it difficult for the guilds to maintain their monopolies.

The growth of Egyptian towns was accompanied by a gradual modernization of certain occupations. How this affected the guilds may be illustrated by the example of the Alexandria water carriers (*saqqāyīn*). A company for water supply had been established in Alexandria during the second half of the century, and in 1894 a decree was published which converted the water carriers into a corporation of wage laborers. No wonder that this portended the guild's end: half a year later a new regulation for water carriers was issued by the Alexandria Municipality, in which the corporation was no longer mentioned at all.[20]

Finally, toward the end of the nineteenth century, Egypt's administration was reorganized and became more efficient. Thus the state could do without the intermediate link of the guilds, and step by step their administrative, fiscal, and economic functions shrank until they lost most of them. About the middle of the nineteenth century, changes in the system of taxation deprived the shaykhs of the function of distributing among the members of the guilds a fixed tax quota imposed on the guild as a whole. Saʿīd officially abolished the monopolies of the guilds (1854–56), but did not succeed in carrying out his decrees in this respect. No further changes in the guilds' functions were introduced during the rule of Ismāʿīl (1863–79). But in the 1880's and the 1890's the government published a whole series of decrees providing for professional permits to be issued by official authority, not by the guilds' shaykhs.[21] Another group of decrees fixed wages for a number of public services, thereby curtailing the shaykhs' function in this matter.[22] In 1881 the shaykhs were relieved of the task of collecting the taxes,[23] and by 1892 all taxes on the guilds, and thereby the remaining fiscal functions

[19] See chapter 8, above.

[20] Compagnie des Eaux, Arrêté du 20 Décembre 1894, P. Gelat, *Répertoire annoté de la législation et de l'administration égyptienne,* III, 1 Alexandria, 1897, p. 534; Majlis Baladī al-Iskandariyya, *lāʾiḥat al-saqqāyīn*, May 29, 1895, *al-Qarārāt waʾl-manshūrāt*, 1895, pp. 272–73. On the decline of the occupation of water carriers in Cairo, see A. Raymond, "Les porteurs d'eau du Caire," *Bulletin de l'Institut Français d'Archaeologie Orientale* 57 (1958): 201–2. However, as late as 1910 there were still water carriers in Cairo and even their guild had survived. See H. Hamilton Fyfe, *The New Spirit in Egypt*, London, 1911, p. 20; and especially Martin, pp. 31 and 48.

[21] For details and documentation, see Baer, *Egyptian Guilds*, pp. 110–11.

[22] For details and documentation, see Baer, *Egyptian Guilds*, p. 104.

[23] Jallād, 3:181.

of the shaykhs, had been abolished.[24] Monopolistic practices of the guilds of undertakers, weighers, and builders were prohibited during the years 1887–90, and in 1890 the complete freedom of all trades was announced.[25] Finally, the last of the more important functions of the guilds' shaykhs, that of supplying labor, disappeared during the first decade of the twentieth century. In 1902 the government issued a regulation laying down rules to be complied with by persons occupied in placing domestic servants. No mention is made of any guild or its shaykh.[26] As to providing other kinds of laborers, by the end of the decade the *khawlī*, a contractor of labor, had replaced the shaykh of the guild. He recruited workers, supervised their work, replaced absentees or sick laborers and paid the wages. It was he who made the contract with the employer in which all particulars concerning the number of workers, the duration of the work to be executed, and the conditions of work were laid down. He received his remuneration from employers and employed alike. In the building trade this function was performed by a person who at the same time was a working foreman.[27] Thus the shaykhs of the guilds were deprived of almost all their functions, partly by explicit official orders and mainly by the fact that these functions were taken over by various government departments or new social and economic institutions.

By that time, however, not many of the guilds had survived. Most of them had died quietly, and their death is not recorded in any of our sources. Some guilds, however, which still existed in 1870 or even later, had vanished at the following dates: slave dealers in 1878, weighers and measures between 1889 and 1895, Cairo butchers by 1893, boatmen between 1893 and 1896, shoeblacks by 1894, interpreters and Alexandria water carriers by 1895, porters in 1898, Manzala fishermen by 1903, and brokers and auctioneers by 1909; the shoemakers' and druggists' guilds too did not exist any longer at the beginning of our century.[28]

But some guilds survived even later. As late as in 1914, the weighers and measurers of Aswān submitted a petition to the Minister of the Interior asking him to appoint a shaykh for each of these two guilds. His answer was

[24] For details and documentation, see Baer, *Egyptian Guilds*, pp. 85–87. Martin, p. 46, says that from 1882 on, i.e., with the British occupation, the guild shaykhs were relieved of their fiscal functions. As we have seen, the two most important functions were no longer in their hands at that time; what remained for Cromer to do was to abolish the last of the taxes affecting the guilds, some of them having been abolished before the British occupation.

[25] *al-Awāmir al-ʿaliyya wa'l-dakrītāt*, 1887, pp. 689–96; 1889, p. 260; 1890, p. 17 (Article 1); *al-Qarārāt wa'l-manshūrāt*, 1889, pp. 495–97 (Article 6).

[26] *Lā'iḥat al-mukhaddimīn*, September 15, 1902, *al-Qarārāt wa'l-manshūrāt*, pp. 411–14.

[27] J. Vallet, *Contribution a l'étude de la condition des ouvriers de la grande industrie au Caire*, Valence, 1911, pp. 23–24, 114–15.

[28] For details and documentation, see Baer, *Egyptian Guilds*, pp. 147–48.

that the official regulation concerning weighing and measuring did not provide for the nomination of shaykhs but left to the administration the control of the work of these corporations.[29] But not only in faraway Aswān did some of the guilds survive. The builders' guilds were officially reorganized in 1889, the guild of public writers of petitions in 1894, that of pilots in 1896, and that of engravers of seals in 1898; and none of the relevant decrees was replaced before World War I.[30] Nubian servants, watchmen, and cooks had maintained their traditional guild organization at the beginning of this century, and so had the Cairo fishermen and guards, guides, and camel drivers at the Pyramids, officially recognized as a guild in 1900. Donkey drivers continued to be officially organized as guilds all over the country, the last decree (for Cairo) mentioning the guild and its shaykh dating from 1910.[31] None of these guilds was abolished before World War I.

It is not known for how long these guilds survived. But after World War I nothing more was heard of appointments of guilds' shaykhs or of any function performed by the guilds in the public life of Egypt, whose towns had been socially and politically completely transformed.

We have tried to show how a large group of writers have been misled by assuming that Egyptian guilds underwent the same process as those of certain European countries. In the course of our study of Egyptian guilds in modern times, we have also come across another misleading conception, that of authors who deal with "Islamic guilds" in general, without taking into account the considerable differences among different Islamic countries. It was particularly Elia Qoudsî's excellent account of the Damascus guilds, presented to the sixth International Congress of Orientalists held in Leiden more than eighty years ago,[32] which has been used again and again for descriptions of the guilds in Egypt or for generalizations about what has been called the "character of Islamic guilds."

Qoudsî's account shows indeed that the structure of the Damascus guilds at that time was very similar to that of Egyptian guilds. The different grades of proficiency from apprentice to master, the elaborate ceremonies of initiation at the transition from grade to grade, and the hierarchy of guild officers

[29] Assemblée Législative, 22me séance, April 18, 1914, *Journal Officiel*, Supplement, No. 67, June 1, 1914.

[30] *al-Qarārāt wa'l-manshūrāt*, 1889, pp. 495–97; 1894, pp. 4–6; Gouvernement Egyptien, Ministére de l'Interieur, *Législation administrative et criminelle*, 3rd ed., Cairo, 1914, 2:392–94; Gelat, III, 2:501–4.

[31] Métin, pp. 288–89, 292; Martin, pp. 28, 48; *al-Qarārāt wa'l-manshūrāt*, 1900, pp. 251–53; *Législation administrative et criminelle*, 2:335–38.

[32] Ilyās Qudsī, (Elia Qoudsî), "Nubdha ta'rīkhiyya fī'l-ḥiraf al-dimashqiyya" ("Notice sur les corporations de Damas"), *Actes du sixième Congrès International des Orientalistes*, deuxième partie, Section 1: Sémitique, Leiden, 1885.

with a shaykh at their head were described in detail by Qoudsî, and we have found a large number of similar terms and ceremonies in sources for our study of Egyptian guilds. Unfortunately, Qoudsî's information on the guilds' functions is not as systematic and detailed as that on their structure. He mentions the shaykh's task of finding work for laborers, and the restrictive and monopolistic character of the guilds is implied in his description of the requirements for exercising a craft or a trade. These were functions which the Damascus guilds and the Egyptian ones had in common. It is remarkable, however, that Qoudsî has nothing to say about the fiscal function of the guilds. In contrast with Egypt, the guild in Syria apparently was not the most important urban unit of taxation. From time to time special taxes were imposed on certain guilds,[33] but it seems that the town quarter remained at least as important a unit of taxation as the guild. Thus, when the Egyptians had occupied Syria and decided in 1833 to impose the *firda* (poll tax), they first tried to have the population registered for this purpose by the shaykhs of the town quarters. When the results appeared to them to be unsatisfactory, they imposed the new tax on the guilds. However, this did not succeed either, and they returned to their original plan and collected the *firda* by using the town quarters as units of taxation.[34]

However, there seem to have been quite significant differences not only between the functions of Egyptian and Syrian guilds but also between their respective processes of decline and disappearance, with which we are concerned here. First of all, in contrast with Egypt, Syrian guilds, like those of other parts of the Ottoman Empire, were abolished by law, while nothing of the kind was ever done in Egypt. After having abolished the traditional guilds of Istanbul in 1910,[35] the Ottoman government abolished those of the provinces in a further law of 1912 which provided at the same time for the establishment of modern professional chambers or syndicates. The formulation in Arabic of the two first articles ran as follows: "Jamīʿ niqābāt al-aṣnāf al-sābiqa mulghāt. Likull ṣinf min jamīʿ arbāb al-ḥiraf wa'l-ṣanā'iʿ an yu'allif niqāba mustaqilla."[36]

The fact that in Egypt the guilds were not abolished by law has been contradicted by a number of writers. The first who put forward the theory

[33] See, e.g., Mikhā'īl al-Dimashqī, *Ta'rīkh ḥawādith al-Shām wa-Lubnān min sanat 1197 ilā sanat 1257*, Beirut, 1912, p. 21.

[34] Qusṭanṭīn al-Bāshā al-Mukhliṣī (ed.), *Mudhakkirāt ta'rīkhiyya . . . biqalam aḥad kuttāb al-ḥukūma al-dimashqiyyīn*, Ḥarīṣā, n.d., pp. 90–92.

[35] Law of 16 Ṣafar 1328 A.H./February 26, 1910, *Düstur, tertīb-i thānī*, vol. 2, Istanbul, 1330, pp. 123–27.

[36] Law of 20 Jumādā al-ūlā 1330 A.H./May 7, 1912, *Düstur, tertīb-i thānī*, vol. 4, Istanbul, 1331, pp. 483–88. Arabic version according to J. Gaulmier, "Notes sur le mouvement syndicaliste a Hama," *Revue des Etudes Islamiques*, 1932, pp. 121–23 (annexe 1).

that the British occupation abolished the guilds in 1882 was Germain Martin.[37] The same view has been advanced by Meyerhof in his article on the druggists.[38] A slightly corrected version of Martin's theory is to be found in Vallet's book on the condition of workers in Cairo industries published in 1911. But Vallet criticizes Martin only for claiming that the corporations were suppressed in 1882. He rightly points out that no such decree was issued either in 1882 or later, but he claims wrongly that the jurisdiction of the guild shaykhs was suppressed by the establishment of the National Courts in 1883 and that the decree of January 9, 1890 which established the Professional Permits Duty not only declared all professions to be free (which it did) but also suppressed the traditional system of apprenticeship and the ritual ceremonies of the guilds[39] (which it did not).

It is on Vallet's version of Martin's theory that most subsequent writers on this subject have based their analyses. Clergé, for instance, in his book on Cairo, reproduces word for word the theory about the effect of the establishment of the National Courts in 1883 and the suppression of apprenticeship and ceremonies by the 1890 decree.[40] The same is reiterated by Dr. Zaki Badaoui in his booklet on labor in Egypt published in 1948.[41]

Obviously, it was neither necessary nor desirable to abolish the guilds in Egypt by decree. As we have seen, the guilds were gradually deprived of almost all their functions, partly by explicit official orders and mainly by the fact that these functions were taken over by various government departments or new social and economic institutions. This process took place partly before and partly after the British occupation. In its course such economically harmful attributes of the guilds as their monopolistic rights and privileges were done away with. On the other hand, in the case of some occupations the guild system apparently still had advantages for effective control by the government up to the time of World War I, so that the wholesale abolition of the guilds was undesirable.

As against this, the decrees by which the guilds were abolished in the Ottoman provinces were part of a comprehensive legislative and administrative action by the government of the Young Turks, the aim of which was to bring about the radical modernization of Ottoman state and society.[42]

[37] Martin, pp. 30, 46.

[38] M. Meyerhof, "Der Bazar der Drogen und Wohlgerüche in Kairo," *Archiv für Wirtschaftsforschung im Orient*, 3 (1918), Heft 1–2:37: "Mit . . . der Besetzung Ägyptens durch die Engländer 1882 wurde das Zunftwesen in Ägypten aufgehoben."

[39] Vallet, pp. 139–40.

[40] M. Clergé, *Le Caire*, vol. 2, Cairo, 1934, pp. 138–39.

[41] Z. Badaoui, *Les Problèmes du travail et les organisations ouvrières en Egypte*, Alexandria, 1948, p. 18.

[42] Cf. B. Lewis, *The Emergence of Modern Turkey*, London, 1961, p. 223.

However, these legislative efforts of the Young Turks were not always effective. Therefore, while in Egypt the guilds completely disappeared after World War I without having been legally abolished, in Syria they seem to have existed in spite of their abolition, though very much weakened, as late as the 1920's. About Ḥamā we are told, "Les vestiges des corporations sont si faibles a Hama que la plupart des gens les ignorent tout a fait."[43] But in Damascus in 1927 about 10 percent of the gainfully occupied population was still organized in the traditional guilds.[44] Although no parallel study of Cairo has been made, from all we know it is highly improbable that such vestiges of the guilds still existed in Egypt after World War I.

It is not at all surprising that the Damascus guilds lingered on much longer than the Egyptian ones. Not only did Egypt's social and administrative transformation take place earlier than that of Syria and was much more thorough, as we have repeatedly shown in this work; in addition, the Damascus guilds were much more autonomous than the Egyptian ones and less dependent on the government and connected with its administrative machine. Thus, after the seventeenth century, Cairo had no institution of a head shaykh of the guilds, while in Damascus there was a *shaykh al-mashāyikh* with strong roots in the local population, its important families, and its guild organization. The post of the guild shaykh in Damascus was either inherited or the shaykh was freely chosen by the elders of the guild, and the election had to be confirmed by the *shaykh al-mashāyikh* but not by the government.[45] As against this, the shaykh of an Egyptian guild was always appointed by the government.[46] It may well be that this is related to the difference between Egyptian and Syrian guilds mentioned above, namely, the fact that, in contrast with Egypt, the Syrian guild was not the most important urban unit of taxation. However that may be, the case of the guilds seems to show again that the more centralized structure of government in Egypt was an important factor in bringing about a quicker dissolution of the traditional units of society than in decentralized Syria.

[43] Gaulmier, p. 96.

[44] L. Massignon, "La Structure du travail a Damas en 1927," *Cahiers Internationaux de Sociologie*, 15 (1953): 34–52.

[45] Qudsī, pp. 9–11, 13–14.

[46] Cf. Baer, *Egyptian Guilds*, pp. 69–72.

10

Slavery and Its Abolition

The Slaves and Their Owners

The most convenient classification of slaves in nineteenth-century Egypt is according to their colors—white, brown or bronze, and black—and according to sex. Egypt had been ruled for about six hundred years by an elite of soldiers who had been white slaves, the Mamluks. Many of the Mamluks who lived in Egypt at the beginning of the nineteenth century and who still partly ruled it, were annihilated in a great massacre carried out by Muḥammad ʿAlī in March, 1811. Nevertheless, Mamluks continued to be bought and owned. Although they no longer constituted a ruling aristocracy, at least during the first half of the century they still occupied important positions as officers in the army, as military guards, and, during the rule of ʿAbbās (1848–54), as governors of provinces.[1] In 1839 their number was estimated at two thousand,[2] but it declined steadily because of growing difficulties of supply (see below) and the increasing employment of native Egyptians as high officials and army officers. They were owned mainly by "Turks," that is, inhabitants of Egypt whose places of origin were in the non-Arab countries of the Ottoman Empire,[3] and among them principally by the ruling Muḥammad ʿAlī family. ʿAbbās alone owned, at the time of his death, about five hundred Mamluks.[4] However, there were also instances of

Originally published as "Slavery in Nineteenth-Century Egypt," *Journal of African History*, 8, no. 3 (1967): 417–41. (Here with some additions.)

[1] John Bowring, *Report on Egypt and Candia*, London, 1840, p. 9; Hekekyan Papers, vol. 5, B.M., Add. 37452, f. 10b (written on February 26, 1851); Bruce to Clarendon, Cairo, August 13, 1854, PRO, FO 78/1036; Alfred von Kremer, *Aegypten*, Leipzig, 1863, 2:86–87.

[2] Bowring; F. Mengin, *Histoire sommaire de l'Egypte sous le gouvernement de Mohammed-Aly*, Paris, 1839, p. 157.

[3] Cf. Bowring; Mengin; E. W. Lane, *The Manners and Customs of the Modern Egyptians*, Everyman's Library, London, 1944, pp. 136–37.

[4] Bruce to Clarendon, Cairo, August 2, 1854, PRO, FO 78/1036. See also Hekekyan Papers, vol. 5, B.M., Add. 37452 f. 10b.

rich Egyptians owning white male slaves, such as the physician Ibrāhīm al-Nabrāwī, who owned "many mamālīk," or a certain Muḥammad Bey Saʿīd, a native of Nawasā al-Baḥr village in the Delta.[5] As late as the 1870's, white boys were occasionally purchased as playmates for the sons of the wealthier beys and pashas,[6] but their number had become so small that among the 8,092 slaves manumitted between August, 1877, and November, 1882, there were no more than twenty-two white male slaves.[7]

A special category of white male slaves was the Greek prisoners of war taken during the campaign of Ibrāhīm Pasha in the years 1825–28. In 1826 their number had been estimated at three thousand (including women and children), and about three thousand more were said to have been brought after the battle of Navarino (October, 1827)—altogether six thousand (females and children included).[8] They were privately sold by their captors to slave dealers who disposed of them, but many of the men were delivered by the soldiers to Ibrāhīm Pasha. Throughout the later 1820's, attempts were made by the consuls and the European communities in Egypt to ransom those among them who had not become Muslims, and even Muḥammad ʿAlī made some attempts to buy them back in order to liberate them according to the conditions imposed on him by Admiral Codrington after Navarino.[9] In 1839 there remained no more than three hundred males (and six hundred females), all of whom apparently had become Muslims.[10]

At the time of the Greek war, many Greek female slaves were brought to Egypt as well, but before and after that short period practically all white female slaves in Egypt were Circassians and Georgians from the Caucasus and from Circassian colonies in Asia Minor.[11] Like white male slaves, they too were owned principally by wealthy Turks, the largest numbers, again, to be found in the harems of the Muḥammad ʿAlī family. Thus Qaṣr al-ʿĀlī, the residence of the Khedive Mother Hoşyar Kadın Efendi, housed three hundred Circassian slaves, and Neşedil, a Circassian slave of the Khedive Ismāʿīl, was established in Zaʿfarān Palace with fifty Circassian and thirty Abyssinian slaves of her own.[12] Ismāʿīl's Minister of Finance

[5] Mubārak, 17:4; Borg to Stanton, Cairo, May 20, 1872, FO 141/78, part 2.

[6] Cf. J. C. McCoan, *Egypt as It Is*, London, 1877, p. 318.

[7] *Further Correspondence respecting Reorganization in Egypt*, Egypt No. 6 (1883), C. 3529, p. 91.

[8] Report by Henry Salt, Alexandria, August 12, 1826, FO 78/147; Report by John Barker, Alexandria, May 17, 1828, Barker to Vice Admiral Codrington, Alexandria, May 24, 1828, and Barker to Vice Admiral Malcolm, Alexandria, November 21, 1828, FO 78/170.

[9] Report by Henry Salt; Barker to Malcolm, Alexandria, October 31, 1828; Amīn Sāmī, *Taqwīm al-Nīl*, part 2, Cairo, 1928, pp. 337, 344.

[10] Bowring; Mengin.

[11] Cf. Lane, p. 191; McCoan, p. 319.

[12] Emine F. Tugay, *Three Centuries: Family Chronicles of Turkey and Egypt*, London, 1963, pp. 191, 179, and *passim*.

Ismāʿīl Ṣadīq (al-Mufattish) left at his death 144 white female slaves.[13] But even Egyptians preferred Circassians to colored concubines whenever they could afford to buy them, or, as in the case of Nabrāwī, the above mentioned physician, when they received them as presents from the viceregal family.[14] During the cotton boom of the 1860's even fellahs tried to acquire Circassian concubines, with amusing consequences in some cases.[15] These concubines did only light work, such as making coffee, preparing and lighting pipes, and occasionally cooking special dishes, while all the coarse work was done by black slaves.[16] In many cases the status of slavery or concubinage of Circassian girls was soon terminated by marriage, often with their master or his son.[17]

However, the high cost of white slave girls placed them beyond the reach of all but the wealthiest, and "middle-class" Egyptians who acquired concubines had to be contented with the second best, that is, Abyssinian (primarily Galla) girls.[18] With regard to both their color and their status, they occupied an intermediate position between white and black slaves. As Lane put it:

> They themselves . . . think that they differ so little from the white people, that they cannot be persuaded to act as servants, with due obedience, to their master's wives; and the black (or negro) slave girl feels exactly in the same manner towards the Abyssinian, but is perfectly willing to serve the white ladies.[19]

There were also Abyssinian male slaves, though fewer than females of this category. Finally, slaves of another kind who were neither white nor black were children of poor Egyptian families who were sometimes sold by their parents into slavery.[20]

However, the bulk of slaves in Egypt were black slaves from different parts of Africa, both male and female. Their main use was in domestic service, where they did the coarse work—except in families where both slaves and free servants were kept; in this case the meanest work was done

[13] Vivian to Derby, Cairo, April 14, 1877, FO 84/1472.

[14] Mubārak, 17:4.

[15] Cf. D. Mackenzie Wallace, *Egypt and the Egyptian Question*, London, 1883, pp. 269 ff.

[16] Tugay, p. 192; see also, for instance, J. A. St. John, *Egypt and Nubia*, London, 1845, p. 240.

[17] McCoan, p. 318, and see examples in Tugay, pp. 184, 202, 305, etc.

[18] McCoan, pp. 319–20; see also M. J. Lapanouse, "Mémoire sur les caravanes venant du royaume de Sennâar. . . ." *Mémoires sur l'Egypte*, vol. 4, Paris, an XI, p. 97.

[19] Lane, p. 190. It is interesting to note that ten Abyssinian girls bought in the Cairo slave market made up the first batch of girl students at Muḥammad ʿAlī's *madrasat al-wilāda* (school of midwifery) established in the early 1830's—since it was not possible, for some time, to get Egyptian girls or women to enter this school of their own free will. See J. Heyworth-Dunne, *An Introduction to the History of Education in Modern Egypt*, London, n.d., p. 132; Sāmī, part 2, p. 479.

[20] For a detailed discussion of this phenomenon see Lane, p. 200.

by the latter.[21] Black slaves of a special kind were eunuchs, who were kept only by the Muḥammad ʿAlī family and the upper class of Turks.[22] Early in the century, between a hundred and two hundred boys of not more than ten years of age were castrated every year at Abū Tīg (or, more precisely, at Dayr al-Jandala, about six miles south of Abū Tīg) on the caravan route from the Sudan to Egypt. Coptic priests were among the most expert operators. This, however, was prohibited later on, and the eunuchs were imported "ready-made" from Kordofan and Darfur.[23] Many of the eunuchs, who were used mainly as guards for the harems and their inmates, were themselves owners of slaves.[24]

Domestic service and concubinage were by no means the only use made of black slaves in nineteenth-century Egypt, as claimed by Egyptian apologists and repeated by most European writers.[25] First, until the British occupation Egypt's rulers persistently tried to use black slaves as soldiers, while white slaves or former Mamluks were employed as officers. Muḥammad ʿAlī's attempts to acquire slaves in the Sudan for his army has been frequently described, and we need not go into detail here.[26] In the late 1830's, their number was estimated at 2,500.[27] In Saʿīd's time (1854–63) slaves were taken mainly for his Sudanese units, even after he had prohibited the slave trade, and also for his bodyguard.[28] But even Ismāʿīl (1863–79) continued to enlist slaves for his troops,[29] and in the 1870's many of the slaves who tried to achieve their freedom through the British consulates were sent by the authorities to the army.[30] Since the government needed

[21] Lane, p. 193; McCoan, p. 320.

[22] Lane, p. 137; Bruce to Clarendon, Cairo, January 17, 1855, FO 84/974. There were 150 eunuchs in Qaṣr al-ʿĀlī alone; see Tugay, p. 191.

[23] Louis Frank, "Mémoire sur le commerce des Negres au Caire . . .," *Mémoires sur l'Egypte*, 4:132 ff.; P. S. Girard, "Mémoire sur l'agriculture, l'industrie et le commerce de l'Egypte," *Description de l'Egypte, état moderne*, 2, Paris, 1812, p. 632; Mubārak, 11:70–71; McCoan, p. 327.

[24] See, for instance, "List of Slaves Freed by Thos. F. Reade," in *Memorandum by Consul Reade on Slave Trade in Egypt*, London, August 13, 1868, FO 84/1290.

[25] See, for instance, McCoan, pp. 315 ff.; Tugay, pp. 303 ff.; and many others.

[26] See, for instance, R. Hill, *Egypt in the Sudan 1820–1881*, London, 1959, pp. 24 ff., 46–48, 62–64, etc.

[27] Mengin, p. 159; Bowring, p. 10.

[28] *Memorandum by Mr. Petherick*, December, 1860, and *Report of Dr. J. Natterer . . . dated 5 April 1860*, inclosure in Colquhoun to Russell, Alexandria, May 29, 1860, FO 84/1120; Colquhoun to Russell, Alexandria, July 1 and August 17, 1863, FO 84/1204; Petherick to Colquhoun, Cairo, March 17, 1865, FO 141/57.

[29] Petherick to Colquhoun; Reade to Stanley, Alexandria, August 9, 1867, FO 141/63; Vivian to Derby, Cairo, December 8, 1876, FO 84/1450.

[30] Omar Bey to Reade, Cairo, May 28, 1868, FO 84/1290; Rogers to Stanton, Cairo, April 23, 1872, FO 141/78, part 2; Harding to Stanton, Mansura, May 30, 1873, and Consular Agent at Mansura to Vivian, June 23 and July 22, 1873, FO 141/82; *Statement by Saîd el Soudani*, inclosure in Borg to Governor of Cairo, April 18, 1878, FO 141/119; etc.

slaves for this purpose, border regions were required to pay their taxes in slaves. Such a system of taxation was practiced mainly during the rule of Muḥammad ʿAlī, but some cases were reported even in the 1860's and 1870's; the regions concerned were the Siwa Oasis, Upper Egypt, Nubia, and the Sudan.[31]

But army service was not the only outdoor activity demanded from slaves in Egypt. Contrary to the prevalent assumption, agricultural slavery was not uncommon. This seems to have been an innovation of the nineteenth century and the result of agricultural development coinciding with a shortage of labor and the availability of slaves. Early in the century, one of the contributors to the *Description de l'Egypte* still wrote with regard to slaves, "La culture des terres et les travaux pénibles lui sont presque étrangers; et si quelques Égyptiens confient à des esclaves le soin de leur chevaux, c'est à peu près la tâche la plus rude de leur condition. . . ."[32] In the 1830's, when peasants were recruited for military service, some European landowners in Asyūṭ attempted to employ slaves for field labor, but the cost turned out to be much higher than that of fellah labor.[33] However, on the large farms of the Muḥammad ʿAlī family, especially on Ismāʿīl's sugar plantations in Upper Egypt, many hundreds of slaves were employed as agricultural laborers at various times during the century.[34] Moreover, between Isnā and Kuruskū in Upper Egypt, fellahs kept slaves to perform agricultural work throughout the century.[35] As late as 1884, nine-tenths of the men who worked the water pumps in Isnā province were slaves.[36] Most of the slaves manumitted in 1885 and 1886 by the government offices established for this purpose were agricultural slaves from Isnā province.[37] In Lower Egypt agricultural slavery was the temporary result of the sudden prosperity in the 1860's which lead to the acquisition of new land and to a tremendous expansion of agriculture.

[31] Campbell to Palmerston, Cairo, March 15, 1839, FO 78/373; Barnett to Aberdeen, Alexandria, April 17, 1842, FO 78/502 (also 84/426); *Memorandum by Mr. Petherick*, December 1860; Vivian to Derby, Cairo, December 8, 1876, FO 84/1450.

[32] De Chabrol, "Essai sur les moeurs des habitans modernes de l'Egypte," *Description de l'Egypte, etat moderne*, 2 (2), Paris, 1812, p. 482.

[33] Bowring, pp. 16, 89.

[34] Hekekyan Papers, vol. 3, B.M., Add. 37450, f. 224 (written in January, 1847); Rogers to Clarendon, Cairo, November 24, 1869, FO 84/1305.

[35] Hekekyan Papers, vol. 2, B.M., Add, 37449, ff. 469–70 (written on September 13, 1844); Mubārak, 17:23.

[36] *Further Correspondence respecting the Finances and Conditions of Egypt*, Egypt No. 4 (1889) C. 5718, p. 44. Cf. della Sala to Riaz, Cairo, September 12, 1880, FO 141/140.

[37] *Correspondence respecting Slavery in Egypt*, Africa No. 4 (1887), C. 4994, pp. 9–12.

> The peasantry of Egypt who suddenly gained extraordinary sums of money for their cotton during the American Civil War, spent some of their profits in the purchase of slaves to help them in the cultivation of their lands . . . nearly all the slaves who had applied at Mansourah for emancipation were agricultural, not domestic slaves.

Similarly, "most of the slaves sold at [the fair of] Tanta are for land labor; the principal purchasers are farmers."[38] It may be added that at that time fellahs also used to evade the *corvée* by sending their slaves as substitutes.[39]

Finally, there were two additional minor instances of the use of slaves for nondomestic work. In the late 1820's the Greek prisoners of war who had become slaves in Egypt were employed in public works,[40] and, later in the century, slaves were employed in Suez for work in coastal sailing vessels. "Dhow and bugla owners equip their vessels almost entirely with slaves."[41] It may be true, as stressed by all the sources, that even in these kinds of work the plight of slaves in Egypt was much better than that of the American slaves. But from the point of view of Egypt's social history, it is important to stress these facts which have so far been neglected by all writers on this subject, the more so as Egypt was one of the few Muslim countries in which nondomestic slavery existed in the nineteenth century. Of Turkey it was said, at that time, that "out of door slavery does not prevail . . . there is enough free labour."[42]

In addition to their practical use, the possession of slaves served as an important social status symbol in nineteenth-century Egypt.

> So inwrought, indeed, is the institution into the domestic and social life of the country, that the possession of one or more slaves is as essential to "respectability" amongst one's neighbours as is that of a servant for menial work in a European family; and this social consideration has, probably, more to do with the maintenance of the institution than any question as to the relative cost of slave and free labour.

[38] Rogers to Vivian, Cairo, September 3, 1873, FO 141/82; *Confidential Memorandum on Slave Dealing in Alexandria* (signed Ali Hassan), Alexandria, June 2 and 6, 1873, FO 141/84 (also 84/1371).

[39] Reade to Stanley, Alexandria, August 9, 1867, FO 141/63.

[40] Report by Henry Salt, Alexandria, July 12, 1827, FO 78/160; Barker to Stratford Canning, Alexandria, October 11, 1828, FO 78/170.

[41] West to Vivian, Suez, July 28, 1873, FO 141/82; "The Slave Trade in Egypt," *Times of India*, quoted in *The Anti-Slavery Reporter*, published in London by the British and Foreign Anti-Slavery Society, 3d ser., 20, no. 5 (September 1, 1876): 128.

[42] Francis to Clarendon, Constantinople, September 28, 1869, FO 84/1305. For other examples of agricultural work in Muslim countries done by slaves (Khiwa, Zanzibar, and beduin Arabia), see R. Brunschvig, "ʿAbd," *Encyclopedia of Islam*, new ed., 1:36. In Mecca slaves were used at that time as builders; see C. Snouck Hurgronje, *Mekka in the Latter Part of the Nineteenth Century*, Leyden and London, 1931, p. 11.

> . . . In most places the position of a person is measured by the number of slaves he possesses—especially is this true in the case of the women who take peculiar pride in telling how many slave girls they have under their command.[43]

Wherever Mubārak, in his geographical-biographical encyclopedia, wants to stress the social importance of notables mentioned by him, he emphasizes the fact that among their following there was a large number of slaves.[44] But the possession of at least one slave was not the privilege of a small upper class. We have mentioned that certain kinds of slaves (white males and females and eunuchs) were owned principally by the Muḥammad ʿAlī family and the upper class of Turks. Black slaves, however, who were not eunuchs were owned by almost all layers of Egyptian society. In our sources we have come across the following owners of slaves: beduins, village notables, fellahs, millers, butchers, shopkeepers, a bookseller, all kinds of merchants, a banker, clerks, all grades of officials and government employees, all ranks of army officers, religious functionaries, some *muftīs*, a judge, a physician, and others.[45] Moreover, many Christians and Jews kept slaves, and while in Turkey Europeans were not allowed to own slaves,[46] they did so in Egypt as long as slavery existed in this country, even such foreigners as the French Consul.[47]

It is definitely impossible to establish the exact number of slaves in Egypt at any time in the nineteenth century. Three different sources (although perhaps not independent from each other) estimated their number in the years 1838–40 at between 22,000 and 30,000, divided as follows: 4,500–5,000 black males, 12,000–20,000 Negro and Abyssinian females, 2,300–

[43] McCoan, p. 317; Letter by N. to Mr. Joseph Cooper, Egypt, November 28, 1872, *The Anti-Slavery Reporter*, 3d ser., 18, no. 4 (January 1, 1873): 104.

[44] Mubārak, 8:82; 9:39; 14:38; etc.

[45] Bowring, p. 9; Hekekyan Papers, vol. 3, f. 329 b; Mubārak, 8:82; 9:39; 14:38; 17:4, 23. Calvert to Reade, Alexandria, July 2, 1867, FO 141/62; Rogers to Stanton, Cairo, February 22, 1872, FO 141/78, part 1; Atkin to Stanton, Mansura, May 12, 1873, and West to Vivian, Suez, August 5, 1873, FO 141/82; Borg to Vivian, Cairo, July 1, 1878, FO 141/120; and, in particular, "List of Slaves . . ." in *Memorandum by Consul Reade*. See also *The Anti-Slavery Reporter*, 3d ser., 18, no. 4 (January 1, 1873): 104; and 20, no. 5 (September 1, 1876): 127, where it is said, about Egypt, that "a poor man, or even the slave of a good indulgent owner, can buy a slave on credit while he can barely feed himself. . . ." Thus with regard to Egypt at least, it seems to be inaccurate to claim that "ownership of slaves tended to be a prerogative, if not a privilege, of the wealthy elite" (C. A. O. Van Nieuwenhuijze, *Social Stratification and the Middle East*, Leiden, 1965, p. 33).

[46] Chabrol, p. 374; Pezzoni to Nesselrode, Alexandria, May 24, 1828, in R. Cattaui, *Le Règne de Mohammed Aly d'après les archives russes en Egypte*, vol. 1, Cairo, 1931, p. 236.

[47] Chabrol, p. 374; Cattaui, pp. 230–66; Lane, p. 104; Mubārak, 14:53; McCoan, pp. 326–67; "List of Slaves . . .," *Memorandum by Consul Reade*; Reade to Stanley, Alexandria, August 9, 1867, FO 141/63; Gilbert to Palmerston, Alexandria, November 7, 1848, FO 84/737; Vivian to Derby, Alexandria, June 30, 1877, FO 84/1472; A. B. Clot-Bey, *Aperçu général sur l'Egypte*, Paris, 1840, 1:274 ff.; N. W. Senior, *Conversations and Journals in Egypt and Malta*, London, 1882, 1:207; *The Anti-Slavery Reporter*, 4th ser., 1, no. 8, (August 15, 1881): 130–31.

4,000 white males and 3,000 white females.[48] According to a census taken some time in the 1850's, the number of slaves in Cairo was 11,481, of whom 8,674 were females and 2,807 males.[49] Thus the ratio between male and female slaves seems to have been about 1:3, a result corroborated, in general, by the estimates for 1838–40. In view of the distribution of manumitted slaves among different areas of Egypt in the years 1877–82, one may assume that roughly a little less than half of Egypt's slaves lived in Cairo, and that therefore the number of slaves in the 1850's too amounted to between 20,000 and 30,000. The same result emerges from the figures of slaves manumitted by the official *Bureaux* which were established after the Treaty of 1877 (see below): they numbered about 18,000 in the years 1877–89,[50] but since many others were directly freed by their masters, we arrive again at an estimate of about 30,000. The conclusion that throughout the century the number of slaves in Egypt did not change considerably is not astonishing. Although the import of slaves continued throughout the first three-quarters of the century, there were many ups and downs in the number of slaves imported (see below). Furthermore, many slaves were manumitted by their masters, according to Muslim practice, a few years after their acquisition, and many children of female slaves were free because they had free fathers. Nevertheless, it may well be that all the figures mentioned above are too low.

The Slave Trade

In the nineteenth century white slaves were brought to Egypt from the lands on the eastern coast of the Black Sea (Circassia and Georgia), and from the Circassian settlements in Anatolia, via Istanbul. Some were kidnapped by organized raids and some taken as prisoners in the wars between rival clans, but most were bought as children from parents who sold them with the intention of bettering their condition. Many Circassian girls were thus sold at the time of the great immigration into Turkey during the late 1850's and early 1860's. The dealers, many of them dependents or servants of the local beys of the Trabzon vilayet, transported them as their wives to Istanbul and there sold them (in the second half of the century—secretly) to certain women, some of them of the upper classes of society, who undertook to educate them. They received religious instruction and were taught to read (but not to write), needlework and embroidery, and sometimes

[48] Mengin, pp. 157–59; Bowring, pp. 9–10; Col. Campbell, *Report on Egypt*, July 6, 1840, FO 78/408 B.

[49] M. J. Colucci Bey, "Quelques notes sur le cholera qui sévit au Caire en 1850 et 1855," *Mémoires . . . présentés . . . a l'Institut Egyptien*, vol. 1, Paris, 1862, p. 607.

[50] *Further Correspondence respecting Reorganization in Egypt*, Egypt No. 6 (1883), C. 3529, p. 91; *Further Correspondence respecting the Finances and Condition of Egypt*, Egypt No. 4 (1889), C. 5718, p. 44.

music. After a period of education they were sold either directly to the viceroy of Egypt or, after having been transported to Egypt (accompanied by a eunuch, who prevented their being inspected on landing by pretending they were the harem of an important personage), to other dignitaries who had ordered them, or to dealers who kept them in private houses, where they were exhibited to prospective buyers. In the course of the nineteenth century this trade declined considerably as a result of Russian expansion and the continuous struggle of the Circassians against Russia, and the principal remaining source of supply were the Circassian settlements in Anatolia.[51]

There are five major areas from which brown and black slaves were brought to Egypt. From each of these areas a route of supply led to Egypt. During the nineteenth century only minor changes occurred in these routes. By far the most important source of slaves for Egypt, regarding both the quantity of annual supply and the persistence of supply throughout the century, was the area south and west of Darfur. At the beginning of the century, the annual caravan from Darfur was the greatest of all caravans reaching Egypt, and its principal merchandise was black slaves, both male and female. Most of them were prisoners taken in the perpetual wars between Darfur and the neighboring tribes. They were brought to the market in Darfur and sold to merchants after one-fifth had been deducted for the Sultan and one-fifth for the chief of his army. The caravan took the direct route to Asyūṭ via Bārīs and Khārja oasis.[52] In the 1850's however, Zubayr Raḥma and his allies the Rizayqāt established a new ruling class of traders and a new overland route for their slave caravans through Kordofan, and from that time onward most of the slaves of the Cairo market who came from the pagan tribes south of Darfur were purchased in El Obeid in Kordofan, although the direct caravan from Darfur to Asyūṭ operated as well.[53]

The second center from which regular slave caravans proceeded to Egypt was Sennar. Here too captives of raids into the area of the Nuba Mountains

[51] Pisani to Elliot, September 14, 1869, inclosure in Elliot to Clarendon, Constantinople, September 14, 1869; Taylor to Clarendon, Erzeroom, September 20, 1869; Palgrave to Clarendon, Trebizond, September 21, 1869; Francis to Clarendon, Constantinople, September 28, 1869; Elliot to Clarendon, October 27, 1869; Rogers to Clarendon, Cairo, November 24, 1869, FO 84/1305; Palgrave to Clarendon, Trebizond, July 6, 1870, FO 84/1324; Bowring, p. 9; McCoan, p. 318; Ch. White, *Three Years in Constantinople*, London, 1845, 2:286, 309; and see especially Tugay, pp. 178–79 for the story of her grandmother Neşedil.

[52] M. J. Lapanouse, "Mémoire sur les caravanes qui arrivent du royaume de Dârfurth . . .," *Mémoires sur l'Egypte*, 4:81–82; Girard in *Description de l'Egypte, état moderne*, 2:630–32; Mubārak, 17:32.

[53] R. Gray, *A History of the Southern Sudan 1839–1889*, London, 1961, pp. 66–69; *Memorandum by Mr. Petherick*, December, 1860, FO 84/1120; Stanton to Clarendon, Alexandria, May 9, 1866, FO 84/1260. For alternative routes from Kordofan to Egypt, see Borg to Vivian, Cairo, August 23, 1878, FO 141/121.

and Abyssinia were sold to dealers, who transported them to Egypt. The route of this caravan ran from Sennar to Berber and from there, under the protection of the shaykh of the ʿAbābda, to Ibrīm (on the Nile, five miles from Kuruskū), Darāw, and Isnā. Black slaves from the Nuba Mountains by far outnumbered the Abyssinians thus brought to Egypt.[54] Slaves continued to be supplied to Egypt from this source at least until the 1860's.[55]

Between these two areas, slave hunters and slave traders of various sorts (among them Danāqla from northern Sudan) captured tribesmen dwelling along the White Nile, Bahr al-Zaraf and Bahr al-Jabal. At certain periods these tribes, mainly the Shilluk and the Dinka, were also forced to pay their taxes in slaves. When the open slave market at Khartoum had been abolished, the Shilluk village of Kaka became the market for slaves from the White Nile.[56] Slaves from this source too were sold in Egypt, but information is not as definite as that concerning the other routes of supply.

The fourth region which supplied slaves to Egypt was Bornu (south-west of Lake Chad) and Wadāy (the eastern part of modern Chad). Slaves from this region were brought to Egypt via Libya and the Western Desert. Apparently, there existed a number of alternative routes. They went either through Fezzān or directly to Cyrenaica. Some of these slaves were sold in Benghazi to beduins or Maghrebis and transported by them to Maryūṭ where brokers from Alexandria took care of them; others were brought from Benghazi straight to Cairo. One route of supply of Bornu and Wadāy slaves was by way of the Kufra and Jalo oases; the latter was, at a time, a principal center of slave trade in the Libyan Desert, where the slaves were dressed after their horrible march of a few months through the desert and taught a few words of Arabic. Other important stations on the Western Desert route to Egypt were Siwa oasis and Kirdāsa or Abū Ruwaysh near Giza.[57]

[54] Girard, pp. 636–67; M. J. Lapanouse, "Mémoire sur les caravanes venant du royaume de Sennâar . . .," *Mémoires sur l'Egypte*, 4:96–98, 116 ff.; L. Frank, p. 138.

[55] Gray, pp. 44–45; *Memorandum by Mr. Petherick*, FO 84/1120.

[56] Gray, pp. 53, 149–50; Colquhoun to Cherif Pasha, Alexandria, June 4, 1862, FO 84/1181; Petherick to Colquhoun, Cairo, March 17, 1865, FO 141/57; *Abstract of Sir Samuel Baker's Report to the Viceroy*, inclosure in Vivian to Granville, Alexandria, September 6, 1873, FO 84/1371. However, in Gray's view, "the impression given (by Baker) to those who directed policy both in Egypt and Europe was that the misery of the situation on the White Nile was solely due to the operations of the slave trade, with the result that their subsequent efforts to suppress it led them to overlook the more serious sources of this trade elsewhere and to ignore the fundamental factors which were creating the disaster on the White Nile." See Gray, p. 84 and *passim*.

[57] L. Frank in *Mémoires sur l'Egypte*, 4:135; Stanton to Derby, Alexandria, September 3, 1874, FO 84/1397; Henderson to Derby, Benghazi, December 24, 1875, FO 84/1412; Cookson to Malet, Alexandria, May 17, 1880, FO 141/138; Robertson Smith to Malet, Alexandria, April 22, 1880, FO 141/140. Cf. Mubārak, 12:112; 15:5.

Finally, Abyssinians and slaves from the east African coast were supplied to Egypt via the ports of Massawa and Zayla by boat through the Red Sea, sometimes via Jidda, arriving near Suez. At times when the Egyptian government took effective measures against the slave trade in the Sudan, this route served also as an alternative for trade in Sudanese slaves. The slaves were carried not only in private sailing vessels but even in the steamers of the ʿAzīziyya Company, the principal shareholder of which was the Khedive.[58]

There are only estimates of the number of imported slaves at different times, and even these are incomplete and often contradictory. At the beginning of the century two French scholars estimated the number of slaves annually brought by the Darfur caravan at 12,000 and 5,000–6,000 respectively, and the number brought by the Sennar caravan at 300–400 and 150 respectively.[59] A third scholar maintained that all these figures were exaggerated and that no more than 3,000–4,000 of these slaves were sold in Cairo in the past, and even less, about 1,200, after the Mamluks had augmented the taxes on slaves. In the past, each caravan brought no more than 1,000–1,500 slaves.[60] In the late 1830's the annual import of slaves was estimated at 10,000–12,000,[61] but during the 1840's and 1850's it seems to have declined to about 5,000 or even less.[62] During the 1860's the import of slaves grew tremendously as a result of the cotton boom, and it was estimated at 25,000–30,000 yearly (10,000–15,000 down the Nile, in addition to the Darfur-Asyūṭ, the Red Sea, and other routes);[63] but at the end of the decade it declined again, and between 1869 and 1880 the following estimates were made by British consuls: by the Red Sea, 500–600 (1869),

[58] L. Frank in *Mémoires sur l'Egypte*, 4:138; Circular of Ragheb Pasha, January 9, 1865; West to Colquhoun, Suez, May 10, 1865; Stanton to Russell, Alexandria, September 26, 1865, FO 84/1246; *Report on the Slave Trade . . . in the Consular District of Jedda*, Raby to Clarendon, Jidda, December 10, 1869, FO 84/1305; West to Vivian, Suez, August 5, 1873, FO 141/82 (also 84/1371); *The Anti-Slavery Reporter*, 3d ser., 20, no. 5, (September 1, 1876):127. Cf. R. Pankhurst, "The Ethiopian Slave Trade in the Nineteenth and Early Twentieth Centuries: A Statistical Inquiry," *Journal of Semitic Studies*, 9, no. 1 (Spring, 1964):225.

[59] Lapanouse in *Mémoires sur l'Egypte*, 4:81, 98; Girard in *Description de l'Egypte, état moderne*, 2:632, 637.

[60] L. Frank in *Mémoires sur l'Egypte*, 4:136. According to this author, the reason for contradictory information on this subject was that the registers were burned every year by the Coptic scribes or the proprietors of the *wakāla* (see below).

[61] Bowring, p. 9, and Bowring to Palmerston, off Tripoli (Syria), April 7, 1838, FO 78/345.

[62] Von Kremer, 2:86 (decline from five thousand in 1847 to no more than one thousand in the late 1850's); *Memorandum on the Slave Trade . . . by Mr. Coulthard*, inclosure in Colquhoun to Russell, Alexandria, June 8, 1860, FO 84/1120 (between three thousand and four thousand in the late 1850's).

[63] Stanton to Clarendon, Alexandria, May 9, 1866, FO 84/1260; Reade to Stanley, Alexandria, August 9, 1867, FO 141/63.

from Darfur and Kordofan, 1,500 (the early 1870's), and through the Western Desert via Siwa, about 2,000 (the late 1870's).[64]

A small number of the brown and black slaves imported into Egypt were reexported, mainly to Turkey (early in the century also some to Cyprus and about 100 yearly to Syria).[65] For a time they were even transported by the steamers of the Egyptian ʿAzīziyya Company, which resulted in persistent protests by the British Consul in Izmir.[66] In the years 1869–73 the Egyptian government and the Alexandria police were repeatedly approached to stop this export.[67]

Throughout the century there were considerable fluctuations in the prices of slaves, sometimes even from one year to another, according to the frequency of caravans, the number of slaves imported, the mortality of slaves in Egypt, and the demand which changed with the economic conditions of the country.[68] Usually the price of black girls was a little higher than that of boys, though exceptions to this rule have been registered. The price of black adults was higher than that of boys by as much as 100 per cent. Eunuchs fetched double or three times the price of black male adults. The price of Abyssinian boys was a little higher than that of Negro boys, and the difference grew with the age of the slave, reaching 100 per cent. There were great variations in the difference between the price of Abyssinian girls and that of Negro girls, figures in our sources showing differences of between 25 and 600 per cent. The highest class was of course that of white females (Circassians), who were sometimes up to ten times as expensive as Abyssinian girls.[69]

Perhaps the least known aspect of the slave trade is its local organization in Egypt. The *jallāba*, that is, dealers in Sudanese merchandise, and in

[64] *Report on the Slave Trade* . . ., Raby to Clarendon, Jidda, December 10, 1869, FO 84/1305; Borg to Vivian, Cairo, August 23, 1878, FO 141/121; Cookson to Malet, Alexandria, May 17, 1880, FO 141/138.

[65] White, 2:285–86; Girard, p. 649; *The Anti-Slavery Reporter*, new ser. 3, no. 30, (June 1, 1848):97.

[66] FO 141/70 (1869); 141/72 (1870); 141/75, part 1 (1871); 141/78, part 2 and 141/79 (1872); 141/90 (1874), *passim*. See also Elliot to Clarendon, Constantinople, June 10, 1869, FO 84/1305.

[67] FO 84/1305, *passim*; FO 84/1324, *passim*; Stanley to Granville, Alexandria, September 10, 1872, FO 84/1354. FO 84/1371, *passim*.

[68] Cf. L. Frank in *Mémoires sur l'Egypte*, 4:145; Lane, p. 190 (decline by 50 per cent in the course of a few years); Sakakini to Malet, Alexandria, June 14, 1880, FO 141/140 (fluctuations of 12–18 per cent from one year to another).

[69] For figures, see, in addition to sources mentioned in the previous note, Girard, pp. 632, 637; Lapanouse in *Mémoires sur l'Egypte*, 4:98; Lane, pp. 191–92; Bowring, p. 89; McCoan, p. 327; *Confidential Memorandum on Slave Dealing in Alexandria*, FO 141/84; *The Anti-Slavery Reporter*, 3d ser., 20, no. 6 (November 1, 1876):149.

particular slave dealers, were known for generations to be "dark-skinned people from the districts of the Oases, Aswān, and Ibrīm."[70] These people continued, apparently, to constitute the main element of slave dealers until the abolition of the slave trade late in the nineteenth century. Slave dealers in the 1880's and early 1890's, whose origin can be established, were first and foremost people from Upper Egypt, Sudanese dwelling in Egypt (mainly in Cairo), beduins, villagers of the Buḥayra province, and Maghrebis. Women also practiced the slave trade.[71] Among the people from Upper Egypt, the most notorious were the natives of Darāw and its vicinity (about twenty-five miles north of Aswān). As late as 1880 Count della Sala, who inspected the area with the aim of suppressing the slave trade, said that in order to implement the orders prohibiting the trade it would be necessary to imprison most of the inhabitants of four large villages near Darāw, including the village shaykhs and government officials.[72] At one time some Persian subjects residing in Egypt also specialized in this occupation.[73] Very few data on their numbers are found in the sources, and we do not know how many persons practiced the slave trade in Egypt at any time in the nineteenth century. Including the participants in caravans, there must have been hundreds. According to two local sources, their number in Cairo (1879) was seventy-eight and in Alexandria (1873) seventy;[74] British sources maintained that, in Cairo, it had declined to thirty-two by 1882 and to zero in the late 1880's,[75] but probably some still practiced the trade underground.

Slave dealers in Egypt were clearly divided into dealers in black slaves (*jallāba*) and dealers in white slaves (*yasīrjiyya*, sing. *yasīrjī*, from Turkish *esirci*).[76] In the past a definite distinction between these two groups was

[70] *Bu Tayife esmerül-levin Elvahî ve Asvanî ve Ibrim vilayetinden âdemlerdir.* Evliya Çelebi Seyahetnamesi: *Mısır, Sudan, Habeş (1672–1680)*, vol. 10, Istanbul, 1938, p. 382.

[71] Our principal source for establishing the identity of slave dealers were their trials as published in *Majmūʿat al-qarārāt waʾl-manshūrāt,* Cairo-Būlāq, 1876–80, p. 94; 1881, p. 93; 1886, p. 713; 1887, pp. 24–25, 52, 101–2, 320, 335, 514, 517, 583, 638, 670, 817; 1888, pp. 23, 30–31, 120; 1889, pp. 183, 467; 1890, pp. 265, 548; 1891, pp. 672, 932; 1892, pp. 4, 132, 273, 407, 602; 1893, pp. 178, 430; 1894, p. 78. For beduins, see also Hogg to Malet, Minya, May 6, 1880, FO 141/140; and for women, Reade to Cherif Pacha, Alexandria, August 8, 1867, FO 84/1277.

[72] Della Sala to Riaz Pacha, Cairo, September 12, 1880, FO 141/140. See also Mubārak, 11:2, mentioning the slave trade as one of the major occupations of the people of Darāw.

[73] Stanton to Granville, Alexandria, August 19, 1872, FO 84/1354.

[74] Borg to Lascelles, Cairo, September 8, 1879, FO 141/129; *Confidential Memorandum on Slave Dealing in Alexandria*, FO 141/84.

[75] *Further Correspondence Respecting the Finances and Condition of Egypt*, Egypt No. 4 (1889), C. 5718, pp. 40, 44; *Correspondence respecting Slavery in Egypt*, Africa No. 4 (1887), C. 4994, p. 7.

[76] Cf. Aḥmad Amīn, *Qāmūs al-ʿādāt waʾl-taqālīd waʾl-taʿābīr al-miṣriyya*, Cairo, 1953, p. 214.

made with regard to social status: while dealers in black slaves were included in a group of "cursed and impious" guilds of low social status, dealers in white slaves were grouped with the highly respected guilds of the Khān al-Khalīlī merchants.[77] This specialization persisted in the nineteenth century, although later there were some dealers in both black and white slaves.[78]

Many slave dealers had associates in various towns, so that they were able to transfer their merchandise according to demand.[79] There were also family firms; the most notorious was that of the al-ʿAqqād brothers, one of whom operated in the Sudan while the other did business in Cairo.[80] Like all other urban professional groups in Egypt, slave dealers were organized in a guild. For many years in the 1860's and 1870's Sulaymān Aghā abū Dawūd was the shaykh of this guild, and when he died in September, 1877, a certain Muḥammad Ṣāliḥ (who married his widow) succeeded him in this position. In 1878 (a few months after the abolition of the trade by the 1877 convention) an official communication stated: "The guild of slave dealers does not exist nor does the Government recognize it in any form. The said Mohammad Aga is known by the Local Authority as Chief of the Merchants trading in Soudan goods such as natron, ostrich feathers, gum, ivory etc."[81] This was an easy excuse of the Egyptian authorities pressed by British diplomatic representations, since it was based on the fact that very often slave dealers also dealt in other products of the Sudan. In the 1860's, however, the title of Sulaymān abū Dawūd clearly was *shaykh al-yasīrjiyya*, and in this capacity he was even charged by the government, at its expense, to lodge and feed liberated slaves until they found the means to fend for themselves.[82] The following relevant account was published in the British press:

> The sales are conducted in well-known localities by men licensed by the Government, and acting under a sheikh appointed by the Zaptieh. . . . The Government now and then makes seizures of slaves entering the town . . . but . . . it sends for

[77] Evliya Çelebi, pp. 382, 376; cf. G. Baer, *Egyptian Guilds in Modern Times*, Jerusalem, 1964, p. 35.

[78] Reade to Cherif Pacha, Alexandria, August 8, 1867, FO 84/1277.

[79] Reade to Cherif Pacha; *Confidential Memorandum on Slave Dealing in Alexandria*, FO 141/84.

[80] *Memorandum by Mr. Petherick*, December, 1860, and *Report of Dr. Natterer*, April 5, 1860, inclosure in Colquhoun to Russell, Alexandria, May 29, 1860, FO 84/1120; Gray, p. 52.

[81] Reade to Cherif Pacha, August 8, 1867, FO 84/1277; Borg to Vivian, Cairo, April 19, 1878, and *Statement by Saîd el Soudani* in Borg to Governor of Cairo, April 18, 1878, FO 141/119; Sami Ibraheem to Borg, May 1, 1878, inclosure in Borg to Vivian, Cairo, May 2, 1878, FO 141/120. Cf. Baer, *passim.*

[82] Reade to Cherif Pacha; Cherif Pacha to Reade, Alexandria, August 18, 1867, FO 84/1277.

the said sheikh, and tells him to put out the seized slaves to Pashas and others, not in the name of slaves, but of servants entirely at their disposal. Of course there is a "consideration."[83]

This was neither the first nor the last instance of official commissions entrusted to slave dealers; for example, in 1860 Saʿīd placed an order for a bodyguard of five hundred Negro soldiers with the slave-trading firm of the above mentioned al-ʿAqqād brothers.[84]

Early in the nineteenth century there was in Cairo a special *wakāla* (caravanserai) for the slave trade, called *wakālat al-jallāba*, which was described as follows:

[il] n'a rien de remarquable que sa caducité et une grande mal-propreté; les deux sexes sont séparés dans de mauvaises petites chambres qui ont une grande analogie avec nos prisons: une autre partie est placée par groupes dans la cour de l'okele [the European pronunciation of *wakāla*], souvent sur les marchandises de leur maître.[85]

For the annual slave caravan, however, other *wakāla*s were specially hired and the newly imported slaves were exhibited there.[86] In the year 1235 A.H. /1819–20 Muḥammad ʿAlī established his monopoly of the Sudanese trade and took possession of the *wakālat al-jallāba* in Cairo;[87] but when his monopolies were abolished the old order was reestablished, except that the number of *wakāla*s grew. The condition of the slaves exhibited there was the subject of complaints of foreigners, and as a result Muḥammad ʿAlī ordered, in September, 1842, to transfer the sale of slaves to the vicinity of the mausoleum of Qāytbāy, on the outskirts of the city.[88] However, it seems to have returned soon to the city center and even spread to various quarters of Cairo—to judge by the list of *wakāla*s in which slaves were sold supplied by Consul Reade in 1867, which included such places as Wakālat al-Maḥrūqī and Wakālat al-Siliḥdār.[89]

Cairo was certainly the great depot of slaves and the center of the slave trade, though it was also pursued in other towns of Egypt. In 1873, the following was reported about Alexandria: "There are no public depots for the sale or exchange of slaves at Alexandria, but there are several slave

[83] Written by "a correspondent from Alexandria" and published in the *Pall Mall Gazette*, September 9, 1867, quoted by *The Anti-Slavery Reporter*, 3d ser., 15, no. 9 (September 16, 1867):208.

[84] *Report of Dr. Natterer* in Colquhoun to Russell, May 29, 1860, FO 84/1120; Gray, p. 52.

[85] L. Frank in *Mémoires sur l'Egypte*, 4:135.

[86] Girard in *Description de l'Egypte*, 2:634.

[87] Sāmī, 2:286.

[88] Sāmī, 2:518.

[89] Reade to Cherif Pacha, Alexandria, August 8, 1867, FO 84/1277; cf. Mubārak, 3:41.

dealers here . . . who carry on the business at their residences, their stock varying from 6 to 15 or 20 slaves, according to their means". The slave dealers met in a certain coffeehouse, and persons who intended to sell a slave invited the dealer to their houses. The slaves were brought to Alexandria by way of Cairo or Siwa.[90]

A very important occasion for trading in slaves was the *mawlid* (anniversary birthday festival of a saint connected with a fair) of Sayyid Aḥmad al-Badawī in Ṭanṭā. Every year hundreds of slaves were brought to this fair; the ordinary black ones were kept in tents erected on the outskirts of the town, while eunuchs, Abyssinian girls, and white slaves were lodged in the *wakālas*, hired in advance by the more important dealers for the duration of the *mawlid*.[91] In 1867 Consul Reade visited the *mawlid* of Ṭanṭā in disguise in order to liberate slaves; he saw five or six hundred slaves and estimated the total number of slaves assembled on this occasion for sale at between 1,500 and 2,000.[92] The slave trade was indeed such an important part of the *mawlid* that its suppression at the end of the century was one of the main causes of the considerable decline in the number of annual visitors to the *mawlid*.

The Disappearance of Slavery and of the Slave Trade

There can be no doubt that official measures taken against the slave trade were among the important causes for the final disappearance of slavery in Egypt. The history of these measures has never been written, but it is beyond the scope of this study to go into details. It is, however, necessary to begin this analysis of the final disappearance of slavery with a short but comprehensive survey of legislation and of official action taken in this matter.

Throughout the first half of the nineteenth century no official measures whatever were taken in Egypt against the slave trade. In conversations with British consuls Muḥammad ʿAlī declared that he was personally in favor of the abolition of slavery, but that he could not do anything about it because the practice was in conformity with Islam and because of the prejudices of the higher classes in Egypt.[93] ʿAbbās was not even reported to have disliked

[90] *Confidential Memorandum on Slave Dealing in Alexandria*, FO 141/84; See also H. de Vaujany, *Alexandrie et la Basse Egypte*, Paris, 1885, p. 160 and *The Anti-Slavery Reporter*, 3d ser., 21, no. 3 (August, 1878), p. 79.

[91] de Vaujany; *Confidential Memorandum on Slave Dealing in Alexandria*.

[92] Reade to Stanley, Alexandria, August 9, 1867, FO 141/63. The slaves who were not sold at the *mawlid* of Ṭanṭā were taken to Disūq in the northern Delta where the *mawlid* of the Saint Ibrāhīm al-Disūqī was held one week after that of al-Badawī in Ṭanṭā. See, for instance, Carr to Rogers, Kafr al-Zayyāt, August 20, 1871, FO 84/1341; Carr to Wallis, Kafr al-Zayyāt, April 23, 1877, FO 141/110.

[93] Barnett to Aberdeen, Alexandria, July 12, 1842, FO 84/426, and August 1, 1843, FO 84/486.

slavery or the slave trade. The first ruler of Egypt to ban the trade was Saʿīd. In December, 1854, half a year after his appointment as *wālī* of Egypt, he issued an order to the governor of the southern province prohibiting the import of slaves from the Sudan into Egypt,[94] and in 1855 he established a control post at Fashoda to check the transport of slaves down the White Nile.[95] To judge by the frequent reiteration of this prohibition, it does not seem to have been effective. In February, 1857, trade in black slaves was banned by the Ottoman Sultan, and a special firman to this effect sent to Saʿīd in the second half of that month opened by stating that former orders to suppress the slave trade had been neglected.[96] On September 14, 1858 Saʿīd issued a new order to the Governor of Alexandria demanding the complete and immediate liquidation of the slave trade. Saʿīd stated in this order that his numerous orders to put an end to the trade had been ignored, although the time during which slave dealers should have finally disposed of the slaves in their possession, namely, until the end of Dhī al-Ḥijja 1272 A.H./end of August, 1856, had expired long ago.[97] A similarly worded order was sent by Saʿīd to the Governor of Sennar and Khartoum on November 27, 1861.[98] However, none of Saʿīd's orders were put into effect, and at the end of his rule (1863) the trade in black slaves flourished as before.[99]

By 1863, however, with the abolition of slavery in America, the British public had become more and more interested in the Arab slave trade, and Britain initiated its official intervention to curb slavery and the slave trade in Egypt.[100] In addition to diplomatic pressure on the Egyptian government, British intervention in the 1860's consisted mainly in direct action by the consuls. At the beginning, some consuls and consular agents used their exterritorial rights to set free any slave who presented himself at the consulate. To this the Egyptian authorities would not agree, and in 1865 an agreement was reached according to which the Consul would request a letter of freedom from the Chief of Police for any slave seeking refuge at the

[94] For Turkish text and English translation of the order dated December 5, 1854, see FO 141/28. See also Hill, p. 102, n. 1, for another reference. Cf. Bruce to Clarendon, Cairo, January 17, 1855, FO 84/974. At that time, the Ottoman Sultan Abdülmecid had prohibited trade in white slaves only (October, 1854). See Brunschvig, p. 37.

[95] Hill, p. 102.

[96] For French translation of the text, see *Recueil de firmans impériaux ottomans adressés aux valis et aux khédives d'Egypte*, Cairo, 1934, pp. 268–70. Cf. Brunschvig.

[97] Sāmī, part 3, 1:299.

[98] Hill, p. 102.

[99] Cf. von Kremer, 2:84–86; Gray, pp. 73–78; Petherick to Colquhoun, Cairo, March 17, 1865, FO 141/57.

[100] For background and implications in the Sudan, see Gray, pp. 166 ff. The British and specific Sudanese aspects of the campaign against the slave trade are beyond the scope of this work.

consulate. The slave would then be accompanied by a representative of the Consul to witness the manumission. The consuls were instructed to keep a register of slaves thus set free and to check their later whereabouts.[101] However, in many cases the consuls continued to take action on their own,[102] which resulted in explicit instructions by the British government that, except in well-authenticated cases of cruelty on the part of masters toward their slaves, the official action of British consular officers should be limited to preventing, as far as possible, the import of slaves into Egypt and to procuring the manumission of those who may have been illegally imported.[103]

The attempt at preventing the import of slaves into Egypt by trying to suppress the slave trade in the Sudan and the Red Sea was indeed considered by the Egyptian government to be all that could be done about slavery during the 1870's. After the failure of administrative and military measures taken in the 1860's, Ismāʿīl tried to solve the problem by appointing European officials, mainly British, as governors and leaders of expeditions against the slave dealers; these foreigners would not be affected by vested interests and corruption, and thus would have better chances of fulfilling their task than the Turkish and Egyptian officials who had failed. Their efforts and the results of their activities belong to the history of the Sudan rather than to that of slavery in Egypt; moreover, they have been dealt with by many writers in great detail. The suppression of the slave trade was one of the main aims of Sir Samuel Baker's expedition (1869–73), and of Charles Gordon's appointment as Governor of the Equatorial Province (1873–76) and of his appointment as Governor-General of the Sudan (1877–80). Two other Europeans, the Italian Romolo Gessi and the Silesian Jew Eduard Schnitzer (Emin Pasha) were appointed by Gordon in Bahr al-Ghazal and Equatoria respectively. In addition, the Swiss J. A. W. Munzinger was appointed in 1871 as Governor of Massawa and in 1873 as Governor-General of the whole Red Sea and Somali coast. Late in 1876 the Scotsman H. F. McKillop, a senior officer in the Egyptian coastal service, undertook to combat the slave trade in the Red Sea with two or three vessels

[101] McCoan, p. 321; Sir Henry Bulwer (British Ambassador in Istanbul) to Stanley (British Consul in Alexandria), Alexandria, March 21, 1865, FO 141/57.

[102] See, for instance, West to Stanton, Suez, January 29 and March 3, 1866, FO 141/59; Rogers to Vivian, Cairo, August 2, 1873, FO 141/82 (relating Consul Reade's activities in 1867).

[103] Egerton to Reade, August 28, 1868, FO 84/1290 and 141/84. McCoan's claim (p. 321) that the Consular agent at Manṣūra "emancipated" no fewer than 1,700 slaves in a single month in 1873 is not accurate. His report reads as follows: "From the 13th July last I have sent to the Moudirieh (seat of the governor) 1,717 slaves. . . . All received letters, with the exception of the last 249." Harding to Vivian, Mansoura, August 25, 1873, FO 141/82.

on which he was to employ Britons.[104] In March, 1877, he was replaced by Captain Morice, R.N., who was in turn replaced by Captain Malcolm, R.N., appointed on January 1, 1878 as Director-General of the Egyptian Anti Slave Trade Police Service in the Red Sea;[105] but in June of the same year Captain Malcolm resigned because of his disagreements with Gordon about the implementation of the recently signed Anti Slave Trade Convention (see below).[106]

Although some of these missions and campaigns succeeded here and there in temporarily reducing the scope of the slave trade, there can be no doubt that on balance they failed. Ismāʿīl had the idea, or at least thought it convenient to declare, that as soon as the slave trade had been suppressed at its source, slavery in Egypt would vanish.[107] As against this, Gordon at some time opined "that the whole germ of the question rests in the demand for slaves and no more will be taken when the demand is removed."[108] In fact slavery in Egypt vanished, two decades later, when there emerged favorable conditions for eliminating both supply and demand. But, for reasons to be explained further on, in the 1870's there was no way out of this vicious circle.

On August 4, 1877 a Convention between the British and Egyptian Governments for the Suppression of the Slave Trade was signed at Alexandria.[109] According to this convention, the import and export of Sudanese and Abyssinian slaves were prohibited. Slave dealers were to be punished heavily, and the slaves owned by them freed. British vessels in the Red Sea were allowed to arrest ships transporting slaves and to set the slaves free. Four special "bureaux" were to be established, in Cairo, Alexandria, the Delta, and Upper Egypt, to register manumissions and to find work for freed slaves and schools for the children among them. Every person depriving a freed slave of his freedom or taking from him his manumission certificate was to be punished as a slave dealer. A special Khedivial decree of the same date fixed the punishment of slave dealers at five months to five

[104] See Vivian to Derby, Cairo, December 8, 1876, FO 84/1450, and January 13, 1877, FO 84/1472.

[105] "Directeur Général du service de l'abolition de la Traite dans la Mer Rouge et sur les côtes qui relèvent de notre jurisdiction." See inclosure in Cherif to Vivian, Cairo, January 9, 1878, FO 141/119. See also Vivian to Derby, Cairo, March 2, 1877, FO 84/1472, and January 8, 1878, FO 84/1511.

[106] FO 84/1511, *passim*. According to Lord Dufferin, "the Red Sea Service was suppressed after it had failed." See *Further Correspondence respecting Reorganization in Egypt*, Egypt No. 6 (1883), C. 3529 (*Dufferin Report*), p. 71.

[107] See Stanton to Granville, Cairo, December 20, 1872, FO 84/1354.

[108] Stanton to Derby, Alexandria, September 9, 1874, FO 84/1397.

[109] For English and French text, see *Blue Book*, Egypt No. 1 (1878). Arabic text in Sāmī, part 3, 3:1485–87.

years of hard labor. On the other hand, it stated that the prohibition of selling slaves from family to family would come into force in Egypt after seven years and in the Sudan after twelve years. Similarly, the trade in white slaves would be finally prohibited only after seven years. Regulations for the implementation of the convention were sent to the administrative authorities.[110]

The officers of the special bureaux were appointed about two months after the convention was signed. At their head was Maẓlūm Bey and the *ma'mūr* of the Cairo bureau was Sāmī Ibrāhīm.[111] In June, 1880, the Service for the Abolition of Slavery was established under Count della Sala, "a man of iron health and immense energy, with a reputation for soldierlike qualities gained in Mexico under Maximilian."[112] His demand that his office, instead of the police, should issue the certificates of manumission was not granted,[113] but he devised efficient plans for fighting the caravans of slave dealers, most of which were stopped by his vigorous action.[114] Moreover, importers of slaves who were caught were heavily punished.[115] In 1883, in the wake of the reorganization carried out after the British occupation of Egypt, the Service for the Abolition of Slavery was incorporated into the police and put under Colonel Schaefer. In 1885 the manumission bureaux were also placed under his orders and their number increased.[116] Another reorganization of the police after General Valentine Baker's death in 1887 resulted in the reestablishment of the Service as an independent department under the Minister of the Interior.[117]

The activity of the manumission bureaux increased gradually. In 1877–78, only 722 slaves were set free, but in the following year the number increased to 1,602. In 1885 and 1886 the number of slaves manumitted by

[110] For Arabic text, see Sāmī, part 3, 3: 1488–91. Both the Convention and the Regulations are recorded by Sāmī under the heading "24 Jumādā al-ūlā 1294," i.e., June 6, 1877, which must be an error. The Regulations themselves are not dated in Sāmī's text. According to another source, they were dated 7 Shawwāl 1294 A.H./October 14, 1877. See Borg to Malet, Cairo, March 1, 1880, FO 141/138.

[111] Vivian to Derby, Cairo, October 9, 1877, FO 84/1473; Borg to Vivian, Cairo, December 13, 1877, FO 141/112, and May 2, 1878, FO 141/120.

[112] *Majmū'at al-qarārāt*, 1880, pp. 98–99; Sir Edward Malet, *Egypt 1879–1883*, London, 1909, p. 63.

[113] Della Sala to Malet, Cairo, October 26, 1880, FO 141/140; della Sala to Riaz, Cairo, March 21, 1881, FO 141/151.

[114] Cf. della Sala to Malet, Assiout, November 8, 1880, FO 141/140; *Dufferin Report*, p. 71.

[115] See, for instance, *Majmū'at al-qarārāt*, 1880, pp. 109; 126–29.

[116] *Report on the Administration and Condition of Egypt and the Progress of Reforms*, Egypt No. 3 (1891), C. 6321, p. 36.

[117] P. Gelat, *Répertoire de la législation et de l'administration égyptienne*, 2 ème période, vol. 1, Alexandria, 1893, p. 588 (Minister of the Interior, Circular of July 21, 1888).

the bureaux had risen to 2,075 and 2,628 respectively. At the beginning, the Cairo and Alexandria bureaux achieved the highest number of freed slaves, but in the middle 1880's the most active bureaux were those of Upper Egypt, and the provinces of Lower Egypt surpassed Alexandria. By 1889 about 18,000 slaves had been manumitted by the bureaux.[118]

On November 21, 1895 a new Convention between Great Britain and Egypt for the Suppression of Slavery and the Slave Trade was signed at Cairo.[119] The new convention itself did not differ very much from the 1877 convention, except that it was more comprehensive, prohibiting as it did the import and export of all kinds of slaves, including white ones, and that a detailed *Règlement* for the control of the Red Sea shipping was appended to it. However, under Article 2, the Egyptian government undertook to publish a special law with detailed penalties for the different delicts connected with the slave trade, providing for the punishment of buyers as well as sellers. Such a *décret* was indeed published on January 21, 1896,[120] and it, rather than the convention, contributed the most important step forward in official measures against the slave trade. The penalty for importers of slaves was raised to as much as fifteen years of hard labor. Different penalties were fixed for buyers and sellers of slaves in Egypt, according to the character of the transaction, and the sale of slaves from family to family was also to be punished. The head of the family was made responsible for transactions going on in his harem. Thus a major problem of implementation of the 1877 law, namely, its vagueness, was overcome. Another obstacle, that of the incapacity of freed female slaves to marry without special sanction of their former masters (see below), was tackled by Article 4, which penalized anybody who prevented a freed slave "de jouir de sa pleine liberté et de disposer de sa personne." For the castration of slaves the death penalty or hard labor was laid down. Penalties were also fixed for complicity in dealing in slaves and for the intention of doing so, as well as for captains and owners of ships transporting slaves. A special decree of the same date specified the courts in which crimes connected with slavery and the slave trade were to be tried.[121] As a result of the laws of 1896 the prosecution of slave dealers, which had been intensified in the late 1880's and the early 1890's, gained

[118] For sources see n. 37 and 50, above; Borg to Vivian, Cairo, August 23, 1878, FO 141/121; Borg to Lascelles, Cairo, September 8, 1879, FO 141/129.

[119] For text, see *Treaty Series* No. 6 (1896), C. 8011. French text also in Gelat, 3 ème période, 1894–96, vol. 1, Alexandria, 1897, pp. 584–90, and in Gouvernement Egyptien, Ministère de l'Intérieur, *Législation administrative et criminelle*, 3d ed., vol. 2, Cairo, 1914, pp. 179–86.

[120] *Législation administrative et criminelle*, pp. 186–89.

[121] *Législation administrative et criminelle*, vol. 1, Cairo, 1912, pp. 464–67.

further momentum.[122] These laws and their vigorous implementation may indeed have been the most effective official measures ever taken to put an end to the slave trade and slavery in Egypt.

However, were it not for the internal development of Egyptian society, the administrative measures against slavery could never have succeeded. This is borne out by the tremendous obstacles the campaign against slavery encountered and by its ineffectiveness for a long time. First of all, the various attempts made prior to the Mahdi's revolt in the Sudan to tackle the slave trade at its source practically failed one after the other. Baker, and later Gordon, did not lack energy to enforce the prohibition of the trade, but neither had at his disposal an administrative machine strong enough to rule the country against the powerful organization of slave-trading interests.[123] The 1877 convention did not change this in the least, and Gordon gradually came to the conclusion that in the Sudan it was a dead letter: in July, 1879, he declared that, under the conditions prevailing in the Sudan, the convention could not be implemented.[124] Secondly, the measures against the slave trade had to be implemented by officials who themselves owned and purchased slaves, received bribes for disregarding the evasion of the law (sometimes in the form of a proportion of the illegally sold slaves), or even traded in slaves themselves and supplied them to influential and rich persons.[125] In the report on his visit to the *mawlid* of Ṭanṭā, Consul Reade wrote: "The Provincial Governor . . . had actually affected the release of a considerable number of slaves when, on the arrival of a higher functionary (the Inspector General of Provinces) the work of emancipation came suddenly to a close." And the Foreign Office added the following note to Reade's report:

> A letter from a "Scandrene" in today's *Times* says that Ismail Pasha Muffetich, or Chief of the Vice Roy's business affairs, went to Tantah and ordered the liberation of the slaves. "Whether" he adds "this was done I cannot say, but it

[122]For trials in the late 1880's and the early 1890's, see sources mentioned in note 71. For the late 1890's, see, for instance, Sir John Scott, "L'abolition de l'esclavage en Egypte," *Revue de l'Islam* (Paris), 6 (1901):91. (This paper was presented by Sir John Scott to the Anti-Slavery Congress which was held in Paris on August 6–8, 1900. The English version was published in *The Anti-Slavery Reporter*, 4th ser., 26, no. 4 (August-October, 1900):118–24).

[123]For a concise treatment of this matter, see P. M. Holt, *A Modern History of the Sudan*, London 1961, pp. 64–70. For details, see especially Gray, *passim.*

[124]Gordon to Consul General, Cairo (telegram), Khartoum, July 28, 1879, FO 141/131.

[125]See Colquhoun to Russell, Alexandria, August 17, 1863, FO 84/1204; Stanton to Clarendon, Alexandria, May 4, 1866, FO 84/1260; Reade to Stanley, Alexandria, August 9, 1867, FO 141/63; Borg to Vivian, Cairo, July 1, 1878, FO 141/120; Borg to Lascelles, Cairo, September 8, 1879, FO 141/129; Cookson to Malet, Alexandria, May 17, 1880, FO 141/138; della Sala to Riaz, Cairo, September 12, 1880, FO 141/140.

is certain that a few hours saw them back in the dealers' hands, and something more than a report added that the Muffetich found himself richer by about £4,000 and two Circassian slaves.[126]

Moreover, the slave traders had deep roots in Egyptian society. This is well illustrated by the case of a caravan importing slaves from Darfur which was caught near Asyūṭ in the spring of 1880. It was established that Maqār Dimyān, one of the richest merchants of Asyūṭ, who was the French Consular Agent and an intimate friend of the Governor, traded in slaves himself, the bulk of his wealth having been gathered from this branch of his business. All the slave dealers in the town were either his partners or in his pay.[127] The notables and shaykhs of Asyūṭ, including the *sartujjār* (chief of the merchants), tried, with the help of the shaykhs of the guardians, to conceal the slaves from the authorities, and even the *ʿumda* (headman) of the town was an accomplice and received a certain payment for every slave sold.[128] European observers had the impression that there existed some kind of solidarity among the Muslim population with regard to slaves and slavery. "Il existe, surtout dans la Haute Egypte, une veritable entente parmi les Mussulmans pour ne prendre, dans aucun cas, à leur service des esclaves affranchis." "It is evident that the hand of the whole Moslem community is raised against the man who in any way assists the Consulate in tracking out a fugitive slave."[129]

This was of course the result of the conflict between Islam and Islamic law, on the one hand, and Western concepts and innovations, on the other hand, in which the abolition of slavery was involved. Many Muslims considered the attempts to do away with slavery an encroachment on Qur'ānic law and tradition.[130] This led to very tangible consequences. For instance, the *qāḍī*s refused to perform marriages of female slaves who had not been

[126]Reade to Stanley, Alexandria, August 25, 1867, FO 84/1277. As late as 1894 it was reported that one of the Egyptian officials who recently had bought slave girls in Cairo was ʿAlī Pasha Sharīf, President of the Legislative Council, who had recommended the Council some months earlier to abolish the slave-trade department, claiming that no slave trade existed in Egypt anymore. See *The Anti-Slavery Reporter*, 4th ser., 14, no. 1, (January and February, 1894):8 and no. 5 (September and October, 1894):253 ff., quoting *The Times*, September 14, 1894.

[127]Borg to Malet, Cairo, May 8, 1880, FO 141/138; Hogg to Malet, Assiout, May 3, 1880, FO 141/140.

[128]Hogg to Malet, Assivut, May 3, 1880, FO 141/140, and April 6, 1881, FO 141/151; Circular of Riaz to governors, Cairo, February 29, 1880, FO 141/139. For the Asyūṭ slave caravan of 1880, see also *The Anti-Slavery Reporter*, 3d ser., 22 (1880): *passim*.

[129]Della Sala to Malet, Cairo, October 26, 1880, FO 141/140; West to Malet, Suez, January 11, 1881, reprinted in Malet, *Egypt 1879–1883*, p. 94.

[130]Cf. Rogers to Vivian, Cairo, August 2, 1873, FO 141/82; Baron de Malortie, *Native Rulers and Foreign Interference*, London, 1882, p. 116.

formally freed by their masters, and completely disregarded official certificates of manumission.[131] Moreover, since most of the slaves were an integral part of the families in which they lived, their manumission involved a breach in the secretiveness of the Arab family, so dear a value to the Egyptian and the Arab in general: instead of being *mastūra* ("covered" or "concealed"), the family would become *makshūfa* and its secrets revealed to the outside world.[132]

This mood was sustained by some very practical considerations. Large sums had been invested in the acquisition of slaves by persons belonging to almost every walk of life who saw no reason why they should be deprived of their property.[133] No wonder, therefore, that all kinds of tricks were used in order to evade the law. The prevalent method to prevent the freeing of slaves was for the master to accuse the runaway slave of theft, so that he could not be freed before he repaid the master.[134] This device became so usual that at a certain time the police, before liberating a slave, demanded that he should bring a person as guarantee that he will appear should his master accuse him of robbery, or arrested him and then made inquiries whether he had stolen something from his master.[135] The regulations for the implementation of the 1877 Convention included a special provision (Article 12) that accusations of theft should be inquired into only after the slave had been given his certificate of manumission;[136] nevertheless, in 1881 this device of slaveowners seems to have been still in use.[137]

To evade the prohibition of the slave trade, various methods were used. In the Sudan, slave dealers could practically move about freely with their slaves. As Gordon stated in 1879, two years after the first Anglo-Egyptian Convention had been concluded: "So long as slavery of any kind is a recognized institution, slave dealers can mask their transactions by declaring the slaves found in their possession . . . to be their personal property, i.e.

[131] Cf. Borg to Vivian, Cairo, August 15, 1878, FO 141/121; Borg to Lascelles, Cairo, September 8, 1879, FO 141/129; della Sala to Malet, Cairo, October 26, 1880, FO 141/140. *The Anti-Slavery Reporter*, 4th ser., 7, no. 1 (January–February, 1887):14–16.

[132] Cf. Borg to Cookson, Cairo, October 21, 1877, FO 141/112. For the concepts of *satara* and *kashafa*, see, for instance, M. Berger, *The Arab World Today*, New York, 1962, pp. 163–65.

[133] Cf. Borg to Vivian, Cairo, September 26, 1877, FO 141/112.

[134] Cf. Cherif to Stanton, Cairo, January 2, 1866, and West to Stanton, Suez, January 10, 1866, FO 141/59; Calvert to Reade, Alexandria, October 4, 1867, FO 141/62; Atkin to Stanton, Mansoura, May 12, 1873; Consular Agent, Mansoura, to Vivian, June 20, 1873; West to Vivian, Suez, August 5, 1873, FO 141/82.

[135] Stanley to Stanton, Alexandria, January 16, 1867, FO 141/62; encl. in Rogers to Stanton, Cairo, February 22, 1872, FO 141/78, pt. 1.

[136] Sāmī, part 3, 3:1489

[137] See della Sala to Riaz, Cairo, March 21, 1881, FO 141/151.

domestic slaves," and it was almost impossible to prove the contrary.[138] As to the import of slaves, we have mentioned above the subterfuge of declaring Circassian girls accompanied by a eunuch to be the harem of an important personage. The owners of caravans provided themselves with certificates of manumission or of marriage, which were supplied easily, for a small payment, by the *maḥkama* (religious court) of Darfur.[139] Another way of contraband was the *ḥajj*, the annual pilgrimage to Mecca. For a long time it was practically impossible to check how many of his slaves or wives a pilgrim had taken with him and how many he had brought back into Egypt. Only in February, 1887, was an order issued which made their registration compulsive for any pilgrim leaving Egypt.[140]

However, the reluctance of Egyptian slave-owning society to forgo the comfort of this institution was not the only obstacle on the way to the abolition of slavery. For at least two decades, beginning with the first attempts at freeing slaves made by British consuls in the 1860's, Egyptian society had not yet adjusted to absorbing a large number of freed slaves. As a result of the *qāḍīs*' attitude to the marriage of freed slave girls, most of the manumitted Circassians and quite a large proportion of black and Abyssinian girls became prostitutes.[141] In Cairo a Home for Freed Women Slaves was established under the auspices of the British and Foreign Anti-Slavery Society. The Egyptian government subscribed £250, which were later augmented by gradually increasing contributions,[142] but this could not solve the more fundamental problem.

As to male slaves, the question of what to do with them after manumission was equally difficult. In the 1860's and 1870's it often happened that slaves freed by the authorities and left alone were soon restored to their former states of slavery (sometimes by fraudulent means).[143] Many did not

138 *Analysis of the Slave Trade Convention of the 4th of August 1877*, Zohrab to Malet, Cairo, January 22, 1880, FO 141/138.

139 Della Sala to Malet, Cairo, October 26, 1880, FO 141/140.

140 *Majmūʿat al-awāmir al-ʿaliyya waʾl-dakrītāt*, Cairo, 1887, pp. 58–59. Cf. Baring to Salisbury, Cairo, February 12, 1887, Africa No. 4 (1887), C. 4994, p. 7.

141 Borg to Vivian, Cairo, February 3, 1879, FO 141/128; Borg to Lascelles, Cairo, September 8, 1879, FO 141/129; della Sala to Malet, Cairo, October 26, 1880, FO 141/140; cf. A. B. de Guerville, *New Egypt*, London, 1905, p. 139.

142 For details on this Home, see *The Anti-Slavery Reporter*, 4th ser., 5, no. 7 (July and August, 1885): 448–51; no. 9 (November and December, 1885): 505, 508; 6, no. 3 (May and June, 1886): 57–59; 9, no. 3 (May and June, 1889): 152–56; 16, no. 2 (March and April, 1896): 118–19; 20, no. 2 (March and May, 1900): 61–64. See also H. Lamba, "L'Esclavage en Egypte," *Revue de l'Islam*, 6 (1901): 69–75. For Egyptian government contributions, see Annexe B and C of the 1895 Convention, *Législation administrative et criminelle*, 2: 183.

143 Reade to Stanton, Cairo, May 28, 1868, FO 141/65; *Memorandum by Consul Reade on Slave Trade in Egypt*, London, August 13, 1868, FO 84/1290; Rogers to Clarendon, November 24, 1869, FO 84/1305; Rogers to Stanton, Cairo, April 23, 1872, FO 141/78, pt. 2.

find work and returned into slavery of their own free will. Describing the sale of Ismāʿīl al-Mufattish's slaves, Consul Vivian concluded: "All the slaves who demanded it were liberated, but the major part preferred to return to slavery to find shelter instead of being thrown upon the streets."[144] In 1878 Sāmī Ibrāhīm, the *ma'mūr* (officer in charge) of the Cairo Bureau for the Suppression of Slave Trade, declared that, because of the absence of a "Home" for manumitted slaves, he had many difficulties in disposing of them.[145] Sometimes they even joined gangs of robbers.[146] The reason for the emergence of this problem was of course the fact that before the 1880's no free labor market had developed in Egypt. Labor was supplied by guilds, each of which monopolized its specific craft or trade, and there were few opportunities for outsiders. At that time many observers expressed the opinion that slavery and the slave trade would flourish in Egypt until there was a complete revolution in Egyptian society.

Whether such a revolution did take place in Egypt in the last two decades of the nineteenth century may be open to controversy; but it is beyond doubt that most of the above mentioned impediments to the abolition of slavery and the slave trade vanished during that period. The Mahdist revolution cut off the principal source of supply, and after the reconquest of the Sudan an effective administration was established capable of suppressing such vestiges of the trade as still existed.[147] But Egyptian society had certainly changed too. The most important change affecting slavery was the emergence of a free labor market in the late 1800's and the 1890's. In contrast with the third quarter of the nineteenth century, in which towns in Egypt did not grow faster than the general population, the percentage of increase of the urban population during the last two decades of the century was twice as great as the total rate of population growth. At that time there was a notable movement of population from country to town. Moreover, those were the years in which the guild system broke down. Between 1887 and 1890 monopolistic practices of specific guilds were prohibited, and in 1890 the complete freedom of all trades was announced. The last function of the guild shaykhs, that of supplying labor, disappeared during the first decade of the twentieth century.[148] Former owners of slaves began to see that free labor was much cheaper and far less troublesome than slave

[144] Vivian to Derby, Cairo, April 14, 1877, FO 84/1472.

[145] Borg to Vivian, Cairo, May 2, 1878, FO 141/120; see also Borg to Vivian, Cairo, August 23, 1878, FO 141/121.

[146] Felice to Borg, Zagazig, March 1, 1882, FO 141/160.

[147] Cf. Holt, pp. 121–22, 148.

[148] Cf. chapters 8 and 9, above.

labor.[149] Thus they gradually replaced their slaves by hired domestic servants. Apparently this change was first visible in Cairo and only later in smaller and more distant towns; it was initiated by the upper and well-to-do class which was influenced by European customs, and later spread to other layers of the society.[150] As early as 1891, Cromer could write in his annual report that relatively few slaves were left in private houses. "Slaves now leave Harems even without coming to Manumission Bureaux." Therefore, buying them was no longer a good investment. "The demand for domestic servants is greater than the Home for Female Slaves can supply."[151]

Similarly, developments in the countryside had created conditions which were unfavorable to the employment of agricultural slaves. Whereas during the first part of the century Egypt had suffered from shortage of manpower, the increase of population had gradually brought about the beginning of a population surplus. Moreover, by the end of the century a large class of landless peasants had come into being as a result of abandonment or confiscation of land for nonpayment of taxes or other burdens (*corvée*, conscription) which the peasants could not bear or as a result of foreclosure for nonpayment of debts.[152] Thus, when a new agricultural boom occurred during the first few years of the twentieth century, landowners expanding their farms had at their disposal plenty of free agricultural labor, and nobody thought about acquiring slaves—as prosperous peasants had done in the 1860's.

At the same time, a small but important section of Egyptians had changed their attitudes toward slavery as a result of their cultural contact with Europe. A representative expression of this new attitude, which was part of the general trend of Islamic modernism, is a small book by Aḥmad Shafiq on Islam and slavery published in Cairo in 1891.[153] After explaining that Islam demands humane treatment of slaves and favors their manu-

[149] Baring to Salisbury, Cairo, February 12, 1887, Africa No. 4 (1887), C. 4994, p. 7; *Report on the Finances, Administration, and Conditions of Egypt, and the Progress of Reforms*, Egypt No. 1 (1896), C. 7978, pp. 22–24.

[150] See G. Schweinfurth to C. H. Allen, Cairo, October 23, 1882, *The Anti-Slavery Reporter*, 4th ser., 2, no. 11 (December 15, 1882):301.

[151] *Report on the Administration and Conditions of Egypt, and the Progress of Reforms*, March 29, 1891, Egypt No. 3 (1891), C. 6321, p. 36; cf. H. Steckner, *Beim Fellah und Khedive*, Halle, a.S., 1892, pp. 177–78.

[152] Cf. G. Baer, *A History of Landownership in Modern Egypt 1800–1950*, London, 1962, pp. 28–38.

[153] Ahmed Chefik, *L'Esclavage au point de vue musulman*, Cairo, 1891; translated into Arabic by Aḥmad Zakī under the title *al-Riqq fī l-Islām*, Cairo, 1892 (references below are to the Arabic translation). The book was written in an apologetic vein as a reply to prominent members of the Catholic Church who had accused Islam and the Arabs for their part in African slavery and the slave trade.

mission.[154] Shafīq concludes that Islam virtually intended to undermine the institution of slavery and to do away with it, but since it could not do so in a sudden and abrupt manner without danger to society as a whole, it contented itself temporarily with laws abolishing the negative aspects of slavery and encouraging manumission.[155] But this was not all. The slaves who were brought to Egypt from Africa were not even lawful slaves, according to the *sharīʿa*, because some of them were Muslims, and because they were not prisoners of a war waged according to the laws of the *sharīʿa*— the only source of slavery recognized by Islam. Therefore, the Egyptian government had the full right to set free all those who were still considered "slaves" in Egypt, and the 1877 Convention was fully in accordance with the *sharīʿa*.[156]

Similar views were apparently voiced at that time even among the Cairo ʿulamāʾ. Although Mr. Wilfrid Blunt's reports often included information based on wishful thinking, the following probably comprised at least a grain of truth:

> According to him [Shaykh Muḥammad al-Anbābī, Shaykh al-Azhar during the ʿUrābī insurrection and again later in the century] and to the vast majority of the Cairene Ulema, slavery was an institution permitted by the Koran only when Islam was in a state of war with idolators. Then captives on the battle-field were, by custom rather than by precept, legitimately enslaved—this for the sole purpose of their conversion to the true faith, and with an advice to pious persons among the captors to give them at the end of a few years their freedom. . . . Now, as no religious war has recently been waged against any idolatrous nation, it follows that no captives have been legitimately made and, therefore, the slaves brought into Mahommedan markets, either openly or clandestinely, are the result of robbery. As such they are in reality free men illegally detained. . . .[157]

This attitude seems to have become widespread among educated Egyptians at that time. A sign of the new mood were the discussions of the January, 1896, laws on slavery and the slave trade in the Legislative Council. Although in the 1890's this Council was very critical of British policy in Egypt and very much influenced in its deliberations by religious feelings and convictions,[158] when the antislavery laws were discussed not

---

[154]Shafīq, *al-Riqq fī'l-Islām*, pp. 67 ff., 85–92.

[155]Shafīq, p. 94. This later became the accepted view of the Islamic Modernists. See, for instance, Rashīd Riḍā, *Tafsīr al-Manār*, vol. 11, 2d ed., Cairo, 1953, pp. 288–89.

[156]Shafīq, pp. 95–96, 101. For a similar opinion expressed by the Egyptian paper *al-Muʾayyad*, see Shafīq, Appendix, p. 124.

[157]Letter from Mr. Wilfrid Blunt to Mr. Charles H. Allen, Secretary to the Anti-Slavery Society, London, March 17, 1882, *The Anti-Slavery Reporter*, 4th ser., 2, no. 4 (April 15, 1882):91.

[158]Cf. J. M. Landau, *Parliaments and Parties in Egypt*, Tel Aviv, 1953, pp. 46–49.

a single view opposing the suppression of slavery and the slave trade was expressed.[159]

Thus the combination of administrative, economic, social, and cultural factors facilitated the suppression of the slave trade and the disappearance of slavery in Egypt toward the end of the nineteenth century. In the twentieth century, slavery no longer constituted a problem in Egypt at all.

[159]See Egypt No. 1 (1896), C. 7978, pp. 22–24.

11

The Beginnings of Municipal Government

It has been often pointed out that, in contrast with the classical Greek city, the Islamic city never developed into an autonomous league of citizens or attained corporate status or rights. It was not independently administered by its inhabitants but by the central government, which created the administrative apparatus of the city and appointed all its important functionaries. Juridically it did not differ from its rural surroundings and it was not distinguished by the grant of privileges. Among other reasons, this was the result of the fact that the Islamic *umma* was an indivisible unit, and the town was first and foremost considered to be the place where the religious duties of the Muslim could best be performed.[1]

The universal validity of this characterization has recently been challenged. In particular, it has been Professor Claude Cahen who has stressed the existence of different types of urban society in different areas of the Islamic world and the emergence of autonomous and popular forces in some of the Islamic cities. However, even he has come to the conclusion that such a development did not take place in Egypt, where no traces of urban popular autonomy or municipal development could be detected.[2] Compared with the countries of the Fertile Crescent, Egypt always has had a much more centralized government. This was the result of the preeminent importance of the government for the economy as a regulator of irrigation

Originally published as "The Beginnings of Municipal Government in Egypt," *Middle Eastern Studies*, 4, no. 2 (January, 1968), pp. 118–40.

[1]See G. E. von Grunebaum, "Die islamische Stadt," *Saeculum*, 6 (1955):138–53; X. de Planhol, *The World of Islam*, Ithaca, N. Y., 1959, pp. 8–9, 14, etc.

[2]C. Cahen, "Zur Geschichte der städtischen Gesellschaft im islamischen Orient des Mittelalters," *Saeculum*, 9 (1958):59–76; C. Cahen, *Mouvements populaires et autonomisme urbain dans l'Asie musulmane du Moyen Âge*, Leiden, 1959.

by the waters of the Nile, of Egypt's relatively easy communications, and of its relatively uniform population.

Whatever the situation may have been in medieval Egypt, in Ottoman Egypt the indigenous town population had no formal share in political power or executive authority. The *dīwān* (council) of Cairo established by Napoleon Bonaparte in 1798 was therefore an important innovation.[3] However, for various reasons it cannot be considered as a beginning of municipal government in Egypt. Not only did it work under close French control and supervision, but, more important, its existence was so short-lived that its influence on later developments was negligible: no connection whatever can be established between Bonaparte's experiment in conferring political power on Cairo's *ʿulamāʾ* and the first municipal institutions which emerged in Egypt generations later.

The long delay in the establishment of municipal institutions in Egypt was certainly not unrelated to a fundamental trait of Egyptian social history: the chiefs of the various basic administrative and economic units in which Egypt's population was organized were all appointed by the government and not freely elected by the members of the units which they headed. The village headman, the *shaykh al-balad* or *ʿumda*, always represented in Egypt the authorities to the villagers rather than the villagers before the authorities. Therefore, he was appointed in the eighteenth century by the *multazim* (tax farmer) and throughout the nineteenth century by the government.[4] Similarly, the *shaykh al-ḥāra*, the chief of the town quarter, was appointed by the authorities of the central government from the beginning to the end of the nineteenth century.[5] The same is true for the shaykhs of the guilds, although the opinions of important members of the guilds were of course taken into consideration when the government chose the person to be appointed shaykh.[6] Thus no indigenous nuclei of self-government existed which were able to develop into municipal institutions.

It is probably true that the first kind of municipal institution in modern Egypt was the so-called *Conseil de l'Ornato* (or *Commission mixte permanente de l'Ornato*; in official Arabic use: *Majlis al-ūrnāṭū*), which was established in Alexandria on September 29, 1834.[7] Unfortunately, information about this commission is very scarce. We know from one source that among its

[3] Cf. P. M. Holt, *Egypt and the Fertile Crescent 1516–1922*, London, 1966, pp. 7–8, 161–62.

[4] See chapter 3, above.

[5] Cf. F. Mengin, *Histoire sommaire de l'Egypte sous le gouvernement de Mohammed-Aly*, Paris, 1839, p. 114; *Majmūʿat al-qarārāt waʾl-manshūrāt*, Cairo, Būlāq, 1887, pp. 69–70; 1890, pp. 444–45.

[6] G. Baer, *Egyptian Guilds in Modern Times*, Jerusalem, 1964, pp. 69–72.

[7] For the date, see Zoulfikar Pasha to Charles Hale (American Agent and Consul General), Alexandria, July 18, 1869, PRO, FO 141/70.

members were the Consuls General of England, Greece, and Sweden,[8] and from another that Shaykh al-Ghazalātī (perhaps Gharayānī) was a member.[9] Among its functions the following have been mentioned—again in different sources: giving names to streets;[10] dealing with violations of building regulations;[11] supervising building activity in general; and organizing a network of streets.[12] There can be no doubt that the establishment of such a council in Alexandria had something to do with the presence of the European consuls and a European merchant community in that town. To call it the "beginnings of municipal government" is certainly an exaggeration.[13] In any case, it remained the only municipal institution in Egypt during the second third of the century. We have found no accounts of its activities, either in the copious literature on Egypt under Muḥammad ʿAlī, ʿAbbās, or Saʿīd or in unpublished consular reports.

Meanwhile, however, the foreign community of Alexandria had grown to a considerable extent, especially as the result of the great influx of foreigners at the end of the 1850's and the beginning of the 1860's. Part of the thirty thousand to fifty thousand foreigners who yearly entered Egypt went to Cairo and beyond, and another part left Egypt again after a short stay. But among those who stayed for a longer time, settlers in Alexandria were the majority. Their number must have amounted to between thirty thousand and forty thousand in 1860 and fifty thousand and sixty thousand at the end of the 1860's; their proportion in Alexandria's total population was variously estimated at between one-quarter and one-third.[14] Many of them had a strong economic and social interest in the development of urban facilities and municipal services in Alexandria.

However, the immediate impetus for the next move to establish municipal institutions in Egypt came from developments elsewhere. In July, 1858, an experimental municipality was established in a "model district" of Pera and Galata in Istanbul, where foreign residents were predominant. A municipal

[8] Zoulfikar Pasha to Charles Hale.

[9] Amīn Sāmī, *Taqwīm al-Nīl*, part 2, Cairo, 1928, p. 538.

[10] Sāmī, part 2, p. 538.

[11] Philippe Gelat, *Répertoire de la législation et de l'administration égyptienne.*Ire période, vol. 1, Alexandria, 1888, pp. 94–95.

[12] Sāmī, part 3, vol. 2, Cairo, 1936, p. 568.

[13] R. L. Hill, "Baladiyya: (2) Arab East," *The Encyclopaedia of Islam*, new ed. (*EI*² in later references), 1:976. It is curious that, on the other hand, the first real municipality in Egypt, namely the Alexandria municipality of 1890, is not mentioned in this article.

[14] See A. von Kremer, *Aegypten*, Leipzig, 1863, 2:134–35; E. de Régny, *Statistique de l'Egypte, Année 1872*, Alexandria, 1872, p. 132; *Année 1873*, Cairo, 1873, p. 19; D. S. Landes, *Bankers and Pashas*, London, 1958, pp. 87–88. Higher estimates are probably exaggerations; see Landes, p. 88, note 2, and also, for instance, Stanley to Clarendon, Alexandria, June 18, 1869, FO 78/2092 ("Europeans form quite half the population of Alexandria").

council, consisting of a chairman and twelve members, was to deal with "all that concerns cleanliness and public amenities"—the latter including a very large list of services. As Professor Bernard Lewis has pointed out, these measures did not yet represent an approach to the European conception of municipal institutions, since the city was not recognized as a corporate person, nor was there any suggestion of election or representation. What was created was a new kind of administrative agency of the government with new kinds of tasks and a measure of budgetary autonomy.[15]

In Egypt, however, conditions were not yet ripe even for such a moderate innovation. Some time after the Pera and Galata municipality had been established, Saʿīd gave an order to implement the Istanbul regulations in Cairo and Alexandria as well. This, however, raised the opposition of the European consuls. As a result Zoulfikar Pasha, Egypt's Foreign Minister, requested on 11 Jumādā al-ūlā 1278 A.H./November 14, 1861 the Viceroy's permission to revise the Istanbul regulations in accordance with the *ornato* regulations in use in Egypt, but without impairing the basic provisions of those regulations. Accordingly Saʿīd issued an order (dated 24 Jumādā al-ūlā 1278 A.H./November 27, 1861) to form a commission, half of its members to be local notables and merchants and the other half prominent European owners of real estate or other highly respected Europeans as well as two or three government officials. The commission was to be headed by the Governor, and it was to submit its draft revision of the Istanbul regulations to the consuls for approval.[16]

It took exactly seven years until this commission was appointed. We have not found a clear indication of the reasons for this delay in any of our sources, but, in view of later discussions with which we shall deal below, they may be guessed. Apparently the Egyptian government did not see, at that time, a chance to overcome the unwillingness of the powers and their consuls to relinquish any of the foreigners' privileges. In any case, in 1864 it preferred to strengthen the existing *majlis al-ūrnāṭū* rather than experimenting with new institutions. On August 25 of that year the Governor of Alexandria was instructed to establish an enlarged *majlis* (council) under the chairmanship of Colucci Bey, the Head of the Sanitary Board, who was involved in all activities connected with the planned Alexandria municipality at that time. The new *majlis* was to be composed of six officials and six foreigners.[17] Again, no reasons are known to us for the abandonment

[15] B. Lewis, "Baladiyya: (1) Turkey," *EI²*, 1:973. For background of this development, see B. Lewis, *The Emergence of Modern Turkey*, London, 1961, pp. 387–94.

[16] Sāmī, part 3, 1:388.

[17] Sāmī, part 3, 2:569.

of this initiative; whatever they may have been, only a few months later, on December 7 of the same year, the whole *ornato* institution was incorporated in the newly created Ministry of Public Works under Nubar Pasha.[18]

A new turn occurred four years later, probably under the influence of the 1868 municipal code of regulations, which attempted to extend the commission system of Pera and Galata to the rest of the fourteen districts of Istanbul.[19] On October 5, 1868 Zoulfikar Pasha, Egypt's Foreign Minister, informed the consuls that a "provisional and preparatory municipal commission of Alexandria" had been appointed, with Colucci Bey as its president.[20] In addition to the president, the commission included thirteen members, eight of them non-Egyptians by origin. It had a secretary, de Régny, and an Egyptian interpreter. The commission met for the first time on October 13, 1868 and for the last time on May 31, 1869. It composed a municipal code with detailed regulations for the projected Alexandria municipality which were approved by the Egyptian government on June 3, 1869.[21] According to this code, the municipality was to be composed of twenty-four councillors and a president to be appointed by the Khedive. The councillors were to be elected by owners or lessees of real estate of a certain value and were themselves to be owners or lessees of real estate of a still higher minimum value. The right to elect and to be elected were both conditioned by a five-year residence in Alexandria. The functions of the municipality were defined as follows (Article 16):

> 1. De pourvoir directement à la voirie, à la salubrité, au bien-être, a l'embellissement de la ville et de ses environs, à l'établissement de l'état civil, et généralement aux intérêts locaux, en tant qu'ils ne rentrent pas dans les attributions du Gouvernement.
>
> 2. De pourvoir indirectement à la police municipale, en se mettant d'accord avec la préfecture de police ou l'autorité supérieure pour tout ce qui se attache à cet objèt.
>
> 3. De créer, percevoir et administrer toutes ressources nécessaires à ses dépenses, comme de gérer les biens qui appartiendront dûment à la ville.[22]

Decisions of the municipal council would have to be sanctioned by the Minister of the Interior; the Governor of Alexandria and the Prefect of Police would be allowed to attend its sessions, with consultative votes. The

[18] Sāmī, part 3, 2:581.

[19] Cf. Lewis, "Baladiyya," p. 974.

[20] See Zoulfikar to Stanton, Alexandria, October 5, 1868, FO 141/66.

[21] Ville d'Alexandrie, *Règlements de la municipalité d'Alexandrie, approuvés par le gouvernement du Khédive d'Egypte au 3 juin 1869*, Alexandria, 1869.

[22] Ville d'Alexandrie, pp. 10–11.

first transitional council would be appointed by the government. According to a "Règlement Intérieur" included in the code, the municipality was to be composed of a general secretariat, a department of roads and streets, a department of public health, as well as sections of administrative services, municipal police, and finance. Appended were a "Règlement de Voirie," a very detailed "Règlement de Salubrité," as well as a "Règlement Municipal des Peseurs et Mesureurs Publics," a "Règlement des Voitures Publiques de Place et de Remise," and a "Arrèté Ministériel instituant une Garde Municipale" dated June 3, 1869. However, the crucial part of the code was the "Règlement Municipal pour l'impôt foncier sur les immeubles d'habitation,"[23] which provided for the establishment of a house tax amounting to 8 per cent of the income from urban property, to be collected by the municipality in the name of the government. A municipal committee was to fix annually the amount to be paid by each property owner and to make final decisions about remissions and exemptions.

On June 8, 1869 the code was transmitted to the consuls together with a circular letter asking them to name the foreign candidates for appointment as councillors of the first municipal council, as laid down in the regulations.[24] During June and July the consuls held consultations at the residence and under the chairmanship of their doyen Charles Hale, the American Agent and Consul General. On July 10, Hale asked the Foreign Minister whether the regulations included in the code had already been approved by the Egyptian government. Zoulfikar replied that the règlement concerning roads and streets was based on measures taken long ago by the *ornato* commission; that the règlement concerning public health was a codification of orders issued by the Board of Health; that the house tax had been established the same year as communicated to the consuls in a circular of January 7, 1869; that the regulation for weighers and measurers had been issued on September 29, 1868 by request of commercial and financial interests of Alexandria; and that the regulation of public vehicles had been issued, in agreement with the consuls, on February 22, 1869, and implemented soon afterward.[25]

These explanations were of no avail. On July 22, 1869 Hale informed Zoulfikar that, at a meeting held the same day at his residence by the members of the consular corps in order to examine the regulations formulated by the preparatory municipal commission, they had come to the

[23] Ville d'Alexandrie, pp. 53–60.

[24] Zoulfikar to Stanley, Alexandria, June 8, 1869, FO 78/2092 and 141/70. For provisions regarding the candidates for the first council, see Ville d'Alexandrie, p. 12.

[25] Hale to Zoulfikar, Alexandria, July 10, 1869; Zoulfikar to Hale, Alexandria, July 18, 1869, FO 141/70. The circular of Zoulfikar dated Cairo, January 7, 1869, is also to be found in FO 141/70.

conclusion "que ces règlements portaient dans leur ensemble de profondes atteintes à la juridiction consulaire et aux usages existants." They had, therefore, to be considered as mere projects which needed the approval of the foreign governments to become definite regulations. Municipal institutions were certainly very useful, but they had necessarily to be limited by the existing treaties. The consuls would be ready to cooperate in drafting new regulations in accordance with the existing principles of consular jurisdiction.[26]

Thus a rather paradoxical situation emerged. The idea of municipal government was certainly a European conception with almost no indigenous root in the Middle East in general and in Egypt in particular. The attempt to implement it was the result of the growth of the foreign community in Egypt, especially in Alexandria. The immediate impetus came from the actual establishment of a municipality in Pera and Galata, where foreign residents were predominant. Yet the factor which frustrated the first practical effort of the Egyptian government to establish municipal institutions was the foreign consuls. What were their reasons, and why was a municipality feasible at that time in Pera and Galata but not in Alexandria?

In their memorandum of July 22, 1869, the consular corps in Egypt rather vaguely explained their opposition to the draft of the Egyptian government by its violation of consular jurisdiction and existing usage. By "existing usage" they probably meant the fiscal immunity enjoyed by foreigners in Egypt. In contrast with other parts of the Ottoman Empire, it was the customary privilege of foreigners in Egypt that no tax whatever could be imposed on them unless it was sanctioned by a specific international convention.[27] It took another fifteen years until the foreign powers sanctioned the imposition of a house tax on foreigners in Egypt, and twenty years until they sanctioned other municipal taxes. In 1869 no sanction of this kind was feasible, and the foreign consuls in Egypt certainly were not ready to waive the special privileges enjoyed by their fellow countrymen; on the contrary, they vied with each other in defending them fanatically. It was of no avail that Zoulfikar Pasha tried to blur the difference between Egyptian and Ottoman usage by declaring that the regulations concerning the new house tax were based "sur des principes qui, depuis des siècles,

[26] Hale to Zoulfikar, Alexandria, July 22, 1869, FO 141/70.

[27] Cf. G. Pélissié du Rausas, *Le Régime des capitulations dans l'empire ottoman*, vol. 2, Paris, 1905, p. 465; M. Bahi ed Dine Barakat, *Des Privilèges et immunités dont jouissent les étrangers en Egypte vis-à-vis des autorités locales*, Paris, 1912, pp. 187–89.

dominent *en Orient*. . . ."[28] Without this tax, however, the new municipality could not exist.

The violation of consular jurisdiction by the draft municipal code consisted, according to Consul Stanton, in the provisions for imposing fines and penalties by local authorities on foreigners, among others. Such fines and penalties were provided for by all the various règlements appended to the code (see above). To this the consuls could not agree so long as no mixed jurisdiction had been created.[29] Nubar Pasha too considered the failure of the attempt to establish, in 1869, a municipality in Alexandria to have been the result of the nonexistence of some system of mixed international jurisdiction at that time.[30] In this connection it should be pointed out that, again in contrast with the usage in other parts of the Empire, it had become the custom in Egypt that any case in which a foreigner was the defendant was to be tried by the consul of the accused foreigner according to the law of his home country.[31] This privilege made it impossible for the consuls to agree that foreigners in Egypt be subjected to any local legislation.

Finally, an important reason for the opposition of the consuls to this scheme was their fear that foreigners would have no control of the planned municipality. Consul Stanton said so in so many words in his memorandum to Lord Clarendon: the president would have too much power, and there would be no guarantee for an adequate representation of the European community.[32] In this respect too the situation in Alexandria was different from that in Galata and Pera: in Galata and Pera Europeans were the predominant element so that they virtually administered themselves, while in Alexandria they constituted only less than a third of the population. This difference already served in 1861 as an explanation for the decision not to implement the 1858 Istanbul order in Egypt automatically but to revise it in accordance with Egyptian conditions.[33]

All these differences between conditions in Turkey and those in Egypt, which resulted in foreign opposition to the establishment of municipalities in Egypt for decades, explain the striking contrast between the revised Ottoman vilayet law of January, 1871, and the Egyptian law of 22 Jumādā al-thāniya 1288 A.H./September 5, 1871 concerning the establishment of administrative and judicial councils in the villages, towns, and provinces

[28] Zoulfikar to Hale, Alexandria, July 18, 1869, FO 141/70 (my italics).
[29] Stanton to Clarendon, Cairo, July 21, 1869, FO 78/2093.
[30] Nubar to Stanton, Cairo, February 14, 1871, FO 141/75, pt. 3.
[31] Pélissié du Rausas, pp. 244 ff.; Bahi ed Dine Barakat, pp. 172 ff.
[32] See note 29, above.
[33] Cf. Colucci Bey in *Bulletin de l'Institut Egyptien*, 1862–63, pp. 45–46.

of Egypt.[34] Although there were numerous divergences in detail which are outside the scope of our discussion, the Egyptian law was certainly influenced by the revised Ottoman vilayet law, especially with regard to its provisions concerning the local administrative councils (Articles 61–110 of the Ottoman law; Chapter 1, parts 1–2 of the Egyptian law). All these councils were no municipalities: they had no separate budget distinguished from the revenue and expenditure of the state and no rights of legislation, and legally they did not constitute a corporate body. In fact their tasks did not exceed assisting government executives in performing their functions. However, Articles 111–29 of the Ottoman law provided for the establishment of municipal councils in provincial cities along the same general lines as the 1868 municipal code of Istanbul. These had at least one important attribute of a municipality, namely, a separate budget with revenue from various taxes and dues—not just voluntary contributions (Article 126). Provisions for the establishment of such municipal councils were completely absent in the Egyptian law. True, apparently this part of the Ottoman law was not carried out,[35] but in 1877 a new very detailed *vilayat belediye kanunu* (provincial municipal code) was enacted.[36] Some attempt seems to have been made to implement parts of this code in Turkey and the Arab provinces[37]—but not in Egypt. This is particularly remarkable in view of the fact that the new system of local councils in the Arab provinces of the Empire had been introduced by the Egyptians during their occupation of Syria.[38]

In fact no municipality was established in Alexandria before 1890, and Cairo had to wait even half a century longer. During the 1870's and 1880's some administrative functions both in Cairo and in Alexandria were performed by what was called *al-dā'ira al-baladiyya* or *ma'mūr al-dā'ira al-baladiyya*, but the former was no more than a department of the central administration, and the latter an appointed government official.

[34] For the revised Ottoman vilayet law of 1871, see *Düstur*, 1:625 ff.; G. Young, *Corps de droit ottoman*, vol. 1, Oxford, 1905, pp. 47 ff.; G. Aristarchi Bey, *Législation ottomane*, vol. 3, Constantinople, 1874, pp. 7 ff.; see also R. H. Davison, *Reform in the Ottoman Empire*, Princeton, 1963, pp. 159–60; B. Lewis, "Baladiyya," *EI*², p. 974. For the Egyptian law of September, 1871, see Sāmī, part 3, 3:943 ff.; and [A. von Kremer?], *Reformen im Verwaltungs—und Finanzwesen Egyptens*, Wien, 1872. Date according to Sāmī; it should be noted, however, that 22 Jumādā II corresponds to September 8, not 5, of that year.

[35] Davison. Lewis.

[36] For text, see *Düstur*, 4:538 ff.; Young, pp. 69 ff.

[37] "Baladiyya," *EI*², pp. 974–95.

[38] Cf. M. Maoz, "The Balance of Power in the Syrian Town during the Tanzimat Period, 1840–61," *Bulletin of the School of Oriental and African Studies*, (University of London), 29, part 2 (1966):280–85 and *passim*.

Meanwhile, however, the Alexandria merchants, in particular the non-Egyptian exporters, took the initiative in establishing an institution for carrying out some functions of a municipality. In 1869 they decided to levy upon themselves voluntarily a tax of twenty *para* per *qinṭār* of exported cotton and ten *para* per *ardabb* of exported cereals for the purposes of paving and draining the roads of Mīnat al-Baṣal and Mīnat al-Sharqāwiyya, the quarters where nearly all the stores for cotton, grain, seeds, and other export articles were situated and where the cotton market was held. This action was taken after they had suffered considerable losses as a result of their carts getting stuck in the mud every winter and being exposed to the rain for days before reaching the shipping quay. After negotiations between the representative of the exporters, Mr. Ludwig Müller, and the government, a committee was appointed on March 14, 1869 consisting of nine members representing the merchants and under the presidency of the Governor of Alexandria. It was called "Commission du Commerce d'Exportation" and its mandate was fixed for a period of ten years.

After completing the paving of all the roads in the two business quarters as well as building up the quays of the Maḥmūdiyya Canal along these quarters, the merchants consented to extend their activity to the town of Alexandria. Thus many streets in the town were paved under an arrangement whereby the committee of exporters paid one half while the owners of the houses in these streets were expected to bear the other half of the expenses. In addition to the expenses of paving, the committee defrayed the cost of repairing the streets already paved and keeping them in order.

The total amount levied by the committee of exporters during the first ten years (March, 1869–March, 1879) ammounted to £216,480. The Egyptian government contributed to the work done by the committee an annual subsidy of £6,250. In March, 1879, when the mandate granted to the committee expired, it was renewed by the government and the name of the body was changed into the "Mixed Provisional Municipal and Commercial Committee," but for another seven years its membership was confined to nine representatives of the exporters under the presidency of the Governor of Alexandria. However, on March 13, 1886, the general assembly of the exporters passed a resolution that, "in view of the great sacrifices which they had already made for the town, the time had arrived for the government to distribute equitably between the exporters, importers, and property owners of Alexandria the burden of executing further necessary improvements." Therefore, a new committee was appointed by the government on December 20, 1886, consisting, in addition to the representatives of the exporters, of three representatives each of the importers and property owners and six Egyptians nominated by the government. The exporters and importers were to continue to pay, as before, a tax of one half per mille on all goods exported and imported and the landlords were to contribute voluntarily a sum of £E 4,000 per annum. The exporters would then contribute a sum equal to the combined shares of the importers and landlords, and, under these conditions, the government would renew the subsidy of £E 6,000 per annum. On May 11, 1887, however, the representatives of the landlords on the committee declared that they were unable to make their contribution of £E 4,000 because of the heavy burden of the newly introduced house tax. The government came to the rescue by consenting to add to the annual subvention one percent of the tax on building property, that is, more than £E 5,000.[39]

These arrangements worked for such a long time mainly because the contributions were voluntary and the control in the hands of the foreign merchants. When, however, the committee ceased to function in 1888, the representatives of the foreign powers agreed that the contributions formerly levied on a voluntary basis become obligatory taxes.[40] This, as well as the general principle of corporate representation as established by the commercial committee, became the basis on which the 1890 Alexandria municipality was founded.[41]

However, even before the establishment of the 1890 municipality in Alexandria municipal government in Egypt developed in some other directions. Apparently under the influence of the activity of the Alexandria merchants, some notables and merchants of Manṣūra had submitted a a petition with the request to make similar arrangements. As a result, a decree was issued on June 8, 1881 authorizing the inhabitants of Manṣūra to levy "voluntary taxes" on goods exported from the town or imported into it in order to enable them to execute works of road paving, the construction of sewers, as well as lighting and maintenance of streets and roads (Article 1). The tax-paying inhabitants were permitted to establish a commission (*qūmisyūn* in Arabic), consisting of the *mudīr* of the province as *ex officio* president, the Chief Engineer and Chief Physician of the province, and eight members elected from among the property-owning literate businessmen of the town (Articles 2, 3, 5). This commission was to decide about the

[39] Report by Consul Cookson, Alexandria, 1876 and 1877, *Commercial Reports*, 1878, 75:134–35;Report by Consul Calvert, Alexandria, 1878, *Commercial Reports*, 1878–79, 71:39–40; Calvert to Vivian, Alexandria, July 5, 1878, FO 141/120; A. Wright and H. A. Cartwright, *Twentieth Century Impressions of Egypt*, London, 1909, pp. 432–33.

[40] D'Aubigny to Flourens, Cairo, Febraury 3, 1888 and April 2, 1888, and d'Aubigny to Goblet, November 16, 1888, Affaires Etrangères, *Documents diplomatiques, affaires d'Egypte 1884–1893*, Paris, 1893, pp. 360–62.

[41] Affaires Etrangères, pp. 362 ff.

taxes to be levied and the works to be executed (which, would have, however, to be approved by the Minister of Public Works) (Article 8). An annually elected three-man committee, also headed by the *mudīr*, was to sign the contracts and orders of payment and to hire and dismiss employees (Article 9).[42] It seems, however, that for at least fifteen years this decree remained a dead letter.[43]

Even more rudimentary municipal arrangements came into being three years later in Ṭanṭā. According to a circular of the Ministry of the Interior dated 5 Dhū al-Qaʿda 1301 A.H./August 27, 1884, the *mudīr* of Gharbiyya province had assembled the notables of Ṭanṭā, and they had decided to organize the cleaning and maintenance of streets by levying a voluntary tax from the owners of houses and shops. For this purpose a special committee of seven notables had been appointed by the *mudīr*. The arrangement was approved by the Ministry, and other *mudīr*s and towns were encouraged to follow suit.[44] This seems to have happened in Damietta, where in 1887 the inhabitants asked to be authorized to impose facultative taxes upon goods imported into their town and exported from it, to be used according to the decisions of a committee of five members under the presidency of the Governor. According to one source, this initiative was of great benefit for the town.[45]

It should be stressed that all these arrangements were far from being municipalities. Not only was it expressly stated that all contributions from the inhabitants were to be voluntary, but no powers of legislation of any kind were vested in the commissions. The range of their activity was extremely small. They did not become a corporate body from the legal point of view, which considerably narrowed the scope of their action. In this respect it is interesting to note that the Manṣūra decree included a provision that all works executed according to the new arrangement would be incorporated in the public domain of the state (Article 1). In general, the central government was predominant in these municipal institutions. They were headed by the governors of the provinces, partly appointed by them, the Minister of the Interior could dismiss the commissions whenever he pleased, and every work had to be approved by the Minister of Public Works before being executed.[46]

[42] *Majmūʿat al-awāmir al-ʿaliyya waʾl-dakrītāt*, Cairo, Būlāq, 1881, pp. 103–6; Gouvernement Egyptien, Ministère de l'Intérieur, *Législation administrative et criminelle*, 3d ed., vol. 1, Cairo, 1912, pp. 157–60.

[43] M. Delcroix, "L'Institution municipale en Égypte," *L'Égypte Contemporaine*, 13 (1922): 281.

[44] For details, see *Majmūʿat al-manshūrāt waʾl-qarārāt waʾl-muʿāhadāt*, Cairo, Būlāq, 1884, pp. 84–85.

[45] Delcroix, p. 281.

[46] Articles 8 and 13 of the Manṣūra decree.

Notwithstanding the predominant function of the central government in these bodies, it cannot be said that the government at that time promoted the establishment of municipal institutions. In Lord Dufferin's scheme for the reorganization of the government in Egypt no mention was made of municipalities and he explained that the consideration of this subject had been postponed.[47] Three years later, in 1886, Sir E. Baring (later Lord Cromer) was still very skeptical with regard to the establishment of municipalities, and in any case he insisted that no portion of the budget could be devoted to this purpose.[48] This attitude found its expression in the circular letter in which authorization for the arrangement in Ṭanṭā was given. It was stressed that the government had sanctioned the arrangement only because it would not cost the treasury anything and on condition that the government would not be officially involved in it in any way.[49]

On January 5, 1890 the decree was published by which the municipality of Alexandria was established—the first veritable municipality in Egypt and for a long time the only one.[50] As we have shown, the Alexandria municipality continued a tradition of local institutions initiated by the activity of the Alexandria merchants. Its establishment became possible when the foreign powers agreed that specific taxes be levied on foreign residents of the town, and it became necessary when the voluntary committee of merchants ceased to function. Some of the principles according to which this committee functioned were incorporated in the 1890 decree. The new municipal commission consisted of twenty-eight members: six *ex officio* members (the Governor of Alexandria [*ex officio* president], the Attorney General of the Mixed Court of Appeal, the Director General of Customs, the Chief Prosecutor [Chef du Parquet] at the native tribunal, the highest medical officer of the Sanitary Service, and the engineer occupying the highest post at the Public Works department in Alexandria); eight members appointed by the government; six members elected by all males over twenty-five years of age occupying buildings of a rental value exceeding £E 75; three members elected by the exporters; three members elected by the importers; and two members elected by the proprietors of real estate

[47] Dufferin to Granville, February 14 and April 28, 1883, *Further Correspondence respecting Reorganization in Egypt*, Egypt No. 6 (1883), C. 3529, pp. 47–49, and Egypt No. 14 (1883), C. 3696, p. 51.

[48] Aunay to Freycinet, Cairo, May 6, 1886, Affaires Etrangères, p. 204; Baring to Norrish, Cairo, May 25, 1886, FO 635/5 (Cromer Papers), p. 43.

[49] "*Naẓaran liʾan hādhā al-ʿamal la yukallif al-ḥukūma shayʾan mā . . . ʿalā sharṭ an lā yakūn liʾl-ḥukūma mudākhala rasmiyya fīhi. . . .*"

[50] For Arabic text of the decree, see *Majmūʿat al-awāmir al-ʿaliyya waʾl-dakrītāt*, 1890, pp. 2–14; for French text, together with further legislation prior to World War I, *Législation administrative et criminelle*, 1:94 ff.

situated in Alexandria. Among the elected members, not more than three were allowed to belong to the same nationality, local or foreign (Articles 2–3).

The decree of January, 1890 (Article 15), invested the new municipality with authority in a much wider range of activities than that of any of its predecessors. This necessitated, of course, a larger budget. The first item of its revenue (Article 40) remained the by now traditional tax of one half per mille on the value of all goods exported or imported through Alexandria. To this was added a tax of 1 per cent on the rental value of buildings, to be paid by the owners, and 2 per cent on rents, to be paid by the lessees. In addition, the municipality received the revenue, in Alexandria, of the tax on carriages and beasts of burden, the income of the Nuzha Gardens, the road tolls, and half the revenue from the Alexandria octroi (with a minimum of £E 31,780 guaranteed by the government). Finally, the 1890 decree provided for further revenue to be authorized in due course. Thus, in 1896 the government ceded to the Alexandria municipality the income of the house tax in Alexandria exceeding the sum of £E 35,000, the income of the Alexandria slaughterhouse and half the net produce of the sales of State Domain in Alexandria (but not more than £E 8,000 for each period of five years).[51] In 1902, when the octroi was abolished in Alexandria, the municipality was granted as a compensation the remaining £E 35,000 of the house tax and the income from rents on State Domain in Alexandria. Moreover, the municipality's share in the produce of sales of State Domain was no longer restricted to a maximum of £E 8,000.[52] Furthermore, Article 31 of the 1890 decree authorized the municipality to introduce purely municipal taxes of a nature strictly defined and enumerated in detail in the decree—which, in fact, the municipality did in due course.

The assent of the Powers that foreigners in Alexandria be taxed did not involve, however, a departure from their position in principle. Therefore, elsewhere the old difficulty persisted.[53] The first attempt to solve the problem was described as follows in Cromer's report for the year 1893:

[51] Decree of January 13, 1896, *Législation administrative et criminelle*, 1:106–7.

[52] Decree of November 29, 1902, *Législation*, 1:107.

[53] The fact that the powers agreed to taxation of foreigners in Alexandria but not elsewhere caused bitter resentment. Thus a committee of the Legislative Council proposed in 1893 to abolish the Alexandria municipality because, among other reasons, the idea had been to establish similar municipalities elsewhere as well, but since the powers had refused to make the financing of them possible, the exclusive existence of the Alexandria municipality meant discrimination against the other towns. (*Majmūʿat al-qarārāt waʾl-manshūrāt*, 1893, pp. 781–82).

> Some two years ago the Egyptian Government prepared a scheme for the creation of Municipalities in the provincial towns of Egypt. Owing chiefly to the fact that it was proposed to tax Europeans, the scheme required the unanimous assent of the Powers. That assent was not obtained. The Egyptian Government, therefore, looking to the practical points at issue, has now decided to grant an additional sum of £E 10,000 a year to be spent on improvements in nine of the provincial towns in Egypt. Small commissions will be appointed in each town to draw up the local Budgets. Should this system work well, it may perhaps be possible to extend it to other towns.[54]

Thus, according to a decree of November 21, 1893,[55] Local Commissions of seven members each were established in nine Egyptian towns (Asyūṭ, Damanhūr, Manṣūra, Damietta, Madīnat al-Fayyūm, al-Maḥalla al-Kubrā, Suez, Ṭanṭā, and Zaqāzīq), consisting of three *ex officio* members (the Governor of the province—*ex officio* president of the commission, the Inspector of Sanitary Services, and the Chief Engineer) and four members elected by all males aged twenty-five years and above and paying house tax of at least £E 5 yearly (amended to £E 2 in January, 1895).[56] The revenue was restricted exclusively to the government grant, to be spent, according to a budget fixed by the Commission, on a limited and specified number of items (Article 21). From 1893 onward, new Local Commissions were created year after year according to the government grants available; until 1914, the period with which we are concerned here, their number amounted to fifty.[57]

However, since these Local Commissions were dependent on government grants their resources were necessarily limited and the results of their activity were poor. The first attempt to change this situation was made by the town of Manṣūra, which demanded, and achieved in 1896, the re-invigoration of the 1881 decree, which had been a dead letter until that time (see above). It will be remembered that that decree had authorized the inhabitants of Manṣūra to levy "voluntary taxes," and this principle became the basis of a new kind of municipal commission established from that year onward. According to Article 4 of the 1896 arrangement,[58] the eight elected members of the municipal commission were to be elected only by those males over twenty-five years of age who, in addition to paying an annual house tax of at least £E 2 and occupying a building with a rental

[54] *Report on the Finances, Administration, and Condition of Egypt, and the Progress of Reforms*, Egypt No. 1 (1894), C. 7308, p. 2.

[55] *Majmūʿat al-qarārāt waʾl-manshūrāt*, 1893, pp. 294–99.

[56] *Majmūʿat al-qarārāt*, 1895, p. 16.

[57] Delcroix, p. 313. (On pp. 308–17 of his extremely valuable study, Delcroix has published detailed statistics and lists of all kinds of municipal commissions in Egypt.)

[58] Arrêté of the Ministry of the Interior, May 22, 1896, *Législation*, pp. 160 ff.

value of at least £E 24, agreed to pay the voluntary taxes laid down in the decree. The second principle of these new municipal commissions in which they differed from the ordinary Local Commissions was the participation of foreigners. As a "compensation" to those foreigners who agreed to pay the voluntary taxes, their representatives were not only admitted into the new commissions but were given equal representation with the Egyptian citizens although they formed only small minorities in most towns, that is, in general four out of eight elected members. Separate electoral lists were drawn up, and Egyptians could vote only for Egyptians, and foreigners for foreigners.

Because of this second principle this new kind of municipality was called a Mixed Local Commission. (In the course of time, the first principle ceased to distinguish these commissions from the ordinary Local Commissions because the latter also gradually adopted the system of voluntary taxes). By 1914, thirteen Mixed Local Commissions had been established in the following towns: Manṣūra (1896), Madīnat al-Fayyūm (1902), Ṭanṭā and Zaqāzīq (1905), Damanhūr and Banī Suayf (1906), al-Maḥalla al-Kubrā (1910), Port Said, Ḥilwān, Minyā, Mīt-Ghamr, Ziftā, and Kafr al-Zayyāt (1911).[59]

A detailed description of these developments would go beyond the scope of a study of the beginnings of municipal government. We shall, therefore, conclude with a short analytical summary.

The first point to be stressed again is the fact that among these bodies of urban administration the Alexandria municipality was the only one which could be called a municipality with some justification. Two important attributes distinguished it from all the Local and Mixed Local Commissions: First, only the Alexandria municipality constituted a corporate body from the legal point of view. Article 13 of the 1890 decree read: "La Commission municipal d'Alexandrie constitue une personnalité civile de nationalité indigène" (in Arabic, *Shakhṣ madanī min raʿāyā al-ḥukūma al-maḥalliyya*) and no such article appeared in connection with any of the other commissions. Secondly, none of these commissions except the Alexandria municipality was authorized to levy obligatory urban taxes. Even the municipality of Alexandria was not allowed to create new taxes or introduce changes into old ones; it could make suggestions in these matters, but the final decision remained with the Council of Ministers of the central government (Article 31). All the other commissions were compelled to content themselves with so-called voluntary taxes—the reason being, as we have explained, that no taxes could be imposed on citizens of foreign

[59] Delcroix, pp. 284–6, 297–98, 312–13; *Législation*, pp. 180–382.

nationality without the assent of all the Powers (which was not given), and therefore such taxes could not be imposed on Egyptian citizens either without causing gross discrimination against them. With these "voluntary taxes" quite important improvements in the services of the towns concerned were carried out, but the difficulties encountered were tremendous; no month passed without one commission or the other informing the Ministry of the Interior that this or that person or group of persons had refused to pay the voluntary municipal taxes, and various means, including litigation, had to be employed in order to make these persons or groups change their attitudes and facilitate the smooth working of the municipal commissions.[60]

It has been frequently stated in this study that the special privileges of foreigners in Egypt had been one of the most important impediments of municipal development in Egypt. We must now add that when part of these privileges were waived in order to make the establishment of the Alexandria municipality possible, the foreign residents of that town received in recompense a preponderance in the municipality which was not proportional to their number. This caused strong resentment among Egyptians. Thus, one of the reasons given for the above mentioned proposal of the committee of the Legislative Council in 1893 to abolish the Alexandria municipality[61] was that the electoral law of this municipality worked in a way to keep the membership of its council exclusively to foreigners, while Egyptian nationals had no say worth mentioning. The same grievance was voiced and argued in detail twenty years later by Maḥmūd al-Dīb, representative of Alexandria in the General Assembly, at the session of March 31, 1912 of that Assembly.[62] Al-Dīb claimed that since the establishment of the municipality there had always been only one Egyptian among the fourteen elected members of the council—as against thirteen foreigners. The reason was, in his view, that most Egyptians had no vote because they did not inhabit the town center, where rents were high, but those parts of the town where rents used to be lower than £E 75. Thus in 1912 there were only 357 Egyptians among the 2,173 voters. Moreover, the provision that not more than three members of the same nationality could be elected worked against Egyptians, who were all of the same nationality, while the foreigners were split into many nations, True, to make up for this deficiency the government used to appoint five Egyptians among the eight appointed members, but the Egyptians, said al-Dīb, had the right to be represented by elected members and not just to be appointed.

[60] Cf. Delcroix, pp. 286, 287, 320.
[61] See above, note 53.
[62] *Journal Officiel*, Supplement to no. 93 of 1912, pp. 21–22.

But not only because of the predominance of foreigners in the council, the Alexandria municipality was far from constituting an institution of self-government for the population of that town. In 1912 there were, in addition to the 2,173 general electors, 489 exporters and importers and 702 proprietors of real estate with the right to vote[63]—together 3,364 voters in a town of about four hundred thousand inhabitants at that time. Moreover, the Alexandria municipality has been frequently criticized because fourteen out of twenty-eight members of the council were either *ex officio* members or appointed by the government. In addition, the governor of the town was *ex officio* president of the council (Article 12); he nominated a secretary and, by virtue of their important executive positions, these two officials exercised practically a controlling influence. This was only slightly mitigated by the creation, in 1904, of the post of Administrator. All decisions of the municipal commission had to be submitted to the Ministry of the Interior and could not be carried out without the approval of the Ministry (Article 19).[64] The same was the case with regard to decisions of Mixed Local Commissions, which, in addition, could be dissolved any time by the Ministry of the Interior (Article 22 of most of the earlier decrees). In the view of some of the critics the powers of the Alexandria municipality and the municipal commissions were too narrowly defined. Thus, some of them censured Article 32 of the 1890 Alexandria decree by which the police was expressly excluded from the spheres of activity of the municipality.[65] In 1913 Aḥmad Luṭfī al-Sayyid expressed the view that elected local councils would be the best bodies to control the schools.[66]

One of the most serious and most persistent shortcomings of the network of municipal councils established in Egypt was the absence of any kind of local government in Cairo, where more than 40 per cent of Egypt's urban population was always concentrated. If no municipality was established in Cairo, it was not because there was no demand. In 1909 it was reported that "Cairo has for some time been agitating for a municipality on the same lines as that of Alexandria, but there is no sign on the part of the authorities

[63]*Journal Officiel*, Supplement to no. 93 of 1912, pp. 21–22.

[64]For the Arrêté of the Ministry of the Interior of June 27, 1904 creating the post of Administrator, see *Législation*, pp. 124 ff. For complaints about the predominance of the central government in the Alexandria municipality, see, for instance, A.D.S., "La Municipalité d'Alexandrie," *Rivista Quindicinale* (Alexandria), vol. 2, no. 8 (1890): 205–6, and reply by G. Sheridan, "Essai sur la municipalité d'Alexandrie," *Rivista Quindicinale*, vol. 2, no. 17 (1890): 422–23; see also Wright and Cartwright, p. 434.

[65]Cf. A.D.S. in *Rivista Quindicinale*, vol. 2, no. 11 (1890): 279–80.

[66]Cf. Jamal Mohammed Ahmad, *The Intellectual Origins of Egyptian Nationalism*, London, 1960, p. 103.

that one is likely to be established at present."[67] The question of the establishment of a municipality in Cairo was frequently raised, before World War I, in the General Assembly, but without avail.[68] Cairo's first municipality was created as late as 1949, the year of the final abolition of the Capitulation regime in Egypt, when the taxation of foreigners had ceased to be a problem, their judicial privileges having been done away with, and when, therefore, the municipality of Egypt's capital could be established without providing for any special position of foreigners in it.[69]

Egypt's administrators have often mentioned the apathy of Egypt's population and its unwillingness to pay taxes for improving municipal services as an important reason for the long delay in the development of municipal government in Egypt. Thus Lord Cromer wrote in 1893:

> Local wants should undoubtedly be met by local rates, but it is to be feared that a considerable time must lapse before the inhabitants of the large towns will recognize the importance of drainage schemes and pure water supply to the extent of desiring, much less imposing on themselves, local taxation for these purposes.

And again in 1898:

> . . . I greatly doubt the advisability of imposing taxation for objects which are in advance of the general public opinion of the country. I do not, of course, go so far as to say that no reform should be undertaken in Egypt unless an active and spontaneous public demand exists for its execution. . . . At the same time . . . if progress in Egypt is to be real and lasting, some little time must be allowed for the population in general to assimilate ideas which . . . are novel to the present generation, and were wholly unfamiliar to their ancestors.[70]

There is, of course, more than a grain of truth in these words, although the inhabitants of Egyptian towns seem to have changed their attitude faster than Lord Cromer believed. M. Delcroix, for some time Director of Municipal Services in Egypt, says that in 1880 they were still ignorant of

[67] Wright and Cartwright, p. 90. See also J. Alexander, *The Truth about Egypt*, London, 1911. pp. 126–27.

[68] For two examples, toward the end of the period dealt with in this study, see *Journal Officiel*, Supplement to no. 65 of 1912, p. 7; Supplement to no. 45 of 1914, April 11, 1914.

[69] Cairo municipality was established according to Law No. 145 of August 25, 1949. Cf. *al-Waqā'i' al-Miṣriyya*, no. 115, September 1, 1949. A detailed discussion of the problems of Cairo municipality is beyond the scope of this study.

[70] *Report on the Finances, Administration and Condition of Egypt, and the Progress of Reforms*, Egypt No. 3 (1893), C. 6957, p. 23; Egypt No. 1 (1898), C. 8815, p. 37. Such views were then reflected in the travel accounts of foreign observers as follows: "They [the Egyptians] cannot see why towns should be drained. . . . Municipal charges for street paving and lighting seem to them to be fantastic waste." (H. Hamilton Fyfe, *The New Spirit in Egypt*, London, 1911, p. 196).

what had been achieved in other countries by municipalities and hostile to a new authority to be established in their midst, and even a decade or two later it often happened that the inhabitants of a town where the establishment of a local commission was planned feared the new charges to be imposed on them and submitted a petition not to establish the commission. As against this, by the time of World War I the same people who two decades earlier had refused to have a municipal commission, even if the government paid all the expenses, now demanded to establish one even if they had to furnish the whole budget.[71] Moreover, the hesitating attitude of the inhabitants of Egypt's towns toward innovations was not peculiar to them. Therefore it cannot explain the remarkable fact that in this sphere, of municipal legislation, Egypt lagged far behind Ottoman legislation in general—while in many other spheres of socio-economic and socio-political legislation the opposite was the case.[72] The explanation, it would seem to us, is to be sought in the traditional predominance of the central government in Egypt over local forces as a result of the economic and geographical structure of the country, as well as in the particular position and exceptional privileges of foreigners in Egypt.

[71] Delcroix, pp. 280–81, 283, 291.

[72] For penal law, see chapter 7, above, and for land tenure, chapter 4, above. In both these chapters we concluded that Egyptian legislation preceded that of the Ottoman Empire by a considerable length of time.

12

Summary and Conclusion: Social Change in Egypt, 1800–1914

Continuity and Change

In a recently published book on the intellectual evolution of modern Egypt the author devotes one chapter to the political, economic, and social transformation between the years 1804 and 1882. Summing up, he arrives at the following conclusions: "The cumulative effect of the development that we have described amounted to nothing less than a complete transformation of the basic character of the life and organization of Egyptian society."[1] This statement surely requires a number of qualifications. So does the opposite view that, except for some superficial borrowing from the French, Egyptian society did not change at all under Muḥammad ʿAlī, ʿAbbās, Saʿīd, and Ismāʿīl.[2] Social change in nineteenth-century Egypt was a complex process which needs to be investigated in detail.

Evidently the traditional structure of the family and the status of women did not undergo any change at all. At the beginning of the twentieth century the extended family was still prevalent in Egypt as a unit of property owning as well as of dwelling, uniting as it did the father of the family, his wife or wives, his unmarried daughters and sons, and his married sons with their wives and children in a single house or in apartments closely grouped or attached to one another. The father of the family owned all the family possessions and controlled the family labor force and its income. Parents

Originally published as "Social Change in Egypt: 1800–1914," in P. M. Holt (ed.), *Political and Social Change in Modern Egypt* (London: Oxford University Press, 1967), pp. 135–61. (Here shortened.)

[1] N. Safran, *Egypt in Search of Political Community*, Cambridge Mass., 1961, p. 8.

[2] See, for instance, Earl of Cromer, *Modern Egypt*, London, 1908, vol. 2, chapter 34.

arranged the marriages of their sons and daughters, who generally were not allowed to make their own decisions in this matter.[3] ("Clan" endogamy, and particularly cousin marriage, was the rule.) The family was divided into seniors and juniors, and the distinction between those of greater or less consideration was based on relative age.[4] Similarly, the family was strictly divided into two worlds—of men and women.

Although the forerunners of a feminist movement had appeared as early as the end of the nineteenth century, the aims of this movement were as yet very modest and its influence on actual life was not felt until much later. At the beginning of the twentieth century, male and female societies were no less segregated from one another than at the beginning of the nineteenth. Urban women did not unveil or emerge from their seclusion before World War I,[5] while in some regions fellah women had not worn a veil even a century earlier.[6] But where peasant women used to veil in the nineteenth century, they continued to do so in the twentieth (for instance, women of well-to-do fellah families in certain parts of Upper Egypt.)[7] The wife was supposed to be submissive, obedient, devoted, and respectful to her husband. He could easily divorce her, and urban husbands frequently used this right. According to authors who wrote at the end of the nineteenth and the beginning of the twentieth century, polygamy was relatively common not only among wealthy families but also among the lower classes.[8] None of the legal reforms relating to the status of Muslim women had been introduced before World War I.

[3] Cf. F. Schwally, *Beiträge zur Kenntnis des Lebens der mohammedanischen Städter, Fellachen und Beduinen im heutigen Ägypten*, Heidelberg, 1912, pp. 5, 9–10, 15–16.

[4] Cf. E. F. Tugay, *Three Centuries: Family Chronicles of Turkey and Egypt*, London, 1963, p. 233. Mrs. Tugay's description relates to Turco-Egyptian families of the upper class at the beginning of the twentieth century, but it is certainly valid for other classes too, and even for a later period. See, for instance, H. Ammar, *Growing Up in an Egyptian Village*, London, 1954, pp. 52–53.

[5] Schwally, pp. 8–9.

[6] U. J. Seetzen, *Reisen . . .*, vol. 3, Berlin, 1854, p. 265 (written 1807–8); J. A. St. John, *Egypt and Nubia*, London, 1845, pp. 97, 186–87, 190, 283–84, 335, 415, 425–26; Mubārak, 12:134; 14:68.

[7] Mubārak, 8:28, 51, 105; 9:88; 11:64; 13:69; W. S. Blackman, *The Fellahin of Upper Egypt*, London, 1927, pp. 37–38; A. Boktor, *School and Society in the Valley of the Nile*, Cairo, 1936, p. 63.

[8] Schwally, pp. 16–17, 20, 34; A. von Fircks, "Stand, Bewegung und wirtschaftlicher Zustand des ägyptischen Volkes 1894," *Zeitschrift des königlichen preussischen statistischen Bureaus*, 35 (1895):154. It is interesting to note that about the middle of the nineteenth century some observers had the opposite impression. Cf. Bayle St. John, *Village Life in Egypt*, London, 1852, 1:55; N. W. Senior, *Conversations and Journals in Egypt and Malta*, London, 1882, 1:65 (written in 1855). A possible reason for a rise in the proportion of polygamous families in the course of the second half of the century is the abolition of slavery. One of the best descriptions in Egyptian fiction of the persistence of the traditional family at that time is in Ṭāhā Ḥusayn, *Shajarat al-bu's*. This has been analyzed in M. Milson, "Ṭāhā Ḥusayn's 'The Tree of Misery': A Literary Expression of Cultural Change," *Asian and African Studies* (Jerusalem) 3 (1967):78–80.

Moreover, not only marriage and divorce continued to be regulated by traditional religious law, but also all other matters of "personal status," such as adoption, guardianship, heritages, wills, and *waqf*. This, however, was not the only field in which religion retained its social function. By the end of the nineteenth century the Ṣūfī *ṭarīqas* (orders) had not yet been superseded as the principal form of organization of the population of Egypt by any kind of secular association; the secret societies at the end of the century were restricted to very small groups. The *ṭarīqa*s constituted the framework of social gathering and played an important role at public festivals, which served as the main expression of social consciousness of the masses. Almost all of these festivals had a religious content, and the most significant of them were the hundreds of *mawlid*s (*mūlid*s), small ones in almost every Egyptian village, and larger ones in provincial towns and the capital. These *mawlid*s had not lost their vitality during the whole period with which we are dealing, nor had the veneration of the shaykhs, in whose honour the *mawlid*s were held.[9] Thus religion, particularly popular religion, was a social factor in which very little, if any, change occurred during the nineteenth century. The same may be said of course about a large variety of customs, such as marriage and funeral rites, which were not always directly connected with religion.

If such institutions as the family, the status of women, and the social function of religion did not undergo any change during the nineteenth century, one can hardly speak about a "complete transformation of the basic character . . . of the Egyptian society." That they did not change is certainly connected with the fact that during that period Egypt was not transformed from an agrarian into an industrial society. Moreover, after the failure of Muḥammad ʿAlī's industrial experiment,[10] no serious industrial development took place in Egypt for decades. Some of Muḥammad ʿAlī's factories were liquidated by ʿAbbās and Saʿīd, and others were sold by Saʿīd or given in *iltizām* to private individuals. These, however, made little headway, since they had to pay a large variety of burdensome taxes.[11] Ismāʿīl tried to revive industrial initiative by privately taking over

[9]For the beginning of the twentieth century, see, for instance, Sayyid Quṭb, *Ṭifl min al-qarya*, Cairo, 1945, pp. 77 ff. For the 1870's and 1880's, hundreds of examples are given by Mubārak, *passim*. See also Milson, pp. 80–87.

[10]For analyses of Muḥammad ʿAlī's failure see A. E. Crouchley, *The Economic Development of Modern Egypt*, London, 1938, pp. 72–76; M. Fahmy, *La Révolution de l'industrie en Egypte . . . (1800–1850)*, Leiden, 1954, pp. 98 ff.; H. A. B. Rivlin, *The Agricultural Policy of Muḥammad ʿAlī in Egypt*, Cambridge, Mass., 1961, pp. 198–200.

[11]See, for instance, Amīn Sāmī, *Taqwīm al-nīl*, Cairo, 1936, part 3, 1:149–50; 2:901–2; Nubar to Stanton, no. 347, Cairo, April 12, 1871, PRO, FO 141/75, part 2; Barr to Stanton, Alexandria, February 24, 1875, FO 141/92; A. von Kremer, *Aegypten*, Leipzig, 1863, 2:35.

government enterprises and by sending missions abroad to acquire new factories. A few were bought (a paper factory, for instance), but production turned out to be uneconomic. Therefore a whole group of factories were liquidated in 1875 and the buildings turned into barracks.[12] Only two branches continued to flourish: the sugar industry, run by the government; and cotton gins, established mainly by foreigners. In general, however, foreign capital was interested in public utility companies (water, gas, and railways) rather than in industry. As to local Egyptian capitalists, in addition to the taxes which discriminated against them, important factors deterred them from investing in industry. Industrial investment involved a great risk, because of the small market and the competition of European products, compared with the large gains of investment in agricultural land, made possible through the vast expansion of agricultural production at the time. The British occupation changed this situation only insofar as most of the oppressive taxes were abolished, but Cromer opposed industrial development, arguing that without introducing protective customs duties such development would be impossible, and that, if he did introduce customs, he would be acting against his free-trade convictions, while Egypt would lose her income from customs on European merchandise.[13] As a result, his economic policy was extremely unfavorable to industrial development.

All this does not mean, however, that during the nineteenth century no changes occurred in the socio-economic structure of Egypt. Although no industry emerged, Egypt underwent a considerable economic development, which has been aptly summarized as follows:

> ... the subsistence economy under which the country had lived for centuries was replaced by an export-oriented economy, the bulk of Egypt's available reserves of land, water, and underemployed labour were brought into use and its total output and exports increased several times, with a consequent rise in real per-capita income and in the level of living.[14]

In addition, during that time Egypt almost suddenly came into close contact with the West which culminated in foreign intervention in Egyptian affairs and in the British occupation of Egypt. The rulers of Egypt attempted to introduce an efficient and modern system of government and tried to achieve independence of the Ottoman Empire. All this had some far-reaching social consequences.

[12] Sāmī, part 3, 2:499, 598–99, 793, 862, 964–96; 3:1,105, 1,253.

[13] Cromer to Bergne, Cairo, May 2, 1901 (Private), FO 633/8 (Cromer Papers), 319–21. For the absence of an Egyptian entrepreneur class, see also C. Issawi, *Egypt in Revolution*, London, 1963, pp. 29–30.

[14] Issawi, pp. 18 ff.

Changes in Rural Society

To begin with, during the nineteenth century Egypt largely solved its problem of nomadic tribes, which cannot be said about any other country of the Middle East.[15] As we have shown, Muḥammad ʿAlī embarked upon a campaign to crush and settle the beduins once and for all. In addition to more violent measures, he and his successors granted the shaykhs large tracts of land as their private property in order to induce them to settle on the land. The most important consequence of this settlement was the break-up of tribal unity. Part of the tribes moved to towns, where the shaykhs became government officials, acquired large mansions, and intermarried with the ruling class, while the "rank and file" of the tribes became part of the lower classes: most of the first railway workers in Egypt were beduins.[16] The development of cash crops and the rising prices of agricultural products were powerful incentives for the shaykhs to acquire large tracts of land, and they emerged as big landowners, while the members of the tribes were "lost among the fellahs." The growing wealth of the shaykhs led to the establishment of luxurious households, and they became alienated from the tribesmen, a process which was bound to create friction between them and their former fellow tribesmen, and there were even cases of revolts against the shaykhs.

A similar process of social differentiation took place among the settled rural population. At the end of the eighteenth century the rulers of the Egyptian countryside were the *multazims* or tax farmers, a great part of whom were town dwellers; the rural population proper was divided into a small layer of wealthy families of village notables and the mass of the fellahs, who did not own the land they tilled and among whom no significant differences seem to have existed. During the nineteenth century a profound change in the social structure of rural Egypt was brought about through the replacement of the traditional subsistence economy by the growing of cash crops, by the transformation of the land from state property into the full private property of individual citizens,[17] and, finally, by the gradual introduction of a modern westernized system of administration.

The *multazims* were liquidated by Muḥammad ʿAlī, and in the course of the nineteenth century other urban groups emerged as big landowners (see below). The socio-economic position of the families of village notables underwent great fluctuations until they reached the apogee of their wealth and power under Ismāʿīl; afterward both their wealth and their power declined,

[15] For detailed treatment of this subject, see chapter 1, above.
[16] Mubārak, 7:91.
[17] See chapter 4, above.

mainly as a result of the restriction of their fiscal and political authority under the British occupation, and most of those who remained wealthy moved to towns.[18] The landed property of many of these formerly prosperous families gradually split up through inheritance. This was one of the factors which caused the emergence of a completely new rural class in Egypt—that of owners of medium-sized landed property. At the end of the nineteenth century these medium-sized properties of between five and fifty feddans covered about 35 percent of the privately owned landed property.[19]

Similarly, the fellahs split into owners of small plots and landless tenants and laborers. This too was the corollary of the development of private ownership of land and of a market economy. In the course of the nineteenth century part of the land gradually was registered in the name of the fellahs who tilled it, but for a variety of reasons many of them lost it again. The burden of taxation often forced cultivators to abandon their land and forfeit ownership rights, and in many cases land was confiscated for the nonpayment of taxes. Another burden that turned many small landowners into landless peasants was the *corvée* (chiefly for public works connected with flood prevention and irrigation) and the levying of men for the army. In addition, in the second half of the century, fellah indebtedness became an acute problem. During the nineteenth century there was a gradual transition from payment of taxes in kind to cash payments, and fellahs began to borrow from moneylenders. This was facilitated by the introduction of modern laws of mortgage with the establishment of the Mixed Courts in 1875. From then on, it became possible for creditors to foreclose on land for the nonpayment of a debt. Recurring slumps, droughts, floods, and cattle plagues aggravated the plight of fellahs, many of whom lost their land to their creditors.[20] At the end of the century there were in Egypt less than a million landowners who, together with their families, cannot have amounted to more than six million persons. Since the total population numbered about ten million, of whom at least eight million lived in villages, by that time between one and two million peasants must have been landless.

While stimulating social differentiation among Egypt's rural classes, the emergence of a market economy also widened the gulf between Upper and Lower Egypt. The greater proximity of Lower Egyptian villages to the mercantile and cultural centers of the country brought with it greater economic opportunities as well as a faster cultural development. According to Mubārak, in the 1870's or 1880's most Azhar students from Lower Egypt

[18]See chapter 3, above.

[19]Cf. G. Baer, *A History of Landownership in Modern Egypt 1800–1950*, London, 1962, pp. 25–26.

[20]Baer, pp. 28–38.

knew the Qur'ān by heart before coming to the Azhar University, while students from Upper Egypt did not, and the latter were much poorer than their fellow students from the Delta.[21] Visiting Egypt in 1883, Mr. Villiers Stuart observed a sharp distinction between the "thriving population of the Delta and the poverty-stricken population of the south."[22] At the end of the century this differentiation led to a considerable migration from Upper Egypt to the Delta (and consequently to the occasional deterioration of security in Lower Egypt.)[23] Between the censuses of 1897 and 1907 the population of Lower Egyptian provinces (the city and desert governorates excepted) grew by 18.7 per cent, while that of the four Upper Egyptian provinces grew only by 12.3 per cent.

The development of a market economy and of private ownership of land, as well as the growth of social differentiation among the village population, effected yet another important change in Egypt's rural society—the dissolution of the village community. Until the middle of the nineteenth century, village lands in Upper Egypt and in some areas of Middle Egypt were periodically redistributed among the villagers, and in Lower Egypt the village shaykh used to reallocate land whenever fellahs failed to pay their share of the taxes. The village was collectively responsible for the payment of a fixed tax quota imposed on it and for the supply of labor for public works. In the 1850's the practice of periodically redistributing village land in Upper and Middle Egypt was discontinued, and Saʿīd's land law of August 5, 1858 considerably extended the individual fellah's property rights to the land he held. At about the same time Saʿīd abolished collective village responsibility for tax payment and introduced individual tax assessments. The remaining function of the village community as a corporate body was abolished in the 1880's, when the *corvée* (and later the obligation to turn out for fighting locusts and floods) became the individual duty of every villager.[24]

Guilds, Town Quarters, and Religious Communities

The dissolution of the village community was only one aspect of a more comprehensive process. There were other corporate bodies which had formed the traditional structure of Egyptian society and which disintegrated in the course of the nineteenth century. Perhaps the most important

[21] Mubārak, 4:28–29.

[22] *Reports by Mr. Villiers Stuart, M.P., respecting Reorganization in Egypt*, Egypt No. 7 (1883), C. 3554, pp. 8–9, 16.

[23] Cf. *Majmūʿat al-awāmir al-ʿaliyya wa'l-dakrītāt*, Cairo–Būlāq, 1888, pp. 499–502; *Report on the Administration, Finances, and Condition of Egypt and the Progress of Reforms*, Egypt No. 3 (1892), C. 6589, pp. 27–28; Sayyid Quṭb, pp. 165–66.

[24] For details, see chapter 2, above.

of these bodies were the urban guilds.[25] We have shown that, although they persisted until the last quarter of the nineteenth century, they finally disappeared as a result of the influx of European goods and of Europeans settling in Egypt, of urbanization, and of the reorganization of the Egyptian administration. Thus the state could do without the link of the guilds, and step by step their administrative, fiscal, and economic functions shrank until they lost most of them.

While the Egyptian government ceased to appoint shaykhs of guilds before World War I, every town quarter was headed by a shaykh (*shaykh al-ḥāra*) even much later. In the course of the nineteenth century the fiscal functions and police duties of these shaykhs were transferred to government departments; on the other hand, they were assigned a large number of new administrative functions, of many of which they were deprived again at the beginning of this century. Some functions still remained in their hands, such as making reports of births and deaths,[26] but the town quarter had lost its significance as a social unit.

The gates by which Cairo's quarters were separated from each other had already been demolished by Bonaparte.[27] However, after the French occupation they were apparently reestablished: some later sources state that they were still closed,[28] others that this practice had ceased;[29] in some distant towns, such as Asyūṭ, it seems to have persisted much longer.[30] In the past each quarter had its gang of youths organized after the pattern of the medieval *futuwwa* associations, and there were frequent fights between the gangs of the different quarters. During the nineteenth century the vigor of these feuds seems to have diminished, although apparently they did not completely disappear, as claimed by Mubārak.[31] One reason for the weakening of solidarity among the inhabitants of a specific quarter was the fact that each of these quarters, once inhabited by people of similar social status, became in the course of time much more heterogeneous: Mubārak tells us about two quarters of Cairo in which only high officials and notables

[25] For details, see chapter 9, above, and G. Baer, *Egyptian Guilds in Modern Times*, Jerusalem, 1964.

[26] Law no. 23 of August 11, 1912, *Journal Officiel*, no. 96, 1912. For parallel developments of the functions of the village shaykh, see chapter 3, above.

[27] Cf. *Histoire scientifique et militaire de l'expédition française en Égypte*, Paris, 1830–36, 4:97.

[28] See, for instance, B. St. John, 1:129; Mubārak, 1:78.

[29] Cf. Dr. Stacquez, *L'Égypte, la Basse Nubie et le Sinai*, Liège, 1865, p. 65. Aḥmad Amīn, *Ḥayātī*, Cairo, n.d., p. 33.

[30] Stacquez, p. 135; G. Charmes, *Cinq mois au Caire*, Paris, 1880, p. 227.

[31] Mubārak, 2:84; Aḥmad Amīn, *Qāmūs al-ʿādāt waʾl-taqālīd waʾl-taʿābīr al-miṣriyya*, Cairo, 1953, pp. 304–5; Amīn, *Ḥayātī*, pp. 39–40. See also J. Berque, *Les Arabes d'hier à demain*, Paris, 1960, pp. 18, 225–26, according to whom the social importance of the town quarter in Damascus seems to have been much more persistent.

had lived in the past and which, about the middle of the century, had become socially mixed.[32]

Even people belonging to different religious communities began to mix and live together in the same quarter. During the first half of the nineteenth century, strict segregation seems to have been the rule, and members of each community inhabited separate quarters.[33] But as early as 1858 the British Consul in Cairo wrote:

> Formerly the Christians were assembled in particular quarters, with a certain amount of organisation for defence: they are now to a considerable extent scattered, and the protection which they have so long enjoyed has led to the abandonment of all organisation . . . even in the quarters which are still exclusively Christian.[34]

Nevertheless, at the end of the nineteenth and the beginning of the twentieth century there were still quarters almost exclusively inhabited by Muslims, such as Khalīfa and Sayyida Zaynab in Cairo or Mīnat al-Baṣal in Alexandria: in 1897 there were 56 *shiyākhāt* (subquarters) in Cairo, out of 195, in each of which lived less than 10 Copts, and in Alexandria 34 out of 108. In smaller towns religious segregation was even more persistent. The overwhelming majority of Copts lived in mixed villages, not in villages inhabited exclusively by Copts: in 1897 and 1907 there were only twelve villages with less than ten Muslims. But usually Copts and Muslims lived in separate parts of the village.[35] In this respect, as in others, we find that the religious community retained much of its social significance throughout the nineteenth century. Generally speaking, all persons engaged in a specific urban occupation belonged to one community; where the trade was practiced by people of more than one community, they usually formed separate guilds.[36] As late as the beginning of the twentieth century about 98 percent of all *ṣarrāf*s (tax collectors) were Copts.[37] By that time a new class of educated Muslims had emerged which attempted to enter many of the occupations formerly monopolized by the Copts, especially certain branches of government employment. This, however, created a sharp antagonism between

[32] Mubārak, 2:28; 3:54.

[33] Cf. J. Bowring, *Report on Egypt and Candia*, London, 1840, p. 8; E. W. Lane, *Cairo Fifty Years Ago*, London, 1896, pp. 60–69.

[34] Walne to Green, Cairo, July 5, 1858, inclosure in Green to Malmesbury, no. 104, Alexandria, July 7, 1858, FO 78/1402.

[35] Cf. Mubārak, 9:87; 12:3; 14:68; etc.

[36] Cf. Mubārak 1:99–100; 3:34; 7:74; 9:85, 87, 92; 10:52; 11:14; 12:44, 95, 104, 148; 14:121; etc.

[37] See K. Mikhail, *Copts and Moslems under British Control*, London, 1911, p. 44, n. 1.

the two communities, culminating in the rival congresses of Copts and Muslims held in 1911.[38]

But even if the religious community kept its vitality as a social unit, the economic position, social status, and political power of the heads and officials of the religious institutions declined considerably during the nineteenth century. Like the village community, the religious community ceased under Saʿīd to constitute a corporate body for administrative purposes, and in January, 1855, the *jizya*, the special tax on non-Muslim communities, was abolished.[39] This deprived the religious functionaries of minority communities of important administrative functions. The Coptic clergy was further weakened by permanent intrigues and quarrels as well as by growing Protestant and Catholic missionary activity. In 1874 the members of the community founded a secular council, *al-Majlis al-millī al-ʿāmm liʾl-Aqbāṭ al-Urthūdhuks*. One of its explicit purposes was to take over the Coptic *waqf*s from the clergy. An official regulation of May 14, 1883 vested the management of all Coptic *khayrī waqf*s in this council. From then on, the power of the Coptic patriarch, the clergy, and the monks was severely undermined by secular organizations.[40]

The Muslim *ʿulamāʾ* did not fare much better. At the end of the eighteenth and the beginning of the nineteenth century the *ʿulamāʾ* were among the chief *multazim*s in Egypt. Like the Mamluk *amīr*s, they built luxurious palaces, surrounded themselves with servants and hangers-on, employed officials, and took enormous interest in their property and wealth. Under Bonaparte they had attained a position of great political importance.[41] But this golden age for the *ʿulamāʾ* did not last longer than it took Muḥammad ʿAlī to consolidate his rule. After he had overcome their opposition and confiscated their *iltizām*s and *rizaq aḥbāsiyya*, a precipitate decline in their position took place.[42] In 1831 the *muftī* of Manṣūra complained that the *ʿulamāʾ* had become poor people, and in 1863 von Kremer wrote that they had completely lost their former influence and importance, and that many of the *ʿulamāʾ* originated from the peasant population.[43] A few years later another author said that "all that he [the *qāḍī*] has saved from the ruins of

[38] Mikhail, *passim*.

[39] Sāmī, part 3, 1:106.

[40] See S. H. Leeder, *Modern Sons of the Pharaos*, London, n.d. (1918?), pp. 255–64; Baer, *Landownership*, pp. 178–81.

[41] Baer, *Landownership*, pp. 60–61; Mubārak, 4:31 ff; 13:63–64; 14:93–94; 15:7, 27–28; 17:10–12.

[42] Rifāʿa al-Ṭahṭāwī's father was forced to emigrate from his town. See Mubārak, 13:53.

[43] Michaud et Poujoulat, *Correspondance d'Orient*, Paris, 1834, 7:12 (April 1831); von Kremer, 2:94–95. The peasant origin of many of Egypt's *ʿulamāʾ* in the nineteenth century is illustrated by Mubārak's numerous biographies.

his former splendour is a certain moral influence among his religious brethren, an influence that is daily declining."[44]

The Decline of the Turkish Element

Another important group whose position in Egyptian society declined during the nineteenth century was the "Turks," later called "Turco-Egyptians." These were people from all over the non-Arab countries under Ottoman rule whose common characteristic was that they spoke Turkish. There were Turkish students at the Azhar University, Turkish dervish convents in Cairo, and Turkish merchants—concentrated in the part of Cairo's market called Khān al-Khalīlī. But the importance of the Turkish element derived from the fact that during the first quarter of the century all officials above the rank of *shaykh al-balad* (village headman) were "Turks"[45] (the fiscal tasks were performed by Copts). Similarly, all army officers of higher rank and most junior officers and noncommissioned officers were Turks, even long after fellahs had been recruited by Muḥammad ʿAlī as soldiers for the first time in the history of Islamic Egypt. Since the ruling dynasty was also "Turkish," the whole ruling class of Egypt was an oligarchy speaking a foreign language.[46] Through grants of large tracts of land they became the most important landowners in nineteenth-century Egypt.[47] Their gradual and partial replacement by Arabic-speaking Egyptians was one of the most significant social changes of the nineteenth century.

The early attempts of Muḥammad ʿAlī to replace the Turks in the lower ranks of the administration with Egyptian village and beduin shaykhs has been often described.[48] The experiment was not entirely successful, and in any case the post of *mudīr* (governor of a province) was retained by Turks.[49] In 1840 Muḥammad ʿAlī tried for the first time to replace Turkish officers in the fleet with "Arab" (Egyptian) ones.[50]

[44] C. B. Klunzinger, *Upper Egypt: Its People and Its Products*, London, 1878, p. 74. On the miserable economic position of the *ʿulamāʾ* at the beginning of the twentieth century, see J. Dorpffer, "Les Revenus de l'Université d'El Azhar," *La Revue Egyptienne*, May 20, 1912, pp. 33–42.

[45] E. W. Lane, *The Manners and Customs of the Modern Egyptians*, Everyman's Library, London, 1944, p. 129.

[46] According to numerous estimates throughout the century, their number did not exceed twenty thousand including of course merchants etc.

[47] Cf. Baer, *Landownership*, pp. 39–49.

[48] See, for instance, Baer, *Landownership*, p. 50, and a detailed account in Rivlin, pp. 109–11. See also chapters 1 and 3, above.

[49] According to a list sent by Consul Murray to Palmerston on May 28, 1847, at that time all the pashas of Egypt were non-Egyptians. See FO 141/14 and 78/707. For the time of ʿAbbās, see Bayle St. John, 1:64–65; and for the early years of Saʿīd's rule, Senior, 1:251–52 (written January, 1856).

[50] Larking to Palmerston, no. 18, Alexandria, October 6, 1840, FO 78/414.

Saʿīd resumed the experiment on a larger scale. He ordered that one-third of all officials acting as *nāẓir qism* (district officer) and one-quarter of those acting as *ḥākim khuṭṭ* (officer in charge of sub-district) be replaced by Egyptians (*abnāʾ al-ʿArab*).[51] In June, 1858, he appointed an Egyptian *nāẓir qism* to the office of *mudīr* of Giza province.[52] Addressing himself to the village shaykhs, Saʿīd reminded them that his father's experiment had failed because of their incompetence, threatened them with severe punishment if they did not succeed, and appealed to their pride by making them responsible, in case of failure, for perpetuating the rule of *abnāʾ al-Turk*.[53] Toward the end of Saʿīd's day the "majority of Turkish employés were dismissed service."[54]

Simultaneously Saʿīd tried to create an Egyptian officer class in the army. For this purpose (among others) he recruited the sons of village shaykhs, who had been exempt from army service till then.[55] One of those recruited was Aḥmad ʿUrābī, who by 1860 had reached the rank of colonel (*qāʾim maqām*).[56] Although Saʿīd tried to instill Arab-Egyptian national feeling into the recruits, many shirked the service or deserted their units, and in 1861 Saʿīd dismissed most of the newly created army.[57]

Ismāʿīl continued Saʿīd's policy, but apparently the result was only a partial replacement of Turkish *mudīrs* by Egyptians.[58] By the end of the 1870's, however, the lower ranks of the administration had been completely Egyptianized. The same was the case in the army,[59] but there the Turks and Circassians succeeded in retaining their monopoly of commanding positions. This was one of the grievances which led to the ʿUrābī revolt.

As a result of this revolt and the British occupation, the Egyptian army was disbanded. The new army consisted of Egyptians under British

[51] Sāmī, part 3, 1:189, 192–93 (October 1856); Harris to Bruce, Luxor, December 19, 1856, FO 141/30 and 78/1222.

[52] Sāmī, part 3, 1:283.

[53] Sāmī, part 3, 1:185–86. This is an extremely interesting and remarkable document.

[54] Hekekyan Papers, vol. 16, B.M. Add. 37463, ff. 121–23 (written on April 10, 1861). Cf. Colquhoun to Russell, Alexandria, November 11, 1861, FO 78/1591. Colquhoun's explanation of this development was Saʿīd's desire to weaken his dependence on the Porte.

[55] Von Kremer, 1:256; Senior, 1:261, 293.

[56] Aḥmad ʿUrābī, *Kashf al-sitār ʿan sirr al-asrār fī l-nahḍa al-miṣriyya* . . ., Cairo, n.d., 1:12–13. Cf. W. S. Blunt, *Secret History of the English Occupation of Egypt*, New York, 1922, pp. 99–100, 367.

[57] ʿUrābī, p. 16; Sāmī, part 3, 1:380–81; Colquhoun to Russell, November 11, 1861.

[58] See lists of *mudīrs* at the beginning of every year in Sāmī, part 3, vol. 3, *passim*. Conflicting views have been expressed by J. C. McCoan, *Egypt as It Is*, London, n.d. (1877), p. 115; Klunzinger, pp. 66–67; and D. Mackenzie Wallace, *Egypt and the Egyptian Question*, London, 1883, pp. 147–48, 152.

[59] For the biographies of a large number of officials and army officers of fellah origin, see Mubārak, *passim*.

command, the Turks and Circassians having lost their controlling position. Similarly, the higher posts of the civil administration were filled with Britons and other Europeans. As a result of the loss of their political power, the Turks also gradually lost their position as the largest landowners: except for some of the *waqfs* they had founded in the nineteenth century, few of their large estates survived. The only exception was the Muḥammad ʿAlī family.[60] It not only continued to own a considerable proportion of Egyptian land, but it also retained its Turkish character. All the members of this family spoke Turkish, and many of them never learned to speak Arabic well; Fārūq was the first ruler of the Muḥammad ʿAlī family at whose court Arabic was spoken.[61]

Most of the other "Turkish" families had in the meantime lost their Turkish character. The supply of new "Turkish blood" gradually ceased, and as early as Muḥammad ʿAlī's time many Turks left Egypt.[62] Many of those who remained married Egyptian women, and the children spoke Arabic.[63] In the 1820's a visitor to Cairo still wrote, "The first thing that astonishes a stranger in Cairo is the squalid wretchedness of the Arabs, and the external splendour of the Turks."[64] Only twenty years later Hekekyan remarked that the dress of the Turks had been adopted by a great number of the Arab inhabitants of Egypt and that there was a gradual approach to equality.[65] Toward the end of the century the character of the remaining Turco-Egyptians grew more Egyptian from year to year.[66]

No wonder, therefore, that in the course of the nineteenth century, Arabic gradually replaced Turkish as the language used in government offices. As early as 1840 Bowring wrote that the use of Arabic for official purposes was growing.[67] In 1858 Saʿīd issued an order to the effect that official correspondence be conducted in Arabic, but that the change should be gradual where Turkish officials were concerned.[68] In 1869 Ismāʿīl renewed this order and even dismissed the Turkish dragomans, but a few

[60] Cf. Baer, *Landownership*, pp. 131–38. See also T. Neumann, *Das moderne Agypten*, Leipzig, 1893, p. 40.

[61] Tugay, pp. 57, 162, 241.

[62] Bowring, p. 9; Senior, 1:252–53; 2:66, 128. Cf. I. Abu-Lughod, "The Transformation of the Egyptian Elite; Prelude to the ʿUrābī Revolt," *Middle East Journal*, vol. 12, no. 3 (summer 1967):329.

[63] Von Kremer, 1:67.

[64] R. R. Madden, *Travels in Turkey, Egypt, Nubia, and Palestine in 1824, 1825, 1826, and 1827*, London, 1829, 1:307.

[65] Hekekyan Papers, vol. 3, B.M. Add. 37450, f. 100 (written October 23, 1845).

[66] Cf. Cromer, *Modern Egypt*, 2:169–70.

[67] Bowring, p. 9. One of the most important reasons was of course the establishment of an Arabic school system by Muḥammad ʿAlī. Cf. Abu-Lughod, p. 337.

[68] Sāmī, part 3, 1:283–85. For the gradual change from Turkish to Arabic in *al-Waqāʾiʿ al-miṣriyya*, the official newspaper of the government, see Abu-Lughod, p. 338.

months later he was compelled to allow the use of Turkish in the army.[69] By the end of the century, however, Arabic had completely replaced Turkish in official use.

Urbanization and the New Urban Society

Traditional Egyptian society comprised yet another essential element which disappeared during the nineteenth century, namely, slavery.[70] We have shown that though official measures taken against the slave trade were one of the most important causes for the final disappearance of slavery, they would never have succeeded were it not for the internal development of Egyptian society. By the end of the century a small but important section of Egyptians had changed their attitude toward slavery as a result of their cultural contact with Europe. However, the most important change was the gradual emergence of a free labor market. This was the result not only of the abolition of monopolies but also of the urbanization which took place in the 1880's and 1890's.[71]

Most of the increase in Egypt's urban population was of course the result of the influx from the countryside which swelled the class of workers, petty traders, and people without any fixed occupation. It often happened that natives of a specific village or district migrated to a specific town and specialized in a particular occupation. In 1907 there lived in Cairo about thirty thousand people born in Asyūṭ province, while a considerable part of the inhabitants of the Suez Canal towns had come from Qenā. Many of Cairo's porters were from Mūsha village (Asyūṭ province), many of the water carriers from Dār al-Baqar (Gharbiyya), and a great part of the building workers were recruited in Tirsa (Gīza).[72] Both government departments and private employers used to recruit their workers through contractors (*khawlī*, colloquial *khōlī*), who supplied the laborers, supervised their work, and paid their wages.[73] By the end of the first decade of this century the nucleus of a new working class had emerged, composed mainly of transport and building workers and of workers in the few industries which had been established: sugar refineries, ginneries, and cigarette factories.[74] However, a large proportion of the new urban lower classes consisted as yet of a fluctuating mass of people without any fixed employment.

[69]H. Stephan, *Das heutige Aegypten*, Leipzig, 1872, p. 201; R. Buchta, "Die Aegypter," *Das Ausland* (1882), 847; Sāmī, part 3, 2:849.

[70]For details, see chapter 10, above.

[71]For details, see chapter 8, above.

[72]Mubārak, 10:31, 100; 16:90.

[73]J. F. Nahas, *Situation économique et sociale du fellah égyptien*, Paris, 1901, p. 170; J. Vallet, *Contribution à l'étude de la condition des ouvriers de la grande industrie au Caire*, Valence, 1911, pp. 23–24.

[74]For details on their conditions, organization, etc., see Vallet, *passim*.

The character of the middle class did not undergo profound changes, although as a whole it grew in size, and a shift took place in the relative importance of some of its components. We have mentioned that in the second half of the nineteenth century Egyptian artisans and merchants, especially small and medium ones, were severely hit by European competition. Even if their number did not decline, they certainly had no ample scope for expansion. Another group of the middle class that did not make much headway during that time was the liberal professions. According to the census of 1907, at that time Egypt had no more than 3,677 architects, engineers, and people with similar occupations, 2,237 lawyers and their clerks, 719 pharmacists and herbalists, 53 veterinary surgeons, and 1,271 physicians and surgeons, that is, about nine thousand inhabitants per physician. Almost half of these were foreigners. Secular education was identified almost exclusively with entrance into government employment.[75] Moreover, once Egyptians were accepted as officials, government employment became the ideal of a large part of the Egyptian population because of the power and social status connected with it. In his autobiography Mubārak says, "I chose not to become a *faqīh* . . . but a clerk (*kātib*) because I saw that clerks were good-looking in appearance, regarded with respect, and near to the rulers."[76] This development is reflected in the comparison between census figures for 1882 and 1907: while the total population grew by 66 per cent, the number of persons employed in public administration grew by 83.7 per cent; the total number of persons engaged in liberal professions (clergy, lawyers, physicians, artists, and the like) grew by only 35.6 per cent.[77]

The main change that occurred in the upper classes (disregarding for the moment foreigners, about whom more will be said below) was the merging of formerly well-defined units in one group. We have seen that in the course of the century differences between "Turks" and "Arabs" were blurred; a parallel process took place in the socio-economic field. At the end of the eighteenth and the beginning of the nineteenth century, the governing class of officials was strictly separated from the urban craftsmen and merchants, and the latter were never landowners. Nor did the governing class own land in the modern sense of the word, although they acted as tax farmers. During the nineteenth century, interpenetration between these different socio-economic groups developed in several ways.

[75] See M. Berger, *Bureaucracy and Society in Modern Egypt*, Princeton, 1957, pp. 28–29.

[76] Mubārak, 9:38. *Fāqīh* may have been used in the literary sense, i.e., a person versed in religious law, or in the coloquial Egyptian meaning of teacher in a Qur'ān school (*fiqī*).

[77] Figures for 1882 according to the unpublished third volume of the census as quoted by A. von Fircks, *Aegypten*, Berlin, 1895, 1:187. These figures are known to be inaccurate, but the comparison certainly indicates the general trend.

First, in the course of the century high officials became large landowners, mainly by receiving land grants from the rulers. On the other hand, village notables and former beduin shaykhs who had become large landowners were appointed in the civil service and moved to towns.[78] Sometimes these landowner-officials also entered other economic spheres, especially as contractors for supplies for the government, transport, and the like.[79] At the end of the century officials were forbidden to have a share in government contracts, or to acquire land sold by the government,[80] but a considerable proportion of the high civil service continued to be recruited from the landowners.[81]

At the same time rich merchants began to acquire large estates, both because agricultural development made investment in land a profitable business and because landownership had become the most important criterion of social status. Two outstanding cases, those of the al-Hajīn and al-Ṭarazī families, have been related in detail by Mubārak.[82] Others were the al-Shanāwīs and Mutawallī Bey Nūr of Manṣūra; Sayyid Aḥmad Bey al-Dīb, Rizqallāh Bey Shadīd, and the Abāẓas of Zaqāzīq; Maḥmūd Pasha Sulaymān of Asyūṭ; and Muḥammad Bey Abū Ḥusayn and many others of Cairo.[83] Many of them, or members of their families, also served as government officials.

As a result of this interpenetration, no urban *bourgeoisie* in the European sense emerged in Egypt. There was no social class of Egyptians whose principal interest concentrated in the towns and in the promotion of urban economy. This is well illustrated by the lack of independent municipal development. Between 1890 and 1911, municipalities were established in many Egyptian towns, but most of their members were appointed by the central government or were government officials, the governor of the province had a decisive vote, and their powers were confined to a small range of activities. Moreover, foreigners were represented in a much higher proportion than their percentage in the population. Indeed, the only municipality with some tradition of independence and a larger scope of activity was that of Alexandria, in which foreigners constituted the majority during the whole period under discussion.[84]

[78] For detailed treatment of this development, see Baer, *Landownership*, pp. 13–15, 17, 45–60.

[79] See, for instance, the interesting biography of ʿAlī Bey al-Badrāwī, Mubārak, 12:49–50. Cf. also Rogers to Stanton, Cairo, November 3, 1871, FO 141/75, part 3.

[80] Cf. Order of June 28, 1896, *Majmūʿat al-qarārāt waʾl-manshūrat*, 1896, pp. 333–34.

[81] See Berger, pp. 45–46.

[82] Mubārak, 3:54–55; 15:96. Cf. Baer, *Landownership*, p. 23; on the interpenetration between landownership and urban business in the twentieth century, see pp. 138–42.

[83] For details on their landed property and urban business see Wright and Cartwright, pp. 384, 389, 481–82.

[84] For details, see chapter 11, above.

Foreigners and Westernization

At the end of the eighteenth century there were in Egypt no more than a few hundred Europeans, including Greeks. During the rule of Muḥammad ʿAlī the number of Europeans grew to about ten thousand, at least half of them Greeks and about two thousand Italians.[85] The great influx of Europeans occurred during the time of Saʿīd and Ismāʿīl, especially in the early 1860's, as a result of the great financial and commercial opportunities connected with the cotton boom and the manifold projects of these two rulers.[86] By 1878 their number had risen to 68,653; by 1897 to 112,574; and by 1907 to 151,414, of whom 62,973 were Greeks, 34,926 Italians, and the rest (53,515) others (excluding Ottoman subjects).[87] A proper evaluation of these figures should take into account that even after the great influx the number of foreigners did not rise above 1.3 per cent of the total population (from less than one-half of one per cent in the 1840's), and that about one-third of the "other foreigners" (16,000 in 1907) were Asians, Maltese, or North Africans.

The contact of the Egyptian population with these foreigners was not the only channel of Western influence on Egyptian society. Between 1813 and 1919 about nine hundred Egyptians were sent on educational missions to Europe,[88] and many others visited Europe on their own. Thousands were educated at foreign schools in Egypt: the number of pupils at these schools was 7,450 in 1875 and 48,204 in 1913–14, many of them Egyptians.[89] In the course of the century hundreds of works were translated from European languages into Arabic, technical and scientific books as well as novels, plays, and the like. Many Europeans were employed in controlling positions of the Egyptian administration, especially after the British occupation.

The contact with foreigners and with Europe expressed itself in many fields with which we are not directly concerned here. During the nineteenth century, especially after 1882, an extensive network of communications was established; parts of Cairo and Alexandria were built or rebuilt after the model of Paris, and supplied with water, gas, and electricity; the administration of Egypt was modernized; and important changes took place in

[85] Estimates vary considerably. Our estimate is based on Mengin, *Histoire de l'Egypte*, 2:269 ff.; Clot, 1:167, 243 ff.; Bowring, pp. 4, 9; Campbell Report.

[86] Cf. D. S. Landes, *Bankers and Pashas*, London, 1958, pp. 87 ff.

[87] Figures for 1878 according to F. Amici, *Essai de statistique générale de l'Égypte*, Cairo, 1879; for 1897, Gouvernement Egyptien, *Recensement général de l'Egypte*, June 1, 1897, Cairo, 1898; for 1907, Egypt, Ministry of Finance, *The Census of Egypt Taken in 1907*, Cairo, 1909.

[88] M. M. Mosharrafa, *Cultural Survey of Modern Egypt*, vol. 2, London, 1948, p. 54; J. Heyworth-Dunne, *An Introduction to the History of Education in Modern Egypt*, London, n.d. [1939], pp. 253, 304, 326, 394.

[89] Sāmī, part 3, 2:1286; R. D. Matthews and M. Akrawi, *Education in Arab Countries of the Near East*, Washington, D.C., 1949, p. 34; Heyworth-Dunne, Appendix.

legislation and the administration of the law. However, it would seem that the most important social change brought about by this contact was the development of education.[90] At the end of the eighteenth and the beginning of the nineteenth century there was no secular education, and learning was confined to the small class of people who were destined to become part of the religious establishment. There are no reliable figures for that period, but the few existing estimates indicate that at the time of Muḥammad ʿAlī not more than 5 per cent of the children between six and twelve years of age received any formal education at all.[91] In the course of the century this percentage rose to about 17.5 in 1875 and a little less than 25 in 1913–14.[92] Part of the elementary and primary education was secularized, and a variety of institutions for secondary, vocational, and higher education was established. According to an estimate by Artin Pasha, the percentage of literate adults increased from 1 in 1830, to 3 in 1850, and 10 in 1881.[93] Thus a growing number of Egyptians were able to read the newly founded newspapers and the growing output of the Arabic printing presses, also an innovation of the nineteenth century.

However, although the above figures indicate progress, they also stress the fact that even at the end of the period under discussion only a very small layer of Egyptian society received any formal education; the number of those who did not forget what they had learned because of lack of practice must have been even smaller. Still smaller was the number of literate people whose education brought them into contact with Western society capable of changing their social attitudes. Education as an instrument of the westernization of Egyptian society was therefore confined to a very small part of the population.

Moreover, many factors reduced the social influence of contact with foreigners residing in Egypt. The overwhelming majority of foreigners lived in Alexandria and Cairo, and, except for the Greeks, most of the rest lived in Port Said and Ismailia. Thus only inhabitants of these towns had the opportunity of continuous contact with foreigners. But even in these towns foreigners generally lived in their own quarters, often secluded from the Egyptian population. In Cairo there was a striking difference between the appearance of the quarters in which the foreigners concentrated and that of the Egyptian quarters: the former were lighted by electricity and gas,

[90] See Heyworth-Dunne, *passim.*

[91] Cf. Heyworth-Dunne, p. 360; Bowring, p. 137. Children in this age group are taken to have constituted 15 per cent of the population.

[92] Figures for 1875 and 1913–14 according to Sāmī and Matthews and Akrawi, as quoted in note 89, above.

[93] Quoted by A. Boktor, *School and Society in the Valley of the Nile*, Cairo, 1936, p. 139.

while the latter were not, and in summer the European quarters were deserted.[94] In Alexandria the two elements mixed to a larger extent, but then the character of the population of Alexandria was typical of that of any Mediterranean port rather than of Egyptian society.[95]

Conclusion

As a result of all these factors "westernization" was confined to a very small layer of Egyptian society. Moreover, the fact that this layer tried to adopt a foreign culture and civilization alienated it more and more from the bulk of the Egyptian population. While at the beginning of the century there were no significant cultural differences among Egyptians, the impact of the West created a gulf between the Europeanized and educated Egyptian officials and other parts of the upper classes and the great mass of fellahs and town dwellers, including the lower middle classes.

As we have seen, the contact with Europe and the economic and administrative development in the nineteenth century only partly changed the life and organization of Egyptian society. The traditional family and religious community remained intact, and the position of women in society did not change. Neither wealthy Egyptians nor the lower classes acquired the mentality of an industrial society. The social change brought about consisted almost entirely in the destruction of the traditional socio-economic framework: the dissolution of the tribe and the village community, the disappearance of the guilds, and the abolition of slavery. Most of these developments occurred during the last two decades of the century. But the creation of modern groupings, such as modern parties or labor trade unions, was left for the twentieth century.

As a result of the destruction of the traditional socio-economic framework, the rigid separation between different units of the socio-economic structure vanished. We have seen that different groups of the upper class merged into one: similarly, mobility between the classes grew. In the eighteenth century everybody was born into his occupational group and there were very few chances for a poor man to become rich. Urbanization, the disappearance of the guilds, the growing demand for officials, the development of private ownership of land, and the great expansion of agriculture—all created opportunities which greatly increased social mobility. We have mentioned that in the second part of the century many officials and army officers were

[94] Wright and Cartwright, pp. 333, 335–36.

[95] Wright and Cartwright, p. 429. See also Landes, pp. 86–89.

of fellah origin. Throughout the century not a few people of humble and poor origin became rich landowners, high officials, wealthy merchants, or or even physicians.[96] However, lack of entrepreneurship among Egyptians, and lack of industrial development, confined mobility within limits which began to disappear only much later.

[96] See biographies in Mubārak, 9:92–93; 11:88; 12:49; 17:4; etc.; Wright and Cartwright, p. 389 (Abū Ḥusayn); Mackenzie Wallace, pp. 197–99. Cf. Baer, *Landownership*, pp. 49–50; Berger, pp. 45–46 (pointing out that the Egyptian higher civil service draws heavily upon the lowest socio-economic groups).

Appendix

ʿAlī Mubārak's *Khiṭaṭ* as a Source for the History of Modern Egypt

ʿAlī Pasha Mubārak's *al-Khiṭaṭ al-tawfīqiyya al-jadīda* (Būlāq, 1304–5 A.H./1886–89) has been the subject of a number of reviews by orientalists and of special chapters in some books on Mubārak by Arab authors.[1] Most of these have stressed the parts of this work that deal with ancient and medieval Egypt. The reviewers were certainly right in saying that Mubārak's account of the history and topography of ancient and medieval Egypt was no more than a compilation based on medieval Arab authors and European orientalists of the nineteenth century.[2] Thus the Egyptologist and the historian of medieval Islam will not find much interesting material in this work. In the nineteenth century, when it was published, it was perhaps of use to educated Egyptians who preferred to become acquainted with Egypt's heritage through the Arabic work of a Muslim, but today it no longer fulfills even this purpose. However, according to Mubārak's words

Originally published as "ʿAlī Mubārak's *Khiṭaṭ* as a Source for the History of Modern Egypt," in P. M. Holt (ed.), *Political and Social Change in Modern Egypt* (London: Oxford University Press, 1967), pp. 13–27.

[1] K. Vollers in *Zeitschrift der deutschen morgenländischen Gesellschaft*, 47 (1893):720 ff.; K. Vollers in *EI*[1] and *EI*[2]; C. Brockelmann, *Geschichte der arabischen Literatur* (*GAL*), 2:634, Supplement(*S*), 2:733; I. Goldziher in *Wiener Zeitschrift für die Kunde des Morgenlandes* (*WZKM*), 4 (1890):347 ff. The first Arabic book on Mubārak was Muḥammad Pasha Durrī, *Taʾrīkh ḥayāt al-maghfūr lahu ʿAlī Mubārak Bāshā*, Cairo, 1311 A.H./1894, based on Mubārak's autobiography in his *Khiṭaṭ*. The best modern Arabic work is Maḥmūd al-Sharqāwī and ʿAbdallāh al-Mishadd, *ʿAlī Mubārak, ḥayātuhu wa-daʿwatuhu wa-āthāruhu*, Cairo, 1962, including on pp. 102 ff. a complete list of Mubārak's works. See also Muḥammad Aḥmad Khalafallāh, *ʿAlī Mubārak wa-āthāruhu*, Cairo, 1957, and Saʿīd Zāyid, *ʿAlī Mubārak wa-aʿmāluhu*, Cairo, 1957. Many other Arabic histories and collections of biographies include sections on Mubārak; most of these are also based on his autobiography. Since all these reviews and books include a general description of the *Khiṭaṭ*, I have refrained from repeating these details here.

[2] Even the classics are often quoted from modern French works; see 17:28.

in his preface, he wrote this work for another important purpose also: like the medieval Arab authors, especially al-Maqrīzī, who wrote the history and described the geography of Egypt in their time, he wanted to give an account of contemporary Egypt as a record for later generations. The result was not only an enormous opus of more than one and a half million words but also a unique and outstanding product of modern Arabic literature. Before trying to answer the question of whether this work is of use to the historians of modern Egypt, I shall first survey the sources on which the parts dealing with modern Egypt are based, and the way in which Mubārak presents his material.

Mubārak's Sources

Official Documents

Prior to the publication of Mubārak's *Khiṭaṭ*, Régny, Amici, and Dor had already published their statistical yearbooks, and in 1884 the government had issued the results of the 1882 census.[3] Moreover, there can be no doubt that Mubārak had access to additional unpublished statistical material—in the course of his career he had been responsible for the ministries or departments of *waqf*, education, public works, and railways. It cannot be said that he has systematically used this material. Here and there he mentions the *dafātir al-taʿdād* (census registers) as a source for the administrative divisions of Egypt (14:140; 17:61) or the spelling of place names (15:17; 17:59); he quotes *kitāb al-iḥṣāʾāt al-miṣriyya li-sanat 1872* (probably Régny's yearbook) for the number of foreigners in Egypt and their geographical distribution (7:65), and he uses Régny's statistics, without mentioning the source, for his figures on the movement of ships and goods and the members of guilds in Alexandria (7:74–75, 79–84).[4] Similarly, he gives population figures for Cairo according to the "censuses" of 1872 and 1882 (1:98).[5] However, Mubārak does not say from what source he derived his figures on the population of other towns and villages. Population figures are given mainly for

[3] E. de Régny, *Statistique de l'Egypte*, Alexandria, 1870–3; F. Amici, *Essai de statistique générale de l'Egypte*, Cairo, 1879; E. Dor, *Statistique des écoles civiles*, Cairo, 1875; Ministère de l'Intérieur, *Recensement général de l'Egypte 1882*, Cairo, 1884.

[4] Régny (1870), pp. 69–72. There are, however, some differences between Mubārak's and Régny's lists.

[5] To the best of my knowledge, no census whatever was taken in 1872. Mubārak's figures are apparently based on Régny (1873), p. 20, whose data were calculated according to official records of population movement.

Sharqiyya province, very few for places in Minūfiyya, Gharbiyya, and Buḥayra, and none at all for Upper Egypt. There can be no doubt that for this purpose he did not use the 1882 census, in which detailed figures on every town and village in Egypt are tabulated. To judge by the ratio of Mubārak's figures to those of the census, the former probably relate to the middle 1870's.[6] Indeed, this seems to be the time at which most of Mubārak's *Khiṭaṭ* was written.[7]

A second type of official documents used by Mubārak are title deeds and the cadastral survey. Although he does not explicitly say so, his detailed figures on the *zimām* (registered area) of many villages obviously derive from the cadaster. On only one occasion he mentions as a source the *ta'rīkh al-masāḥa li-sanat 1228*—that is, Muḥammad ʿAlī's cadastral survey (14:116). Apparently he is on much firmer ground when he speaks about urban real estate. Urban title deeds (*ḥujaj amlāk*) are used for locating buildings and institutions which no longer existed in Mubārak's time (for example, 2:82), and on the basis of the *dafātir al-dā'ira al-baladiyya* (municipal records) he prepared a list of buildings in Cairo according to their different types, their use, and the number of their owners (1:94). However, Mubārak's most important source of this kind is *waqfiyyāt*, *waqf* documents to which he had access as Minister of Waqfs. In no other modern Arabic work known to me have *waqf* documents been used so extensively as in the *Khiṭaṭ*. They serve Mubārak in various ways: to locate buildings, streets, and institutions (2:36; 3:65; and so on); to discover facts about prices and currencies in the eighteenth century (20:150f.); and even as a source for the history of the Bakrī family (3:121). Moreover, Mubārak has published in full (or almost in full) seven *waqfiyyāt* from the nineteenth century and thirteen from the eighteenth century in addition to thirty-two older ones. This is doubtless first-rate material for the economic, social, and cultural history of Egypt.

Mubārak also had recourse to the archives of the Wafā'ī order of *sharīf*s (*dafātir al-sādāt al-wafā'iyya*). But, unfortunately, these documents are used only in the part dealing with currencies and prices (20:151ff.) and not as a source for the history of the order and the family; in the chapter on the Sādāt (5:138f.) they are not mentioned, and the narrative is based on other sources.

[6] We have arrived at this conclusion by calculating the ratio of Régny's figures for the early 1870's and Amici's for the late 1870's to those of the census (both Régny and Amici give only totals for provinces).

[7] See, for instance, 18:34: *al-ān yaʿnī sanat iḥdā wa-tisʿīn wa-mi'atayn wa-alf*—that is, 1874; 10:21 and 12:105: *al-ān aʿnī sanat 1293* (1876). However, in the parts on Cairo and on the Nilometer, later data have been used; for instance, the 1882 census (see above); see also 3:124, where the events that occurred in 1880 are related, and 18:109–10 (data for the year 1887–88).

Personal Observation

Both Goldziher and Brockelmann[8] affirm that most of Mubārak's demographic, topographic, economic, and anthropological data are based on personal observations made in the course of his many official tours through the country. Others claim that Mubārak obtained most of his facts from engineers and officials of the Ministry of Public Works.[9] It seems that, although he benefited from the knowledge of many assistants, his personal experience certainly served as a most important source for writing the *Khiṭaṭ*.

The principal part of his work based on personal experience is his extensive autobiography (about seventeen thousand words, 9:37–61). It includes most interesting personal observations on the condition of the rural population in Muḥammad ʿAlī's day, education in Egypt throughout the century, the educational missions to Europe, literary activity in Egypt, engineering works and communications, *waqf*, the army, the higher bureaucracy of Egypt, the *ʿulamāʾ*, and many other subjects.

In many cases Mubārak explicitly states that a specific fact came to his knowledge through personal observation. These include the description of mosques and mausoleums (2:25, 62, 199), the location of schools (2:7, 46), the development of railway stations (7:90), and questions connected with a slaughterhouse (1:104). In many other cases he does not definitely say so, but since these also concern *waqf*, public works, railways, education, and the army, he must have come across these matters in the course of his official career. Almost all the personal observations made on matters that were not connected with his career concern buildings he saw or persons he met in Cairo or Alexandria but not in provincial towns or villages.

Oral Evidence

Mubārak frequently relates what he was told by his contemporaries. Many of these supplied him with their biographies: officials (8:18, 22; 10:98), the manager of a *waqf* (10:40), *ʿulamāʾ* (8:73, 74; 9:2, 86, 87; 11:9; 12:118; 14:141; 15:11), army officers (7:85; 11:86), engineers (9:7; 12:143), interpreters and writers (11:68; 17:62), physicians (11:88; 14:125), and even a sailor (14:100). Many biographies of *ʿulamāʾ* were supplied by their sons, most of them students or teachers at the Azhar (4:41; 8:27, 29; 9:33; 11:14; 12:19; 14:96, 140; 15:40). In some cases Mubārak made special inquiries to obtain a biography (4:38).[10]

[8] *GAL*, 1st ed., 2:482.

[9] Cf. Vollers in *EI*[2]; ʿAbd al-Raḥmān al-Rāfiʿī, *ʿAṣr Ismāʿīl*, 2d ed., Cairo, 1948, 1:240; Khalafallāh, p. 154.

[10] Sharqāwī and Mishadd, p. 110, belittle the importance of these biographies. The reason seems to be the above-mentioned controversy about Mubārak's original contribution (see references in preceding note).

Obviously Mubārak tried to continue the famous tradition of Arabic biographical literature, and particularly to collect biographies of the *ʿulamāʾ* of his time, completing thereby the collections of his predecessors (al-Sakhāwī, al-Shaʿrānī, al-Jabartī, and others), whom he frequently quotes. But it is also evident that *ʿulamāʾ* were in a better position than anybody else to supply him with information on the subjects in which he was interested. According to his own evidence, *ʿulamāʾ* were the source for his accounts of a *mawlid* (13:50) and of the history of the Bakrī family (3:121). Similarly, in reply to his inquiry Coptic priests supplied him with information about their community, churches, convents, and so on (6:72).

However, Mubārak's oral sources include not only *ʿulamāʾ*. He received information about the exploration of the Suez area from Gastinel Bey[11] (12:76) and about the Eastern Desert from somebody who had toured the area in search of marble (10:21–24). A detailed description of the *ḥajj* was supplied by a person who for fourteen years had served as *kātib al-ṣurra*[12] (9:22). In some cases Mubārak merely quotes a "reliable source" (2:112; 11:84; 12:63).[13]

In addition, Mubārak asked the inhabitants of a town quarter or a village about many things that interested him (6:25). For example, he asked a native of a village who had become an Azharī (8:30), an official of the Public Works Department born in a neighboring village (13:41), and the head of the most important family of the village and the owner of its land (12:96–97). Such witnesses and others supplied him with information about wells and pools (9:19), the local saint and his tomb (14:99), local customs (15:73), and so on. At one place his local witness gave him an interesting and detailed account of a *mawlid* (12:96–97). In another case Mubārak states that his witness supplied him with the general description of the village related in the *Khiṭaṭ*. Scores of similar descriptions are scattered throughout this work without their sources being mentioned; many of them are probably based on information supplied by the natives of the villages.

Written Arabic Sources

The eighteenth and nineteenth centuries are not rich in Arabic historical and geographical literature on Egypt. Nevertheless, Mubārak could have used more Arabic works on these subjects than he did. He does not mention Niqūlā Turk's history of the French occupation (published in Paris in 1839),

[11] A teacher of chemistry in Egyptian military schools.

[12] The clerk responsible for the money paid by Egypt to the Ḥijāz on the occasion of the *ḥajj*.

[13] *Balaghanī mimman athiq, akhbaranī man athiqu bihi, akhbara bihi thiqātuhum*, and so on.

Iskandar Abkārius's history of Ibrāhīm Pasha (published in Cairo six years before the publication of the *Khiṭaṭ*), Muḥammad Amīn Fikrī's geography,[14] al-Sharqāwī's history,[15] or Salīm al-Naqqāsh's book.[16]

Admittedly, all these books are much inferior to the outstanding work of that period, al-Jabartī's history, which is frequently mentioned and quoted by Mubārak. If a village or a town had been mentioned by al-Jabartī, Mubārak in his section on that village or town generally quotes from al-Jabartī the whole passage on the event connected with the place. Thus a large number of passages from al-Jabartī are scattered throughout the *Khiṭaṭ*, among them scores of biographies, especially of *ʿulamāʾ*.

Another book by an Arabic author of the nineteenth century is al-Tūnisī's travels,[17] quoted by Mubārak for the description of the desert routes between the Nile, the oases, and the Sudan, including a detailed description of the oases (and a biography of al-Tūnisī) (17:33). Besides al-Jabartī and al-Tūnisī, the only modern Arabic author mentioned by Mubārak is Buṭrus al-Bustānī, from whose encyclopedia Mubārak quotes almost exclusively biographies of medieval Arab scholars.

Finally, there is no indication in Mubārak's *Khiṭaṭ* that he used the Arabic press of Egypt, which by his time had already developed to a considerable degree.

Works in European Languages

Among the European sources used by Mubārak for his account of modern Egypt the *Description de l'Egypte* occupies the first place. He calls it *Khiṭaṭ al-faransāwiyya* or *Kutub al-faransāwiyya* or *Kitāb al-jamʿiyya al-faransāwiyya al-khāṣṣ bi-khiṭaṭ Miṣr*.[18] It is frequently quoted for matters concerning both

[14] Muḥammad Amīn Fikrī, *Jughrāfiyyat Miṣr*, Cairo, 1296 A.H./1879. The reason was perhaps that Fikrī himself had extensively used the manuscript of the *Khiṭaṭ* for his book. See his introduction, p. *jīm*. However, in the second volume there is a long biography of Fikrī (2:46 ff.), and his help is acknowledged by Mubārak in his *ʿAlam al-dīn*, Alexandria, 1299 A.H./1882, pp. 7–8.

[15] ʿAbdallāh al-Sharqāwī, *Tuḥfat al-nāẓirīn fī man walā Miṣr min al-wulāt waʾl-salāṭīn*, Cairo, 1281 A.H./1864–65. This is a remarkable omission, because Mubārak has a biography of al-Sharqāwī, including a long list of his works (13:63 f.). The biography is based on al-Jabartī. On al-Sharqāwī's history, see D. Ayalon, "The Historian al-Jabartī and His Background," *Bulletin of the School of Oriental and African Studies*, University of London, 23, no. 2 (1960):248–49, and sources quoted there.

[16] Salīm al-Naqqāsh, *Miṣr liʾl-Miṣriyyīn*, Alexandria, 1884. This omission may be explained either by the fact that by 1884 the manuscript of the *Khiṭaṭ* was already more or less completed or by Mubārak's aversion to anything connected with the ʿUrābī movement (see below).

[17] *Tashḥīdh al-adhhān bi-sīrat bilād al-ʿarab waʾl-sūdān: Voyage au Darfour . . . par le Cheykh Mohammed ibn-Omar el-tounsy, autographié et publié par M. Perron*, Paris, 1850; (cf. *GAL, S*, 2:748–49).

[18] European books in general are designated *kutub al-Faranj* (see below).

ancient Egypt and Egypt at the time of the French occupation. Mubārak uses the *Description* for information on the topography and economic conditions of Egyptian towns and villages at the time of the French occupation (for instance, 11:60; 12:98, 102; 15:70, 94; 16:52), on population figures and administration at that time (1:98; 12:47), on mosques, hospitals, and convents (1:96–97; 2:104; 12:54), on the Nilometer (18:34, 93), and on various other topographical and historical subjects. With the exception of one or two of these quotations, no volumes and pages are given.

The works of European officials who served the Muḥammad ʿAlī family are used by Mubārak rather sporadically and, surprisingly enough, more often than not in connection with matters which are not their principal concern. Dr. Clot-Bey, for instance, who established the medical school at the time of Muḥammad ʿAlī and laid the foundations of a health service in Egypt, wrote a book about the plague in Egypt[19] which is not quoted by Mubārak. He uses Clot's *Aperçu général*[20] not for its detailed sections on health and hospitals but for such subjects as the digging of the Maḥmūdiyya Canal (7:50), Muḥammad ʿAlī's navy (7:52–54), figures on Egypt's religious and ethnic communities (7:54, without mentioning that they are taken from Clot), Muḥammad ʿAlī's army (7:55–57), Suez (7:75), and industry at the time of Muḥammad ʿAlī (15:91). It is interesting to note that most of this material is concentrated in the seventh volume of the *Khiṭaṭ* dealing with Alexandria. The book of Linant de Bellefonds,[21] who was Director of Public Works in Egypt at the time of Muḥammad ʿAlī and who made the first plans for the Delta barrage, is mentioned by Mubārak only in connection with various topographic questions (14:74; 17:27, 28, 65) but not with public works and irrigation.

However, two other European officials are quoted on matters with which they were concerned in Egypt. One is Hamont, the manager of Muḥammad ʿAlī's private estates. His book[22] is mentioned exclusively in connection with horse breeding and sheep raising (12:120; 15:30); but then Hamont was not an admirer of Muḥammad ʿAlī, and his book is full of severe accusations against him. It was therefore no suitable material to be quoted by Mubārak,

[19] A.-B. Clot-Bey, *De la Peste observée en Égypte*, Paris, 1840. For publications of Clot in Arabic, see Yūsuf Sarkis, *Muʿjam al-maṭbūʿāt al-ʿarabiyya wa'l-muʿarraba*, Cairo, 1928, p. 1567. None of these is quoted in the *Khiṭaṭ*.

[20] A.-B. Clot-Bey, *Aperçu général sur l'Egypte*, Paris, 1840, 2 vols. The author's name is rendered *Qūlūṭ*, although in the section on Cairo we find *Shāriʿ Klūt* (3:112). The book is called *ta'rīkhuhu li-Miṣr* (7:52).

[21] M. A. Linant de Bellefonds, *Mémoires sur les principaux travaux d'utilité publique exécutés en Egypte depuis la plus haute antiquité jusqu' à nos jours*, Paris, 1872–73.

[22] P. N. Hamont, *L'Egypte sous Méhémet-Ali*, Paris, 1843. On its background, see J. M. Carré, *Voyageurs et écrivains français en Égypte*, Cairo, 1956, 1:293–94.

who was a loyal servant of the Muḥammad ʿAlī family. The second is Cailliaud, who was employed by Muḥammad ʿAlī to explore the Eastern Desert in search of emeralds. Mubārak translates his account of this expedition (13:21).[23]

Like his quotations from European officials, Mubārak's use of books written by European consuls and travelers seems to have been only occasional. Beginning with the eighteenth century, the first is de Maillet, the French Consul in Egypt during the years 1692–1708. His book[24] is also mentioned in connection with emeralds (13:23); the same author seems to be meant when, instead of *Māyyh*, we find *Māny* (7:39, 40, 42), *Māby* (7:44, 48), or *Māly* (7:38), since all these passages deal with Alexandria at the beginning of the eighteenth century (on misprints of foreign names, see below). Emeralds are also the subject of a quotation from Bruce,[25] one of the two British travelers mentioned by Mubārak (who probably used the French translation of Bruce's book).[26] The letters of Savary,[27] who toured Egypt in 1776–77 are cited only in connection with two subjects: the description of Rosetta (11:75; 15:4), and the monasteries near Suez (12:76). But even more astonishing is the scanty use made of the famous travels by Volney[28] (spelled *Wūlny* or *Fūlny* or *Wlyn* or *Flyn*). The curious thing is that Mubārak twice quotes medieval Arabic authors according to Volney (7:16; 13:10) and twice questions of Egyptology (7:33; 16:9), but he does not mention him at all in connection with the conditions of Egypt at the end of the eighteenth century, except for the Nilometer (18:92–93).

The first European traveler of the nineteenth century mentioned by Mubārak appears in the *Khiṭaṭ* as *al-dukdū Ra'jūs* or *al-dūk dū Rājūs*. This is no other than Maréchal Auguste Marmont, duc de Raguse, who in 1843 traveled in eastern Europe, southern Russia, Turkey, and Egypt.[29] He is quoted on springs and monasteries near Suez (12:70, 75), the battle of

[23] F. Cailliaud, *Voyage à l'Oasis de Thèbes et dans les déserts situés à l'Orient et à l'Occident de la Thébaïde fait pendant les années 1815–1818. Rédigé et publié par M. Jomard . . . contenant: . . .* 3° *Des Recherches sur les oasis, sur les mines d'émeraude, et sur l'ancienne route du commerce entre le Nil et la Mer Rouge*, Paris, 1822–24, 2 vols. Cf. Carré, 1:225–28. The author's name is spelled by Mubārak *Kābū*, but this seems to be a misprint of *Kāyū*.

[24] *Description de l'Egypte . . . composé sur les mémoires de M. de Maillet par l'Abbé Le Mascrier*, Paris, 1735. Cf. Carré, 1:56–63.

[25] James Bruce, *Travels to Discover the Source of the Nile, in the Years 1768, 1769, 1770, 1771, 1772 and 1773*, London, 1790, 5 vols.

[26] James Bruce, *Voyage en Nubie et en Abyssinie*, Paris, 1790–92, 5 vols. Thomas Shaw's travels, which had also been translated into French, are quoted once, in connection with the Nilometer (18:92).

[27] C. E. Savary, *Lettres sur l'Egypte*, Paris, 1785–86, 3 vols. Cf. Carré, 1:80–104.

[28] C. F. C. Volney, *Voyage en Syrie et en Egypte, pendant les années 1783, 1784 et 1785*, Paris, 1787. This is the original form of the title, which is usually cited as *Voyage en Égypte et en Syrie*.

[29] *Voyage du Maréchal duc de Raguse*, Paris, 1837–40, 5 vols. Cf. Carré, 1:279–84.

Shubrākhīt in 1798 (12:119), the artillery school at Ṭurā (13:32), and the natron concession (13:34). The next is Ampère, son of the famous physicist, who traveled in Egypt in 1844–45 (not in 1830, as stated in Mubārak).[30] In the *Khiṭaṭ* we find the translation of part of his description of Alexandria (7:30). *Jrky al-Firinsāwī* seems to be Gisquet (cf. 7:39—*Kitāb Jsky*), who traveled in Egypt a few months prior to Ampère and whose book[31] is also mentioned in the part of the *Khiṭaṭ* dealing with Alexandria (7:37). That Mubārak quotes the superficial account by H. Bernard of the campaign of Muḥammad ʿAlī against the Wahhābīs (12:81) may be explained by the fact that he found it in Arabic translation.[32]

In addition to these European authors who are mentioned by name, Mubārak frequently uses travel accounts without citing their authors. He says merely that a specific bit of information is taken from *baʿḍ al-sayyāḥīn*, *baʿḍ man sāḥa fī Miṣr*, *baʿḍ al-faransāwiyya fī siyāḥatihi*, or *baʿḍ man sāfara fī tilka al-jihāt fī waqtinā hādhā* (8:100; 14:121; 16:20; 17:30, 39, 55, and so on). Moreover, he sometimes says only that his information is derived from a European source—*baʿḍ kutub al-Ifranj* (for instance, 17:7, 38). Similarly, his biographies of some orientalists and travelers are taken from what he calls *qāmūs al-Ifranj* or *al-qāmūs al-ifranjī* or *qāmūs jūghrāfiyyat al-ifranjī* [*sic*][33] (10:52; 11:68, 75; 12:38, and so on).

Finally, Mubārak apparently had access to some journals in European languages. He mentions two of them: the Egyptian *Moniteur*[34] (14:133), and the *Journal Asiatique* (12:40, 83). However, neither is used for information on modern Egypt.

Summary

The European sources used by Mubārak are all French works, either written by French authors or translated into French. Yet from the vast literature on modern Egypt written in French, Mubārak made a very small selection; some of the most important are not on his list. Moreover, he uses the sources in a rather capricious way: generally, each is quoted on only one subject, not always the principal contribution of the author to the knowledge of modern Egypt. He never mentions the title of the works he cites, let alone the pages on which the quoted passage is found.

[30] J. J. Ampère, *Voyage en Egypte et en Nubie*, Paris, 1868. First published in *Revue des deux mondes* (1846–49). Cf. Carré, 2:49 ff.

[31] J. H. Gisquet, *L'Egypte, les Turcs et les Arabes*, Paris, 1848. Cf. Carré, 1:295 f.

[32] ʿAbdallāh Abū'l-Suʿūd, *Ta'rīkh al-diyār al-miṣriyya fī ʿahd al-dawla al-Muḥammadiyya al-ʿAliyya, ta'līf Barnār wa-tarjamat Abū'l-Suʿūd*, Cairo, 1292 A.H./1875. French original: H. Bernard, *Notices géographiques et historiques sur l'Egypte*, Paris, 1867, part 3.

[33] Probably P. Larousse, *Le Grand dictionnaire universel du xix*e *siècle*, 1865–76.

But even Arabic written sources, official and nonofficial, published and unpublished, are used by Mubārak in a rather irregular manner. They do not, therefore, make a significant contribution to the importance of the *Khiṭaṭ* as a source for modern Egyptian history. This statement must be qualified by citing two important exceptions: urban title deeds, and *waqf* documents.

As against this, much of the information which is based on oral evidence and on his own personal experience makes a substantial contribution to our knowledge of nineteenth-century Egypt, although the way he presents this material is in many instances unsatisfactory.

Presentation of Material

Arrangement

In the arrangement of the vast material contained in the *Khiṭaṭ*, Mubārak does not deviate from the tradition of medieval Arabic works of a similar kind. He deals with each Egyptian town or village in alphabetical order—with the exception of Cairo (1–6) and Alexandria (7). All the information on a specific place available to Mubārak—its topography, economic conditions, ancient, medieval, and modern history, the biographies of prominent people born in the place, and so on—is presented under one heading: the name of the place. Mubārak must have worked with the aid of an enormous card index or an equivalent apparatus. He did not try, however, to arrange his material according to subjects—with the exception of some parts of the volumes dealing with Cairo and the last three volumes, dealing respectively with the Nile, the canals, and coins and currencies. In general the result is a compilation pieced together from heterogeneous items. Only in a few instances does he critically compare different accounts of the same event or different sets of data.

The arrangment of the material according to towns and villages made it difficult for Mubārak to deal with general subjects which are not connected with a particular place. Many of these subjects, especially in the field of political history, are simply omitted; others are dealt with incidentally, when a slight connection with a particular place could be established. Thus Mubārak gives an account of Muḥammad ʿAlī's army, the conquest and exploration of the Sudan, and various other subjects in the volume dedicated to Alexandria (mostly according to Clot, as we have seen). The discussion of many places includes the biography of persons who had almost no connection at all with these places: they are mentioned only incidentally (10:17–21, 37, and so on). For instance, Mubārak tells us that the inhabitants of

Nazlat Sīdī ʿĪsā (Minyā province) falsely claim that Maʿrūf al-Karkhī, a *Ṣūfī* of the eighth century, is buried in a tomb near this village. This does not deter him, however, from taking the opportunity not only to relate the biography of that *Ṣūfī* but also to describe Karkh, a quarter of Baghdad, and even Baghdad itself (12:37). A few pages further on he says that a certain al-Sinjārī was not connected with a place in Egypt called Sinjār in medieval times but with Sinjār in the Iraqi-Syrian Jazīra; nevertheless, *lā baʾsa bi-sawq tarjamatihi* . . . (there is no harm in relating his biography) (13:46).

Thus much interesting information is scattered throughout the volumes of the *Khiṭaṭ*, but it is often impossible to guess where to find it. The *Khiṭaṭ* has of course no index, a shortcoming of which Jurjī Zaydān has already complained.[35] True, there are at the beginning of each of the twenty volumes very detailed tables of contents, which include not only the names of the towns and villages which are described in the volume but also the biographies and other subjects dealt with in connection with the description of the various places. But it is not always easy to use these tables of contents, and they certainly do not compensate for the lack of an index. Moreover, they are not complete; to give only one example out of many: the table of contents of the ninth volume does not include the interesting description of the great *mawlid* annually held in Upper Egypt, to be found on pages 61–62 of that volume.

Accuracy

Unfortunately, accuracy is not one of the merits of Mubārak's *Khiṭaṭ*. Many of the errors are obviously misprints. As we have seen, only rarely is a foreign name printed in the same transliteration when it is mentioned more than once, and many of these names are not easily recognizable. But the distortion of foreign names is by no means the only type of misprints, as stated by Goldziher.[36] If in fact there had been a *maʿmal zujāj* (glass factory) in Bīr Shams (Minūfiyya) in the nineteenth century, this would have been very important for the industrial development of Egypt (10:25); unfortunately, it was certainly only a *maʿmal dajāj* (a building for the hatching of fowls' eggs by artificial heat) like those that existed in many Egyptian villages at that time.[37] The discrepancy between Régny's and Mubārak's figures on the

[34] First published in 1874; from 1885, an official publication.

[35] Jurjī Zaydān, *Taʾrīkh ādāb al-lugha al-ʿarabiyya*, 2d ed., Cairo, 1937, 4:252. This is certainly one reason why only few authors have used the *Khiṭaṭ*. The preparation of such an index would be an important service to the study of modern Egypt.

[36] "Störende Druckfehler kommen nur in den häufigen fremden Eigennamen vor" (*WZKM*, *supra*).

[37] Cf. 10:4–7 and *passim*; see also E. W. Lane, *An Account of the Manners and Customs of the Modern Egyptians*, Everyman's Library, London, 1944, pp. 317–19.

members of Alexandria's guilds may also be the result of misprints.[38] Similarly, some errors in topographic and geographic data may be explained by misprints: *fī al-shimāl al-qiblī* (14:97) is certainly a printing error, and so probably are *Snūr* instead of *Sīnarū* (8:26) and *al-Mndīsha* instead of *al-Mūshiyya* (17:31).

There are, however, many topographical and geographical errors which definitely cannot be explained as misprints. The most frequent are wrong bearings of a place in relation to other places; I have noted more than forty errors of this kind. It is improbable that they resulted from the use of wrong maps: Mubārak certainly had access to the map of his colleague Maḥmūd al-Falakī published in 1872–73[39] and to that of Jacotin which was published together with the *Description de l'Egypte*.[40] The examination of these maps shows that they were not the source of Mubārak's errors. The *Khiṭaṭ* is not provided with a map.

There are also topographical errors of various other kinds. In some instances Mubārak locates a village on the wrong side of the Nile (for example, Dandara—11:60); sometimes he confuses two different villages which have similar names (for example, Minyat Ḥabīb al-Gharbiyya and Minyat Ḥabīb al-Sharqiyya—16:61); in some instances he gives a wrong name (for example, Banī Mazār instead of Banī Ṣāliḥ—7:15; Khārija instead of Dākhila—15:70; Baḥr Rashīd instead of Baḥr Dimyāṭ—16:60). There are even villages which are altogether wrongly located or about which a number of wrong data are given (for example, Shabās al-Shuhadā—12:115; Maḥallat Diyāy—15:29).

Many of the statements about distances between two places are wrong. The distance between Burdayn and Shubrā al-Nakhla is not 1,500 meters (9:15) but at least nine kilometers; between Bulqīna and Dār al-Baqar al-Qibliyya not two (9:80) but six kilometers; between al-Kawm al-Akhḍar and Abī Ḥummuṣ not five (15:12) but approximately seventeen kilometers; between al-Manāja and Ṣān al-Ḥajar not four (15:74) but about twenty kilometers; and so on. But in most instances he states distances in terms of time, and the time one needs to travel from one place to another depends of course upon the vehicle one uses.

Finally, there is at least one grave error concerning the number of inhabitants of a town. Mubārak writes that al-Maḥalla al-Kubrā has about fifty thousand inhabitants and is the greatest town of Lower Egypt except

[38] See note 4, above.

[39] Maḥmūd Bey al-Falakī, *Kharīṭat al-wajh al-baḥrī li'l-aqālīm al-Miṣriyya*, Cairo, 1289 A.H./1872–73.

[40] Jacotin, *Carte topographique de l'Egypte et de plusieurs parties des pays limitrophes, levée pendant l'expédition de l'armée française*, Paris, 1821.

for Alexandria (15:18). This cannot have been correct. According to the 1882 census, al-Maḥalla al-Kubrā had 27,823 inhabitants, and even in the more accurate 1897 census no more than 31,100 were counted. Both censuses showed that both Ṭanṭā and Damietta were larger than al-Maḥalla al-Kubrā, and in 1897 it was surpassed also by Manṣūra, Damanhūr, and Port Said. Similarly, Mubārak claims that the town of Rashīd (Rosetta) continuously grew and developed (11:75). In fact, the construction of the Maḥmūdiyya Canal and the development of Alexandria caused the decline of Rosetta throughout the nineteenth century; from the middle of the century onward, even the absolute number of its inhabitants continuously declined.

Critical Approach and Prejudices

Referring to the information on ancient times in the *Khiṭaṭ*, Goldziher pointed out as a remarkable fact that Mubārak sometimes expressed critical opinions of texts and their contents.[41] The same may be said with regard to some of the information of modern Egypt. For instance, comparing data on mortality at the time of the French occupation with those of the second half of the nineteenth century, Mubārak remarks that since they show a rise in the mortality rate, they cannot be correct, because the improvement of health conditions certainly brought about a decline in the rate of mortality (1:98–99). However, his critical approach is considerably limited by certain social and political prejudices.

Mubārak accepts without hesitation the genealogies of his contemporaries who supplied him with their biographies. Many of them claimed of course that they were descended from Arab tribes, holy shaykhs, or the family of the Prophet (for example, 4:41; 9:7; 10:98; 11:68; 14:96). Mubārak's criterion for the truth of information about individual persons is often their social status. For instance, he does not believe a story told by al-Jabartī which disparages the Bakrī family, because "it is inconsistent with the honor of this highly respected house" (3:113). Moreover, he relates as an undisputed fact that whenever a member of this family is nearing death, there appears on his heel a scar like that caused by the bite of a serpent. The reason is that their ancestor Abū Bakr was bitten by a serpent in a cave. In 1297 A.H./1880 ʿAlī al-Bakrī died, and a few days before his death the scar had appeared (3:124). As against this, he condemns many superstitions and

[41] *WZKM*, *supra*, p. 349. However, in each of these cases one should examine whether or not Mubārak copied the criticism from the European works which he used as sources for the classics. See note 2, above, and note 42, below.

beliefs in supernatural forces current among the lower classes (for example, 2:75, 113).[42]

An equally important limit of Mubārak's critical approach is his prejudice in favour of the Muḥammad ʿAlī family. He glorifies without reservation Egypt's rulers of the nineteenth century (for example, 7:57, 60, 65; 10:80, 82, 83). There is no ground for Sharqāwī's and Mishadd's assertion that the praise was modified by criticism;[43] in the passage adduced by Sharqāwī and Mishadd (18:138), Mubārak states only that the expenses on the celebration of the opening of the Suez Canal amounted to about one-sixth of Egypt's annual revenues, but his account of the celebration leaves no doubt that he did not disapprove of this fact, or for that matter, of Ismāʿīl's wastefulness. The following is an interesting illustration of Mubārak's loyalty to the Muḥammad ʿAlī family. In connection with the town of Banhā, Mubārak quotes from al-Jabartī a long paragraph about Shaykh ʿAbdallāh al-Banhāwī (9:89). He omits, however, from al-Jabartī's account the passages in which al-Jabartī describes the corruption of the ruling class during the early years of Muḥammad ʿAlī's rule.[44]

Mubārak does not laud all the rulers of Egypt in the nineteenth century with equal fervor, but he seems to distribute his praises according to subjective criteria. To judge by the *Khiṭaṭ*, it was ʿAbbās and, later, Ismāʿīl who continued Muḥammad ʿAlī's work of developing and modernizing Egypt, while Saʿīd is not mentioned at all in this connection (7:60–65). The obvious reason for this view of modern Egyptian history is the fact that Mubārak was in ʿAbbās's favor, while he fell into disgrace at the time of Saʿīd.

Similarly, opponents of the Muḥammad ʿAlī family are punished by the omission of their biographies from the *Khiṭaṭ*. Sharqāwī and Mishadd have dealt in detail with the omission of ʿUmar Makram's biography,[45] and we find a similar attitude toward all those who had any connection with the ʿUrābī revolt.[46] Neither Hirriyya near Zaqāzīq, the native village of

[42] Mubārak also criticizes many popular customs (for example, 4:112, 119; 11:15). However, the criticism of some customs connected with the *mawlid al-Badawī* at Ṭanṭā (15:29) mentioned by Goldziher (p. 351) is not an opinion originally expressed by Mubārak but is quoted by him, together with the whole passage, from his source. Cf. ʿAbd al-Wahhāb al-Shaʿrānī, *al-Ṭabaqāt al-kubrā* (Cairo, n.d.) Maṭbaʿat Ṣabīḥ wa'awlāduhu, 2:120–21.

[43] Sharqāwī and Mishadd, p. 205. Sharqāwī and Mishadd (p. 89) claim that in his *ʿAlam al-dīn* Mubārak is more critical, but even there we find no more than moralizing, which may be understood as indirect criticism of the rulers. It is interesting to note that Sharqāwī and Mishadd justify Mubārak's unreserved loyalty to the Muḥammad ʿAlī family by the benefits he received from its ruling members.

[44] Cf. Jabartī, 4:64.

[45] Sharqāwī and Mishadd, pp. 149–51.

[46] On the relation between Mubārak and ʿUrābī's group, see Sharqāwī and Mishadd, pp. 191 ff. See also his own account, 9:55–58. For Mubārak's general political, religious, and cultural attitudes, his other works are more important than the *Khiṭaṭ*.

ʿUrābī, nor Maḥallat Naṣr, the village in which Muḥammad ʿAbduh was born, is mentioned in the *Khiṭaṭ*, and there are no biographies of ʿUrābī, Muḥammad ʿAbduh, ʿAbdallāh Nadīm, or other prominent persons connected in some way with the revolt.

The Subject Matter of the Khiṭaṭ

Paradoxical as it may sound, the principal importance of Mubārak's *Khiṭaṭ* is not its contribution to the historical geography and topography of Egypt. The main reason for this is its lack of accuracy and the numerous mistakes dealt with above. Moreover, it should be pointed out that while in 1882 there were in Egypt 3,651 towns and villages (3,692 in 1897) and about 8,600 smaller places (more than 14,000 in 1897), Mubārak discusses only 1,155 of them.[47] This is by no means a negligible number, but one should not forget that the majority of Egyptian villages are not included in this geographical encyclopedia.

The study of Egypt's political history benefits even less from Mubārak's *Khiṭaṭ* than does the study of geography and topography. Although the detailed enumeration of administrative institutions and the description of local government in every town and village is useful, little other political information is included in the *Khiṭaṭ* which may not be found elsewhere. Here and there Mubārak relates events connected with the Muḥammad ʿAlī family, but his original contribution is rather small. Generally he contents himself with copying al-Jabartī's account of events connected with a specific place. As we have seen, the arrangement of his material according to towns and villages made it difficult for him to include in his work much of Egypt's political history.

There is much material on economic history in the *Khiṭaṭ*, though not to an equal extent on its different subdivisions. Except for coins and currencies, few financial questions are dealt with by Mubārak. As against this, the work is rich in information on agriculture; land tenure and ownership; rural trade; the specific crafts of many of Egypt's villages, towns, and districts; and the general economic development of various towns. Commerce, transport, and communications are also treated in detail, but while there is copious information on internal commerce and trade routes, one finds comparatively little on maritime transport and foreign trade.

The *Khiṭaṭ* supplies essential information on the social structure of the Egyptian village and town in the nineteenth century. Subjects dealt with are, for instance, the various kinds of dwellings; the division into quarters

[47] In this count we have included villages discussed in detail by Mubārak under the heading of another place but not villages mentioned only by name on which no details are given.

and the social character of the different quarters of specific towns and villages; the split of the rural population into two factions; the foundations of new villages; rural and urban institutions (the *maḍyafa*, the *sūq*, and so on); and the urban guilds. In addition, many towns and villages are described in detail, and comparison with their present structures may yield interesting results for the study of their social development.

Of major importance is Mubārak's material on the various social groups and classes in nineteenth-century Egypt. We find in the *Khiṭaṭ* unique information on Egypt's tribes and the process of their settlement; on rural families and notables; on merchants, officials, army officers, physicians, engineers, and particularly *ʿulamāʾ*. A great part of this information is included in biographies and autobiographies which shed light on the origin and social background of members of these groups, their position in society, and their rise or decline.

Other aspects of social life frequently dealt with by Mubārak are religious and ethnic communities (Copts, foreigners, and so on); the position and status of women; health conditions; and—particularly—education, one of the main fields of his official activity. In connection with education (and some of the biographies), we find also interesting information on cultural and literary development—Mubārak even reproduces a number of poems written by his contemporaries—but in this respect the *Khiṭaṭ* is certainly no more than a minor source of secondary importance. On the other hand, the descriptions of marriage and funeral rites, food and dress, reception of guests, and various customs serve as a substantial addition to Lane's work and the *Description de l'Egypte*.

It would seem, however, that the preeminent importance of the *Khiṭaṭ* consists in the abundant and interesting information on various aspects of religious life in Egypt in the nineteenth century. From *waqf* documents and Mubārak's personal experience as Minister of Waqfs we receive a clear picture of the situation and problems of this institution at that time. A most illuminating section on the Azhar includes, among other things, descriptions of social life at this institution, material conditions of the students, and relations between different groups of students. Furthermore, there is much information on other religious institutions in Egyptian towns and villages, such as religious courts, mosques, and convents. However, Mubārak's treatment of popular religion is at least as illuminating as that of orthodox Islam. He describes hundreds of saints' tombs in towns and villages, their history and the beliefs and customs connected with them; the religious and social position of the *sharīfs*; the various *Ṣūfī* orders and their shaykhs; scores of *mawlid*s and the customs and rites connected with each of them, as well as changes that occurred in their celebration. Goldziher was certainly right when, in the first review of the *Khiṭaṭ* ever published, he decidedly stressed this aspect of Mubārak's work.

To summarize, the importance of Mubārak's *Khiṭaṭ* is in the field of social history.[48] It goes without saying that, in this field too, Mubārak's shortcomings have to be taken into account; but there can be no doubt that his work is an indispensable and unique source for the study of the social history of Egypt in the nineteenth century.

[48] There can be no doubt that social anthropologists could use this work to a much larger extent than they have done until now. For instance, in a recently published bibliography in the field of social anthropology (L. H. Coult, Jr., *An Annotated Bibliography of the Egyptian Fellah*, Coral Gables, Florida, 1958), Mubārak's *Khiṭaṭ* is mentioned (no. 102, p. 31), but the compiler was content with reading a sample. In the subject index, the *Khiṭaṭ* appears under the headings: historical background; topography; settlement patterns; marriage· ceremonies; and death, burial, and funeral (in contrast with other references, no page numbers are given). But the *Khiṭaṭ* is not indexed under building construction, dress, agricultural methods, landownership, crafts and rural industries, administration, inter-village quarrel, religion, education, *mawlid*s, and many other subjects on which there is important material in Mubārak's work.

Author-Title Index

Subject Index